# MINNEAPOLIS & ST. PAUL

TRICIA CORNELL

Jul 2019

# CONTENTS

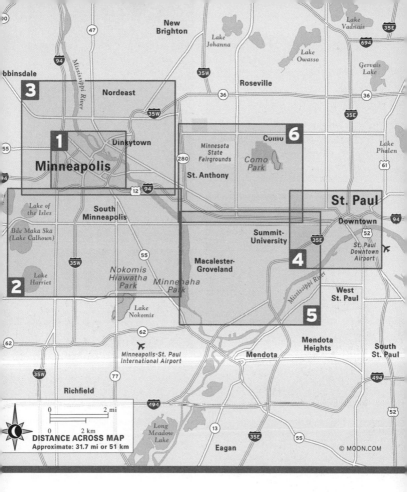

# MAPS

1 Minneapolis waterfront along the Mississippi River

2 farmers market in Minneapolis

3 Minnehaha Falls

4 the St. Anthony neighborhood

5 Scandinavian-style sandwich

6 Lake Harriet

# DISCOVER
# MINNEAPOLIS & ST. PAUL

"I like Hollywood. I just like Minneapolis a little bit better." Those are the immortal words of Minnesota's favorite son, Prince Rogers Nelson, who famously made his home and recorded his music in the suburb of Chanhassen. You'd be hard-pressed to find a native Minnesotan who disagreed. Nothing against the rest of the world: We just like it a lot here. That kind of hometown pride is visible on T-shirts and caps you'll see all around town. And it's also evident in the way we live our lives. We're out, enjoying what every corner of the cities has to offer. That means hitting the trails, seeking out the water (you won't have to look far), finding a festival, going to a play or a concert every night, becoming a regular at a taproom, and developing strong opinions on the best *bánh mì* in town.

St. Paul is compact, pretty, and offers plenty in the way of sights and classic neighborhood bars. Minneapolis is the glitzy twin and the hub of the arts and music scene. Both cities are buzzing year-round. Far from hibernating, we embrace the winter. Joggers put on an extra layer, windsurfers transform into ice surfers, cyclists install winter tires, and skiers exult. And when temperatures climb back above freezing, the whole process begins again: the lakefronts, river paths, and outdoor restaurants fill with people who enjoy spring more than anyone else on earth. Yes, it can get a little cold here. And we love it.

You know how they say that the best part of having out-of-town guests is getting to play tourist in your own home city? Well, in Minneapolis and St. Paul, people turn that aphorism on its head: The best part of being a tourist in the Twin Cities is pretending you're a local. The truth is, there aren't any touristy areas here, because the best things to do are what the locals do.

# 10 TOP EXPERIENCES

**1** **Get Out on the Water:** Whether you're interested in paddling and cruising or strolling and bicycling alongside the water, you've got options aplenty here, from the **Chain of Lakes** (page 31) to the **Mississippi River** (page 156).

**2** **Experience Life in the Skyways:** It's a whole world up there in the elevated walkways connecting buildings in downtown Minneapolis and St. Paul, where you can shop, dine, and watch the locals in their native habitat (page 28).

**3** **See Live Theater:** On any given night you can choose from a dozen or more shows ranging from the pioneering to the world-renowned (page 115).

GUTHRIE
THEATER

**4** **Enjoy Summer Festivals:** From events celebrating arts and music to the Minnesota State Fair, you'll find a festival nearly every weekend in the season (page 141).

**5** **Sample Diverse Cuisine:** From multiethnic **Eat Street** (page 62) and **Midtown Global Market** (page 74) to **Hmong marketplaces** (page 78), the Twin Cities benefit from their immigrant communities.

<<<

**6** **Go Bicycling:** With hundreds of miles of bike trails, Minneapolis and St. Paul offer great options for exploration on two wheels (page 149).

**7** **Crawl the Brewpubs and Taprooms:** With dozens of breweries in the Twin Cities, it's not hard to find a taproom to fit your style (page 93).

**8** **Browse Farmers Markets:** Farmers markets are beloved here, and on weekends especially it seems the whole city converges on neighborhood outposts to shop, snack, and schmooze (page 174).

**9** **Discover the Walker Art Center and Sculpture Garden:** One of the premier contemporary art museums in the country is an indoor and outdoor delight right on the edge of downtown Minneapolis (page 24).

> > >

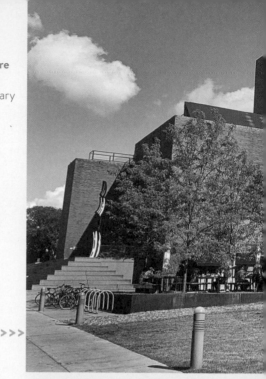

**10** **Embrace the Cold:** Whether enjoying the **Winter Carnival** (page 139), **skating** (page 160), or **cross-country skiing** (page 164), the Twin Cities sinks into the wintry weather.

> > >

# EXPLORE
## MINNEAPOLIS & ST. PAUL

## THE BEST OF THE TWIN CITIES

Divide and conquer is the best way to squeeze the best the Twin Cities have to offer into just two days. If you go by foot, plan on three or four miles of walking a day.

### DAY 1

Start your tour where Minneapolis began, on the Mississippi River. On a summer Saturday, grab a pastry, coffee, and even an early-morning bratwurst at the **Mill City Farmers Market.**

There's plenty right on the riverfront to fill a morning: the **Guthrie Theater**'s endless bridge, the 1.8-mile **St. Anthony Falls Heritage Trail**, the stunning **Stone Arch** and **Hennepin Avenue Bridges, Mill Ruins Park,** and the **Mill City Museum** (don't miss the film *Minneapolis in 19 Minutes Flat*).

To get an even closer view of **St. Anthony Falls,** the only waterfall on the Mississippi, stop at **Water Power Park.**

Spend the afternoon strolling down **Nicollet Mall.** Start at the **Minneapolis Central Library** and head southeast. Along the way, see

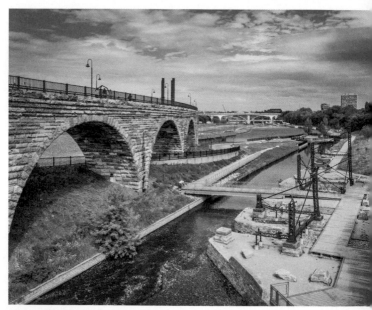

Mill Ruins Park and the Stone Arch Bridge

# GET OUTSIDE

### BEST LAKES
In Minneapolis, busy **Bde Maka Ska (Lake Calhoun)** is where to go to walk, jog, bike, play volleyball, sunbathe, slackline, or just hang out in a hammock. **Lake Harriet** is popular with serious speed walkers. **Lake of the Isles** is for quiet contemplation, though **Cedar Lake** is the place to find true solitude (private enough, notoriously, for skinny-dipping). **Lake Como** is the center of outdoor recreation in St. Paul.

### BEST SUMMER RECREATION
Rent a bicycle from any of the many **Nice Ride** stations throughout the cities. Or if you're a seafaring type, rent a kayak, paddleboat, or stand-up paddleboard from **Wheel Fun Rentals,** which has outposts on most of the cities' biggest lakes. For a true Minnesota water adventure, rent a kayak from **Mississippi River Paddle Share** for a paddle down the Mississippi itself. Inveterate strollers can head to the **Minnesota Landscape Arboretum,** where you can walk for miles among beautiful and varied gardens.

### BEST WINTER RECREATION
Join the skaters at **Rice Park** or many of the city's frozen lakes. For some downhill action, ski the easy hills at **Como Park** or the tougher slopes at **Hyland Ski and Snowboard Center.** If moguls are calling your name, they're calling you from **Buck Hill,** where top racers train. If you're all about the skinny skis, hit the groomed trails at **Theodore Wirth Park** or blaze your own trail across any city lake. And if skiing's not your style, the park is also the best place to fly downhill on a snow tube.

Nicollet Mall

between two high-rise condo buildings—to **Loring Park.**

Directly across the park from the greenway is the yellow-and-blue **Irene Hixon Whitney Bridge,** which leads to the **Walker Art Center and Sculpture Garden,** home of the iconic *Spoonbridge and Cherry,* by Claes Oldenburg and Coosje van Bruggen.

Your evening options from here are great: Treat yourself to fine dining at **Burch** steak house or at one of the half dozen restaurants ringing Loring Park. For less expensive ethnic fare, head to **Eat Street** (Nicollet Ave. between 13th St. and 29th St.).

After dinner, if you don't have theater tickets, the **bars along 1st Avenue** are always hopping. Or unwind with lawn bowling on **Brit's Pub's** rooftop or a jazz show at the **Dakota Jazz Club and Restaurant.**

## DAY 2

Start your day in St. Paul with Swedish pancakes at the **St. Paul Hotel,** then step right outside and enjoy beautiful **Rice Park,** flanked

the **skyways** by ducking into just about any store or office building and following signs. On Thursdays between May and October, the **Nicollet Mall Market,** a farmers market, sets up along most of the mall. At 12th Street, head down the **Loring Greenway**—a parklike path

Cathedral of St. Paul

by some of the city's most recognizable buildings. Spend a few minutes admiring the interior of the **Landmark Center** or spend an hour or so at one of the small museums inside. Before leaving the park, take a peek inside the reference library at the **James J. Hill Center**, find out what's showing at the **Ordway Center for the Performing Arts**, and snap a few pictures with F. Scott Fitzgerald and his friends the *Peanuts* characters, cast in bronze.

Your next stop is the **Minnesota History Center**, which deserves as much time as you're able to give it (the gift shop is a great place to get souvenirs).

The **Cathedral of St. Paul**, a short walk away, welcomes both the faithful and the respectfully curious.

A little less than a mile away, the **Minnesota State Capitol** offers tours on the hour, or you can wander on your own. Leave a little time to explore the memorials on the grounds.

For dinner and entertainment, head back to downtown St. Paul proper. The classic American **St.**

## TWIN CITIES ON A BUDGET

### SIGHTS
You can absorb most of the history of St. Paul without ever paying anything at the door: It's always free to tour the **Minnesota State Capitol, Landmark Center,** and **Cathedral of St. Paul.** And, while there's plenty to do that costs money at the **Mall of America,** many use it as a free indoor entertainment venue on cold winter days. If you've got kids in tow, you'll be happy to hear that the **Como Park Zoo and Conservatory** doesn't charge admission.

### RESTAURANTS
For inexpensive (and delicious) eats, tour the Vietnamese, Thai, and Hmong restaurants on **Eat Street (Nicollet Avenue)** in Minneapolis or **University Avenue** in St. Paul, or find plenty of Mexican-American choices on **Lake Street** in Minneapolis and St. Paul's **District del Sol.**

### NIGHTLIFE
If you've got a fiver in your pocket, that's enough to buy one of the area's best improv troupes at the **Brave New Workshop** (Friday-Sat. 9:45pm).

### ARTS AND CULTURE
Two top destination museums—the **Walker Art Center and Sculpture Garden** (Thurs. 5pm-9pm). and **Minnesota History Center** (Tues. 3pm-8pm) waive admission fees one night a week to attract a younger evening crowd. The Walker also hosts free first Saturdays with special hands-on activities for children. Some museums never ask a penny at the door: The **Frederick R. Weisman Art Museum** showcases contemporary art, the **Minneapolis Institute of Art** reaches across nearly every era of art history and every continent, and the **Minnesota Museum of American Art** may be smaller in scale but it isn't lesser in quality.

### RECREATION
A stroll around **Bde Maka Ska (Lake Calhoun)** or **Lake Harriet** costs nothing, as does a self-guided tour of Minneapolis's downtown riverfront or the view over St. Anthony Falls from the **Guthrie Theater**'s endless bridge (open to the public without a theater ticket).

# BEST VIEWS

view from Indian Mounds Park

### STONE ARCH BRIDGE
From the sweeping curve of the Stone Arch Bridge, you can see St. Anthony Falls and the downtown Minneapolis skyline (page 25).

### FOSHAY TOWER
The 32-story Foshay was once the tallest building between Chicago and the West Coast, and its observation deck is still a classic spot from which to view Minneapolis (page 27).

### INDIAN MOUNDS PARK
Indian Mounds Park sits high on a bluff over the city and offers wonderful views of the downtown St. Paul skyline and river (page 41).

### 6SMITH
Grab a seat on this restaurant's dockside patio or rooftop and take in expansive views of Lake Minnetonka (page 86).

### SCIENCE MUSEUM OF MINNESOTA
From the public patio outside the museum, you can see the bridges crossing the Mississippi River, bluff to bluff (page 131).

Paul Grill and the French Meritage are on Rice Park. For something way more fun than classic, try the New American dining at Saint Dinette.

Most of the Twin Cities' livelier nightlife takes place in downtown Minneapolis, but a couple of taprooms, including Tin Whiskers Brewing Company, have opened in downtown St. Paul, and Vieux Carre hosts live jazz nearly every night.

## DAY 3
If you've got an extra day in the Twin Cities and you've exhausted those rather ambitious itineraries for the first two days, it's time to head out of the two downtown cores.

Get some fresh air on the walking paths around the Chain of Lakes in Minneapolis or in St. Paul's sprawling Como Park. Take a short hike around Minnehaha Falls, which inspired Henry Wadsworth Longfellow's epic poem *The Song of Hiawatha*.

On warm days, dine alfresco at Sea Salt in Minnehaha Falls Park.

If you're in the mood to shop, then

orchids at the Minnesota Landscape Arboretum

Minnehaha Falls

St. Paul's **Grand Avenue** is your best bet. To venture any farther out of town, you'll need your own car. The only real exception to this is the **Mall of America,** which is a good option on a cold winter day.

For some kid-friendly sightseeing, head west to the **Minnesota Landscape Arboretum** or south to the **Minnesota Zoo.**

## BEST PEOPLE-WATCHING

### THE SKYWAYS
Grab a seat in one of the many skyway-level restaurants and notice people scurrying from place to place. You can also find a skyway over Nicollet Mall to watch the street life below (page 28).

### BDE MAKA SKA (LAKE CALHOUN)
Stretch out on the grassy lawns on the south side of Bde Maka Ska and you'll be in a hive of activity, with people engaging in volleyball, lawn games, slacklining, and occasionally juggling or yoga (page 31).

### MALL OF AMERICA
Everybody comes to the Mall of America, from teens lining up to get their idol's signature to parents letting toddlers run the wiggles out to tourists lugging suitcases to inveterate mall walkers in sensible sneakers. Park yourself on a bench anywhere on the outer ring, or find a seat in the central amusement park (page 44).

### GRAND AVENUE
This St. Paul shopping district holds indie stores and dozens of restaurants. Take a seat outdoors at one of the latter and watch the world go by (page 172).

### 50TH AND FRANCE
Grab a window seat at one of the chic restaurants along 50th Street, as people with fresh blowouts happily swinging shopping bags walk past (page 172).

# NEIGHBORHOODS

## DOWNTOWN MINNEAPOLIS

Raised indoor walkways, known as skyways, connect 70 downtown city blocks, creating an indoor network of offices, shops, restaurants, theaters, hotels, and condos. Outside, there's even more to discover: the **Mississippi riverfront,** the hip shops and restaurants of the **North Loop,** the **Guthrie Theater,** the **Walker Art Center and Sculpture Garden,** and **Nicollet Mall,** home to some of the best dining and bars in the Twin Cities. Three of the Twin Cities' four **major sports franchises**—the Twins, Vikings, and Timberwolves—have their homes downtown, too.

## SOUTH MINNEAPOLIS

The leafy green neighborhoods of South Minneapolis, popular with families and young professionals alike, are home to the **Chain of Lakes,** the **Minneapolis Institute of Art,** the **Children's Theatre Company,** and **The Museum of Russian Art.** Recent college grads gravitate to the Uptown neighborhood, at the intersection of Lake Street and Hennepin Avenue, for shopping and nightlife. The residents of South Minneapolis love to eat well, and the area is packed with great dining options, including the multiethnic **Midtown Global Market.**

## NORDEAST AND DINKYTOWN

Nordeast, or northeast Minneapolis, was once home to a thriving community of Eastern European immigrants, still reflected in the area's landmarks, including **Surdyk's** wine

Mississippi riverfront at Stone Arch Bridge

store and **Kramarczuk's** deli. Today the area, still largely middle class, is also home to Somali, Middle Eastern, and Latin American communities. The area has also welcomed many of the artists forced out of the gentrified Warehouse District. Dinkytown, once Bob Dylan's haunt, is inseparable from **University of Minnesota** student life.

## DOWNTOWN ST. PAUL AND WEST SIDE

St. Paul is known as the slower-paced twin but has plenty to offer in terms of culture, including the **Ordway Center for the Performing Arts**, the **Science Museum of Minnesota**, and the **Minnesota Children's Museum.** The heart of downtown is **Rice Park**, bordered by the architecturally stunning **Landmark Center.** West 7th Street, heading southwest from the **Xcel Energy Center**, is a great destination for a night on the town. The **Lowertown** neighborhood anchors the eastern side of downtown St. Paul, centered on **Mears Park** and bordered by the Mississippi River.

Landmark Center

Rice Park

Artists' lofts, trendy apartments, and hip restaurants have moved into former warehouses here. St. Paul's West Side, southeast of downtown, now rebranded as the **District del Sol**, is the home to St. Paul's deep-rooted Latino community.

## SUMMIT-UNIVERSITY AND MAC-GROVELAND

The St. Paul neighborhoods west of downtown are home to five colleges and universities, with all the bookstores and coffee shops you expect. **Summit Avenue** is the historical seat of St. Paul's moneyed elite and still a wide, lovely boulevard for strolling. **Grand Avenue** is excellent for boutique shopping and people watching. Just north of I-94, which cuts St. Paul decisively into northern and southern halves, runs the more ethnically and economically diverse **University Avenue,** known for dive bars and great Vietnamese food.

## COMO AND ST. ANTHONY

The northern neighborhoods of St. Paul feel about as removed from urban bustle as you can get. **St. Anthony Park**, with its compact shopping and dining district, is almost like a separate small town, where you can browse a small selection of shops like

Como Conservatory

**Micawber's Books.** The "garden district" of **Como Park** attracts people from around the Twin Cities who want to run, boat, fish, ski, golf, or enjoy the **Como Park Zoo and Conservatory.**

## GREATER TWIN CITIES

The older first-ring suburbs around Minneapolis and St. Paul are hard to distinguish from their gridded and green counterparts within the city limits. Once you hit the second ring and the exurbs, however, the streets start to curve, and suddenly the buildings all seem newer and more spread out. There are plenty of good reasons to venture beyond the cities proper, including **Historic Fort Snelling,** the **Minnesota Zoo,** and the excellent **Minnesota Landscape Arboretum.** And how could you go home from Minnesota and tell your friends you missed the **Mall of America,** in the southern suburb of Bloomington?

# SIGHTS

When Minnesotans want to play or relax they head for the water, and visitors should do the same. The Mississippi River and lakes scattered throughout the Twin Cities are intertwined with daily life here. Both Minneapolis and St. Paul grew up on the riverfront.

Minneapolis City Hall

The river creates the northern and eastern boundaries of Minneapolis's downtown zone, running downstream from the historic Warehouse District and past the eastern edge of downtown at the Guthrie Theater and adjoining parkland. Once powered exclusively by the mighty Mississippi River and St. Anthony Falls, many of the flour mills and silos that put Minnesota on the map still stand but have been converted into lofts, art galleries, and museums, joined by recreation areas and restaurants.

St. Paul sits high on bluffs a few miles downstream from Minneapolis; the river separates the two cities for the most part. The stately Cathedral of St. Paul is perched on one hill to the west of St. Paul's downtown, facing the Minnesota State Capitol, which is on another hill across the interstate. The central business district lies below these two domes, centered on Rice Park.

Getting oriented on foot in both downtowns is fairly easy and an enjoyable form of sightseeing in itself. See Minneapolis by strolling Nicollet Mall, starting from rolling Loring Park and heading toward Minneapolis Central Library. Move easily between the two downtowns using the light rail Green Line.

## HIGHLIGHTS

✪ **BEST PLACE TO SEE CONTEMPORARY ART:** The **Walker Art Center and Sculpture Garden** brings leading artists and performers to the Twin Cities (page 24).

✪ **BEST PLACES TO WITNESS THE POWER OF HYDROELECTRICITY:** Minneapolis as we know it today got its start at **St. Anthony Falls** (page 25), the only waterfall on the Mississippi. You can also see the falls from the **Stone Arch Bridge** (page 25) and easily fill a day with all there is to see and do on the riverfront.

✪ **BEST PLACE TO SEE TWIN CITIANS IN THEIR NATURAL ENVIRONMENT:** In just about any weather, locals are drawn to the **Chain of Lakes** in South Minneapolis to walk, bike, canoe, sail, and sit in the sun (page 31).

✪ **MOST PEACEFUL CULTURAL LANDMARK:** With its stunning architecture, the **Cathedral of St. Paul** generously welcomes all, from the faithful to the curious visitor (page 35).

✪ **MOST ENJOYABLE WAY TO LEARN ABOUT MINNESOTA'S PAST:** History becomes fun at the well-curated **Minnesota History Center** (page 36).

✪ **BEST PLACE TO START A TOUR OF ST. PAUL:** So much of downtown St. Paul's architectural beauty is arranged around tiny **Rice Park** that a thoroughly enjoyable tour can be had within a single block (page 36).

✪ **BEST PLACE TO ASPIRE TO THE LIFE OF A RAILROAD BARON:** St. Paul's toniest address has long been **Summit Avenue.** A stroll along the shady streets is a treat for history and architecture buffs (page 41).

✪ **BEST PLACE TO ENJOY WINTER ESCAPISM:** It's no surprise that the **Mall of America,** while popular year-round, is busiest on frigid winter days (page 44).

✪ **BEST PLACE TO WITNESS THE CHANGING SEASONS:** Just a short drive from Minneapolis, the **Minnesota Landscape Arboretum** shows off our state's beauty, from manicured gardens to wild groves (page 45).

✪ **BEST GUIDED TOUR:** Rather than trudge along on your own two feet, take the **Human on a Stick** tour and ride a Segway along the Mississippi River or through St. Paul (page 49).

# Downtown Minneapolis    Map 1

## ✪ Walker Art Center and Sculpture Garden

Like a giant tinfoil marshmallow floating on the southeast corner of downtown, the Walker Art Center makes an impression. It's known as one of the best places to experience multidisciplinary contemporary art in the country, having built its reputation over nine decades. When it opened in 1927, it was the first public gallery of art in the Upper Midwest. Today it holds works by Pablo Picasso, Henry Moore, Alberto Giacometti, Claes Oldenburg, Chuck Close, Roy Lichtenstein, Yoko Ono, Andy Warhol, and others in its permanent collection and hosts consistently forward-looking exhibitions combining visual arts, sound, and movement.

The 11-acre **Minneapolis Sculpture Garden,** a joint project of the Walker and the Minneapolis Park Board, opened in 1988 adjacent to the Walker itself and underwent a complete overhaul completed in 2016. The highlight of the park and beloved symbol of Minneapolis, Oldenburg and Coosje van Bruggen's *Spoonbridge and Cherry,* has been joined by Katharina Fritsch's joyful Hahn/Cock, a cobalt blue rooster standing proudly over the other pieces.

The **Irene Hixon Whitney Bridge**—two linked yellow-and-blue arches—connects the sculpture garden to **Loring Park** across 16 lanes of traffic. To keep yourself from looking

Walker Art Center and Sculpture Garden

down as you cross the bridge, you can read John Ashbery's specially commissioned untitled poem, which begins: "And now I cannot remember how I would have had it. It is not a conduit (confluence?) but a place."

To get to the art center, take bus 4 or 6 to the Vineland stop (southbound) or the Oak Grove stop (northbound). **MAP 1:** 1750 Hennepin Ave., Minneapolis, 612/375-7600, www.walkerart.org; gallery Tues.-Wed. and Sun. 11am-5pm, Thurs. 11am-9pm, Fri.-Sat. 11am-6pm; garden daily 6am-midnight; gallery $15 adults, $13 seniors, $10 students, children under 18 free; garden free

## ✪ St. Anthony Falls

Right here, on the banks of the Mississippi, is where Minneapolis began. The only waterfall on the Mississippi River, St. Anthony Falls powered the city's birth and growth and continues to provide enough electricity for downtown Minneapolis. The falls originated nearly nine miles downriver, near what is now downtown St. Paul, and migrated upstream as the soft sandstone underlayer eroded and the limestone top layer collapsed. Had this erosion continued, the waterfall, which was moving a few feet to a hundred feet every year, would have disappeared altogether, and Minneapolis wouldn't exist. But human industry intervened, and today the waterfall flows over a concrete apron.

The Mdewakanton Dakota people, who dominated the area before the arrival of Europeans, called the falls *mnirara* (curling waters) and considered many locations in the area sacred, including the now-vanished Spirit Island.

Father Louis Hennepin, a Belgian priest, was the first European to see the falls, in 1680, just three years after he was the first to set eyes on Niagara Falls. He sent home enthusiastic (perhaps overly so) descriptions of a 50-foot cataract, attracting explorers and a growing stream of settlers. The waterfall was first harnessed for industrial use in 1848, when the first sawmill was built, and the logging industry drove rapid development until the 1880s, when flour milling took over. By that time, there were 25 flour mills on the river's banks, as well as the North Star Woolen Mill, which later became one of the first condo developments in downtown Minneapolis.

The best view of the falls is from **Hennepin Island,** home to Xcel Energy's hydroelectric plant and **Water Power Park,** where it almost feels like you could reach out and touch the foam from the observation platform. University of Minnesota scientists also use the island to study the falls at the **Saint Anthony Falls Laboratory,** home to the National Center for Earth-surface Dynamics. You can also get a good look at the falls from the **Stone Arch Bridge.**

The falls are five blocks north of the Government Plaza station on the Blue and Green light-rail lines. Or, take bus 7 or 22 along Washington Avenue to the Park Avenue stop. **MAP 1:** West River Pkwy. between Hennepin Ave. S. and Portland Ave. S., Minneapolis, 612/333-5336; visitors center Apr.-Nov. daily 10am-5pm; free

## ✪ Stone Arch Bridge

When railroad baron James J. Hill completed the Stone Arch Bridge in 1883, the state's railway commissioner said the limestone structure had been "constructed for a thousand years." Well into the bridge's second century, his prediction is holding true.

Built as the first rail connection from the industry on the east side of the Mississippi to the growing metropolitan hub on the west side, it led right to the Union Depot. Its unique and impressive design was dictated by the location: Hill's Great Northern Railway needed to connect a point on the east bank below the falls to a point on the west bank above the falls. It couldn't cross the falls diagonally, and engineers feared that if the bridge sat entirely above St. Anthony, the falls would collapse. So it skirts the downstream edge of the falls for most of its length, and then goes into a beautifully engineered and fairly sharp curve on the west side. The metal trusses were incorporated into the western end of the bridge in the 1960s to accommodate boats. The beloved Minneapolis landmark carried trains until 1978, then opened to pedestrians and bikes in 1994. The bridge is part of a self-guided walking tour along the falls area, with excellent interpretive signs and one of the most beloved views of the downtown skyline.

The bridge is five blocks north of the Government Plaza station on the light-rail Blue and Green Lines. Or, take bus 7 or 22 along Washington Avenue to the Park Avenue stop.

**MAP 1:** Portland Ave. S. and West River Pkwy., Minneapolis

## Basilica of St. Mary

Many of the earliest European settlers in Minnesota were Catholic, including the Belgian priest Father Louis Hennepin, who was the first European to see St. Anthony Falls. In fact, the first Catholic Church west of the Mississippi was built in Minneapolis in 1868, several blocks northeast of where the Basilica of St. Mary stands now.

Stone Arch Bridge

Construction on the basilica began in 1908, at the same time as the cathedral in St. Paul, and it served as a co-cathedral within the archdiocese. In 1926, it officially became the first basilica in the United States (there are now 58). The basilica, which is on the National Register of Historic Places and has been called one of the finest examples of beaux arts in the country, was designed by the principal architect of the 1904 St. Louis World's Fair, Emmanuel Masqueray. Look for the many symbols of Mary in the stonework and windows, including pomegranates, doves, and fleurs-de-lis.

When Highways 94 and 394 were built in the 1960s, the parish splintered and the congregation dwindled. By the 1980s, the building itself was seriously suffering. But as downtown Minneapolis revived, so did the basilica; a full restoration was completed in the 1990s, along with a new dome. Today the basilica is known not only as a spiritual home, but also as the host of the rockingest block party in town every July.

While there are works of art to see and experience throughout the building, you can visit the **John XXIII Gallery** (Sat. 10am-6:30pm, Sun. 7:30am-8pm) to see intriguingly and intellectually curated exhibits of sacred art, both contemporary and historical.

Buses 4 and 6, both of which run along Hennepin Avenue in downtown Minneapolis and Uptown, stop right in front of the basilica.

**MAP 1:** 88 17th St. N., Minneapolis, 612/333-1381, www.mary.org; Mon.-Fri. 6:30am-5pm, Sat. 8am-6:30pm, Sun. 6:30am-7pm; 15-minute tours Sun. after 9:30am and 11:30am masses; call 612/333-1381 to schedule group tours during the week; free

## Foshay Tower

Funny story about the Foshay: It was meant to be a homage to the Washington Monument and an art deco shrine to its owner, Wilbur Foshay. Instead what people remember is this: the $20,000 check to John Philip Sousa that bounced. That's right, bounced. Real estate and utilities mogul Foshay went all out for the official opening of his new building in 1929, even commissioning the "Foshay Tower-Washington Memorial March" from Sousa for the occasion. But six weeks after the gala, Foshay lost his entire fortune and then spent 15 years in Leavenworth prison for fraud. Sousa, so the story goes, refused to allow the march to be played until his debt was repaid. In 1999, a group of Minnesotans paid back the composer's estate.

Minnesotans of several generations remember the 32-story Foshay Tower as the tallest building in downtown Minneapolis, which it was until 1972, when the 55-story IDS Tower surpassed it. There are now well over a dozen buildings in Minneapolis taller than the Foshay, but generations of families remember riding the elevator to the observation deck to look out over the city. The W Minneapolis

hotel now occupies the tower. It preserved the 31st-floor observation deck, along with a small collection of artifacts from the building's heyday, and added a layer of 21st-century opulence that would have made the bankrupt mogul proud.

The Foshay is three blocks south of the Nicollet Mall station on the light rail's Blue and Green Lines and one block east of Nicollet Mall, where the 10, 11, 17, 18, 25, and 59 bus lines run.

**MAP 1:** 821 Marquette Ave., Minneapolis, 612/215-3783, www.foshaymuseum.com; Mon.-Wed. 10am-6pm, Thurs. 10am-9pm, Fri.-Sat. 10am-6pm, Sun. 11am-5pm; $10 adults, $6 children 4 to 14

public seating on Nicollet Mall

## Nicollet Mall

Pick your anatomical metaphor: Nicollet Mall is the backbone of downtown Minneapolis and the heart of the city. The mile-long pedestrian and transit corridor stretches from the **Loring Greenway** (a shady, park-like walkway that connects to **Loring Park**) at the south end to Washington Avenue at the north end. This is where Mary Tyler Moore famously tossed her tam-o'-shanter into the air in front

# SKYWAYS: MAIN STREET ON THE SECOND FLOOR

In the 1960s, the business leaders of downtown Minneapolis realized they needed to compete with the expanding parking lots and indoor amenities of the suburbs (Southdale, the nation's first enclosed shopping mall, opened in Edina, Minnesota, in 1956). Their solution has become one of the Twin Cities' most recognizable traits: the skyway system. In Minneapolis, second-floor glass-enclosed walkways total 9.5 miles and connect more than 80 blocks—nearly every building in downtown's central business district, including 4,000 hotel rooms. It's the nation's first and most extensive system of its kind. St. Paul's slightly smaller and less lively system totals about 5 miles.

Detractors say moving people up to the skyways kills street-level businesses. Others argue that you have to redefine "street-level." About 200,000 pedestrians walk the skyways in Minneapolis every day, patronizing small shops, restaurants, and businesses of all kinds. The skyway-level restaurants are a great place to people-watch, and the passageways also offer fun windows onto street life below; find a skyway crossing Nicollet Mall for the prettiest street views. Skyway maps are posted throughout each system.

**Minneapolis skyway**

of Dayton's department store (now Macy's). But Mary herself wouldn't recognize much of the landmark street now. Where downtown office workers once power-walked, a $50 million renovation, started in 2015, brought public seating, public art, lighting installations, and glades of trees. Stroll by on Thursdays from May to October for the **Nicollet Mall Market,** or enjoy lunch, dinner, or drinks at one of the dozens of outdoor restaurants.

The light-rail Blue and Green Lines stop at the north end of Nicollet Mall, and the 10, 11, 17, 18, 25, and 59 bus lines run along it.

**MAP 1:** Nicollet Ave. between 4th St. S. and 12th St. S., Minneapolis; store hours vary

## Minneapolis Central Library

Even if you don't have any literary or reference needs during your visit to the Twin Cities, the Minneapolis Central Library is worth a look for the architecture and atmosphere alone. A four-story glass atrium joins two buildings: one with four floors of open stacks and sunny work spaces, the other with stacks, meeting rooms, and more secluded work spaces. The 350,000-square-foot building, completed in 2006, occupies a whole block and was designed by Argentine-born

**Minneapolis Central Library**

## WHO CAN TURN THE WORLD ON WITH HER SMILE?

When that small-town girl with big dreams first saw the lights of the big city in TV's *The Mary Tyler Moore Show,* she was heading into the Twin Cities, of course. The series, which ran from 1970 to 1977, was filmed on a soundstage in Studio City, California, but memorable parts of the opening credits were filmed on location in Minneapolis. Mary walks around Lake of the Isles in South Minneapolis and throws her hat in the air on downtown's Nicollet Mall in front of what was then Dayton's department store. A statue, depicting the famous tam toss, now stands in at Nicollet Avenue and 7th Street. Mary's house, which was shown from the outside in between scenes, was at 21st Street and Kenwood Parkway. The old Victorian, a private residence, has tripled in size and is now tan instead of white, but it's still there for old TV buffs to see.

architect Cesar Pelli. Finding it is easy: Look for the massive metal wing floating out over Hennepin Avenue.

Teens and younger kids will each find their own space in the library: Teens can hang out, read, and work on multimedia and tech projects (adult mentors are on site Mon.-Thurs. 3-8pm) in **Teen Central,** with wraparound bookshelves and all kinds of places to sit. The Children's Library on the ground floor has the largest public collection of children's books in the Midwest, including books in more than 30 languages. There's space for families to curl up with a book together and recharge, and even room for little ones to get some wiggles out.

**Cargill Hall** hosts a half dozen art exhibits annually. Special collections in the **James K. Hosmer Special Collections** (Mon.-Thurs. 10am-4:30pm, 1st and 3rd Sat. 10am-4:30pm, free tours 1st and 3rd Sat. 11am) on the fourth floor focus on abolitionism, Mark Twain, local history, and more. Piano players can reserve a beautiful, airy room with a grand piano and floor-to-ceiling windows for practice. Free library tours are offered on the second and fourth Mondays of the month at 1pm, the first and third Wednesdays of the month at 6:30pm, and the last Sunday of the month at 2pm; no registration is required.

You don't need a library card to visit the library or browse, but you do need one to check out materials or use one of the 300 computers available for free public use. There is one particularly modern feature of the library you'll probably never see: an 18,000-square-foot green roof planted with ground cover, reducing heating and cooling costs for the building.

The library is one block north of the Nicollet Mall station on the light-rail Blue and Green Lines.

**MAP 1:** 300 Nicollet Mall, Minneapolis, 612/543-8000, www.hclib.org; Mon.-Thurs. 9am-9pm, Fri.-Sat. 9am-5pm, Sun. noon-5pm; free

### Minneapolis City Hall and Hennepin County Courthouse

When the Municipal Building, as it is also known, was completed in 1888, it boasted the biggest public clock in the world (beating out Big Ben's diameter by six inches). With a 345-foot tower, it also remained the tallest structure in Minneapolis for four decades. (The Foshay Tower topped it in 1929.) The building, with its Romanesque gables and green copper roof, still houses the Minneapolis City Council offices and meeting rooms, but many of Hennepin County's court functions have moved across the street to the Hennepin County Government

*Father of Waters* statue inside Minneapolis City Hall

Center, built in 1977 (look for the twin towers placed so close to each other that together they resemble a toaster). The main draw in the city hall, and definitely worth a brief stop as you walk through downtown, is *Father of Waters,* the massive statue of a Neptune-like figure representing Minneapolis's status as the City of Lakes. (Rub his toe for good luck.) "Father of Waters" is also one of the many names for the Mississippi River. City hall, for architectural reasons, was never connected to the downtown skyway system but can be accessed by tunnels from the Hennepin County Government Center.

Tours are offered on the third Wednesday of the month at noon. Gather at the *Father of Waters* statue. Brochures for self-guided tours are available at the security desk. (Can you spot the fossil in the marble walls?) The tower bells ring on the hour, half hour, and quarter hour and play hour-long concerts to mark special occasions throughout the year.

With 15 bells in all, this is believed to be the only set of bells in the United States that can play the "Star-Spangled Banner" on key.

The light-rail Blue and Green Lines stop directly in front of the courthouse at Government Plaza Station.

**MAP 1:** 350 5th St. S., Minneapolis, 612/596-9535, www. municipalbuildingcommission.org; Mon.-Fri. 6am-6pm, limited access on weekends and later in the evening; free

### Hennepin Avenue Bridge

The first bridge to cross the Mississippi River was completed right on this spot in 1854 and hailed at the time as the "Gateway to the West." The current bridge, completed in 1990, is the fourth in this location, an impressive art deco-influenced suspension bridge paying homage to the wooden suspension bridge the ambitious first engineers constructed, even though the site doesn't necessarily call for this expensive type of construction (in fact, this is the shortest suspension bridge in the country). Underneath its six lanes of traffic, you can explore some remnants of the bridge's predecessors in **First Bridge Park,** including the original footings and the massive iron anchors for the cable suspension system. Interpretive signs include pictures of the bridge's predecessors. And kids can have fun counting the whimsical metal worms set in the pavement.

The bridge is five blocks north of the Warehouse and Hennepin Avenue station on the light-rail Blue and Green Lines. Buses 6 and 4 run across the bridge.

**MAP 1:** Hennepin Ave. and West River Pkwy., Minneapolis

# South Minneapolis

**Map 2**

SIGHTS

SOUTH MINNEAPO_IS

## ✪ Chain of Lakes

One of the greatest gifts Minneapolis's early civic leaders secured for future generations is the treasured Chain of Lakes. Whereas in other cities lakeshore trades hands privately, limiting enjoyment of the water to a few public-access beaches, in Minneapolis nearly every inch of land bordering the city's dozen lakes is public parkland. (The notorious exception is a short piece of private land on the east side of Cedar Lake.) The land was acquired piece by piece through market-rate purchases and private donations starting in the early 1880s by the Minneapolis Park Board. The jewel of this ambitious system is the Chain of Lakes, four interconnected bodies of water: Cedar Lake, Lake of the Isles, Bde Maka Ska, and Lake Harriet.

Today, parkways encircle the lakes, along with more than 13 miles of walking and biking paths. Bike paths run one-way around each lake and are separated from the walking paths. Residents take advantage of the paths and parks year-round, but on especially beautiful days the heavy foot and wheel traffic can resemble a parade.

**Bde Maka Ska (Lake Calhoun)** is the largest of the four, with just over three miles of paths surrounding it. The state officially returned the lake to its Dakota name, Bde Maka Ska (pronounced "bid-EH ma-KAH skuh") in 2018 in response to a public movement, as the name Calhoun refers to

Bde Maka Ska (Lake Calhoun)

Secretary of State John C. Calhoun, a rabid proponent of slavery. The broad, unshaded swathes of grass here, along with a couple of sand volleyball courts, attract a young and fit crowd. Small sand beaches on the south and east sides are popular with families, and canoes and paddleboats can be rented at the north end.

**Lake Harriet** is slightly smaller and shadier. During the summer, concerts are held daily at the bandshell on the north end. The Lake Harriet Yacht Club holds regattas and lessons. Children can hunt for the home of the Lake Harriet elf on the south end.

Surrounded by marshy lowlands, **Lake of the Isles** (2.6 miles around) makes up for what it lacks in recreation opportunities with great bird-watching. **Cedar Lake,** the smallest at 1.7 miles, is the quietest but has two terrific beaches. No swimming is allowed outside of marked areas.

To start exploring, take bus 17 to the north side of Bde Maka Ska or bus 6 to the south side.

**MAP 2:** 612/230-6400, www. minneapolisparks.org; daily 6am-10pm

## Como-Harriet Streetcar Line

At its peak, the Twin Cities Rapid Transit company's streetcars traveled from Stillwater (east of St. Paul) to Excelsior (west of Minneapolis), well over 50 miles. Today two portions of that track remain, lovingly and expertly tended to by volunteers, and both are open for rides. One portion is in Excelsior, on the shores of Lake Minnetonka. The other runs here, between **Lake Harriet** and **Bde Maka Ska (Lake Calhoun)** in Minneapolis. The mile-or-so round-trip takes about 15 minutes. Trolleys

sunset at Bde Maka Ska (Lake Calhoun)

board at the station (a faithful replica of one of the originals, rebuilt in 1990) and run through a glade of trees, under an old stone bridge, and past **Lakewood Cemetery,** until the track emerges opposite Bde Maka Ska. Then the car backs up along the same single track and returns to the station. Along the way, a volunteer in a conductor's uniform tells the story of the Como-Harriet Streetcar Line, beloved in the Twin Cities for its scenic views and high speeds along dedicated rights of way. It was the last line to close when the streetcar system was dismantled in 1954. The current track, relaid by the train buffs themselves, follows the original line until it reaches the cemetery, which has since annexed part of the land where the trolley once ran.

Three of the museum's eight cars run on the line, including the all-wood No. 1300—the car that started it all. In the 1960s, trolley enthusiasts formed a nonprofit organization to save the car—an organization that later became the Minnesota Transportation Museum. One of only two of its type to survive (of 1,140 built by Twin Cities Rapid Transit), No. 1300 celebrated its 100th birthday in 2008. The museum's car No. 322 is an art deco beauty. The all-steel body with clean, modern lines was created in the 1930s and 1940s to combat the streetcar's reputation as an outmoded form of transport and to compete with the sleek automobiles and buses of the day. Vintage ads line the insides of both cars.

Take bus 6 to the Richfield Road and Trolley stop.

**MAP 2:** 42nd St. and Queen Ave., Minneapolis, 952/922-1096, www.trolleyride.org; May-Aug. Sat.-Sun. 12:30pm-8:30pm, Sept. Sat.-Sun. 12:30pm-7:30pm, Oct. Sat.-Sun. 12:30pm-4pm, plus Memorial Day-Aug. Mon.-Fri. 6:30pm-8:30pm and June-Aug. Wed. 1pm-4pm; $2.50, children 3 and under free

# Nordeast and Dinkytown   Map 3

## Ard Godfrey House

Sitting on an improbable patch of green amid the rising condos just across the river from downtown Minneapolis is an improbable little yellow house. This is the Ard Godfrey House, the oldest surviving wood-frame house in Minneapolis. In 1848, millwright Ard Godfrey, who supervised the building of the timber mill at St. Anthony Falls, built this house (originally at Main Street and 2nd Avenue, a couple of blocks closer to the river) with the first lumber sawed at the mill. Today the Women's Club of Minneapolis operates the house as a museum, open in the summer and the holiday season. The 1.5-story house is decorated with period furnishings and photos. One fact you'll be sure to learn is that gardeners of Minnesota have Ard's wife, Harriet, to thank for the humble dandelion. It seems she missed things like dandelion bread, tea, and wine and had seeds shipped from Maine. The small park surrounding the house, **Chute Square,** is where the University of Minnesota got its start in 1851, before moving a couple of miles east.

Take bus 6 or 10 to the Central Avenue and University Avenue stop.

**MAP 3:** 28 University Ave. SE, Minneapolis, 612/813-5300, www.womansclub.org; June-Aug. Sat.-Sun. 1pm-4pm; free

## Our Lady of Lourdes Church

The skinny spire poking up behind the restaurants and bars of St. Anthony Main, just across the Hennepin Avenue Bridge from downtown Minneapolis, is on the oldest continuously operated church in Minneapolis, Our Lady of Lourdes Church. The building was built by the First Universalist Society in 1854 and later sold to the French Canadian Catholic community, which worships there today. The original part of the building, which faces the street, was built in the Greek temple style, and most of the stained-glass windows date to the early 1900s. The congregation's claim to fame is

Ard Godfrey House

its *tourtierres,* French Canadian meat pies, which volunteers make in great quantities both to raise funds for the continued refurbishment of the church and to feed the hungry. Pick one up at the parish house (Sun. 9am-4pm, $20, serves 6-8). Keep in mind that Our Lady of Lourdes is an active church, not a museum.

Take bus 4 or 6 to the Hennepin Avenue and 2nd Street stop.

**MAP 3:** 1 Lourdes Pl., Minneapolis, 612/379-2259, www.ourladyoflourdesmn. com; mass Mon.-Wed. and Fri. 12:05pm, Sat. 5pm, Sun. 8:30am, 11am, and 7pm

## University of Minnesota

The University of Minnesota was founded as a secondary school in 1851, seven years before Minnesota became a state, and became a land grant university in 1869. Today, with more than 50,000 students, it is the fourth-largest university in the country.

The U of M, as it is known locally—or sometimes just "the U"—is divided between the St. Paul campus, where most of the agricultural disciplines are based, and the much larger and busier Minneapolis campus. The Minneapolis campus is further split by the Mississippi River into the West Bank, where the arts departments and law school are located, and the East Bank, the heart of the university. The U's answer to the classic quadrangle is **Northrop Mall,** designed by the legendary architect Cass Gilbert in 1908. The broad lawn is headed by the stately columns of Northrop Memorial Auditorium and lined by classic physics, chemistry, and administrative buildings. Directly across Washington Avenue, accessible by a pedestrian bridge, is **Coffman Memorial Union,** the student activities center. A visitor who wants to get a small taste of life at the U would do well to start here and combine that with a trip to the **Frederick R. Weisman Art Museum,** the shiny metal maze on the banks of the Mississippi. The Weisman sits on Washington Avenue, where the **Washington Avenue pedestrian bridge** crosses the river to the West Bank. Walking or biking across the double-decker bridge, which is one-fifth of a mile long with a shelter running the length of the middle of it for pedestrians, is a daily part of university life for tens of thousands of students and faculty.

The U's oldest buildings are in the Old Campus Historic District, known to most as **The Knoll,** north of Northrop Mall. While the U got its start in 1851 on a patch of land now known as **Chute Square,** it moved to the current location a couple of miles to the west after the Civil War. Now 13 of the buildings in this part of campus, dating as far back as 1886, are listed on the National Register of Historic Places. **Pillsbury Hall** (310 Pillsbury Dr. SE), with its two-tone sandstone and artful mix of Romanesque, prairie school, and arts and crafts elements, is a particular favorite.

To get here, take the light-rail Green Line, which stops at both the East Bank and the West Bank.

**MAP 3:** 612/625-5000, www.umn.edu

# Downtown St. Paul and West Side

Map 4

## ✪ Cathedral of St. Paul

Sitting on the highest point in downtown St. Paul, the Cathedral of St. Paul is the city's most visible and memorable landmark. The beaux arts building is an especially impressive sight at night, when it is illuminated on all sides with electric lights. The cathedral itself gave the city of St. Paul its name. When Father Lucien Galtier arrived in the unfortunately named riverside settlement of Pig's Eye, his first task was to build a log church, which he dedicated to St. Paul. It was Galtier who began writing "St. Paul" as the location on wedding certificates and other church documents. Three successively bigger cathedrals were built on different sites after that first humble building. The current building was built concurrently with the **Basilica of St. Mary** in Minneapolis and completed in 1915. Both buildings were designed by Emmanuel Louis Masqueray.

The cathedral is built as a symmetrical cross and topped by a copper dome. The massive open interior seats 3,000 and was designed to give everyone in the congregation a clear view of the altar. The interior of the dome is entirely open to view from the floor. At 96 feet in diameter and 175 feet high, it dominates the sanctuary. In recognition of the many immigrant groups that have come to Minnesota since that first humble log church, the six shrines behind the sanctuary are dedicated to the patron saints of various countries: Saint Anthony of Padua (Italy), John the Baptist (France and Canada), Saint Patrick (Ireland), Saint Boniface (Germany), Saints Cyril and Methodius (Slavic nations), and Saint Therese (protector of all missions).

More than 200,000 people a year take advantage of the free tours offered Monday-Friday at 1pm (call to arrange a private tour). While the building is open to visitors every day, tourists are asked to stay out of the main sanctuary (unless they are there to worship) and refrain from flash photography during mass and other ceremonies. Daily schedules are posted at the entrance.

The Cathedral Museum (open as volunteers are available; call for details) is in the lower level of the building. Photographs and documents from the cathedral archives are on display, along with occasional traveling exhibits.

Take bus 21 to the Selby and Summit Avenues stop, directly in front of the cathedral, or the light-rail Green Line to the Capitol and Rice stop, then walk 0.75 mile south, across Highway 94.

Cathedral of St. Paul

MAP 4: 239 Selby Ave., St. Paul, 651/228-1766, www.cathedralsaintpaul.org; Sun.-Fri. 7am-6pm, Sat. 7am-8pm

## ✪ Minnesota History Center

The Minnesota Historical Society formed nine years before the state of Minnesota itself, in 1949, but it moved into its impressive granite and limestone home on the hill across from the Minnesota State Capitol in 1992. The building houses the society's administrative offices, massive collections, a research library, and a museum that offers an excellent introduction to Minnesota's past, from distant prehistoric times to the recent development of the suburbs. Exhibits are designed to engage and teach all generations: In Grainland, children can climb through the kid-size model grain elevator for what seems like hours. In Weather Permitting, they can try on warm-weather gear from previous eras or sit in a re-created Minnesota basement during a simulated tornado. And in Open House, they can learn about the actual residents of a typical St. Paul home through several generations of immigrant families. The center's two gift shops are excellent places to find Minnesota-themed souvenirs, and the café focuses on reasonably priced fresh, local fare.

The historical society's library (Tues. 9am-8pm, Wed.-Sat. 9am-4pm) houses over half a million books and 45,000 cubic feet of government records, along with maps, photographs, and more. The public is welcome to use the library free of charge, and it is a popular place to research family history.

Take bus 16 to John Ireland and Kellogg Boulevards or the light-rail Green Line to the Capitol/Rice Street station, then walk 0.5 mile south.

Minnesota History Center

MAP 4: 345 Kellogg Blvd. W., St. Paul, 651/259-3000, www. minnesotahistorycenter.org; Tues. 10am-8pm, Wed.-Sat. 10am-5pm, Sun. noon-5pm, Mon. (holidays only) 10am-5pm; $12 adults, $10 seniors and students, $6 children 6-17, free Tues. 5pm-8pm

## ✪ Rice Park

Though tiny, Rice Park offers prime views of some of downtown St. Paul's most pleasing architecture and public art. The irregular park is surrounded by beautiful buildings, including the Saint Paul Hotel, Landmark Center, Ordway Center for the Performing Arts, and the Central Library, as well as some of St. Paul's finest restaurants. The centerpiece of the park is The Source, a fountain designed by the prolific Wisconsin-born sculptor Alonzo Hauser. A young woman cavorts in the center of the broad pool of water, invoking Minnesota's beloved summers on the lake. But the park may be best known as the home of sculptures of Peanuts characters. While the sculptures are beloved by locals, it's worth noting that Peanuts creator Charles Schulz was never particularly fond of his hometown, St. Paul. A bronze of F. Scott Fitzgerald also commemorates a native son with mixed emotions.

Adjacent to Rice Park (you may not even notice it's a separate tract of land)

# FAVORITE LITERARY SONS

In Rice Park, in the heart of St. Paul, are modest and playful monuments to two of St. Paul's favorite literary sons—men who were, in truth, a little ambivalent about the city of St. Paul itself.

**F. Scott Fitzgerald** was born in St. Paul in 1896. He spent much of his childhood on the East Coast but attended St. Paul Academy for three years. After three years at Princeton, a couple in the army, and a couple at an ad agency in New York, Fitzgerald returned to his parents' house in St. Paul to revise his first novel and, having sold it, to convince Zelda that he would be able to support her. He spent the remainder of his too-brief adult years on the East and West Coasts. Fitzgerald is honored with a life-size statue by artist Michael Price. He stands casually, coat over arm.

**Charles Schulz** was born in St. Paul a generation later, in 1922. His first comic strip, *Li'l Folks*, was published in the *Pioneer Press*. He moved to California permanently in his 30s, after he had hit it big, and made it known that much of the darkness in the early strips came from his bitter memories of his childhood in St. Paul. Despite that, St. Paul has maintained a deep fondness for Schulz. A public art project that ran from 2000 to 2004 featured individually decorated *Peanuts* characters you're likely to see around town. In Rice Park, a bronze Marcie reads on a bench with Woodstock, Schroeder plays the piano while Lucy listens, Peppermint Patty kicks a football, Sally and Linus lean on a wall, and Charlie Brown sits under a tree with Snoopy.

is **Landmark Plaza,** an elegant public art installation, where documents reproduced in the pathway ask visitors to consider some tough questions: "What are you willing to do for your country?" "What are the true costs of war?"

Take the light-rail Green Line to Central station and walk three blocks west, or ride bus 64 or 70, which stop right on the corner of Rice Park. **MAP 4:** 4th St. W. and Market St., St. Paul; daily 7:30am-9:30pm; free

## Minnesota State Capitol

St. Paul's native son, architect Cass Gilbert, wowed the local crowds and observers around the country when the new State Capitol was unveiled in 1905. The most remarkable feature of St. Paul's capitol is its gleaming white dome, the second largest self-supporting marble dome in the world. Local stone was used in the steps and interior, which is rich with carvings, portraits, and sculptures by some of the favorite artists of the early 20th century.

Renovations completed in 2017 polished and shined the whole place up, from the quadriga—the gold leaf-covered horses on the roof—to the Rathskeller Café in the basement. The decorations were all restored to their original 1905 look. Guided tours include a chance to walk out on the roof and see the quadriga up close, weather permitting.

There are several memorials worth visiting on the 18-acre State Capitol grounds, including statues of several former governors and the Norse explorer Leif Ericson. Minnesota's veterans are honored in several memorials as well, including the **Minnesota Vietnam Veterans Memorial,** which opened in 1992. The memorial is just south of the capitol building itself and behind the Veterans Administration building. It includes elements evocative of home for all Minnesotans and a wall inscribed with the names of Minnesota's fallen fighters. The **Minnesota Korean War Memorial** includes evocative twin sculptures of a young soldier and an empty silhouette. A spiral of obelisks memorializes local civil rights leader Roy Wilkins, who led the NAACP for 22 years. And

Minnesota State Capitol

a stark arch, the **Minnesota Peace Officers Memorial**, honors law enforcement officers who gave their lives in the line of duty.

Take the light-rail Green Line to the Capitol/Rice Street Station.

MAP 4: 75 Rev. Dr. Martin Luther King Jr. Blvd., St. Paul, 651/296-2881, www.mnhs. org/capitol; Mon.-Fri. 8:30am-5pm, Sat. 10am-3pm, Sun. 1pm-4pm; guided tours Mon.-Fri. 10am-2pm on the hour; free, $5 suggested donation for guided tours

### Western Sculpture Park

The 4.5-acre park just west of the Minnesota State Capitol grounds is perhaps one of St. Paul's best-kept secrets. Shady, intertwining paths lead visitors to 20 large-scale sculptures, most of which were created by local sculptors, both established and emerging. Perhaps the most prominent are *Grace à Toi,* by Mark di Suvero, a tripod of leaning I-beams with eerily moving parts suspended overhead, and *Walking Warrior I,* by Melvin Smith, a solemn black metal human figure. Families have fun with *Frame,* by Shaun Cassidy, which is just what it sounds like: a large, cheeky white frame. Neighbors and visitors make use of the volleyball court and playground as much as they enjoy the art.

To get here, take the light-rail Green Line to the Capitol/Rice Street station, then walk a third of a mile west and south, or take bus 16 to the Marion Street and Fuller Avenue stop, right at the park.

MAP 4: 387 Marion St., St. Paul, 651/290-0921, www.publicartstpaul.org; daily dawn-dusk; free

### James J. Hill Center

Railway baron James J. Hill gave much to this area: a rail connection to both coasts that turned both cities into 19th-century boomtowns, the magnificent Stone Arch Bridge in Minneapolis, and the James J. Hill Reference Library, one of the foremost collections of business literature in the country. Although Hill first envisioned it as a more general collection, the library decided to focus on business references in the 1970s as a tribute to Hill's legacy. The building, completed in 1921, has been called one of the finest examples of beaux arts architecture in Minnesota, and the striking Great Reading Room is a popular spot for weddings and receptions. Today the library is heavily used by students, researchers, entrepreneurs, and others, but visitors are welcome to look around respectfully as well, free of charge. If you need a space to work or meet with others while you're in town, the Hill welcomes you (and your coffee mug) with open arms. The Hill Center is connected to the equally beautiful **George Latimer Central Library** (Mon. noon-8pm, Tues.-Fri. 9am-5:30pm, Sat. 11am-5pm, Sun. 1pm-5pm), also worth a stop.

Take the light-rail Green Line to Central station, then walk three blocks west. Buses 64 and 70 stop right on the corner of Rice Park.

MAP 4: 80 4th St. W., St. Paul, 651/265-5500, www.jjhill.org; Mon.-Thurs. 10am-5pm; free

James J. Hill Center

## St. Paul City Hall and Ramsey County Courthouse

This stunning example of art deco architecture represents an unusual case of a city benefiting from the Great Depression. The money for the building was approved in 1928, before the 1929 Black Tuesday crash. Even though the costs of materials and labor dipped dramatically, the city let the original $4 million appropriation stand, ensuring a building that was, and remains, truly opulent inside and out. The strong vertical lines of the 21-story exterior stand out in a city that has very few examples of this style of architecture. Inside, the 3-story Memorial Hall is an art deco marvel, rich with mirrors, inlaid wood, and black marble. The room is dedicated to Ramsey County soldiers who died in World Wars I and II, Korea, Vietnam, and Grenada. Their names are inscribed on the walls. The centerpiece of the hall is *Vision of Peace,* by Carl Milles, the largest white onyx sculpture in the world. The massive sculpture depicting Native Americans smoking peace pipes (it was originally called *The Indian God of Peace*) rotates on its motorized base once every 2.5 hours. Visitors are welcome to take self-guided tours and view the distinctive details, right down to the elevator doors and the door handles. Ask at the front desk about drop-in guided tours, or call 651/266-8000 to schedule a tour. Be sure not to miss the views from the 18th-floor law library of the Mississippi River, Cathedral of St. Paul, and the State Capitol.

Take bus 62 or 75 to the Wabasha and 4th Street stop, or the light-rail Green Line to the Central stop, then walk one block south and west.

MAP 4: 15 Kellogg Blvd. W., St. Paul, 651/266-8266; Mon.-Fri. 8am-4:30pm; free

## Union Depot

St. Paul's neoclassical Union Depot, with its severe columns, was completed in 1923, after the original 1871 depot burned down and World War I delayed reconstruction. In its heyday, it saw 282 trains and 20,000 passengers coming through every day. But passenger rail service abandoned Union Depot in 1971, when Amtrak moved to a train station in St. Paul's Midway neighborhood. The massive building didn't sit empty, however, and wasn't allowed to fall into disrepair, but it was, sort of, forgotten, sitting on a far edge of St. Paul's downtown. The U.S. Post Office used the concourse area for mail handling, private offices and condos moved in, and a couple of restaurants filled up the lobby.

In 2012, after a $250 million renovation, Amtrak brought train service back, and Union Depot is once again a transportation hub and an architectural jewel welcoming visitors and locals alike. Stroll through at your leisure, or take an hour-long tour every other Tuesday at 11am. Meet under the clock in the eastern end. Tours are free, but you can secure a space through a reservation form on its website.

The Amtrak train the Empire Builder stops here twice a day (once headed east, once west); the light-rail Green Line, connecting downtown Minneapolis with downtown St. Paul, stops here, and long-distance Greyhound, Megabus, and Jefferson Lines buses use the building as a hub. As part of the building's gold LEED certification, ample bike parking and storage, a Nice Ride bike rental station, and electric car charging stations were included.

Union Depot is the last stop on the light-rail Green Line.

MAP 4: 214 4th St. E., St. Paul, www. uniondepot.org; daily 24 hours; free

Wabasha Street Caves

## Wabasha Street Caves

This complex of caves on St. Paul's West Side has lived many lives: Originally silica mines, the caves have also housed a mushroom farm, a nightclub that saw figures famous in the jazz world and in the underworld, and, currently, an event space specializing in themed tours. The nightclub Castle Royal, which opened in 1932 and closed in the 1960s, is reputed to have welcomed both Cab Calloway and John Dillinger. Today, swing-dancing parties on Thursday nights (6pm-10pm, $8) bring the big hardwood dance floor back to life. Popular 40-minute cave tours (year-round Thurs. at 5pm, Sat. and Sun. at 11am, plus Memorial Day through Labor Day Mon. 4pm, $8) feature a little bit of history mixed with a little bit of sass. Learn all about the various otherworldly sightings in the caves on the Lost Souls Tour (last Sun. of the month, 12:30pm, $10). The caves also host Halloween- and Christmas-themed events.

Take bus 62 or 75 to the Wabasha and Vision Loss Resources stop.

MAP 4: 215 Wabasha St. S., St. Paul, 651/292-1220, www.wabashastreetcaves. com; hours vary; cave tours $8-10

Indian Mounds Park

## Indian Mounds Park

The first European explorers to come to this part of the Mississippi marveled at the mysterious symmetrical mounds they found high up on the bluff overlooking the river. These burial mounds predate even the Dakota tribes, who had been living in the area since sometime before the 17th century, and may be as old as 2,000 years. Historians and archaeologists believe the mounds were built by the Native American tribes known collectively as the Hopewell culture, who traveled north up the Mississippi around that time. As many as 37 mounds in two locations were mapped out by 19th-century scientists, on what is now Dayton's Bluff and Indian Mounds Park. All of these were destroyed in the late 19th and early 20th centuries except for the six that are now the centerpiece of the park. Much of what we know about the mounds comes down from T. H. Lewis, who excavated the mounds, sometimes at breakneck speed, in the early 1880s. He found bones, masks, pottery, and other artifacts, as well as graves created in a variety of ways, indicating that the mounds had been in use over a very long period of time. Unfortunately, nearly all these items have now disappeared.

The remaining mounds—the largest of which is 260 feet in circumference and 18 feet high—are fenced off but visible within the park, with a few interpretive signs nearby. The park is also a popular recreation area and offers fantastic views of the river and downtown St. Paul. Visitors are asked, however, to respect the fact that the mounds are grave sites.

Take bus 70 to the Burns Avenue and Earl Street stop to get here.
**MAP 4:** 10 Mounds Blvd., St. Paul, 651/632-5111, www.ci.stpaul.mn.us; daily sunrise-11pm; free

# Summit-University and Mac-Groveland

Map 5

## ✪ Summit Avenue

For most of its 150-year history, Summit Avenue has been among St. Paul's most sought-after addresses. Even for those who can't quite afford one of the stately homes, a stroll or a jog along the broad, elm-lined boulevard in the center of the avenue is among the chief pleasures of living in or visiting St. Paul. The 4.5-mile avenue stretches from the edge of downtown St. Paul in the east to the Mississippi River in the west. The entire length is part of one of two National Historic Districts and includes fine examples of nearly every type of residential architecture from the past century.

The parklike divided boulevard begins at the intersection with Lexington Avenue and continues west. But the stretch of Summit Avenue east of Lexington is rich with interesting historical homes, especially as the street starts to curve and climb up tony Crocus Hill. This neighborhood remains largely as it was in the early 1900s. At 312 Summit Avenue, the oldest extant house on the avenue and one of the oldest in St. Paul is the Stuart House. It, like most of the buildings, is a private residence. Other private buildings of interest include 516 Summit, where Minnesota author Sinclair Lewis lived for a time, and 599 Summit, where local boy F. Scott Fitzgerald wrote his first published novel, *This Side of Paradise*. The governor's residence—not open to the public—is at 1006 Summit, near the intersection with Lexington. You can tour the museum in the **James J. Hill House,** the largest single-family residence in Minnesota. You can also peek inside the **Germanic American**

James J. Hill House on Summit Avenue

**Institute** (301 Summit Ave., 651/222-7027, www.gai-mn.org; Mon.-Thurs. 9am-5pm, Fri. 9am-4pm; free).

The only park along the length of Summit Avenue is **Lookout Park** (also called Summit Overlook Park), a neat little triangle of land with benches and tidy gardens at the intersection with Ramsey Street. Here you can enjoy views from the Mississippi River bluffs that once belonged to rail and timber barons.

Take bus 21 from Summit and Cretin on the western end to Selby and Summit on the eastern end.

**MAP 5:** Summit Ave. between Selby Ave. and Mississippi River Blvd.

# Como and St. Anthony     Map 6

## COMO PARK

The nearly 400-acre Como Park has been a center for recreation and family fun in St. Paul since the late 1800s. Today more than 2.5 million people come to the park every year to picnic, walk, run, bike, ski, fish, and visit the attractions: the Como Park Zoo and Conservatory, Cafesjian's Carousel, Como Town, and the big pool and water park, with its aquatic zipline and lazy river. Bus 3 stops right in the park.

### Como Park Zoo and Conservatory

The Como Zoo holds a treasured place in many Minnesotans' hearts— so much so that Apple Valley's larger Minnesota Zoo, built in 1978, is still occasionally referred to as "the new zoo." Como's history goes back much longer than that, all the way to 1897, and several of the buildings were built in the 1930s by the Works Progress Administration. Generations of

Minnesotans have come to see tigers, wolves, penguins, gorillas, giraffes, and more, as well as the beloved seal and sea lion shows. One of the newest and most up-to-date areas is the spacious, naturalistic Polar Bear Odyssey. The Tropical Encounter in the Marjorie McNeely Conservatory is an innovative collaboration with the zoo. Visitors see fish, birds, and other small animals interacting with the tropical plants almost as they would in the wild. A sloth even wanders freely, if slowly, throughout the "tropical forest."

MAP 6: 1225 Estabrook Dr., 651/487-8200, www.comozooconservatory.org; Apr.-Sept. daily 10am-6pm, Oct.-Mar. daily 10am-4pm; free

Cafesjian's Carousel in Como Park

### Cafesjian's Carousel

Cafesjian's Carousel was built on the Minnesota State Fairgrounds in 1914. In 1988, when owners unexpectedly announced plans to close the beloved annual attraction, a group of neighbors banded together to save it. The carousel operated for 10 years in downtown St. Paul and moved to Como Park in 2000. Gerard Cafesjian, for whom the carousel is named, donated $1.2 million to finance its restoration and move in the late 1990s. Its new home, a beautiful copper-roofed pavilion, has massive doors that can open on summer days and close to extend the season in the fall. Sixty-eight hand-carved horses in four rows ring the carousel, which is 50 feet in diameter. A restored Wurlitzer band organ, while not original to this carousel, sounds appropriately old-fashioned as it calls out across the park, playing paper rolls of classic carousel tunes.

MAP 6: 1245 Midway Pkwy., St. Paul, 651/489-4628, www.ourfaircarousel. org; May-Labor Day Tues.-Fri. 11am-4pm, Sat.-Sun. 11am-6pm; Sept.-Oct. Sat.-Sun. 11am-4pm; Memorial Day and Labor Day 11am-4pm; $2

### Como Town

Como Town offers pint-size excitement, with rides and play structures for toddlers through tweens and one or two rides for adults to enjoy as well. Most rides are old-school, like the teacups, the swings, and the train, but all is not passive entertainment: Kids can climb, swing, explore, and dig in Hodge Podge Park. Como Town's size and energy level are well suited to the littlest ones, who will be able to take it all in without getting overwhelmed. Opening hours are shorter in May and down to weekends only in September, after which the park closes for the winter.

MAP 6: 1301 Midway Pkwy., St. Paul, 651/487-2121, www.comotown.com; Jun.-Aug. Sun.-Thurs. 10am-7pm, Fri.-Sat. 10am-8pm, May and Sept. limited hours; free admission, rides $0.75-3

GREATER TWIN CITIES

## ✪ Mall of America

Visitors come to the Mall of America to gawk, to say they've seen the largest mall in the United States, and, yes, to shop. There's no reason to be intimidated by the mall's layout: Stores are arranged on three levels of an oval, with three large department stores anchoring the corners (Macy's, Nordstrom's, and Sears, with L.L. Bean in the fourth corner). The sides are all labeled north, south, east, or west, so if you know what side and what level you're on, there's no way to get lost.

The Nickelodeon Universe theme park (952/883-8800, www.nickelodeonuniverse.com) occupies the center, with a full-size Ferris wheel, roller coaster, and log chute, as well as milder rides that thrill little ones with references to Dora the Explorer and Diego. Other thrilling experiences in the mall include Flyover America (5120 center court, www.

Nickelodeon Universe inside the Mall of America

flyover-america.com; Mon.-Sat. 10am-9:30pm, Sun. 11am-7pm; $19 ages 13 and up, $15 children 12 and under), a virtual aerial tour of the country's landmarks; Smaaash (E402, www.smaaashusa.com; Mon.-Thurs. 11am-11pm, Fri.-Sat. 10am-midnight, Sun. 10am-10pm; prices vary), a collection of virtual reality experiences and games; and the Crayola Experience (S300, www.crayolaexperience.com; Mon.-Fri. 10am-6pm, Sat. 10am-8pm, Sun. 10am-7pm; $21, children 2 and under free), where you can play with colors in myriad ways.

If you see a large blue shark wandering the mall, it's advertising Sea Life (952/883-0202, www.visitsealife.com/Minnesota, Mon.-Thurs. 10am-7pm, Fri. 10am-8pm, Sat. 9:30am-8pm, Sun. 10am-6:30pm; $24.25 ages 13 and up, $17.25 ages 3-12), a full-size aquarium located under the mall. Walk through a 300-foot glass tunnel under sharks and rays, pick up starfish and coral in touch tanks, and learn about endangered turtles.

While sheer density makes the mall a shopper's mecca, you won't necessarily find any particular deals or very many shops outside the usual mall standards. For Minnesota souvenirs like Minnetonka Moccasins and wooden loons, check out Love from Minnesota (W380, 952/854-7319, www.lovefrommn.com) and Minnesot-ah! (E157, 952/858-8531, www.lovefrommn.com). Nonshoppers enjoy combining a nice dinner with a movie on one of 13 screens at the CMX Mall of America (612/263-9302, www.cmxcinemas.com) on the fourth floor. You can stay at the Radisson Blu

# THE GREAT INDOORS

Not everyone wants to revel in the cold. Even those who love a good snowstorm may need a break from the long gray stretches of winter or the rainy patches of summer. Smart locals know where to find a bit of the tropics right in the Twin Cities, and visitors can have a great time here even in the worst weather.

While much of the **Minnesota Zoo** is outside, the Tropics Trail and aquariums are all indoors, with hundreds of mammals, birds, fish, and plants from warmer climes on display. You could skip the outdoor trails entirely and still spend a happy and full morning or afternoon at the zoo, especially if you catch an IMAX film.

The **Como Park Zoo and Conservatory** in St. Paul has a much smaller tropics display uniquely combining botanical and zoological exhibits. Keep your eye out for the resident sloth.

All of Minnesota's cultural institutions are, of course, indoors and excellent ways to escape the elements. But if you like your escapism untainted by high culture, there is no better place to run away to than the **Mall of America.** Keep in mind that everyone else in the metro area is likely to hit upon this very idea when the mercury plunges, and the 13,000 on-site parking spaces have actually been known to fill up on the coldest days, forcing chilly shoppers into the 7,000 overflow spaces across the street. The west side of the mall opens at 6am every day of the week so mall walkers can get a few laps in before the stores open (one pass around the first level is 0.57 mile).

Thanks to Minneapolis and St. Paul's **skyways,** you can combine shopping, dining, and a little indoor exercise. St. Paul has 5 miles of indoor walkways and Minneapolis has 9.5. If you can bear to brave the elements for a single block, the **Minneapolis Central Library** is just off the skyway system and a worthwhile escape, especially if you have small children.

or **JW Marriott,** attached to the mall. The mall, in fact, is on an expansion and redevelopment tear; watch for even more retail, hotel, office, and exhibit space in years to come.

The west side of the mall opens at 6am every day of the week so mall walkers can get a few laps in before the stores open (one pass around the first level is 0.57 mile). Keep in mind that after 4pm on Friday and Saturday, everyone age 16 and under must be accompanied by an adult. Mall security guards aren't shy about asking for ID.

The light-rail Blue Line ends at the Mall of America.

MAP 7: 60 Broadway E., Bloomington, 952/883-8800, www.mallofamerica. com; stores Mon.-Fri. 10am-9:30pm, Sat. 9:30am-9:30pm, Sun. 11am-7pm

### ✪ Minnesota Landscape Arboretum

The Minnesota Landscape Arboretum is the largest public garden in the Upper Midwest: a massive and varied collection of display gardens as well as cultivated and wild landscapes. Beyond allowing visitors to wander beautiful paths among well-labeled flowerbeds, the arboretum curates innovative exhibits that combine gardening with sculptures, activities, mazes, and more. Nearly every exhibit includes a component to engage children. The arboretum was established as part of the University of Minnesota's horticultural department in 1907 and has produced such objects of Minnesotans' undying pride as the Honeycrisp apple, a cold-hardy—and very tasty!—variety. Many visitors choose to wander the gardens nearest the welcome center on foot. The herb gardens, annual and perennial demonstration gardens, and Japanese gardens, for example, can all be easily taken in by walking a less-than-two-mile loop. Others like to drive a three-mile loop through prairies, woodlands, and marshes. (Guided tours are available for an additional

Minnesota Landscape Arboretum

fee.) While the grounds are open long hours every day except Christmas and Thanksgiving, the hours of the conservatory and welcome center, including the cafeteria and gift shop, are shorter (Mon.-Sat. 8am-6pm, Sun. 10am-6pm). Admission is free on the third Monday of the month 8am-5pm. In the winter, November-March, buildings close at 4:30pm.

No public transportation runs to the arboretum.

MAP 7: 3675 Arboretum Dr., Chaska, 952/443-1400, www.arboretum.umn.edu; daily 8am-8pm or sunset, whichever comes first; $15 adults, children 15 and under free

### Excelsior Streetcar Line

On the shores of Lake Minnetonka, one of the vestiges of the Twin Cities' once-vast streetcar line still operates. The same volunteers who work tirelessly on the Como-Harriet Streetcar Line also run four trolleys on a short stretch of track in pretty downtown Excelsior. The conductor is sure to tell you stories about the days when

everyone rode the trolleys and will give you a tour of the car barn where they keep and restore the trolleys if you ask. Combining a ride with a round-trip ride on the **Steamboat Minnehaha** (952/474-2115, www.steamboatminnehaha.org, $15 adults, $5 children), which once ferried trolley commuters and vacationers across the lake and now docks near the Old Excelsior Road end of the trolley line, is a great way to spend a summer weekend afternoon.

Commuter bus lines 670 and 671 run to Excelsior, but only for the afternoon commute.

MAP 7: Water St. and George St., Excelsior, 952/922-1096, www.trolleyride.org; May-early Sept. Sat. 10am-4pm, Sun. 1pm-4pm, Tues. 2pm-6pm (through Oct.); mid-Sept.-mid.-Oct. Sat. 11am-3pm; $2.50

### Valleyfair

Valleyfair prides itself on being the largest amusement park in the Upper Midwest, with 75 rides on 90 acres. Popular thrillers include the spinning

RipTide, the Xtreme Swing (which launches riders into the air), and the wooden roller coaster Renegade. Tickets include unlimited rides and as much time as you want to spend in the 3.5-acre Soak City Waterpark, with five water slides and plenty of other soaking wet fun. (Swimsuits are required; changing facilities and lockers are provided. Soak City opens later and generally closes earlier than the rest of the park.) Challenge Park lets visitors indulge their competitive spirits with a zip-cord ride, minigolf, go-carts, and bumper boats, all for an additional fee. The park also puts on one of the area's most popular haunted houses, dubbed "Valleyscare." Note that Valleyfair's hours vary, with the park staying open until 11pm a few weekends in late summer and closing between 5pm and 10pm on weekdays at the beginning and end of the season. Discounts are available after 4pm. Call ahead or check the website.

Commuter bus 499 stops at Valley Industrial Boulevard and Valley Park Drive.

**MAP 7:** 1 Valleyfair Dr., Shakopee, 952/445-7600, www.valleyfair.com; mid-May-Aug. daily 10am-10pm, summer Fri.-Sat. 10am-11pm; $35-55, with discounts for seniors and anyone under 48 inches

## Minnesota Zoo

The Minnesota Zoo offers a wide variety of experiences for all sorts of animal lovers. In the outdoor exhibit, the Northern Trail, the animals are all native to climates very similar to Minnesota's own, from the native moose to the Siberian tiger. Most have plenty of room to roam (and hide from visitors) in enclosures spread wide across the zoo's 500 acres. The Northern Trail loops around the grounds and leads to the Family Farm, where cows, pigs, goats, chickens, and sheep live. The farm is especially popular in the spring, when baby animals draw tens of thousands of visitors.

Inside the zoo building, you'll find the Tropics Trail, with a collection of very different animals, from the rare sun bear to ring-tailed lemurs from Madagascar. The Minnesota Trail starts with our very own raccoons and includes everything from walleye to wolves and from eagles to lynx. In Discovery Bay, a massive tank of sharks and other large fish stops kids cold. Charming Hawaiian monk seals have taken over the living space that opened up when the zoo chose to stop exhibiting dolphins. African penguins live near the south entry in a very informative display.

The zoo's most stunning exhibit is Russia's Grizzly Coast, with 3.5 acres representing three distinct landscapes of Russia's far east: the Pacific coast, the volcanic Kamchatka Peninsula, and the taiga forests of Primorsky Krai. Visitors get an amazing up close look at northern sea otters, brown bears, wild boars, and vanishingly rare Amur leopards in a beautifully designed space.

Buses 440 and 475 run directly to the zoo.

**MAP 7:** 13000 Zoo Blvd., Apple Valley, 952/431-9200, www.mnzoo.com; year-round daily 9am-4pm; extended hours (9am-6pm) Labor Day-Memorial Day and weekends in May and Sept.; $18 adults, $12 seniors and children 3-12, free for children 2 and under

## Historic Fort Snelling

Fort Snelling marks the beginning of an important era in Minnesota's history. The U.S. military arrived here in 1819 to wrest control of the increasingly lucrative fur trade from the

## THE MEANING OF FREE SOIL:
## THE STORY OF DRED AND HARRIET SCOTT

One of the most infamous U.S. Supreme Court cases in history had its roots right here in Fort Snelling. In 1836, Dred Scott came to Minnesota with his owner, John Emerson, the fort's physician. There, he married Harriet, who was owned by the local Indian agent, Lawrence Taliaferro. Slavery was prohibited in the area that now includes Minnesota under the Northwest Ordinance of 1787 and the Missouri Compromise of 1820, but this law was often ignored. Emerson's family, along with Dred and Harriet Scott, later moved back to Missouri (a slave-owning state).

After Emerson died in 1843, the Scotts sued for their freedom on the grounds that they had lived in a free state. They won their first round, but Emerson's widow appealed and the case went all the way to the Supreme Court, which, in 1857, ruled against the Scotts seven to two. Dred Scott died the next year and Harriet died in 1876.

British. Construction on the fort at the confluence of the Mississippi and Minnesota Rivers began in 1820 and was completed in 1824. The soldiers themselves, far from the relative civilization of the East Coast, needed to be self-sufficient and so began much of the development that led to the establishment of Minneapolis at St. Anthony Falls, building mills and roads. The fort even played a bit part in American civil rights history as the home of Dred and Harriet Scott while they lived in Minnesota, forming the base of their claim that they should be allowed to live as free citizens.

Fort Snelling continued to be an active military base, including housing the Military Intelligence Language School during World War II. It was decommissioned in 1946 and started to fall into disrepair, a process Minnesotans are still fighting to reverse. The National Trust for Historic Preservation has placed Fort Snelling's Upper Post on its list of America's Most Endangered Places.

Today the fort sits within the Fort Snelling Unincorporated Area, bordered by both Minneapolis and St. Paul (as well as three suburbs) but inside neither city. The Minnesota Historical Society operates the fort as a living history center, where costumed guides help visitors imagine the year is 1827. The guides act out both military and everyday life, from musket drills to mending clothes, with plenty of hands-on activities for the whole family.

**Fort Snelling Military Cemetery** is adjacent to the fort and open to visitors. **Fort Snelling State Park** (www.dnr.state.mn.us), surrounding the fort, includes 5 miles of paved bicycle trails, 12 miles of groomed cross-country ski trails, a nine-hole golf course, and swimming, boating, and fishing opportunities on Snelling Lake.

The Fort Snelling Station on the light-rail Blue Line is about two-thirds of a mile from the park itself. Bus 7 stops right in the park parking lot. **MAP 7:** Hwy. 5 and Hwy. 55, 612/726-1171, www.historicfortsnelling.org; Memorial Day-Labor Day Tues.-Sat. 10am-5pm, Sun. noon-5pm; Sept.-Oct. Sat. 10am-5pm; $12 adults, $10 seniors and students, $6 children 6-17

# Sightseeing Tours

### ✪ Human on a Stick

Ride a Segway on a three-hour Minneapolis tour following a seven-mile loop from St. Anthony Main to the Stone Arch Bridge, past the Guthrie Theater and Mill City Museum, and up to Boom Island and Nicollet Island. The similar-length St. Paul tour spins over downtown and the State Capitol. A third tour, also leaving from Minneapolis, covers the Minneapolis Sculpture Garden at the Walker Art Center. For all three, knowledgeable guides introduce you to the highlights of the area's history and the beauty of the sites. Plus, you get to say you rode a Segway. All tours start with training, and helmets are provided. Riders must be 13-80 years old and weigh less than 280 pounds. (The human-on-a-stick joke, by the way, refers to Minneapolis's beloved State Fair, where all manner of edibles are served impaled.)

**Various locations:** Downtown Minneapolis meeting/sales point 125 Main St. SE, Minneapolis, 952/888-9200, www.humanonastick.com; Downtown St. Paul meeting/sales point St. Paul Curling Club, 470 Selby Ave., St. Paul; Mar.-Oct. daily; $90

### The Fit Tourist

The best way to see downtown Minneapolis is under your own power. The Fit Tourist leads walking and biking tours that, despite the name, aren't too strenuous. Two walking tours, about 2.5 hours long, cover highlights in downtown's Mill City and downtown core areas. Reserve online to get exact information on meeting places.

**Downtown Minneapolis:** 952/888-9200, www.thefittourist.com; $38

### Landmark Center Tours

An ideal place to start your exploration of St. Paul, the Landmark Center offers free public tours Thursdays at 11am and Sundays at noon. Most tours leave from the Landmark Center foyer, but on the first Wednesday, tours meet at Upper Landing Park, near the Science Museum of Minnesota, and explore the river's influence on the city. Check the Landmark Center's schedule for occasional specialty tours or call to schedule a private Gangster Tour with two weeks advance notice.

**Downtown St. Paul and West Side:** Landmark Center, 75 5th St. W., St. Paul, 651/292-3225 ext. 4, www.landmarkcenter.org; free

### Mill City Museum Tours

On most summer Saturdays and Sundays, and a few Wednesdays and Fridays as well, you can leave the Mill City Museum for walking tours directed by capable and enthusiastic guides from the Minnesota Historical Society. The tours cover downtown's riverfront district, focusing on historical topics from women's work to railroad history to geeky engineering details. See the website for a full schedule and to book online.

**Downtown Minneapolis:** Mill City Museum, 704 2nd St. S., Minneapolis, 612/341-7555, www.millcitymuseum.org; June-Sept. most Thurs., Sat., and Sun.; $14 adults, $12 seniors and college students, $10 children 5-17

### MSP Tours

If you've got a three-hour layover in Minneapolis, you've got enough time to see at least a little bit of the city.

MSP Tours offers three self-guided tours ranging from two hours to half a day. You don't even need a car: These tours are all based around stops on the light-rail and bus systems, which, fortunately, include so much of what makes Minneapolis a great place to visit, from Minnehaha Falls to the Mall of America and the Mississippi River. Pick up maps and audio devices in Terminal 1 of the Minneapolis-St. Paul Airport (along the main mall) or in downtown Minneapolis (220 6th St. S.) and return them to the same location when you're done. It is recommended to reserve in advance. For an additional fee, audio devices can also be delivered to your hotel. The price includes tickets for the Hiawatha light-rail line, which leads from the airport to downtown Minneapolis.

**Various locations:** airport 612/229-9945, downtown Minneapolis 612/232-7814, www.exploreminnesota.com; $27.50 per audio rental (usable by two people)

### St. Paul Gangster Tours

Your guide, "Dapper Dan Hogan," leads the two-hour bus tour in character as the proprietor of a real 1920s joint called the Green Lantern. Prohibition was authored by teetotalers in St. Paul's Landmark Center, and its eventual passage left a brutal mark on the city: an extensive kickback and protection racket involving the St. Paul police, shootouts with John Dillinger, and a whorehouse

rumored to be connected to the State Capitol by a secret but well-traversed tunnel. The tour, by air-conditioned coach, includes parks and facades around St. Paul (where, often as not, villainy of some sort once happened) and also covers a general history of the city through the mid-20th century. Reservations are required. The company also offers a more detailed tour of historic Summit Avenue and a Minneapolis Gangster tour, as well as specialty seasonal tours.

**Downtown St. Paul and West Side:** meeting point 215 Wabasha St. S., St. Paul, 651/292-1220, www.wabashastreetcaves. com; May-Sept. Sat.-Sun. noon; $27

### Taste Twin Cities

The Twin Cities are a fantastic place to enjoy great food and, believe it or not, pretty good local wine. You could go it on your own and do pretty well, or you could entrust yourself to local experts. Taste Twin Cities leads walking tours through downtown Minneapolis, the skyway system, and northeast Minneapolis. Tours take about three hours, including plenty of walking and about five stops for food (plenty to fill you up like a real meal). If you'd rather drink than walk, there are five-hour bus tours of wineries just outside the Twin Cities or breweries within the cities. Buy tickets in advance online.

**Various locations:** 612/280-4851, www. tastetwincities.com; costs vary depending on tour, generally $40-130

# RESTAURANTS

The Twin Cities are a fantastic place for people who love food. Throw out your images of meat-and-potatoes farm food and underseasoned ghosts of Nordic fare. The Upper Midwest's connection to farming serves eaters well. With young chefs—some of whom regularly show up on the list of James Beard Award nominees—leading the way, "local," "seasonal," and "sustainable" have become more than buzzwords. Knowing exactly where your vegetables, beef, chicken, and pork come from has become de rigueur for fine dining. The upshot of the focus on chef-driven short menus is that unless the chef is personally dedicated to a less-meat lifestyle, vegetarians often get shortchanged with an afterthought pasta or salad. (Of course, it will likely be a salad of local butter leaf lettuces.)

Meritage

Diners in the Twin Cities also benefit from the robust Laotian, Vietnamese, and East African communities here. Spring rolls and *bánh mì* (Vietnamese stuffed baguettes) show up on menus all over town. And the fragrant *phô* soup and noodle salads have become local staples.

Minnesotans eat early. Most restaurants open for dinner at 5pm, and the busiest seating is likely to be 6pm. That's good news for people who would rather eat around 8pm but bad news for those who like to dine later—many kitchens close 9pm-10pm. It's another vestige of the farming culture. Adapt by joining the crowds for breakfast and brunch, a Midwesterner's favorite meal.

## HIGHLIGHTS

✪ **BEST PLACE FOR PASTA:** Find flavor-packed plates like gnocchi with cauliflower and orange at **Bar La Grassa** (page 55).

✪ **BEST PLACE TO TASTE MINNESOTA'S IMMIGRANT PAST:** Links of Polish sausage and plates of butter-soaked *pelmeni* fueled Nordeast Minneapolis's Eastern European immigrant families—and at **Kramarczuk's** they keep hungry tourists and locals fed, too (page 72).

✪ **BEST PLACE TO TASTE MINNESOTA'S IMMIGRANT PRESENT:** A trip down University Avenue in St. Paul or Nicollet Avenue in Minneapolis (also known as Eat Street) will take you past dozens of hole-in-the-wall Vietnamese restaurants. **Quang** is a particular local favorite (page 62).

✪ **BEST PASTRIES:** The international experts have spoken: For croissants and patisserie as good as or better than those found in Paris, head to **Rose Street Patisserie** (page 69).

✪ **BEST FARM-TO-FORK MENU:** Whatever is truly at the peak of its season is what you'll find on the constantly changing prix-fixe menu at **Alma** (page 71).

✪ **BEST PLACE TO LIVE YOUR FRENCH BISTRO DREAM:** You might just swear that's Edith Piaf herself enjoying her *soupe à l'oignon* at St. Paul's gilded and now classic **Meritage** (page 76).

✪ **BEST PLACE TO IMPRESS YOUR DATE:** Enjoy French cuisine from a two-time James Beard Award winner in a charming space at **Bellecour** (page 86).

## PRICE KEY

| | |
|---|---|
| **$** | Entrées less than $10 |
| **$ $** | Entrées $10-20 |
| **$ $ $** | Entrées more than $20 |

## CONTEMPORARY AND FUSION

### Bar and Café Lurcat $$$

This is where you will find Minneapolis's beautiful people, arranged artfully on Lurcat's exquisite collection of couches and chaise longues. The people-watching provides delightful entertainment while you eat. In the bar, that means small plates, like rave-worthy miniburgers and decadently golden fries. In the café, you'll find creative contemporary American fare with a touch of French influence: buckwheat crepes, several cuts of steak, butter-poached prawns, and foie gras.

MAP 1: 1624 Harmon Pl., Minneapolis, 612/486-5500, www.cafelurcat.com; Mon.-Thurs. 5:30pm-10pm, Fri.-Sat. 5:30pm-midnight, Sun. 5pm-9pm

### Borough $$$

High-flown, inventive cuisine is served in a high-ceilinged, classically beautiful room. Entrées with dabs and swoops of trendy flavors, from chimichurri to lavender, are big on technique and carefully composed, while the burger at the downstairs cocktail lounge, **Parlour** (same hours), is beloved.

MAP 1: 730 Washington Ave. N., Minneapolis, 612/354-3135, www.boroughmpls.com; Mon.-Thurs. 11am-2pm and 5pm-10pm, Fri. 11am-2pm and 5pm-11pm, Sat. 5pm-11pm, Sun. 10am-2pm

### Butcher and the Boar $$$

Big, primal, meaty dishes make a meal at Butcher and the Boar feel like a feast. This is a great place to accommodate a big group, with plenty of six-tops and a menu ripe for sharing: The roasted long rib is a local classic, and the sausage and charcuterie plates include a fantastic variety of meats cured in-house, from head cheese to, yes, wild boar. If you can't get a seat in the beer garden in back, the dark wood interior is still a beautiful and festive choice.

MAP 1: 1121 Hennepin Ave., Minneapolis, 612/238-8888, www.butcherandtheboar.com; Sun.-Thurs. 5pm-10pm, Fri.-Sat. 5pm-11pm

Spoon and Stable

### Spoon and Stable $$$

In casual, comfort-loving Minnesota, Spoon and Stable is one of just a couple of places offering an elegant, elevated, impress-at-all-costs experience. Nationally lauded young chef Gavin Kaysen creates precise, intricate plates like seared duck breast with burned honey jus, lamb with baby fennel, and bison with king oysters, served by some of the best-trained waitstaff in the cities. And, when you're ready to go beyond Benedict for brunch, Spoon and

Stable is where you come for grilled oysters, tartare, and handmade pasta.

MAP 1: 211 1st St. N., Minneapolis, 612/224-9850, www.spoonandstable. com; Mon.-Thurs. 4pm-midnight, Fri.-Sat. 4pm-1am, Sun. 10am-2pm and 5pm-midnight

### 112 Eatery $$

What would hungry cooks or servers want to eat after a long shift? Probably a hearty egg sandwich with tangy *harissa*, meatballs made with foie gras, perfect steak tartare, or a plateful of light-as-air parmesan gnocchi. They'd want the best ingredients served up in comforting dishes. That's what you get in this tiny Warehouse District space, a favorite among late-night diners.

MAP 1: 112 3rd St. N., Minneapolis, 612/343-7696, www.112eatery.com; Mon.-Thurs. 5pm-midnight, Fri.-Sat. 5pm-1am, Sun. 5pm-10pm

## NORDIC
### The Bachelor Farmer $$$

When the New Nordic trend swept into the United States, this is what it produced in Minneapolis. (The *New York Times* even featured its famous rooftop garden on the front page.) Brothers and heirs to the local department store fortune, Eric and Andrew Dayton opened The Bachelor Farmer (and the Marvel Bar downstairs) as an homage to their Minnesota home. The menu changes constantly, but expect plenty of cod, roe, rye, caraway seeds, sauerkraut, and pork in unexpected modern combinations. Next door, the Bachelor Farmer Café (Mon.-Fri. 6am-5pm, Sat.-Sun. 8am-5pm) serves rigorously crafted coffee and pastries for breakfast, and Nordic-inspired open-faced sandwiches for lunch.

a Scandinavian-style, open-faced sandwich at the Bachelor Farmer Café

MAP 1: 50 2nd Ave. N., Minneapolis, 612/206-3920, www.thebachelorfarmer. com; Mon.-Thurs. 5:30pm-9:30pm, Fri.-Sat. 5:30pm-10:30pm, Sun. 5pm-9:30pm

# ASIAN

## Kado no Mise $$$

Everything at Kado no Mise, from the long, bright dining room to the brief menu to the flavors on your plate, is a study in understated sophistication. The sushi bar is open to walk-ins; order à la carte or *omakase* (chef's choice, which can run well north of $100). For the traditional hours-long parade of tiny, intricate courses known as *kaiseki*, make a reservation upstairs at Kaiseki Furukawa ($125 per person, Thurs.-Sat. 6pm-11pm). Also upstairs, stop in for a sip of Japanese whisky at the semi-secret bar, Gori Gori Peku.

MAP 1: 33 1st. Ave. N., Minneapolis, 612/338-1515, www.kadonomise. com; Mon.-Wed. 4pm-10pm, Thurs.-Fri. 4pm-11pm, Sat. 5pm-11pm, Sun. 5pm-10pm

## Jun $$

Who says authenticity always comes from a little hole in the wall? Sometimes you get it in a swanky, dark-wood dining room like Jun. Find a full range of Sichuan cuisine, from moo shu pork to smoked pig's ears, at every spice level, as well as a brief dim sum menu available all day every day and hand-pulled noodles on the weekends.

MAP 1: 730 Washington Ave. N., Minneapolis, 612/208-0706, www. junnorthloop.com; Sun.-Thurs. 11am-10pm, Fri.-Sat. 11am-11pm

## Zen Box Izakaya $$

At a Japanese pub, or *izakaya*, tables of friends order rounds of beer and sake along with little plates of snacks. That's the best way to enjoy Zen Box, too. From crispy little chicken *kara-age* (the original popcorn chicken) to juicy braised short ribs to classic chilled tofu, most—but not all—of the menu is made to be shared. If you want a hearty meal all to yourself, you can't go wrong with the deep, dark, rich ramen, especially the kimchi ramen.

MAP 1: 602 Washington Ave. S., Minneapolis, 612/332-3936, www. zenboxizakaya.com; Mon.-Thurs. 11:30am-2pm and 5pm-10pm, Fri. 11:30am-2pm and 5pm-midnight, Sat. 5pm-midnight

# ITALIAN

## ✪ Bar La Grassa $$

You know those movie scenes with large, happy Italian families squeezed around tables overflowing with food and reaching across each other for one more bite of pasta, while all talking at once? That may be a stereotype, but that's exactly what your table should look like at Bar La Grassa. Don't expect red sauce Italian and don't expect huge platters of pasta. Instead, the shareable dishes, like the must-order gnocchi with cauliflower and orange, are small, rich, and intensely flavored. Plan to order for the table so you can taste as many things as possible.

MAP 1: 800 Washington Ave. N., Minneapolis, 612/333-3837, www. barlagrassa.com; Mon.-Thurs. 5pm-midnight, Fri.-Sat. 5pm-1am, Sun. 5pm-10pm

## Black Sheep Pizza $$

While Neapolitan devotees will tell you that wood-fired ovens are where it's at, lovers of New York-style pizza will disagree: Coal is what makes a pizza crust great. Black Sheep Pizza brought the first coal-fired oven to the Twin Cities, along with a killer recipe for chewy, flavorful dough—a little thicker than a Neapolitan crust but still eminently foldable. Definitely get the house-made fennel sausage and whatever market salad is on the menu that day. You can now get your coal-fired pizza in St. Paul (512 Robert St. N., St. Paul, 651/227-4337, Sun.-Thurs. 11am-10pm, Fri.-Sat. 11am-11pm) and on Eat Street (2550 Nicollet Ave. S., Minneapolis, 612/886-1233, daily 11am-2am).

MAP 1: 600 Washington Ave. N., Minneapolis, 612/342-2625, www. blacksheeppizza.com; Sun.-Thurs. 11am-10pm, Fri.-Sat. 11am-11pm

## Monello $$

Although it's conveniently located in the Ivy Hotel, Monello is more than just a hotel restaurant. The menu focuses on the seafood-based cuisine of Italy's Campania region, with a parade of crudos and small plates. Come on Sundays for Mama DeCampo's Sunday Supper, featuring homey ziti, lasagna, and piccata. Start or end your meal at the basement cocktail bar, **Constantine** (Sun. 5pm-midnight, Mon.-Thurs. 5pm-1am, Fri.-Sat. 5pm-1:30am).

MAP 1: 1115 2nd Ave. S., Minneapolis, 612/353-6207, www.monellompls.com; Mon.-Thurs. 6:30am-2pm and 5pm-10pm, Fri. 6:30am-2pm and 5pm-11pm, Sat. 7am-2pm and 5pm-11pm, Sun. 7am-2pm and 5pm-10pm

## Zelo $$

Power lunchers and anniversary celebrators love the dark wood and rich ambience at Zelo. The menu is primarily Italian, with touches of Asian flare (calamari *fritti* with lemon aioli, for example, lives comfortably next to ahi spring rolls with wasabi and soy). While the steak and veal entrées are understandably pricey, Zelo's tasty pastas and pizzas, as well as the lunch menu, are actually quite affordable, and you get the same great service. For Zelo taste on the go, head around the corner (same building, different entrance) to Zelino for takeout soups and sandwiches.

MAP 1: 831 Nicollet Mall, Minneapolis, 612/333-7000, www.zelomn. com; Mon.-Thurs. 11am-11pm, Fri. 11am-midnight, Sat. 11:30am-midnight, Sun. 4pm-10pm

## Pizza Lucé $

A little thicker, a little sweeter, a little breadier than your average pie, Pizza Lucé's crust is in a category all its own. And the toppings blow attempts at categorization out of the water: Garlic mashed potatoes, black beans and pico de gallo, and mock duck and pineapple on barbecue sauce are just a few choices on the long menu. This is also a great place for hearty salads and pasta dishes. Vegans and vegetarians will love it here, as will any hungry soul wandering out after bars close at 2am. Lucé has six other locations in the Twin Cities and Duluth.

MAP 1: 119 4th St. N., Minneapolis, 612/333-7359, www.pizzaluce.com; Sun. 10am-2:30am, Mon.-Thurs. 11am-2:30am, Fri. 11am-3:30am, Sat. 10am-3:30am

# STEAK
## Murray's $$$

For more than 60 years, the Silver Butter Knife Steak at Murray's has been one of the classiest ways to say "I love you" to your meat-eating Minneapolis sweetheart. The Silver Butter Knife—you'll recognize it from the picture on the classic neon sign out front—is a 28-ounce cut of meat meant for two, so tender you barely need the titular carving implement. You can also choose among more than a

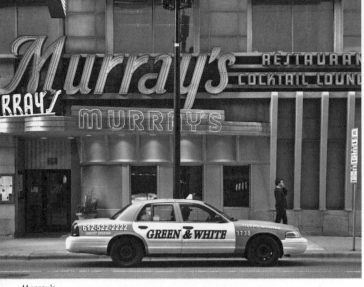

Murray's

dozen other cuts of meat and nearly as many luxurious seafood dishes. Vegetarians . . . well, the only things for vegetarians to enjoy at Murray's are the suave service and timeless setting. **MAP 1:** 26 6th St. S., Minneapolis, 612/339-0909, www.murraysrestaurant. com; Mon.-Thurs. 11am-2:30pm and 5pm-10pm, Fri. 11am-2:30pm and 5pm-10:30pm, Sat. 5pm-10:30pm, Sun. 5pm-10pm

## SEAFOOD
### Sea Change $$$

Whether you're having dinner at the Guthrie or not, whether you care about sustainable fishing or not (they do)— as long as you love seafood, this is the place to go. The raw bar is known for having some of the freshest choices around (from oysters to Hawaiian poke), and the entrées include classic preparations of swordfish and scallops, always with a light touch. The nonseafood options are limited and not nearly as exciting. The large room can feel a little cold and impersonal

(and, bafflingly, there are televisions always on at the bar), but the food will make up for that.
**MAP 1:** Guthrie Theater, 806 2nd St. S., Minneapolis, 612/225-6499, www. seachangempls.com; Tues.-Thurs. 11:30am-3pm and 5pm-10pm, Fri. 11:30am-3pm and 5pm-11pm, Sat. 11am-3pm and 5pm-11pm, Sun. 11am-3pm and 4:30pm-9pm

### Smack Shack $$

You're not supposed to find excellent lobster rolls this far from New England's rocky shores, but here they are. Smack Shack's signature dish is an extra-thick slice of brioche, split through the top, buttered and toasted, and stuffed to the gills with cool lobster salad. In the butter-vs.-mayo debate, Smack Shack lets the diner choose, but either way the sweet claw meat shines through. The rest of the miles-long menu is New Orleans-inspired and very heavy on the seafood, from crab po'boys to a French Quarter-inspired brunch on

57

## LET'S DO BRUNCH

brunch sandwich

Weekend brunch—best enjoyed at an hour that in many cities would be considered "breakfast"—is a beloved ritual in the Twin Cities. This is an early-rising town, even on the weekends. Great bets for hearty breakfasts built on local ingredients include downtown Minneapolis's **Hell's Kitchen** and South Minneapolis's **The Zumbro** and **French Meadow Bakery and Café.** For a morning repast focused more on pastries than on eggs and bacon, head for the French-inspired **Rustica** or to one of **Turtle Bread**'s (www.turtlebread.com) three tasty locations (3421 44th St. W., Minneapolis, 612/924-6013, daily 6:30am-8pm; 4762 Chicago Ave. S., Minneapolis, 612/823-7333, daily 6am-9pm; and 4205 34th St. E., Minneapolis, 612/545-5757, daily 6am-6pm).

weekends. This is one of the few places to get truly late-night eats, with a special menu starting at 10pm Sunday-Thursday and 11pm Friday-Saturday.
**MAP 1:** 603 Washington Ave. N., Minneapolis, 612/259-7288, www.smack-shack.com; Mon.-Thurs. 11am-midnight, Fri. 11 am-1am, Sat. 10am-1am, Sun. 10am-midnight

## VEGETARIAN
### Spoonriver $$
Spoonriver is elegant, urbane, mostly vegetarian, and a popular choice for pre- or post-theater dining—something you should keep in mind if you're hoping to get a table. The menu changes with the season and the trends, always focused on the fresh and flavorful rather than the filling. Weekend brunches are just a tiny bit

more decadent, with omelets, French toast, and buckwheat crepes.
**MAP 1:** 750 2nd St. S., Minneapolis, 612/436-2236, www.spoonriver.com; Tues.-Fri. 11:30am-2pm and 5pm-9pm, Sat. 10am-2pm (8:30am-2pm in summer) and 5pm-9pm, Sun. 10am-2pm and 5pm-9pm

## BREAKFAST AND BRUNCH
### Hell's Kitchen $
Hell's Kitchen is open late into the evening, but it built its reputation and fan base on breakfast: ethereal lemon-ricotta pancakes, a plate of huevos rancheros as big as your head, local bacon cut seemingly a quarter-inch thick, and a popular wild rice porridge you won't find anywhere else. At 11am the menu switches to lunch—hearty sandwiches and burgers, including

bison—with a few hours of amnesty for the best breakfast items. Be sure to pick up a jar of homemade peanut butter on the way out. Renowned road foodies Jane and Michael Stern can't get enough of it. Next door, the eatery's **Angel Food Bakery** (Mon.-Fri. 7am-6pm, Sat.-Sun. 9am-5pm or until sold out) serves up croissants and other treats.

MAP 1: 80 9th St. S., Minneapolis, 612/332-4700, www.hellskitcheninc.com; Mon.-Fri. 7am-10pm, Sat. 7:30am-11pm, Sun. 7:30am-10pm; Thurs.-Sat. includes music until 2am

# South Minneapolis     Map 2

## CONTEMPORARY AND FUSION

### Grand Café $$$

Settle in for an exquisite experience, down to the last detail, from the armory of very specific vintage tableware (there's a mismatched tiny fork for everything) to the warm and attentive service. Chef and owner Jamie Malone is recognized locally and nationally for her French techniques and a seafood focus.

MAP 2: 3804 Grand Ave. S., Minneapolis, 612/822-8260, www.grandcafemn.com; Mon.-Sat. 5pm-10pm, Sun. 10am-1pm and 5pm-9pm

### Tenant $$$

Put yourself in the inventive and exacting hands of this team of up-and-coming chefs (who double as your servers). Tiny Tenant hosts about a dozen people at three seatings a night for six-course tasting menus ($50, reservations only). The room is as spare as the menu.

MAP 2: 4300 Bryant Ave. S., Minneapolis, 612/827-8111, www.tenantmpls.com; Tues.-Sat. 6pm-10pm

### Blackbird $$

Blackbird pulls influences from all over the map and all over the culinary spectrum: rabbit empanadas, locally inspired *bánh mì*, and locally beloved fries with rosemary aioli. Casual and friendly, Blackbird is the ultimate neighborhood place, where everyone can feel like a regular, whether for brunch, lunch, or dinner.

MAP 2: 3800 Nicollet Ave., Minneapolis, 612/823-4790, www.blackbirdmpls.com; Mon.-Thurs. 8am-9pm, Fri.-Sat. 8am-10pm, Sun. 8am-2pm

### Chino Latino $$

Big, bold, beautiful, and brassy: That's Chino Latino and most of its clientele. Once you get a table (reservations are recommended, but waiting to be seated is one of the most popular ways to see and be seen in Uptown), choose "little plates to share" (appetizers) or "big plates to share" (mains that serve three-five). The flavors may look like a multiculti mishmash on the menu, but they make sense once they hit your table: hot tastes from the hot parts of the world, like the calamari with jalapeños. Wash them down with selections from one of the longest and craziest cocktail menus in town.

MAP 2: 2916 Hennepin Ave. S., MInneapolis, 612/824-7878, www.chinolatino.com; Sun.-Thurs. 4:30pm-midnight, Fri.-Sat. 4:30pm-1am

## LAKESIDE DINING

Minnesotans love three things: lakes, summer, and eating by lakes in the summer. And there is excellent and varied dining to be found on all of the Twin Cities' favorite lakes. The opening of these seasonal restaurants, all of which replaced outdated concessions in Minneapolis and St. Paul parks, is an eagerly awaited sign of spring each year, and their closing each fall is a sad rite of passage into the colder, darker days.

lakeside meal by Bde Maka Ska

For casual, picnic-type fare, including a grass-fed burger and sweet-savory truffle popcorn, head to Lake Harriet's **Bread and Pickle** (4135 Lake Harriet Pkwy. W., Minneapolis, 612/767-9009, www. breadandpickle.com, late Apr.-Oct. daily 7am-9pm). For summer food with a sense of fun—fried cheese curds and a hot dog topped with a fried egg and kimchi—sit down by Lake Nokomis, about five miles east of the Chain of Lakes, at **Sandcastle** (4955 Nokomis Pkwy. W., Minneapolis, 612/722-5550, www.sandcastlempls.com, late Apr.-Oct. daily 11am-8pm). At St. Paul's Lake Como, **Spring Café at Como Lakeside Pavilion** (1360 Lexington Pkwy. N., St. Paul, www. springcafestp.com, Memorial Day-Labor Day Mon.-Fri. 11am-9pm, Sat.-Sun. 9am-9pm) serves brisket sandwiches and wild rice brats.

On Bde Maka Ska (Lake Calhoun), **Lola's on the Lake** (3000 Calhoun Pkwy. E., Minneapolis, 612/824-0516, www.lolascafmn.com, late Apr.-Memorial Day daily noon-8pm, Memorial Day-Labor Day daily 11am-9pm, Labor Day-Oct. daily noon-7:30pm) serves up signature smoked wings and pulled pork sandwiches. And, yes, despite the distance from the ocean, people here enjoy the time-honored simple pleasure of sitting by a body of water and eating a fine piece of fish. **Sea Salt** (4801 Minnehaha Ave. S., Minneapolis, 612/721-8990, www.seasalteatery.com, Apr.-Oct. daily 11am-9pm) fills the pavilion at Minnehaha Falls with the scent of fish tacos and lines of eager eaters.

### Corner Table  $$

Corner Table is where neighbors in the know come for fine dining with a little swagger: French techniques, local ingredients, a Minneapolis casual vibe, an ever-changing menu (always prix fixe, 3 courses for $45 or 10 for $145). Chef Thomas Boemer is a near-constant and welcoming presence in the dining room, where it always feels like a cozy dinner party.

MAP 2: 4537 Nicollet Ave., Minneapolis, 612/823-0011, www.cornertablerestaurant. com; Mon.-Thurs. 5pm-10pm, Fri.-Sat. 5pm-11pm

### Harriet Brasserie  $$

It's pretty clear the chef has some Latin roots when you see the beloved Brazilian steak sandwich, the *bauru*, on the dinner menu and a *tres leches* cake on the dessert list, but Harriet draws inspiration from all over the world, from steak au poivre to risotto. The cozy interior and the leafy deck are both excellent places to linger over crab Benedict and a bloody sake for brunch.

MAP 2: 2724 43rd St. W., Minneapolis, 612/354-2197, www.lakeharrietbrasserie. com; Mon.-Thurs. 10am-9pm, Fri. 10am-11pm, Sat. 8am-11pm, Sun. 8am-3pm

## Kenwood $$

What a lucky neighborhood, to have a neighborhood haunt like this. On a surprising little commercial block in shady, solid, upscale Kenwood, chef and owner Don Saunders makes beet carpaccio, veal sweetbreads, and mussels in pistou that feel like just the homey Tuesday supper you were looking for. Not feeling particularly upper-crust? Order the Kenwood burger, a delightfully sloppy concoction with pork belly and a fried egg, made on one of the best burger buns in the city. And bring the kids, because not only are they welcome, they will also find a kids' menu that takes their tastes seriously.

MAP 2: 2115 21st St. W., Minneapolis, 612/377-3695, www.thekenwoodrestaurant. com; Tues.-Thurs. 8am-9pm, Fri.-Sat. 8am-10pm, Sun. 8am-9pm

## Tilia $$

Tilia doesn't take reservations and you probably will have to wait for one of the 40 seats, but take heart: It will be worth it. Chef Steven Brown kicked around just about every decent restaurant in the Twin Cities before pouring his heart and soul into his own place. The menu is a mix of high and low, from the fish taco *torta* to the halibut in shiitake broth. Parents: Tilia has a terrific children's menu, well beyond the usual mac and cheese. And for weekend brunch, the lobster eggs Benedict on cornmeal waffles cannot be beat.

MAP 2: 2726 43rd St. W., Minneapolis, 612/354-2806, www.tiliampls.com; Mon.-Fri. 11am-1am, Sat.-Sun. 9am-1am

## Wise Acre Eatery $$

You've heard of farm to table? This is *one* farm (mostly) to one table—well, a restaurant full of tables. At Wise Acre, about 90 percent of the beef, pork, chicken, eggs, vegetables, and berries comes from Tangletown Farm in Plano, Minnesota, owned and operated by the folks behind the restaurant and the garden shop across the street. Smart summer preserving and greenhouses keep the food flowing throughout the Minnesota winter. The menu is elevated stick-to-your-ribs stuff, drawing on influences well beyond Minneapolis, with curry and *phô* (Vietnamese soup) and pasties. The room is small and energetic, and waits for a table can be long.

MAP 2: 5401 Nicollet Ave. S., Minneapolis, 612/354-2577, www.wiseacreeatery.com; Sun. 9am-8pm, Mon.-Sat. 9am-9pm

# ASIAN

## Fuji Ya $$

Before you could get sushi in every grocery store, you could get it right here, at Fuji Ya. Well, not here exactly—the restaurant has moved a couple of times since it first shocked Minnesotans with raw fish—but from the same family. You'd never know Fuji Ya has five decades under its belt: It's still fresh and young and pulling in a hip crowd. On summer evenings, the secluded patio is a great place to score a seat, but your party may also request a tatami room for the most authentic experience.

MAP 2: 600 Lake St. W., Minneapolis, 612/871-4055, www.fujiyasushi.com; Tues.-Thurs. 5pm-9:30pm, Fri.-Sat. 5pm-10:30pm

## Kyatchi $$

Kyatchi is totally unique on the Twin Cities food scene for the way it pushes modern Japanese cuisine not in an American or fusion-y direction but

# EAT STREET

If you can't decide exactly what you want for dinner and you're up for a bit of a culinary adventure, point your feet south from downtown Minneapolis, along Nicollet Avenue. The stretch from around 13th Street to around 28th Street is known as Eat Street. That mile-or-so walk will take you past Indian, Vietnamese, Chinese, and Mexican restaurants—from holes-in-the-wall to large and well-established places like Vietnamese eatery **Quang.** Almost universally speaking, what you find will be inexpensive, authentic, and tasty.

If your itinerary keeps you on the St. Paul side of things, head west on University Avenue and keep your eye out for Vietnamese restaurants; **Ngon Bistro** offers a contemporary take. Or check out **Cheng Heng,** which serves Cambodian soul food.

classic Vietnamese pho

toward more daring Japanese flavors and textures. In the *nigiri*, sashimi, and *oshizuki* (pressed sushi) expect fish and flavors that play toward an Asian palate. Even the hot dogs—a nod, perhaps, toward the chef's previous life as a private chef for a Japanese baseball player—are more Japanese than American.

**MAP 2:** 3758 Nicollet Ave., Minneapolis, 612/236-4429, www.kyatchi.com; Mon.-Fri. 4pm-midnight, Sat.-Sun. noon-midnight

### Naviya's Thai Brasserie  $$

You've never had Thai food like this before. Every dish is heavy on the vegetables and extraordinarily light on the sauces and grease. An extra-hot grill adds extra flavor to everything from the vegetables to the fried rice (nongreasy fried rice—it's a revelation!). The hot plates and *massaman* curry are great favorites here. While the atmosphere isn't very child-friendly (there are a lot of seats packed into a relatively small space), the kids' menu is one that both parents and children will love, with plenty of healthy, tasty choices.

**MAP 2:** 2812 43rd St. W., Minneapolis, 612/276-5061, www.naviyas.com; Mon.-Fri. 11:30am-9pm, Sat.-Sun. noon-9pm

### ✪ Quang  $

This is where big Southeast Asian families gather to celebrate and dine together. It's also popular with office workers looking for an inexpensive, healthy lunch, and with young Vietnamese couples on a date. Heck, just about everybody eventually comes to bright and friendly Quang for their first or their 4,000th bowl of *phô* (Vietnamese noodle soup with a deep, rich broth). (If you've had enough *phô*, try the barbecue pork salad.) The line may stretch out the door, but you probably won't have to wait long. Service is unbelievably fast.

**MAP 2:** 2719 Nicollet Ave. S., Minneapolis, 612/870-4739, www.quang-restaurant. com; Mon. and Wed.-Fri. 11am-9pm, Sat. 10:30am-9pm, Sun. 10:30am-8:30pm

### Himalayan Restaurant  $

The nourishing cuisines of Nepal, Tibet, and India have a lot in common. They all use complex spiced sauces, and all are pretty vegetarian friendly. The samosas and lentil pancakes are delicious, as are the curries. And, of course, you have the famous Tibetan/Nepali dumplings, *momos*, even with traditional yak. Himalayan Restaurant's lunch buffet is a nice change from the typical Indian buffet.

MAP 2: 2910 Lake St. E., Minneapolis, 612/332-0880, www.himalayanmomo.com; Tues.-Sun. 11am-9:30pm

### Jasmine Deli  $

With just a half dozen tables and a spare, no-nonsense aesthetic, Jasmine Deli won't wow you until the food arrives: fragrant *phô* soup, bright noodle salads, and perfectly sized *bánh mì* (stuffed baguette sandwiches) are the things to order. Linger a little longer over a Vietnamese coffee-drip—brewed right at your table over sweetened condensed milk (iced in the summer).

MAP 2: 2532 Nicollet Ave. S., Minneapolis, 612/870-4700, www.jasminedelimpls.com; Tues.-Sat. 10am-8pm, Sun. 10am-6pm

## NORDIC
### Fika  $

In Sweden, *fika* is the beloved art of the afternoon coffee break, a time and a place for a hot drink and a little something sweet. In the American Swedish Institute, Fika is a destination in its own right, a place to sit down for an elegant midday meal. The salads, small plates, and open-faced sandwiches are artfully composed, showing off the flavors Sweden is known for: meatballs, lingonberries, gravlax, and more. The café's few tables are right in the museum's lobby. If the weather is nice, take a seat in the serene, green courtyard instead.

MAP 2: 2600 Park Ave., Minneapolis, 612/871-4907, www.asimn.org; Sun. 11am-5pm, Tues. and Thurs.-Sat. 8:30am-5pm, Wed. 8:30am-8pm

## LATIN AMERICAN
### Martina  $$

A big, joyous room with a view of a wood fire, where octopus, swordfish, steaks, and scallops crackle on the grill—that's Martina, a little piece of Argentina (with a splash of southern Italy) in southwest Minneapolis. Plates of pastas in pungent sauces follow funky appetizers (tongue bruschetta, leek and onion empanadas). The cocktails are both remarkably well priced and well composed.

MAP 2: 4312 S. Upton Ave., Minneapolis, 612/922-9913, www.martinarestaurant.com; Mon. 5pm-10pm, Tues.-Thurs. 5pm-11pm, Fri. 5pm-midnight, Sat. 10am-2pm and 5pm-midnight, Sun. 10am-2pm and 5pm-10pm

### Hola Arepa  $

The only entrée on the menu at Hola Arepa is the namesake Venezuelan corn cake—the size of a saucer, soft on the inside, crunchy on the outside, and split to make room for oodles of filling. Get your arepa stuffed with chicken in adobo or chimichurri sauce, slow-roasted pork, chorizo, or black beans, along with pickled vegetables and house-made fresh cheese. Absolutely do not say no to the yucca fries or a cocktail.

MAP 2: 3501 Nicollet Ave. S., Minneapolis, 612/345-5583, www.holaarepa. com; Tues.-Fri. 3pm-midnight, Sat. 10am-midnight, Sun. 10am-midnight

### Manny's Tortas  $

A *torta* is a complex thing. Layers of flavor pile up on a wide, thick baguette that barely seems to be able to contain it all. No matter what you order, there will be lettuce, tomato, avocado, peppers, mayo, and cheese. There may be beans and roasted vegetables. There may be several kinds of meat. You may think it will never come together into a single tasty whole, until it goes into the sandwich press and comes out born anew. The chorizo and egg sandwich will cure whatever ails you. Another branch is in the Midtown Global Market (920 Lake St. E., Minneapolis, 612/870-3930, daily 10am-8pm).

MAP 2: Mercado Central, 1515 Lake St. E., Minneapolis, 612/728-5408, www.mannystortas.com; daily 8am-8pm

## Maria's Café $

*Norteamericanos* have no monopoly on the best breakfasts. Maria Hoyos, a native of Colombia, serves up a mix of morning classics from North and South America. You've got your basic two eggs, toast, and bacon. But then there's *cachapas venezolanas* (Venezuelan corn pancakes), so tender they fall apart at the sight of a fork (sprinkled with Cotija cheese, they're the perfect combination of salty and sweet), and sautéed plantains and yucca (available on weekends). Breakfast is served all day, and the lunch menu includes sandwiches and burgers.

MAP 2: 1113 Franklin Ave. E., Minneapolis, 612/870-9842, www.mariascafe.com; Mon.-Fri. 7am-3pm, Sat.-Sun. 8am-3pm

## Sonora Grill $

Three friends from the Mexican state of Sonora take their inspiration from all over Latin America and make everything from scratch, from the skewers of meat known as *pinchos* to the breaded eggplant fries to the aioli dipping sauce. The eggplant *bocadillo*, a good-size sandwich, is a favorite, as is everything that comes with the delicious beans cooked with guajillo peppers.

MAP 2: 3300 Lake St. E., Minneapolis, 612/722-2500; Mon.-Thurs. 10am-10pm, Fri. 10am-midnight, Sat. 9am-midnight, Sun. 9am-10pm

## Taqueria Los Ocampo $

Spanish-language talk shows and *telenovelas* blare from two television sets, and the happy crowds move noisily in and out. Tortillas, gorditas, arepas, and more are made on-site; you'll notice the woman behind the counter slapping disks of masa into shape. Another branch is just across Lake Street in the Midtown Global Market (920 Lake St. E., Minneapolis, 612/872-8562, Mon.-Sat. 9am-8pm, Sun. 9am-6pm).

MAP 2: 809 Lake St. E., Minneapolis, 612/825-4978, www.taquerialosocampo.com; Sun.-Thurs. 9am-midnight, Fri.-Sat. 9am-3am

## Victor's 1959 Café $

A tiny shack painted very un-Minnesotan colors, Victor's has a subversive, makeshift feel to it. But it's actually a long-standing favorite, attracting people willing to wait in lines out the door for the corn pancakes and yucca and eggs in the morning, the authentic Cuban sandwich (ham, pork loin, pickles, and condiments pressed together in a soft, slightly sweet bun) at lunch, and the homey *ropa vieja* (shredded flank steak tossed with vegetables) at dinner.

MAP 2: 3756 Grand Ave. S., Minneapolis, 612/827-8948, www.victors1959cafe.com; Sun.-Mon. 8am-2:30pm, Tues.-Sat. 8am-2:30pm and 4:30pm-9pm

Food trucks have taken the Twin Cities by storm.

Like any American city with a population greater than 72, Minneapolis and St. Paul have been bitten by the food truck bug. Office workers line up at trucks parked the length of Marquette Avenue in downtown Minneapolis and along the edges of Rice Park in St. Paul. Breweries and tap rooms invite trucks to park outside on summer evenings, and every farmers market has at least one or two on weekend mornings.

Several trucks that still prowl the streets have led to bricks-and-mortar restaurants, including **World Street Kitchen** (www.eatwsk.com).

## MIDDLE EASTERN
### World Street Kitchen $

To understand World Street Kitchen, you have to understand its pedigree: Chef Sameh Wadi pioneered high-end, date night-worthy Middle Eastern before he brought the wildly popular World Street Kitchen food truck to the streets to show he could also do fun and funky. From that the truck's brick-and-mortar doppelganger was born. The menu capitalizes on the big, bold flavors that Korean, Thai, and Middle Eastern food share, served up in bowls, burritos, tacos, and wraps.

Finish a meal with one of the dozen flavors of ice cream (Thai tea, chanterelle and caramel, fruity cereal) at World Street Kitchen's **Milkjam Creamery** (612/424-4668, www.

milkjamcreamery.com, Sun.-Thurs. noon-10pm, Fri.-Sat. noon-11pm), next door

MAP 2: 2743 Lyndale Ave. S., Minneapolis, 612/424-8855, www.eatwsk.com; daily 11am-11pm

## FRENCH
### Barbette $$

The sign over the back door beckons: "French Fries Here." And many a wanderer has been lured into the rich, warm, lounge-like room for a big plate of *pommes frites* with béarnaise sauce or a frisée salad with poached egg and lardoons or a plate of mussels. Everything at Barbette is comforting, classically French, and frankly perfect, from breakfast right on through to late-night snacks. Save room for carrot cake.

MAP 2: 1600 Lake St. W., Minneapolis, 612/827-5710, www.barbette.com; Sun.-Thurs. 8am-midnight, Fri.-Sat. 8am-1am

### St. Genevieve $$

St. Genevieve is a bubbly little place with a lot of verve and a lot of fine bubbly on the menu. Sit down here and your "just a drink and a bite" might just turn into a meal, as your oysters on the half shell lead to plate of mussels then to a crepe or a tartine. And then another round of bubbly. Linger at the friendly bar or in the romantic corner in the back.

MAP 2: 5003 Bryant Ave. S., Minneapolis, 612/353-4843, www.stgmpls.com; Sun. 9:30am-9:30pm, Mon.-Fri. 11am-11pm, Sat. 9:30am-midnight

## ITALIAN
### Broder's Pasta Bar $$

House-made pasta cooked to order and tossed to order with individually composed sauces—that's why South Minneapolis diners line up and cheerfully accept the no-reservations policy. Look for terrific dinner-for-two deals after 8pm on Sunday and before 6pm on weekdays, available seasonally. Across the street, at **Broder's Cucina Italiana** (612/925-3113, daily 11am-9pm), you can pick up pizza by the slice or the pie, Broder's famous (in these parts) lasagna and Bolognese, as well as dried pasta and other imported goodies.

MAP 2: 5000 Penn Ave. S., Minneapolis, 612/925-9202, www.broders.com; Mon.-Thurs. 4:30pm-9:30pm, Sat. 4pm-10pm, Sun. 4pm-9:30pm

### Pizzeria Lola $$

The giant copper pizza oven at the center of this beloved southwest Minneapolis spot is always busy. Diners line up (or take one of the limited reservations) for daring pizza (kimchi, Korean short ribs, olives and almonds) on delightfully chewy crust. Be sure to end the meal with house-made soft-serve and a trip to the photo booth.

MAP 2: 5557 Xerxes Ave. S., Minneapolis, 612/424-8338, www.pizzerialola.com; Sun.-Thurs. 11am-10pm, Fri.-Sat. 11am-11pm

## SOUTHERN
### Revival $

Sometimes what you really need is two pieces of fried chicken with a thick, crunchy crust (order them Tennessee hot if you want) with collard greens and golden rice on the side. That is what Revival does best— so well, in fact, that there are lines out the door and occasional backups in the kitchen. There are other entrées on Revival's menu with an unmistakable Southern twang—catfish, shrimp and grits—but nearly everyone comes here for the fried chicken. There's also a location in St. Paul (525 Selby Ave., St. Paul, 651/340-2355, Sun.-Thurs. 11am-10pm, Fri.-Sat. 11am-11pm).

MAP 2: 4257 Nicollet Ave. S., Minneapolis, 612/345-4516, http://revivalmpls.com; Mon.-Fri. 11am-2pm and 4pm-10pm, Sat. 11am-10pm

## STEAK
### Burch $$$

Before you order a steak at Burch, you need to ask yourself a handful of questions, beyond what cut you like— grass-fed or grain? Prime or Wagyu? Domestic or imported? All told, you have nearly three dozen options, including some appealing six- and eight-ounce options. The really interesting stuff, however, is happening on the other side of the menu, where famed

Minneapolis restaurateur Isaac Becker throws out the usual steak house creamed spinach and green beans amandine in favor of a selection of complex dumplings and chef-ed up vegetables. Downstairs, Burch becomes an entirely different restaurant altogether, a dim, cozy hangout with a menu of thin-crust pizzas.

**MAP 2:** 1933 Colfax Ave. S., Minneapolis, 612/843-1515, www.burchrestaurant. com; Mon.-Thurs. 5pm-10pm, Fri.-Sat. 5pm-midnight, Sun. 10am-2pm and 5pm-10pm

## VEGETARIAN
### Birchwood $

The Birchwood isn't strictly vegetarian, but vegetarians, vegans, and their fish- and poultry-eating friends will all find common ground in this cheery neighborhood gem. The atmosphere is casual—you order at the counter and the place is teeming with kids—but pizzas, burgers, and light entrées are all a step above what you'd expect at a casual joint. Make it a pizza party on Saturday night, when two individual pizzas and two glasses of wine are $30. There's live music on Monday nights.

**MAP 2:** 3311 25th St. E., Minneapolis, 612/722-4474, www.birchwoodcafe.com; Mon.-Fri. 7am-9pm, Sat.-Sun. 8am-9pm

## BREAKFAST AND BRUNCH
### French Meadow Bakery and Café $$

For breakfast, French Meadow's plate-sized whole-grain pancakes are legendary. For lunch they're known for tempeh Reubens on sprouted-grain bread, and for dinner line-caught salmon and local chicken. For a more chic, sit-down experience, head around back to French Meadow's sister restaurant **Bluestem Bar** (www. bluestembarminneapolis.com, Sun.-Thurs. 8am-10pm, Fri.-Sat. 8am-11pm). Or check them out in St. Paul (1662 Grand Ave., St. Paul, 651/789-8870, Sun.-Thurs. 7am-9pm, Fri.-Sat. 7am-10pm). The main themes remain the same: virtuous, locally sourced, vegan-friendly, globally inspired.

**MAP 2:** 2610 Lyndale Ave. S., Minneapolis, 612/870-7855, www.frenchmeadowcafe. com; Sun.-Thurs. 7am-10pm; Fri.-Sat. 7am-11pm

### Common Roots $

When you move to a new town and can't find a decent bagel, what do you do? You make your own, or at least that's what Danny Schwartzman did. And, along the way, he challenged himself to make and sell them in the most sustainable way possible: At last count, 90 percent of his ingredients are local, fair trade, or organic. Get a bagel or *shakshuka* (eggs with a tomato and red pepper sauce) in the morning and a burger or sandwich in the afternoon, washed down with a Surly brew.

French Meadow Bakery and Café

Common Roots

MAP 2: 2558 Lyndale Ave. S., Minneapolis, 612/871-2360, www.commonrootscafe. com; Mon.-Fri. 7am-9pm, Sat.-Sun. 8am-9pm

### The Lynhall $

You've just found your new happy place in Minneapolis: long reclaimed-wood tables for sharing, cozy corners for conversation, plenty of space to plug in your laptop, and a menu that goes from soft-scrambled eggs in the morning to short ribs in the evening.

The Lynhall

Come grab a pastry as big as your head (sweet or savory) and stay all day.

MAP 2: 2640 Lyndale Ave. S., Minneapolis, 612/870-2640, www.thelynnhall.com; daily 7:30am-9pm

### Sun Street Breads $

At breakfast, Sun Street can't be beat: big, flaky biscuits topped with eggs, gravy, or roasted veggies, or maybe a fresh pastry (don't miss the *laugen-croissants*, a cross between a pretzel and a croissant). At lunch there's a small roster of excellent sandwiches (the Susan is a meatloaf sandwich with all the fixings) made with Sun Street's own bread. Pick up a loaf or two to take with you.

MAP 2: 4600 Nicollet Ave., Minneapolis, 612/354-3414, www.sunstreetbreads.com; Tues.-Sun. 6:30am-2pm, pizza night Thurs. 5pm-8pm

### The Zumbro $

Somehow this small breakfast-and-lunch place feels sunny even in the winter. It may be all the blond wood, or it may be the happy diners and the always-cheery clatter of latte cups. The Zumbro has mastered the fine art of the frittata and serves a variety alongside tender potatoes and, if you choose, fantastic slices of thick-cut bacon. Keep in mind: It's small and popular, meaning this may not be the best choice for larger groups, active kids, or people in a hurry.

MAP 2: 2803 43rd St. W., Minneapolis, 612/920-3606, www.thezumbro. com; Tues.-Fri. 7am-2:30pm, Sat.-Sun. 7:30am-2:30pm

## SWEETS

### ✪ Rose Street Patisserie $

The very first American chef to join the society known as the Relais Desserts is right here, baking in this kitchen, turning out award-winning patisserie, perfect Parisian baguettes, and flaky croissants that attract aspiring bakers all the way from Paris. The two-story windows and long tables make this an ideal meeting spot. Rose Street also has a location in St. Paul (171 Snelling Ave. N., St. Paul, 651/556-4488; Tues.-Sat. 7am-6pm, Sun. 7am-3pm).

MAP 2: 2811 43rd St. W., Minneapolis, 612/259-7921, www.rosestreet.co, Sun. and Tues. 7am-2pm, Wed.-Sat. 7am-5pm

croissant from Rose Street Patisserie

### Patisserie 46 $

It doesn't get any better than this: croissants with a crackling buttery crust, crisp baguettes with a cloud-like interior, French macarons that would sell out in any Parisian patisserie, and breads you can't wait to take home and slice into—including a six-pound rustic sourdough miche. While most people come for cappuccinos and treats, you can also get a French-style salad, *tartine* (open-faced sandwich), panini, or pizza for lunch.

MAP 2: 4552 Grand Ave. S., Minneapolis, 612/354-3257, www.patisserie46.com; Tues.-Sat. 7am-6pm, Sun. 7am-2pm

### Rustica $

Serious coffee drinkers and serious pastry lovers feel right at home at Rustica. You'll find *kouign-amann*, a buttery, flaky specialty from Breton, cherry clafouti, baguettes, and a handful of lunch sandwiches. This is the sort of place where laptops abound, and it can be hard to find a seat on the worn wood benches.

MAP 2: 3220 Lake St. W., Minneapolis, 612/822-1119, www.rusticabakery.com; Mon.-Fri. 6:30am-8pm, Sat.-Sun. 7am-8am

### Sebastian Joe's $

The signature flavor at Sebastian Joe's is Pavarotti, an addictive blend of caramel, banana, and chocolate. But the raspberry chocolate chip has partisans, as well. Other than that, you never know what you'll find in the ice cream case—cinnamon? green tea? malted vanilla? mango? Sebastian Joe's is a neighborhood family fixture and a favorite stop after soccer and T-ball games. But don't rule it out in the winter: In fact, as the temperature dips below freezing, the prices drop as well! There's another branch in the neighborhood of Linden Hills (4321

## WHEN YOU REALLY JUST NEED A DOUGHNUT

The national doughnut frenzy hit the Twin Cities—and hit it hard. Sure, trends come and go, but the truly good doughnut shops—the ones that brought something special to the doughnut table—those are the ones that stuck around.

Local favorite **Baker's Wife** (4200 28th Ave. S., Minneapolis, 612/729-6898, Tues.-Sat. 6:30am-6pm, Sun. 6:30am-3pm) has been making a classic old-fashioned for years, along with a whole pastry case of turnovers, muffins, and scones.

**Bogart's Doughnuts** (904 36th St. W., Minneapolis, 612/886-1670, www. bogartsdoughnutco.com, Tues.-Fri. 6:30am-noon, Sat.-Sun. 7:30am-noon, or until sold out) bet on its batter, making just a handful of deceptively simple doughnuts with a rich brioche dough. Bogart's also has a cart in the IDS building in downtown Minneapolis.

treats from Bogart's Doughnuts

But if you want all that crazy stuff—maple bacon and Trix toppings and the like—head to **Angel Food Bakery** (86 9th St. S., Minneapolis, 612/238-1435, www. angelfoodmn.com, Mon.-Fri. 7am-6pm, Sat.-Sun. 9am-5pm, or until sold out). And if you want your crazy doughnut for dessert instead of breakfast, **Glam Doll Donuts** (2605 Nicollet Ave., Minneapolis, 612/345-7064, www.glamdolldonuts.com, Mon.-Thurs. 7am-9pm, Fri.-Sat. 7am-1am, Sun. 7am-3pm) is the place for you.

And for a classic doughnut shop in the burbs, where you can not only pick up a box but also hang out to eat and chat, there's **YoYo Donuts** (5757 Sanibel Dr., Minnetonka, 952/960-1800, http://yoyodonuts.com, Mon.-Sat. 6am-9pm, Sun. 7am-9pm).

Upton Ave. S., Minneapolis, 612/926-7916, Mon.-Thurs. 6:30am-9pm, Fri. 6:30am-10pm, Sat. 7am-10pm, Sun. 7am-9pm).
**MAP 2:** 1007 Franklin Ave. W., Minneapolis, 612/870-0065, www. sebastianjoesicecream.com; Sun.-Thurs. 7am-11pm, Fri.-Sat. 7am-midnight

### Sonny's Cafe $

For years Sonny Siron himself made Italian-style ice cream for fancy restaurants in the Twin Cities and as far afield as Chicago. Then, by popular demand, he opened this Tuscan-style jewel box with a hidden garden patio, where neighbors could enjoy his tiny, intensely flavored scoops of cabernet chocolate chip, basil balsamic vinegar, green tea, cardamom black pepper, blackberry cassis, and an ever-changing list of other imaginative flavors.
**MAP 2:** 3403 Lyndale Ave. S., Minneapolis, 612/824-3868, www.sonnysicecream.com; Sun. noon-11pm, Mon.-Thurs. 5pm-11pm, Fri. 5pm-11:30pm, Sat. noon-11:30pm

# Nordeast and Dinkytown   Map 3

## CONTEMPORARY AND FUSION
### ✪ Alma $$

While chef and owner Alex Roberts has twice been nominated for a James Beard Award and the *Washington Post, Gourmet,* and *Bon Appetit* have all taken note of Alma's strengths, this restaurant still has the feel of a cozy neighborhood bistro. It serves an ever-changing three-course prix-fixe menu with carnivore and vegetarian-friendly options. The café next door (Sun.-Thurs. 7am-9pm, Fri.-Sat. 7am-10pm) is open all day for everything from a cup of coffee and a pastry to a cocktail to a jaw-dropping burger.

**MAP 3:** 528 University Ave. SE, Minneapolis, 612/379-4909, www. restaurantalma.com; Sun.-Thurs. 5pm-9pm, Fri.-Sat. 5pm-10pm

Alma

### Betty Danger's Country Club $$

Meet Betty, sister of Suzi (of Psycho Suzi's Motor Lounge) and Donny (of Donny Dirk's Zombie Den). The fictional family keeps Minneapolis—or, at least, artier, hipper Nordeast—entertained and well-fed. Betty's imagined home is Mexampton: Mexico plus the Hamptons, all wrapped up in Minnesota nice and plenty of hot dish. Your ride on the Ferris wheel—the "vertically rotating patio" for zoning purposes—comes with a drink, as does your round of golf. Add snacks for the full experience, or sit down at a stationary table for indulgent enchiladas or overstuffed sandwiches—mildly spicy and covered in cheese, as befits Mexampton. To make a night of it, ride the Tiki Tram shuttle among all three siblings' establishments.

**MAP 3:** 2501 Marshall St. NE, Minneapolis, 612/315-4997, http://bettydangers.com; Mon.-Thurs. 11am-close, Fri. 11am-1am, Sat. 10am-1am, Sun. 10am-close

### Red Stag Supper Club $$

(If you're tired of hearing about green this and local that, avert your attention for a moment.) Red Stag is the first LEED-certified restaurant in Minnesota—which means it was built using environmentally friendly building techniques—and buys as much of its meat and produce as possible from local farmers. But even if that does not interest you, you'll enjoy the food: updated renditions of supper club classics, from mac and cheese with truffle oil to liver and onions with green garlic gravy. Locals love the smelt fries, and this may be the only place this far from the North Shore to find them. Friday is fish fry day, with an extensive menu of battered and fried in-season seafood, including tiny crispy smelt and whole trout.

71

MAP 3: 509 1st Ave. NE, Minneapolis, 612/767-7766, www.redstagsupperclub.com; Mon.-Wed. 11am-1am, Thurs.-Fri. 11am-2am, Sat. 9am-2am, Sun. 9am-1am

## Young Joni $$

Young Joni, which topped many national best new restaurant lists when it opened in 2017, serves a long list of classic and innovative pizzas, but it's about so much more than just the pies. Think of what else a wood-fired oven and grill can do: add a smoky, rustic touch to cauliflower, eggplant, shrimp, and wings. If the red neon light in the alley is lit, that means that Young Joni's **Back Bar** is open. Array yourself on vintage divans and order artsy cocktails (along with a handful of pizzas).

MAP 3: 165 13th Ave. NE, Minneapolis, 612/345-5719, www.youngjoni.com; Sun. noon-10pm, Mon. 4pm-10pm, Tues.-Thurs. 4pm-10pm, Fri. 4pm-midnight, Sat. noon-midnight

# STEAK
## Jax $$$

When Jax first opened in this largely Eastern European neighborhood in 1933, "What dining out was meant to be" was a formal occasion, one you couldn't possibly replicate at home. And that's what you still get at Jax: dark wood, rich food (lots of steak and lobster), and bygone pomp. But even the most formal of dining institutions occasionally lets down its hair: At Jax, you can net your own trout, while they're in season, from a built-in brook in the restaurant's charming back garden.

MAP 3: 1928 University Ave. NE, Minneapolis, 612/789-7297, www.jaxcafe.com; Tues.-Thurs. 11am-9:30pm, Fri.-Sat. 11am-10pm, Sun. 10am-1:30pm and 3:30pm-9pm

## Erté $$

A supper club doesn't have to be stuffy. Erté takes luxurious, filling classics like filet mignon, shrimp cocktail, and Cobb salad and serves them with a touch of humor on the side. You'll find northeast Minneapolis's more fortunate young professionals here enjoying the juxtaposition of the dark wood, white tablecloth atmosphere and their own hip selves. Vegetarians won't find much at all to satisfy them: even most of the salads come packed with animal protein. Hear live music Friday and Saturday nights 7pm-10pm in the Peacock Lounge.

MAP 3: 323 13th Ave. NE, Minneapolis, 612/623-4211, www.ertedining.com; Mon.-Thurs. 4pm-9pm, Fri.-Sat. 4pm-10pm

# EASTERN EUROPEAN
## ✪ Kramarczuk's $

Pick up sausages, cheese, and sweet pastries in the deli, or grab a tray and join the cafeteria line. Either way, you'd better be hungry. Kramarczuk's has served hearty Ukrainian specialties to the Eastern European residents of Nordeast for decades: potato- and cheese-filled *pelmeni* (dumplings nearly the size of a tea cup), cabbage leaves stuffed with ground meat and swimming in tomato sauce, schnitzel, and hearty borscht (red and white).

MAP 3: 215 Hennepin Ave. E., Minneapolis, 612/379-3018, www.kramarczuk.com; Mon.-Wed. 8am-8pm, Thurs.-Sat. 8am-9pm, Sun. 10am-4pm

# ASIAN
## Hai Hai $$

From the dynamic duo behind Hola Arepa, Hai Hai makes Southeast Asian cuisine hip and fun and serves it up in an energetic dining room filled with palms, sunlight, and soothing colors. Think authentic flavors with a twist:

Kramarczuk's landmark sign

fried wontons with liver pâté, fried potatoes with lime-leaf tofu sauce, snap peas in adobo sauce. Hai Hai fills up fast and only takes reservations for groups of six and more.

**MAP 3:** 2121 University Ave. NE, Minneapolis, 612/223-8640, www. haihaimpls.com; Tues.-Fri. 3pm-midnight, Sat.-Sun. 10am-midnight

### Masu Sushi and Robata  $$

The sushi here is nationally recognized, but the fun parts are the *izakaya* (Japanese pub) snacks and *robata*. Robata are skewers of meat, vegetables, and rice balls that you order singly or in collections, or just tell the kitchen to keep 'em coming, while you chat and drink with friends well into the evening if you want, since the kitchen stays open late. Masu is also in the Mall of America (Mon.-Thurs. 11am-9pm, Fri.-Sat. 11am-10pm, Sun. 11am-7pm). Find it on the south side of the third floor (S344).

**MAP 3:** 330 Hennepin Ave. E., Minneapolis, 612/332-6278, www. masusushiandrobata.com; Mon.-Thurs. 11am-midnight, Fri. 11am-1am, Sat. 4pm-1am, Sun. 4pm-11pm

### Sen Yai Sen Lek  $

Sen Yai Sen Lek (big noodle, little noodle) is a little different from other Thai restaurants in the area. You can still get your favorite *tom yum* soup and pad Thai, as well as some curries and stir-fries, but the real emphasis is on noodle dishes inspired by Thai street food. The lettuce wraps with dried shrimp are a flavor-packed favorite. Parents looking for a little change from the usual also appreciate Sen Yai Sen Lek's child-friendly atmosphere.

**MAP 3:** 2422 Central Ave. NE, Minneapolis, 612/781-3046, www.senyai-senlek.com; Mon.-Thurs. 11am-9pm, Fri.-Sat. 11am-10pm

## AFRICAN
### Afro Deli  $

Afro Deli is a bright and cheerful representation of the way Minnesota's newest immigrants are making their mark. Minnesota is home to the largest Somali population in the United States, and Afro Deli is many non-Somalis' first, friendly introduction to *sambusas* (fried dough pockets filled with meat or beans) and *suqaar* (Somali stew), served here alongside hamburgers and falafel. Another location is in St. Paul near the University of Minnesota (5 W. 7th Pl., St. Paul, 651/888-2168, Mon.-Fri. 10:30am-9pm, Sat. 11am-9pm).

Afro Deli

# MIDTOWN GLOBAL MARKET

What to do with the second-largest building in the state (after the Mall of America)? The city of Minneapolis puzzled over this after the closure of its 1.2-million-square-foot catalog order-processing facility in 1994. The massive building, with its landmark 16-story tower, sat empty until 2006, when the **Midtown Global Market** (Lake St. and 10th Ave., Minneapolis, 612/872-4041, www.midtownglobalmarket.org, Mon.-Sat. 7am-8pm, Sun. 7am-6pm) opened on the ground floor. (Condos and office space occupy the rest of the building.) The lively market, the result of the joint effort of neighborhood groups, the African Development Center, and the Latino Economic Development Center, was modeled on successful community markets like Seattle's Pike Place.

Today the Midtown Global Market is a great place to grab a meal—especially if you're with a group of people who can't decide on a particular cuisine. From Latin (try **Manny's Tortas**) to Middle Eastern (**Holy Land** is a solid bet), you'll find something to sate every craving.

The market also houses a dozen specialty and ethnic grocers and dozens of booths selling jewelry, crafts, and art from all over the world. A central stage area sees frequent casual music concerts, and a small children's play area keeps restless little ones amused.

MAP 3: 720 Washington Ave. SE, Minneapolis, 612/871-5555, www.afrodeli.com; Mon.-Fri. 10am-9pm, Sat. 10am-9pm, Sun. 11am-8pm

## MIDDLE EASTERN
### Holy Land $

Don't worry, you're in the right place: Holy Land looks like a big, chaotic grocery store because it is one. But, just to the right as you walk in is the counter where you can order massive plates of gyros, kebabs, and falafel. And there in the center is the buffet. That's what you came here for. And I hope you came hungry. Ultrafresh pita and hummus (the best in town), made on-site, flank a long line of chicken, beef, and lamb entrées—and sometimes even goat. You can also find Holy Land in the **Midtown Global Market** (920 Lake St. E., Minneapolis, 612/870-6104, Mon.-Sat. 9am-8pm, Sun. 9am-6pm).

MAP 3: 2513 Central Ave. NE, Minneapolis, 612/781-2627, www.holylandbrand.com; Sun.-Thurs. 9am-9pm, Fri.-Sat. 9am-9:30pm

## LATIN AMERICAN
### Brasa $$

Brasa is the mostly Latin version of a meat-and-three: Pick your protein (spit-roasted chicken or pork) and your sides (fried yucca, creamed spinach, an ethereal muffin made with creamed corn). That's it, unless you'd like to turn that juicy chicken or pork into a sandwich or construct a meal entirely out of side dishes—which isn't a bad idea either. Or, get it to go and walk the mile to the Mississippi River for a picnic. Brasa is now in St. Paul, too (777 Grand Ave., St. Paul, 651/224-1302, Sun.-Thurs. 11am-9pm, Fri.-Sat. 11am-10pm).

MAP 3: 600 Hennepin Ave. E., Minneapolis, 612/379-3030, www.brasa.us; Sun.-Thurs. 11am-9pm, Fri.-Sat. 11am-10pm

## GREEK
### Gardens of Salonica $$

This is the lighter, more Mediterranean side of Greek cuisine. The best things to eat are the small *meze*-like plates. Fill your table with them and share: hummus with pillowy

Greek pita and olives, ultragarlicky *skordalia* potato dip, pizzas built on pita bases, and the savory flaky pastries they call *boughatsa*. Of course, you can also build a traditional three-course meal and make a long, comfortable evening of it in the spare, serene dining room.

MAP 3: 19 5th St. NE, Minneapolis, 612/378-0611, www.gardensofsalonica.com; Tues.-Thurs. 11am-9pm, Fri.-Sat. 11am-10pm

## ITALIAN
### Pizza Nea $

True Neapolitan pizza is baked in a 900°F wood-fired oven, just as it is here at Pizza Nea. The pies fall somewhere between individual and sharing size (depending on how hungry and how generous you are), and the crust is a bit thicker and chewier than the classic Neapolitan crust. It holds the toppings well, from the basic Margherita with basil to an inspired pie with two fried eggs and sharp parmesan cheese. Pizza Nea also has a great list of local brews.

MAP 3: 306 Hennepin Ave. E., Minneapolis, 612/331-9298, www.pizzanea. com; Mon.-Fri. 11am-2pm and 5pm-10pm, Sat. 11am-10pm, Sun. 11am-9pm

## SEAFOOD
### The Anchor Fish and Chips $

Minnesota doesn't have chippies—late-night English fish-and-chip shops—but it does have The Anchor, which helps fill that need. The menu is short, but it could be even shorter. All you really need to order is a half pound of Alaskan cod and thick french fries cut right here. Some malt vinegar and you're done. If fish isn't your thing, you could also get shepherd's pie, pasties, or even a plain old burger. This pub-like joint is also a great place to go just for a beer. Note the hours: This is one of your few good options for late-night eats.

MAP 3: 302 13th Ave. NE, Minneapolis, 612/676-1300, www.theanchorfishandchips. com; Tues.-Wed. 4pm-10pm, Thurs.-Fri. 4pm-11pm, Sat. 10am-11pm, Sun. 10am-10pm

## SOUTHERN
### Breaking Bread $

Breaking Bread has a two-fold mission: First, feed people from all over the city delicious food; second, help revitalize its own north-side neighborhood with jobs and a community gathering space. The long communal tables are filled with people enjoying smoked brisket, pulled pork, fried chicken, po'boy sandwiches, and (to balance things out) a bright kale salad.

MAP 3: 1210 Broadway Ave. W., Minneapolis, 612/529-9346, www. breakingbreadfoods.com; Mon.-Fri. 8am-3pm, Sat.-Sun. 9am-4pm

## BREAKFAST AND BRUNCH
### Wilde Roast $$

In the spirit of its namesake writer, Wilde Roast is sensuous (with its plush, lounge-like interior) and decadent (with its spare-no-calorie menu). While it's hopping all year long, this is an especially good place to spend a winter afternoon looking out over the ice-flecked Mississippi, eating the creamiest macaroni and cheese and the richest bread pudding in the Twin Cities.

MAP 3: 65 Main St. SE, Minneapolis, 612/331-4544, www.wilderoastcafe.com; daily 7am-11pm

### Al's Breakfast $

Just 11 stools—that's it, 11—are arranged along the single counter stretching from the front of the room to the back. In front of the counter are the grills, where the cook runs back and forth, conducting a symphony of short orders. And behind the stools stand all the people waiting to grab your seat as soon as you're gone. Al's is a University of Minnesota institution, known for its pancakes and its character.

MAP 3: 413 14th Ave. SE, Minneapolis, 612/331-9991; Mon.-Sat. 6am-1pm, Sun. 9am-1pm

# Downtown St. Paul and West Side

## Map 4

## CONTEMPORARY AND FUSION

### Forepaugh's $$$

Forepaugh's is truly of another time. The setting is a three-story 1870s mansion with a grand portico, antique tchotchkes, and several working fireplaces. The menu is the best of what was considered truly fine dining a couple of generations ago: beef Wellington, duckling pâté, escargot, baked Alaska. The service is formal and well trained. Forepaugh's even comes with a ghost story: Molly, an Irish maid in the household of Joseph Forepaugh, reputedly makes her presence known in the bar.

MAP 4: 276 Exchange St. S., St. Paul, 651/224-5606, www.forepaughs.com; Tues.-Thurs. 4pm-9pm, Fri.-Sat. 4pm-10pm

### W. A. Frost and Company $$$

Three decades ago, W. A. Frost, in the 100-year-old building where a pharmacist of the same name once ran his store, was a pioneer in the revival of the Cathedral Hill neighborhood. Today, with its arched stained glass windows, pressed-tin ceilings, and Oriental rugs, it's still a great place to take your mom or grandma out to dinner and enjoy the elegance of a bygone era. Frost's menu, however, is a little more up-to-date, focusing on local ingredients served in modern ways. If the beautiful patio and dining room are full, you can enjoy a full dinner in the bar. Sunday brunch at Frost is an institution.

MAP 4: 374 Selby Ave., St. Paul, 651/224-5715, www.wafrost.com; Mon.-Fri. 11am-1:30pm and 5pm-10pm, Sat.-Sun. 10:30am-2pm and 5pm-10pm

### Saint Dinette $$

"Dinette" is underselling things a bit: This is no humble lunch counter, but a refined dining room. While the plates are perfectly composed, the inspiration comes from the humble, homey food of North America, from Montreal (house-made bagels and the classiest bologna sandwich you've ever had) to New Orleans (shrimp and grits with succotash) to Mexico (chile relleno) to, well, whatever magic place salt cod churros come from.

MAP 4: 261 5th St. E., St. Paul, 651/800-1415, www.saintdinette.com; Tues.-Thurs. 5pm-10pm, Fri. 5pm-11pm, Sat. 10am-11pm, Sun. 10am-9pm

## FRENCH

### ✪ Meritage $$$

Mix a little joy and a little warm camaraderie with formal tableside service and serious culinary chops, and you have Meritage (rhymes with "heritage," a nod to the California Bordeaux-style wines of the same name). From the amusements—two-bite appetizers like the "tiny tuna tartare taco on a taro chip" (try to say that without smiling)—to the starters (don't miss the baby beet salad) and the entrées (steak frites, roast chicken, sole), straight through to the marble-topped cheese cart, this is serious fine dining that doesn't take itself too seriously. Meritage also has a casual raw bar, with more than a dozen varieties of fresh oysters available daily.

MAP 4: 410 St. Peter St., St. Paul, 651/222-5670, www.meritage-stpaul.com; Tues.-Thurs. 11:30am-2pm and 5pm-10pm, Fri. 11:30am-2pm and 5pm-11pm, Sat. 10am-2pm and 5pm-11pm, Sun. 10am-2pm and 5pm-10pm

## ITALIAN
### Cossetta Alimentari $$

For more than 100 years, the Cossetta family has been selling Italian delicacies in downtown St. Paul, from imported pastas to salami. Downtown workers, families, and others needing something fast and filling also come to Cossetta's for a cafeteria-style lunch and dinner, with pizzas, sandwiches, pastas, and salads. You may have to throw some elbows to get around in here during the busiest times. Upstairs in **Louis Ristorante** (Mon.-Thurs. 3pm-11pm, Fri.-Sat. 3pm-midnight, Sun. noon-9pm), get an old-school Italian meal, from antipasti to primi to secondi, in a dark-booth atmosphere that would have made Sinatra feel right at home.

MAP 4: 211 7th St. W., St. Paul, 651/222-3476, www.cossettas.com; Mon.-Thurs. 11am-9pm, Fri.-Sat. 11am-10pm, Sun. 11am-8pm

### Mucci's Italian $$

Deep-fried pizza. Did you stop reading there and start navigating to Mucci's? Well, there's a lot more to this place, including a lasagna so addictive they started selling it to heat at home (along with a handful of other menu items) and lemon potatoes that I now regret telling you about because there will be less for me. About the pizza: It's Montanara-style, meaning the dough is fried, then topped with sauce and cheese.

MAP 4: 786 Randolph Ave., St. Paul, 651/330-2245, www.muccisitalian.com; Tues.-Thurs. 5pm-10pm., Fri. 5pm-11pm, Sat. 8am-noon and 5pm-11pm, Sun. 8am-noon and 5pm-10pm

## ASIAN
### Sakura Restaurant & Bar $$

Frequently named the best Japanese restaurant in the Twin Cities, Sakura has a little something for everyone, including inexpensive and filling *teishoku* dinners (like hearty, everyday combo plates), an elaborate sushi menu, and quick bento lunches. The dining room is bright and cheery—more the place for lively conversation than a romantic evening.

MAP 4: 350 St. Peter St., St. Paul, 651/224-0185, www.sakurastpaul. com; Mon.-Thurs. 11:30am-2:30pm and 4pm-10:30pm, Fri.-Sat. 11:30am-2:30pm and 4pm-11pm, Sun. noon-2:30pm and 4pm-9:30pm

### Cheng Heng $

In an area where *phô*, *bánh mì*, and spring rolls are truly universal comfort food, much of the menu at Cheng Heng is familiar. But this isn't the Vietnamese food you can find along much of University Avenue in St. Paul or Nicollet in Minneapolis. This is authentic Cambodian food,

# NEW MINNESOTA CLASSIC: HMONG FOOD

The Twin Cities' large Hmong population's cooking traditions have started to come out of home kitchens and into the public. Start your exploration of Hmong cuisine at one of two massive marketplaces. **Hmong Village** (1001 Johnson Pkwy., St. Paul, 651/771-7886; daily 9am-7pm) is a complex of small stores selling everything from clothes to kitchenware, along with about two dozen restaurant stalls in an industrial area of St. Paul. **Hmongtown Marketplace** (217 Como Ave., St. Paul, 651/487-3700, www.hmongtownmarketplace.com; daily 8am-8pm) is even bigger, with more than 200 stalls, indoors and out—and plans to grow. Bring a sense of adventure and a willingness to mime your order (not everybody you meet will speak fluent English).

Look for rich barbecue, stuffed chicken wings, fruity bubble teas, fried noodles, papaya salads, *laab* (meat salads, some raw, some cooked), and chicken feet. The cooking is 100 percent authentic and cooked to please a Hmong eater, with one exception: The real heat is often toned down, with chili sauce served on the side.

Both markets host cultural events and celebrations that are open to all.

right down to the curried fish (*amok*), which is practically the Cambodian national dish. Fans also come here for the curry noodle soup: a bright red bowl of comfort, a little sweet, a little spicy. The decor is unpretentious, and the staff are exceedingly warm and friendly.

**MAP 4:** 448 University Ave. W., St. Paul, 651/222-5577, www.chengheng448.com; daily 9:30am-9:30pm

### Trieu Chau $

In the string of gritty Vietnamese holes-in-the-wall along University Avenue, Trieu Chau is particularly beloved. It's tiny, and often packed, but the kitchen moves fast enough that waits aren't long. The menu holds few surprises for fans of this sort of food, but the sweet-and-spicy *phô* soup and vermicelli salads can't be beat—and neither can the prices. A packed house has other advantages: a steady stream of freshly rolled spring rolls.

**MAP 4:** 500 University Ave. W., St. Paul, 651/222-6148; Sun.-Mon. and Wed.-Thurs. 10am-8pm, Fri.-Sat. 10am-9pm

# LATIN AMERICAN
## Pajarito $$

Street food goes sleek. Pajarito's menu starts with the tacos, but you shouldn't stop there. Most of the fun and delicious stuff is on the *platillos* list: small plates (some smaller than others) like *queso fundido* (melted cheese) and *shishito* peppers served *elote*-style (with Cotija cheese and lime). The drinks are especially good, with refreshing rather than heavy-handed cocktails.

**MAP 4:** 605 7th St. W., St. Paul, 651/340-9545, www.pajaritostp.com; Mon.-Thurs. 11am-10pm, Fri.-Sat. 11am-11pm, Sun. 11am-9pm

### Boca Chica $

The Frias family has been serving the well-established Mexican American community of St. Paul's District del Sol since 1964. This is classic old-timey Mexican American cuisine, the better-executed forerunner of every family taco night: flour and corn tacos, chiles rellenos, tamales, flautas, and tostados. Come hungry for the generous, filling lunchtime buffet, or hang out at the bar on weekend evenings while neighbors and visitors clutch buzzers waiting for a table. Yep, those tamales are good enough to pack the massive bright yellow dining room with happy eaters.

MAP 4: 11 Cesar Chavez St., St. Paul, 651/222-8499, www.bocachicarestaurant.com; Mon. 11am-9pm, Tues.-Thurs. 11am-10pm, Fri.-Sat. 11am-11pm, Sun. 10am-9pm

### El Burrito Mercado $

In the back of a grocery store, in the heart of St. Paul's Mexican American community, you will find some of the biggest, best burritos this side of the border. To put together your lunch or dinner—or your filling single meal of the day—pick a *guisado* (a flavorful stew of pork, beef, or chicken) and then decide whether you want it in a taco, burrito, or gordita. It's all made fresh on-site, right down to the generous selection of salsas.

MAP 4: 175 Cesar Chavez St., St. Paul, 651/227-2192, www.elburritomercado.com; Mon.-Sat. 7am-9pm, Sun. 7am-8pm

## MIDDLE EASTERN
### Babani's Kurdish Restaurant $$

Babani's has long claimed to be the first Kurdish restaurant in the United States, a claim few are in any position to dispute. Some dishes are recognizable: tabouli, stuffed grape leaves, the yogurt dip called *jaajic* here and *tzatziki* in Greece, the salty yogurt drink called a *lassi* in India and *dugh* in Iran. Others are entirely unique: *dowjic*, a lemony, yogurty chicken soup; grilled rice balls stuffed with ground meat; and the house specialty, Sheik Babani, an eggplant stuffed with tomato and meat sauce. It all comes

with the warm welcome you might expect from a wandering people. The restaurant itself is small and comfortably worn about the edges.

MAP 4: 544 St. Peter St., St. Paul, 651/602-9964, www.babanis.com; Mon.-Fri. 11am-2:30pm and 5pm-9pm, Sat. 5pm-9:30pm

## STEAK
### Mancini's Char House $$$

If Frank Sinatra himself were to appear in Mancini's maroon and brass dining room, in your steak-stuffed state you might not even blink. Ol' Blue Eyes might even imagine himself to be in old-time Vegas. Mancini's is the place in downtown St. Paul to celebrate anniversaries and big corporate deals with slabs of meat, lobster tails, and carb-heavy sides of potatoes and rolls. There's live music Wednesday-Saturday and a small dance floor.

MAP 4: 531 7th St. W., St. Paul, 651/224-7345, www.mancinis.com; Sun.-Thurs. 4:30pm-10pm, Fri.-Sat. 4:30pm-11pm

### St. Paul Grill $$$

This is old-school, make-a-grown-up-impression dining in the St. Paul Hotel. The dinner menu is almost entirely steaks, chops, and high-end seafood, with formal service in high-backed booths. (Did I say "almost?" Make that "entirely.") If you're not wearing your power suit, loosen your tie at the bar, where you can get an excellent burger.

MAP 4: 350 Market St., St. Paul, 651/224-7455, www.stpaulgrill.com; Mon.-Thurs. 11am-2pm and 5:30-10pm, Fri. 11am-2pm and 5:30pm-11pm, Sat. 11am-2pm and 5pm-11pm, Sun. 10:30am-2pm and 5pm-10pm

St. Paul Grill

and the four booths are filled, and the orders of pancakes, potatoes O'Brien (hash browns with the works), and tuna melts are flying off the griddle. In a world of slick, modern-retro diners, Mickey's is the real thing. And Hollywood has taken notice, giving Mickey's a role in the *Mighty Ducks* and *Jingle All the Way*.

MAP 4: 36 7th St. W., St. Paul, 651/698-0259, www.mickeysdiningcar.com; daily 24 hours

## BREAKFAST AND BRUNCH
### Buttered Tin  $

Lucky Lowertown residents: They get to wake up to this cozy neighborhood café and call it their own. While the sweets are not too sweet—including the bananas Foster French toast—the savory side of the menu has more zing than you might expect from a humble Minnesota brunch, with huevos rancheros Benedict and a breakfast hash studded with artichokes, grape tomatoes, and kalamata olives. Whatever the breakfast hot dish is, get that.

MAP 4: 237 7th St. E., St. Paul, 651/224-2300, www.thebutteredtin.com; daily 7am-3pm

## SWEETS
### Salty Tart  $

Pastries both savory and sweet, from veggie turnovers to Guinness cupcakes, have made Salty Tart a beloved place to take a little break. Brunchy things like eggs, salmon, and avocado toast are served until 2pm.

MAP 4: 289 5th St. E., St. Paul, 612/874-9206, www.saltytart.com; Mon.-Fri. 8am-4pm, Sat.-Sun. 7am-4pm

## SEAFOOD
### OCTO fishbar  $$$

Restaurateur Tim McKee is the unrivaled king of hospitality in the Twin Cities, so expect service that Gets Things Right and still makes you feel at home while you revel in dishes inspired by all of the Seven Seas, from lobster rolls with a Japanese kick to *pozole verde* (green-chile stew) made with fish. The extensive raw bar includes showy themed towers of shellfish. Octo is the anchor tenant in the Market House Collaborative, which also houses premium fish and meat counters, along with Salty Tart.

MAP 4: 289 5th St. E., St. Paul, 651/202-3409, www.octostp.com; Mon.-Fri. 4pm-10pm, Sat.-Sun. 10am-2pm and 4pm-10pm

## DINERS
### Mickey's Diner  $

In 1937, a prefab diner was shipped in from New Jersey and set up in downtown St. Paul. It hasn't closed since. Day and night the seats at the counter

## MINNESOTA CLASSIC: WALLEYE AND WILD RICE

You undoubtedly have heard some snickering about Midwestern food—about hot dish and Jell-O salad, perhaps. And, as is often the case, there's some truth behind the jokes. Yes, as a rule, Minnesotans are a people grown hardy on hot dish (that's "casserole" to the rest of the country) and "salads" that are green only because they are made from green Jell-O (and fruit and marshmallows, and served at dinner, not for dessert).

But all that is home cooking. (Or, more accurately, church supper cooking.) When you are out at a restaurant and want to order something particularly Minnesotan, order the walleye. Walleye, the Minnesota state fish, is a mild, tasty freshwater species beloved by anglers and by eaters. It's often breaded and fried, usually in a sandwich. You'll find it on the menu in corner bars, in bowling alleys, and in white-tablecloth restaurants.

The irony here is that when you do order the Minnesota state fish in a Minnesota restaurant, what you're most likely eating is imported zander (also known as pike perch) from Canada or Europe. Because commercial fishing is strictly limited in Minnesota, walleye can't be caught in sufficient quantities to feed the local market. While this revelation caused a big stink locally a few years back, in the end most restaurant eaters realized that if they couldn't tell the difference, it probably didn't make a very big difference. If you want to be sure that the walleye you're eating is truly walleye, you'll need a fishing line. Or go to **Hell's Kitchen** in downtown Minneapolis, where you'll find the real deal crusted with parmesan, covered with bacon, and sandwiched between two slices of sourdough bread.

If you don't like fish but still want to choose a local flavor, order the wild rice. But here as well we have some nomenclature issues. The Minnesota state grain, wild rice, is actually more closely related to oats than to rice. The Ojibwe, who call it *manoomin,* harvest the long, thin grains by knocking the stalks gently over canoes. It's a labor-intensive process and requires very specific growing conditions. More and more Native American-grown wild rice is available in specialty stores and direct from the tribes, but you have to seek it out. What you're more likely eating is not *manoomin* but a relative of it grown commercially in a paddy (Minnesota law requires commercially grown wild rice to be labeled "paddy rice"). Hell's Kitchen also serves authentic *manoomin* porridge for breakfast with nuts and blueberries.

# Summit-University and Mac-Groveland    Map 5

## CONTEMPORARY AND FUSION

### The Lexington $$$

The Lex looks like a place where deals and careers are made—because it is. Wing-backed leather chairs. Dark wood. Dim light. And upgraded classics like Pot au Pho (Vietnamese-spiced stew) and lobster imperial. In a town where dining tends to be "come as you are," the Lex decidedly isn't. A little spit and polish is required.

**MAP 5:** 1096 Grand Ave., St. Paul, 651/289-4990, www.thelexmn.com; Mon.-Thurs. 4pm-11pm, Fri. 4pm-midnight, Sat. 10am-midnight, Sun. 10am-10pm

### Stewart's $$

The neighbors are fiercely loyal to this cozy underground restaurant—and perhaps a little possessive. If the secret gets out, competition for seats and parking spots might get even worse. The menu celebrates what "American food" means today, from grass-fed

Stewart's

steaks to kimchi fries to a not-so-humble patty melt.

MAP 5: 128 Cleveland Ave. N., St. Paul, 651/645-4128, www.stewartsminnesota. com; Tues.-Fri. 11am-10pm, Sat. 10am-10pm, Sun. 10am-9pm

## RUSSIAN
### Moscow on the Hill $$

Nobody does long, lavish celebrations better than the Russians. If you're looking for a quick bite before a show, go elsewhere. If you're looking for an experience that will last all evening long, there is nothing better than Moscow on the Hill. Russian meals are five courses long: soup, salad, *zakuski* (appetizers, served family style), main dish (often the least significant part of the meal), and dessert, with frequent stops for vodka in between. Musicians stroll the dining room, and as the evening wears on, it turns into one big party.

MAP 5: 371 Selby Ave., St. Paul, 651/291-1236, www.moscowonthehill.com; Mon.-Thurs. 11am-11:30pm, Fri. 11am-1am, Sat. 10am-1am, Sun. 10am-11pm

## ITALIAN
### Punch Pizza $$

Pizza—especially when it takes about four minutes to cook in an 800°F oven—is the ultimate fast food. But it doesn't feel like fast food when it's got gorgonzola and roasted red peppers on it and is served in a classy—but extremely family-friendly—dining room with a beer and wine license. This, the original Punch Pizza, has table service, unlike the other nine locations, including one in Minneapolis (3226 Lake St. W., 612/929-0006, daily 11am-10pm) and another in St. Paul's Grand Avenue shopping district (769 Grand Ave., 615/602-6068, daily 11am-10pm).

MAP 5: 704 Cleveland Ave. S., St. Paul, 651/696-1066, www.punchpizza.com; Mon.-Fri. 4pm-10pm, Sat.-Sun. 11am-10pm

## ASIAN
### Everest on Grand $$

Nepali cuisine is a cross between northern Indian and Chinese, based on lots of ghee and very mild spices. *Momos,* Tibetan dumplings served either steamed or fried, are the highlight of the menu and reason enough to come. The curries, *pakoras* (batter-fried vegetables), and samosas will feel like milder versions of familiar Indian favorites. Keep in mind that this is hearty cuisine: The "lighter" side of the menu is a selection of fried rice dishes.

MAP 5: 1278 Grand Ave., St. Paul, 651/696-1666, www.everestongrand.com; Mon.-Thurs. 11:30am-3pm and 5pm-9pm, Fri. 11:30am-3pm and 5pm-10pm, Sat. 11:30am-10pm, Sun. 11:30am-9pm

### Ngon Bistro $$

Traditional Vietnamese flavors meet colonial French influences meet American cuisine in the farm-to-fork era—that's Ngon Bistro. From the

## THE JUICY LUCY: MINNESOTA'S UNOFFICIAL STATE BURGER

Sandwich a bit of cheese inside a burger before you cook it and you have a remarkably simple Minnesota classic: the Juicy Lucy, or "Jucy" (presumably so it mimics the spelling of "Lucy"). The cheese gets volcanically hot and tends to squirt out in dangerously random trajectories. And a good Lucy is delicious.

Two Minneapolis neighborhood bars lay claim to the Lucy. **Matt's Bar** (3500 Cedar Ave. S., Minneapolis, 612/722-7072, www.mattsbar.com, Sun.-Wed. 11am-midnight, Thurs.-Sat. 11am-1am) takes a certain corporate pride in the misspelling "Jucy." The **5-8 Club** (5800 Cedar Ave. S., Minneapolis, 612/823-5858, www.5-8club.com, Sun.-Wed. 11am-10pm, Thurs.-Sat. 11am-11:30pm) makes burgers that are just as good but spelled correctly.

a classic Juicy Lucy

Although it can't claim to have been there at the Juicy Lucy's birth, **Blue Door Pub** (1811 Selby Ave., St. Paul, www.thebdp.com, daily 11am-1am) has perfected the art of the cheese-stuffed burger. The menu goes beyond cheddar and American to the "Blucy" (blue cheese) and a dozen other variations, and includes an array beers on tap to boot. Blue Door also has locations in Minneapolis's Longfellow neighborhood (3448 42nd Ave. S., Minneapolis, 612/315-2470, daily 11am-11pm), Lyn-Lake (3006 Lyndale Ave. S., Minneapolis, 612/353-4838, Sun.-Thurs. 11am-1am, Fri.-Sat. 11am-2am), and near the U of M (1514 Como Ave. SE, Minneapolis, 612/367-4964, Sun.-Thurs. 11am-11pm, Fri.-Sat. 11am-1am). Many are also fervent fans of **Casper & Runyon's Nook** (page 84), prized for its "Juicy Nookie Burger."

---

polished, kitsch-free dining room to the mussels and smoked trout on the menu, this is definitely not your typical hole-in-the-wall Asian joint. You can scratch your itch for *phô* (soup) or *bún* (noodles), or you can order a Vietnamese-spiced local pork shoulder. Weekend brunches are a treat, with everything from rabbit dumplings to an excellent local smoked trout omelet.
**MAP 5:** 799 University Ave. W., St. Paul, 651/222-3301, www.ngonbistro.com; Sun.-Thurs. 11am-9pm, Fri.-Sat. 11am-11pm

### SEAFOOD
#### Grand Catch $
Ordering at Grand Catch is super simple: Choose your shellfish. Choose your sauce. Tell your server how spicy you want it to be. That's your seafood boil. This is one of just a few places to

scratch that particular itch in the Twin Cities. The atmosphere is down-home and the spice level is high.
**MAP 5:** 1672 Grand Ave., St. Paul, 651/348-8541, www.grandcatchmn.com; Sun.-Thurs. 11am-10pm, Fri.-Sat. 11am-11pm

### DELIS
#### Cecil's Delicatessen $
Cecil's isn't kosher, but it is an undeniably authentic Jewish deli, from the mile-long menu exhorting you to "Eat, eat!" to the crisp latkes and sweet cheese blintzes. Get your sandwich "New York style"—just the meat, a heaping cup of it, and the bread—or with more Midwestern-style fixings. You know all those arguments about what really belongs in a Reuben? You can settle them here, as Cecil's serves several variations on the classic

sandwich. You can also buy excellent pastrami and corned beef (kosher available) and house-baked loaves of pumpernickel and rye in the deli.

MAP 5: 651 Cleveland Ave. S., St. Paul, 651/698-6276, www.cecilsdeli.com; daily 9am-9pm

## BURGERS
### Casper & Runyon's Nook  $

There is some dispute over the origin of the Jucy Lucy—an inside-out cheeseburger that when made properly sears the roof of your mouth in a delightful way—and there are even a few holdout partisans of other Jucy Lucys about town. But there is no disputing the fervent love St. Paulites hold for the Nook's burgers. The bar itself is tiny (and this is a bar, but it's unlikely that anyone has ever ordered a beer here without a burger), and during peak burger-eating hours you will have to wait. But you will know when the hot cheese hits your mouth that it has been worth it. The bar is open until 2am.

MAP 5: 492 Hamline Ave. S., St. Paul, 651/698-4347, www.crnook.com; Sun.-Thurs. 11am-1am, Fri.-Sat. 11am-2am

## CAFÉS
### Cafe Latte  $

Ladies who lunch love to lunch at Cafe Latte. Students, families, and young lovers also love it, along with anyone hungry for a relatively quick and relatively healthy bite. Choose pasta salads, tossed salads, soups, and sandwiches made to order as you slide your tray along the cafeteria side, or order wood-oven pizza specialties on the other side. Fair warning: Although service is quick, the line sometimes snakes out the door. Stop by on weekday afternoons for a refreshing plate of sweets and savories in the style of an English afternoon tea.

MAP 5: 850 Grand Ave., St. Paul, 651/224-5687, www.cafelatte.com; Sun.-Thurs. 9am-10pm, Fri.-Sat. 9am-11pm

## SWEETS
### Grand Ole Creamery  $

The smell of hot, fresh waffle cones is the smell of summer, and it flows out onto Grand Avenue, along with the overflow crowd of ice cream fiends. The flavors rotate daily, with 31 of a possible 200 on offer at any one time. Most are classics, with a few surprises like birthday cake and honey crunch. If you feel like jumping into the middle of a Twin Cities controversy, visit here and Minneapolis's Sebastian Joe's on the same day and declare your allegiance for one over the other. Winter hours may be shorter.

MAP 5: 750 Grand Ave., St. Paul, 651/293-1655, www.grandolecreamery. com; Sun.-Thurs. noon-10pm, Fri.-Sat. 11am-11pm

### Izzy's Ice Cream Café  $

Can't choose just one of Izzy's one-of-a-kind flavors, like key lime pie, Norwegian chai, or dark chocolate zin? Get two. Every scoop of ice cream comes with an "Izzy scoop"—a melon ball-size bonus. Jeff Sommers, the man behind this beloved neighborhood ice cream shop, believes in high-quality ingredients and treading a little more lightly on the earth (Izzy's is entirely solar powered). When the Food Network's Bobby Flay challenged him to an ice cream-making contest, Izzy's hot brown sugar flavor won handily. Izzy's is also in Minneapolis, near the Guthrie Theater (1100 2nd St. S., Minneapolis, 612/206-3356, daily 11am-11pm).

MAP 5: 2034 Marshall Ave., St. Paul, 651/603-1458, www.izzysicecream.com; daily 11am-11pm

## FROSTY TREATS IN FROSTY WEATHER

Don't expect the Twin Cities' beloved ice cream parlors to close up shop during the winter. The lines might be shorter—just a little—but the joints will still be hopping. In fact, Minneapolis's **Sebastian Joe's** offers ever-greater discounts as the mercury dips, and customers are always on hand to take advantage of them. Although there's no winter discount at the other ice cream shops in town, you don't want to miss the innovative flavors at **Izzy's Ice Cream Café**, the Old World elegance at **Sonny's Cafe,** or the small-town atmosphere at **Grand Ole Creamery.**

# Como and St. Anthony    Map 6

## AFRICAN
### Fasika $

The center of the Twin Cities' large and growing Ethiopian community is right here. On weekends, especially, the tables are filled with large groups of family and friends, and if you're an Ethiopian cuisine newbie, you're likely to be the only newbie in the restaurant. Not to worry. The menu includes full descriptions in English, along with photos. Everything starts with *injera*, the spongy fermented bread that serves as both plate and wrap for the warmly spiced stews. You'll also find a real rarity: Ethiopian wine.

MAP 6: 510 Snelling Ave. N., St. Paul, 651/646-4747, www.fasika.com; daily 11am-midnight

## ASIAN
### Mirror of Korea $

From *dolsot bibimbap* (rice topped with pickled vegetables and an egg, served in a hot stone bowl) to barbecued beef and pork to *yook hae* (sharply seasoned steak tartare with fresh garlic and cucumber and topped with an egg yolk), Mirror of Korea serves Korean classics with a strong eye toward tradition. The table full of pickled accompaniments, far beyond kimchi, pleases even the pickiest fan of Korean food. And since 1988, Mirror of Korea has created a lot of those fans.

MAP 6: 761 Snelling Ave. N., St. Paul, 651/647-9004, www.mirrorofkorea.com, Mon. and Wed.-Fri. 11am-9:30pm, Sat.-Sun. noon-9:30pm

## NORDIC
### Finnish Bistro $

Finnish transplant Soile Anderson has brought some of the best of her homeland's cuisine to this friendly, elegant bistro in the leafy St. Anthony neighborhood, where the atmosphere, too, is pleasantly Scandinavian. Finnish-style breakfast is served all day, including oatcakes, plates of lox and veggies, and *pulla* French toast, made with a traditional Finnish cardamom bread.

MAP 6: 2264 Como Ave., St. Paul, 651/645-9181, www.finnishbistro.com; daily 6:30am-8:30pm

## HOME OF BETTY CROCKER AND THE BUNDT CAKE

In the late 1800s, Minneapolis leaped to the top of the flour-milling world with the invention of a new milling technique. Rather than stone grindstones, Minnesota's Washburn-Crosby Mill started using metal and porcelain rollers and then blasting the wheat with air to remove the bits of shell and bran left behind. The pure white flour swept the world, and Minneapolis produced more flour than any other city for several decades.

In 1921, Washburn-Crosby introduced the persona of Betty Crocker to help answer baking questions from customers. An artist created Betty's portrait, and a secretary contributed her signature, which is still used today. Betty has had radio and TV shows and published cookbooks and even been voted the second most famous woman in America (in 1945, after Eleanor Roosevelt). She's gotten a makeover seven times, most recently in 1996, but she's still the most recognizable face in baking.

Another baking icon that got its start here is the Bundt cake. In 1950, the Minneapolis chapter of the Hadassah Society, a Jewish women's aid organization, approached the Nordic Ware company, which is still based in the Minneapolis suburb of St. Louis Park, and asked for a lightweight, fluted, high-sided pan for baking ring-shaped coffee cakes. In 1966, a Bundt cake won the Pillsbury Bake-Off, and the new pan quickly became the most-sold pan in the United States. Today, Nordic Ware has sold more than 50 million pans.

# Greater Twin Cities          Map 7

## CONTEMPORARY AND FUSION

### ✪ Bellecour $$$

When star chef Gavin Kaysen of downtown Minneapolis's Spoon and Stable decided it was time to conquer the suburbs, he went full-on classic French—trout amandine, duck, steamed mussels—in a space as bright and beautiful as a French farmhouse. Bellecour's bakery (open daily 7am-5pm) is equally as French and inviting, with a crepe cake that will haunt your dreams (in a good way). The bar is open an hour later and an hour earlier than the dining room.

MAP 7: 739 Lake St. E., Wayzata, 952/444-5200, www.bellecourrestaurant. com; Mon.-Fri. 5pm-10pm, Sat. 10am-2pm and 5pm-10pm, Sun. 10am-2pm and 5pm-9pm

### 6Smith $$$

Can't afford a home with a lake view? You're not alone. So make this expansive view of Lake Minnetonka yours for the evening, whether you take a seat right on the dock or on the rooftop staring far out over the horizon. The menu is as indulgent as the location: steak, lobster, oysters, scallops, and overstuffed, over-the-top burgers. It's like everything is carefully calculated to make sure every guest leans back and sighs, "This is the life."

MAP 7: 294 Grove Ln. E., Wayzata, 952/698-7900, www.6smith.com; Mon.-Thurs. 11am-11pm, Fri.-Sat. 11am-midnight, Sun. 10am-9pm

### CōV $$

Quick: Name some dishes you can improve upon with lobster. Macaroni and cheese? Sure. Cobb salad? Why not. Cioppino? Classic. Guacamole? Turns out the diners at the upscale CōV in the posh suburb of Wayzata can't get enough of it. It's become de rigueur to start a meal here with that over-the-top mash-up. Like the massive 200-person dining room, every dish at CōV is dressed to impress—and not

# RIDING COFFEE'S THIRD WAVE

If you're serious about coffee—no, really, really serious—you're going to feel right at home in the Twin Cities. If you care about single-origin beans and pour-over techniques and want to have a serious conversation about the benefits of the Clover—you can find your people. Not at every neighborhood coffeehouse, to be sure. But you won't have to look far.

While it's a close race, the most hardcore of the hardcore coffee shops may be **Five Watt** (3745 Nicollet Ave. S., Minneapolis, 612/259-7519, www.fivewattcoffee.com, daily 6am-10pm). In addition to the myriad ways the baristas will brew up your coffee, they also take a mixologist's approach to your morning drink, with bitters, herbs, and more. **Spyhouse** (945 Broadway St. NE, Minneapolis, 612/345-4348; 2451 Nicollet Ave. S., Minneapolis, 612/871-3177; 2404 Hennepin Ave. S., Minneapolis, 612/377-2278; all locations: http://spyhousecoffee.com, Mon.-Fri. 6am-11pm, Sat. 7am-11pm, Sun. 8am-11pm) is a serene home away from home for freelancers and students.

Peace Coffee

A few mini coffee empires known for carefully sourced and exquisitely roasted small-batch beans each have multiple locations, including **Dogwood** (3001 Hennepin Ave. S., Minneapolis, 612/354-2952, www.dogwoodcoffee.com, Mon.-Fri. 7am-9pm, Sat. 8am-9pm, Sun. 9am-6pm; 4021 Lake St. E., Minneapolis, 612/886-1585, Mon.-Fri. 6:30am-7pm, Sat. 8am-7pm, Sun. 8am-6pm; 825 Carleton St., St. Paul, 651/340-9248, Mon.-Fri. 7am-7pm, Sat. 8am-7pm, Sun. 8am-6pm). And people who care as much about coffee growers as coffee beans choose **Peace Coffee** (www.peacecoffee.com, 3262 Minnehaha Ave. S., Minneapolis, 612/877-7760, Mon.-Fri. 6:30am-8pm, Sat. 7am-8pm, Sun. 8am-8pm; Lakewinds Co-Op, 6420 Lyndale Ave. S., Minneapolis, 612/814-8079, daily 7am-8pm; Capella Tower, 225 6th St. S., Minneapolis, 612/248-8677, Mon.-Fri. 6am-5:30pm). Peace Coffee got its start as a bike-delivered bean business and now draws coffee drinkers to its own doors.

---

with fancy reductions and swirls but with luxury ingredients, like truffle oil, prime rib, and swordfish.
**MAP 7:** 700 Lake St. E., Wayzata, 952/473-5253, www.covwayzata.com; Mon.-Fri. 11am-1am, Sat. 10am-1am, Sun. 10am-midnight

## Lyn65 $$

Lyn65 takes its culinary cues from all over the world: kimchi, fried chicken, 'nduja (a spicy, spreadable sausage), masa cakes, flan. But what ties it all together is a simple formula: comfort + big flavor = oversize indulgence. The ambience is intimate and dimly lit, but early in the evening you would still feel comfortable bringing the whole family. The menu changes often, but you'll always find a selection of flatbreads and the excellent Lyn65 burger, unapologetically topped with American cheese.
**MAP 7:** 6439 Lyndale Ave. S., Minneapolis, 612/353-5501, http://lyn65.com; Tues.-Thurs. 4pm-11pm, Fri.-Sat. 4pm-midnight, Sun. 4pm-9pm

## Pig Ate My Pizza $$

The world needs a new category of pie to describe Pig Ate My Pizza. It's cooked in an ultrahot oven, Neapolitan-style.

But you can also get some pies baked on a brioche crust. The pizzas are close to personal-size, but you're definitely going to want to order a round of several to share, so you can experience the full range of wild kitchen creativity. If it's ever been dreamed up in a kitchen, somebody here has tried to put it on a pizza: mussels, pickles, chicken tikka, a pickled egg. And the atmosphere is just as raucous as the menu.

MAP 7: 4154 Broadway Ave. W., Robbinsdale, 763/537-7267, http://pigatemypizza.com; Wed.-Sat. noon-2pm and 5pm-10pm

## Travail Kitchen and Amusements $$

Playing with food is not only allowed, it's the entire ethos at Travail. A meal here comes out in more than a dozen stages—sometimes up to 20—each one attempting to turn some principle of flavor or texture on its head. Molecular gastronomy fans will recognize a few of the tricks, but Travail's air of happy chaos takes itself less seriously than some other cities' modern hot spots. Buy tickets online (yes, tickets for dinner) up to two months in advance. To get a seat without tickets and to order these "micro plates" à la carte, get a seat at Travail's sister restaurant, **The Rookery** (4124 Broadway Ave. W., Robbinsdale, 763/535-1131, www.travailkitchen.com, Wed.-Sat. 5pm-close), next door.

MAP 7: 4154 Broadway Ave. W., Robbinsdale, 763/535-1131, www.travailkitchen.com; Tues.-Sat. 5pm-10pm

# NIGHTLIFE

In Minneapolis and St. Paul, people are tribal in their loyalty to their neighborhood bars. Each is unique to its own fierce partisans but may seem similar to the untrained eye. We've listed those that attract patrons from a wider area, but an adventurous visitor could easily have fun seeking out the best joints on their own.

For a DIY pedestrian bar crawl, start at Psycho Suzi's in northeast Minneapolis and work your way south down Marshall Street or University Avenue. You can continue into downtown Minneapolis. In St. Paul, turn your back to the Xcel Energy Center and head straight down West 7th Street.

You'll also find brewpubs and taprooms aplenty to explore in the Twin Cities, which are happily experiencing a craft beer boom.

The nightclub scene in downtown Minneapolis—and thus the scene in the whole of the Twin Cities, because that's the sum of it—is fluid. As soon as you think you've got the hot spots figured out, they change hands, names, and decor. But locations stay the same (outfitting a

First Avenue and 7th St. Entry

dance club being an expensive endeavor). So do as the locals do: Put on your dancing shoes, head for the intersection of 1st Avenue and 5th Street, and see what looks happening.

Generally speaking, the Twin Cities are gay-friendly. And gay bars and clubs here are some of the most open, friendly, and downright rocking hangouts in town, no matter your persuasion.

# HIGHLIGHTS

✪ **BEST PLACE TO HEAR NATIONAL JAZZ ACTS:** In downtown Minneapolis, the **Dakota Jazz Club and Restaurant** has the market cornered on both great jazz and great dining (page 91).

✪ **BEST PIECE OF MINNEAPOLIS'S MUSICAL PAST, PRESENT, AND FUTURE:** Prince got his start at **First Avenue and 7th St. Entry,** where you can still hear the musical greats of today and the stars of tomorrow (page 91).

✪ **BEST PLACE FOR LAWN BOWLING:** In truth, **Brit's Pub** has the *only* place for lawn bowling in town, but that doesn't diminish it in any way (page 94).

✪ **BEST PLACE TO EXPERIENCE THE LOCAL COCKTAIL REVOLUTION:** The bartenders at **Marvel Bar** know their way around a shaker, a muddler, a bitters dropper, and a long list of local ingredients (page 94).

✪ **BEST DRAG SHOW:** You don't have to be gay to appreciate a good drag show . . . and you don't have to be gay to have fun at the **Gay 90s** (page 96).

✪ **BEST HIDEAWAY:** Look for the blue light, knock on the door, head downstairs, and keep an eye out for trap doors at **Volstead's Emporium,** the worst-kept secret in town (page 99).

✪ **BEST PLACE TO HEAR AN ELECTRIC HURDY-GURDY:** The not-for-profit **Cedar Cultural Center** is the best place to hear world music (page 102).

✪ **BEST PLACE TO RUB ELBOWS WITH POWER BROKERS:** You never know what kind of important deals are going down at the **St. Paul Grill**'s polished oak bar (page 106).

✪ **BEST DESTINATION FOR LOCAL BREWS:** If you've only got an afternoon or evening to spend drinking up the Twin Cities, head to **Surly Brewing Company** (page 108).

✪ **BEST PLACE TO BE A KID AGAIN (WITH OR WITHOUT THE KIDS):** Putt putt through a magical world at **Can Can Wonderland** with a boozy malt in one hand and mini donuts in the other (page 109).

## LIVE MUSIC
### ✪ Dakota Jazz Club and Restaurant

The Dakota is Minnesota's premier jazz club, known as one of the best in the country. Local and national headliners perform every night in a lavish hall before a crowd with a bit of local glamour. The Dakota is a great place to eat, too, whether you munch smoked fish and fries with béarnaise sauce in the club or order a full, luxurious meal in the dining room. Look for early-evening and late-night happy hour deals. Shows generally start at 7pm, 9pm, and 11:30pm and cost $5-75.

MAP 1: 1010 Nicollet Mall, Minneapolis, 612/332-1010, www.dakotacooks.com; Mon.-Thurs. 11:30am-4pm and 5pm-9pm, Fri. 11:30am-4pm and 5pm-10pm, Sat. 5pm-10pm, Sun. 5pm-9pm (later on nights with two shows); tickets vary, generally $5-75

### ✪ First Avenue and 7th St. Entry

First Avenue is a pilgrimage and a rite of passage for young Minnesotans—and those not-so-young who remember seeing U2 or Prince here for the first time (yep, that's First Avenue in *Purple Rain*). You can search out names of your favorite headlining acts on the curved outer walls of this former Greyhound station. Most nights see two or three shows in the Main Room, VIP Room, and the smaller

First Avenue and 7th St. Entry

Entry. Look for midweek, DJ-led dance nights, including Ritmo Caliente.

MAP 1: 701 1st Ave. N., Minneapolis, 612/332-1775, www.first-avenue.com; opening hours depend on show times, only open when there is a show; tickets vary, generally $5-30

### Bunker's

Are you watching the next Prince on stage at Bunker's? Pretty likely. Or, even more likely: another local legend with a reputation of their own. Prince himself used to jam on stage here, and, yes, it does feel like it's been around that long. In a good way. Live music plays every night. After 6pm, the kitchen serves up burgers—and nothing else.

MAP 1: 761 Washington Ave. N., Minneapolis, 612/338-8188, www. bunkersmusic.com; daily 11am-1am; tickets vary, generally $5-8

Fine Line Music Café

### Fine Line Music Café

When the Pixies got back together in 2004, the Fine Line is where they launched their reunion tour. The dance floor isn't big (you can always escape to the balcony), but it has seen big names in music history since 1987, from Sheryl Crow to Bill Clinton. Look for shows nearly every night. For a taste of Minnesota's music scene right now, look for local music showcase nights (usually Tuesday, Wednesday, and Thursday). Shows are 21-plus unless otherwise noted and are general admission. Get there early if you want a table.

MAP 1: 318 1st Ave. N., Minneapolis, 612/338-8100, www.finelinemusic.com; opening hours depend on show times, only open when there is a show; tickets vary, generally $5-35

## BREWPUBS AND TAPROOMS

### Day Block Brewing Company

Day Block is so much more than a taproom. Live music, a wine list, a raft of hip cocktails, and a full menu made on-site all set it apart. Nevertheless, it keeps up its beer bona fides with a half dozen of its own craft beers on tap, including the locally loved Frank's Red Ale.

MAP 1: 1105 Washington Ave. S., Minneapolis, 612/617-7793, www. dayblockbrewing.com; Sun.-Wed. 11am-11pm, Thurs.-Sat. 11am-1am

### Freehouse

Big and usually hopping, the Freehouse is the creation of the local Blue Plate Group, restaurateurs who know how to keep crowds happy. They keep the house-made list of beers short and focused—about a dozen—and the menu long, from breakfast through lunch and dinner. This is an excellent place to bring a large group of diners and drinkers with diverse tastes for a long, lingering meal.

MAP 1: 701 Washington Ave. N., Minneapolis, 612/339-7011, www. freehousempls.com; daily 6:30am-2am

# CRAFT BEER IN THE TWIN CITIES

Once upon a time, state law mandated that liquor had to take three distinct steps on the way to the consumer: from brewers to distributors to retail outlets. No company was allowed to do more than one of those things. But the craft beer revolution brought small—and tiny—brewers who needed an easy and inexpensive way to get their brews into the hands of enthusiastic fans. They lobbied successfully for the right to sell directly to consumers both to drink on-site and to take home.

The taproom was born—and immediately exploded into a veritable boom. Within a few years, dozens of taprooms had opened their doors in the Twin Cities. Some look and feel like retail outlets where you could sit and have a drink if you really wanted to. Others feel like neighborhood pubs. And a few of them are like playgrounds for the beer-loving populace.

Find your perfect pint at a Twin Cities taproom

If you want to talk local beer or try a flight, a taproom or brewpub is the place to go. Most offer tours or have the brewers available to chat. They're all filled with beer nerds. And they sell growlers (half-gallon glass bottles to go). While some have kitchens and full menus, most invite food trucks to park outside or have delivery agreements with nearby restaurants. And, while some brewpubs and taprooms have decidedly grown-up vibes, others are child-friendly, with games to play and sodas on tap and families happily whiling away the afternoon. Here are some spots to get started:

- **Fulton Beer:** Drink on a friendly deck in the shadow of Target Field before, after, or during a Twins game (page 93).

- **Bauhaus Brewlabs:** They're bright, bold, and inviting—both the beer hall and the German-style lagers served here (page 102).

- **Summit Brewing Company:** Enjoy local beer at its blue-collar roots, bellied up to one of this brewery's long, friendly beer hall tables (page 107).

- **Surly Brewing Company:** Beloved local behemoth of craft brewing, Surly is a destination where you could spend all day: Take a tour, try some beer, play yard games, drink more beer, then order elevated bar snacks or pizza (page 108).

## Fulton Beer

Fans of the Minnesota taproom boom will remember Fulton as the team that started it all. Hobby brewers that started in a garage, they moved into a warehouse space on the edge of downtown the moment it was legal. The space is barebones, welcoming, and well lived-in, and the deck, under the shadow of the Twins' stadium, could conceivably be your new home away from home in Minneapolis. Order burgers and fries from the Airstream parked outside.

**MAP 1:** 414 6th Ave. N., Minneapolis, 612/333-3208, www.fultonbeer.com; Wed.-Thurs. 3pm-10pm, Fri. 3pm-11pm, Sat. noon-11pm, Sun. noon-6pm

## Inbound BrewCo

Somehow this big, industrial space with a two-story ceiling and floor-to-ceiling windows still manages to feel convivial. Maybe it's the blond wood and beer hall seating. Maybe it's the dog lovers who bring their pooches. Maybe it's the crowds after a Twins game. There are 30 beers on tap and usually at least one food truck parked outside.

MAP 1: 701 5th St. N., Minneapolis, 612/615-8243, www.inboundbrew. co; Mon.-Fri. noon-midnight, Sat.-Sun. 11am-midnight

### Lakes & Legends

Get the Minnesota lakeside experience without leaving downtown Minneapolis. In Lakes & Legends' giant room, decorated with nods to the Northwoods, you can settle into an Adirondack chair, toss bean bags, or play *hammerschlagen* (a nail-driving game). There are a half dozen beers on tap and often, but not always, a food truck parked out front.

MAP 1: 1368 Lasalle Ave., Minneapolis, 612/999-6020, www.lakesandlegends. com; Mon.-Thurs. 3pm-10pm, Fri. 3pm-midnight, Sat. noon-midnight, Sun. noon-10pm

## BARS

### ✪ Brit's Pub

Footie and rugby on the telly, fish-and-chips, Scotch eggs, even the odd outdoor Shakespeare production. You might say Brit's has gone a smidge too far in its British pub theme—except that this is the real deal, with real English punters behind the scenes. The big attraction is the second-floor rooftop deck with 12 lanes of lawn bowling and numerous exhortations not to be "a tosser." Watch for open bowling nights when the leagues aren't playing and grab a lane for $5 per person per hour.

MAP 1: 1110 Nicollet Mall, Minneapolis, 612/332-3908, www.britspub.com; daily 11am-2am

### ✪ Marvel Bar

The Bachelor Farmer brought the New Nordic dining trend to the Twin Cities, and Marvel, its basement bar, is riding the craft cocktails trend. Ignore the fact that the basement has no windows and little light. Think of it as your own personal speakeasy. Order an oliveto (olive oil, gin, and lemon shaken with an egg white) or a classic old-fashioned. Bartender Pip Hansen is among the cities' best.

MAP 1: 50 2nd Ave. N., Minneapolis, 612/206-3929, www.marvelbar.com; Sun.-Thurs. 5pm-midnight, Fri.-Sat. 5pm-1am

### Bar Lurcat

The thing to do at Bar Lurcat (opinions differ on the correct pronunciation) is to drape yourself over a vintage settee under a crystal chandelier and try to look as beautiful as the surroundings. Failing that, you can enjoy watching all the other artsy types trying to do the same thing. Order small plates from a kitchen run by one of the best food outfits in town (D'Amico and Sons) and choose from an extensive wine list (more than 40 served by the glass).

MAP 1: 1624 Harmon Pl., Minneapolis, 612/486-5500, www.cafelurcat.com; Mon.-Thurs. 4:30pm-10pm, Fri.-Sat. 4:30pm-midnight, Sun. 4:30pm-9pm; cover charges for special events

### Dalton and Wade

Dalton and Wade (extra points if you get the Patrick Swayze reference) pitches a big tent for whiskey lovers: Irish, Scotch, bourbon, rye, even a fair selection of Japanese pours. The cocktail list is also whiskey-focused, with some specialty Manhattans on tap. If you're coming for a meal, the menu is full-on American South: biscuits, brisket, hush puppies, pimento cheese, and grits.

MAP 1: 323 N. Washington Ave., Minneapolis, 612/236-4020, www. daltonandwadempls.com; Mon.-Thurs. 11am-midnight, Fri.-Sat. 11am-1am, Sun. 10am-3pm

Kieran's Irish Pub

### Kieran's Irish Pub
Whether or not there's someone on stage playing an Irish jig (and more often than not there is), there's a big, friendly energy to Kieran's. Founder Kieran Folliard, who himself came across the pond from Ireland, created a place where you want to spend time, not just fill up or drink up. Come for music, for readings, for poetry slams, for rugby on the big screen. Or, come for a surprisingly healthy menu, with big, creative salads and mini plates in addition to the expected shepherd's pie and corned beef and cabbage. While the row of taps is impressive, the thing to order is a 2 Gingers whiskey, created by Kieran himself.

MAP 1: 85 6th St. N., Minneapolis, 612/339-4499, www.kierans.com; Sun.-Mon. 11am-11pm, Tues.-Thurs. 11am-midnight, Fri.-Sat. 11am-2am (open at 10am for noon Twins games)

### The Local
The Local is the best place in town to watch international soccer, rugby, and hurling (it might be the only place for hurling), with screens showing Premiership and Champions League games and plenty of enthusiastic fans. It's also a great place to see young Minneapolis office denizens in their natural environment after work and to enjoy what is known as a giant pint o' prawns. And, for the morning after, a hearty brunch is served on Saturday and Sunday.

MAP 1: 931 Nicollet Mall, Minneapolis, 612/904-1000, www.the-local.com; Mon.-Fri. 11am-2am, Sat.-Sun. 9am-2am

### Monte Carlo
Once a bar for the Warehouse District working class, the Monte Carlo is now a swank bar and restaurant for the Warehouse District young professional class, known for the best martini in town and the wall of bottles stacked to the ceiling behind the copper-topped bar. If drinking makes you hungry, you'll find plenty of filling eats, including a famed Monte Cristo and a meatloaf sandwich with grilled onions.

MAP 1: 219 3rd Ave. N., Minneapolis, 612/333-5900, www.montecarlomn.com; Mon.-Sat. 11am-1am, Sun. 10am-midnight

### Parlour
Downstairs from the very of-the-moment North Loop dining destination, Borough, Parlour is an intimate place to settle in for the evening. A leader

in Minneapolis's cocktail revolution, bartender Jesse Held creates drinks that draw on nationwide trends and local food culture, like the Prairie in Bloom, which mixes tart rhubarb and bitter Cynar. Locals know this is the place to get one of the best burgers in town, made with a mix of sirloin, rib eye, and brisket.

MAP 1: 730 Washington Ave. N., Minneapolis, 612/354-3135, www. boroughmpls.com; Sun.-Mon. 5pm-midnight, Tues.-Sat. 5pm-2am

## WINE BARS
### Bev's Wine Bar

Don't be fooled by the dark windows: Bev's is still open. Most nights the tea lights on the tables and the bar provide most of the light—and the ambience works. The wine list isn't long, but it is carefully chosen and well-priced. This is the perfect escape when a glass of peppery sangiovese and a plate of little cheeses in a quiet room is what you need.

MAP 1: 250 3rd Ave. N., Minneapolis, 612/337-0102, www.bevswinebar.com; Mon.-Fri. 4:30pm-1am, Sat. 6:30pm-1am

## GAY AND LESBIAN
### ✪ Gay 90s

The party never stops at the Gay 90s, a sprawling complex with six bars and three dance floors. And even those not drawn by the "gay" part of the name know they'll find unstoppable dance music and a we're-all-friends-now atmosphere. Watch for karaoke nights, drag shows, and male strippers. Six nights a week, some of the most professional, best-dressed, and best-coiffed drag queens in the Midwest strut their stuff in the La Femme lounge.

MAP 1: 408 Hennepin Ave., Minneapolis, 612/333-7755, www.gay90s.com; Mon.-Sat. 8am-2am, Sun. 10am-2am; cover $5

### The Eagle/The Bolt

The Eagle and Bolt are one and the same establishment, but the Eagle is for drinking and chatting people up, while the Bolt is for dancing. DJs and VJs (that's video jockey) rev up the crowd. The scene is grown-up, casual, and friendly, so no wonder it gets very crowded, as well. There's always the year-round patio if you need a break. Come back for brunch on Saturday or Sunday for a bit of the hair of the dog.

MAP 1: 515 Washington Ave. S., Minneapolis, 612/338-4214, www. eagleboltbar.com; Eagle Mon.-Fri. 11am-2:30am, Sat.-Sun. 10am-2:30am; Bolt Wed.-Sat. 7pm-2:30am, Sun. 4pm-2:30am; cover $5

### 19 Bar

The 19 Bar dates to a time in the Twin Cities when the marginalized gay community was centered right here in the Loring Park neighborhood near downtown. (In fact, some say it's the oldest gay bar in the cities.) As doors have opened and closets closed down for good, 19 has survived and remains a welcome and welcoming haven in what can otherwise be a wild scene. This is just a bar, very much like any other small-town bar, with a crowd of regular young professionals.

MAP 1: 19 15th St. W., Minneapolis, 612/871-5553; Mon.-Fri. 3pm-2:30am, Sat.-Sun. 1pm-2:30am; no cover

### The Saloon

Did old Western saloons have dance floors like this one? Highly unlikely. The focus here is on dancing, not drinking, and several evenings

a week there are go-go boys to keep the crowd going. The back patio is secluded enough for things to get a little rowdy. Spend afternoons enjoying more sedate pursuits, like parlor games, trivia, and bingo. The Saloon is the old-school cornerstone of the Twin Cities' long-standing gay community.
MAP 1: 830 Hennepin Ave., Minneapolis, 612/332-0835, www.saloonmn.com; Mon.-Wed. noon-2am, Thurs.-Sat. noon-3am, Sun. 11am-2:30am; no cover

## DANCE CLUBS
### Aqua
Aqua has a high-end, beautiful-people vibe (watch for pro athletes here during the season). In two big dance rooms, DJs play house and current hits. Thursdays and Sundays are 18-plus, Fridays and Saturdays are 21-plus. There's a pretty strict dress code (nothing baggy or torn, no baseball hats), so go dressed to impress.
MAP 1: 400 1st Ave. N., Minneapolis, 612/232-3232, www.aquampls.com; Thurs.-Sun. 10pm-2am; cover $5-10

### Music Hall MPLS
From 1980s alt-rockers (think Jane's Addiction and Public Image Limited) to solid up-and-comers, Mill City Nights books rock acts on most weekends. Owned by LA entertainment conglomerate AEG, Mill City has an easy pipeline to acts that people want to see. The venue opened in 2012 and doesn't have the history or inspire the love and nostalgia that First Avenue does, but the owners are definitely trying to take it in that direction. The industrial space accommodates 1,200 people and includes risers and screens to help make sure everyone can see the action on stage.

MAP 1: 111 5th St. N., Minneapolis, 612/333-3422, www.musichallmpls.com; most shows start at 8pm; tickets vary, generally starting at $25

### Rouge at The Lounge
As other clubs come and go, The Lounge has endured since 1995, thanks to a loyal after-the-work-day professional crowd and, at least in part, to some original programming. The Lounge will see your go-go dancers (they've got those) and raise you a magician and a fire dancer. Pick your scene among the several rooms, each like a smaller club in itself and each spinning different music, from Top 40 to underground electronica. Keep the dress code in mind—no white sneakers or white T-shirts, nothing saggy.
MAP 1: 411 2nd Ave. N., Minneapolis, 612/333-8800, www.theloungempls.com; Thurs. 10pm-2am, Fri.-Sat. 9pm-2am; cover varies, generally $15, more for live bands

## COMEDY
### Acme Comedy Company
Acme has the classic brick wall (well, Warehouse District limestone), the loyal following (open since 1991), and some of the smartest comics working today. The club brings in national acts and fosters local talent, notably in its annual summer-long search for the funniest person in the cities—rank amateurs only, please. Open mic night is every Monday, and it's free. Combine your laughs with a casual dinner at Sticks, Acme's restaurant.
MAP 1: 708 1st St. N., Minneapolis, 612/338-6393, www.acmecomedycompany.com; check calendar for hours; cost varies depending on event

# South Minneapolis

**Map 2**

## LIVE MUSIC

### El Nuevo Rodeo

Wear your cowboy hat and boots and get ready to line dance, two-step, and let loose on the dance floor to live Mexican bands (on the second floor) and DJs playing *banda, norteño, corrido,* and more. The restaurant on the ground floor serves up standard Mexican fare for lunch and dinner all week.

MAP 2: 2709 Lake St. E., Minneapolis, 612/721-6808, www. elnuevorodeorestaurant.com; Fri.-Sat. 9pm-4am, Sun. 9pm-1am; cover varies, generally $15

### Famous Dave's

Blues, jazz, and salsa acts take the stage at Famous Dave's, with a big dance floor and instructors on hand for salsa nights. Sit down to a plate of ribs and a sweet corn muffin while you're here, but what attracts people—crowds of young professionals—to this Famous Dave's location is the music. In fact, it's been named the Twin Cities' best blues bar more than once.

MAP 2: 3001 Hennepin Ave. S., Minneapolis, 612/822-9900, www. famousdavesbluesclub.com; Mon.-Thurs. 11am-1am, Fri.-Sat. 11am-late, Sun. 10am-midnight; cover varies, generally $5-8

### Icehouse

If your evening plans include dinner and music, there's no better place for both than Icehouse. The menu goes way beyond bar food, with refined takes on American classics like brisket and Caesar salad. And the live stage hosts both local favorites and national touring acts, from contemporary rock to jazz, almost every night of the week. Come on Sunday mornings for some soulful music with your brunch.

MAP 2: 2528 Nicollet Ave., Minneapolis, 612/276-6523, www.icehousempls.com; Mon.-Fri. 11am-2am, Sat. 10am-2am, Sun. 10am-1am; cover varies, generally $0-20

## BREWPUBS AND TAPROOMS

### The Herkimer

While the classic brewpub look involves a lot of dark wood, low light, and low-hanging lights, The Herkimer has decided to go in the opposite direction: It's bright and cheery, with bold colors and big windows. The brewery rotates its two dozen brews through the taps, along with a few outside beers. Some patrons come more for the food than the beer; it tends toward the indulgent, like fancy mac and cheese or a bratwurst burger.

MAP 2: 2922 Lyndale Ave. S., Minneapolis, 612/821-0101, www.theherkimer.com; daily 10am-2am

### LynLake Brewery

This hundred-year-old theater is now on its third life. For years the home of a beloved antiques store, it has now been transformed into a stunning space with exposed brick, industrial lighting, and the glow of a hip, happy crowd. On summer nights, the front windows are wide open and the rooftop patio is the place to be. If you need something to wash down with your beer, you can order pizza, hot dogs, tacos, and tasty bowls of fusion food from four local delivery partners.

MAP 2: 2934 Lyndale Ave. S., Minneapolis, 612/224-9682, www.lynlakebrewery.com; Tues.-Thurs. 5pm-11pm, Fri. 2pm-1am, Sat. noon-1am, Sun. noon-10pm

## Northbound Smokehouse and Brewpub

Two great tastes that go great together: hoppy brews and hot smoked meat. Northbound brings you both. The room is barebones, but the vibe is lively, especially when it fills up (which is often). No matter what you're ordering as a main, do not miss the smoked wings or whitefish dip.

MAP 2: 2716 38th St. E., Minneapolis, 612/208-1450, www.northboundbrewpub. com; Mon.-Thurs. 11am-1am, Fri.-Sat. 11am-2am, Sun. 10am-1am

# BARS

### ✪ Volstead's Emporium

Volstead's is hard to find—and that's part of the fun. Enter through the alleyway and look for the blue light over the door. Knock, speakeasy style, and you're in. The interior is overstuffed Prohibition-era chic, with private booths, hidden nooks, and mirrors that turn out to be something completely different. While the cocktails are definitely what you're here for, the menu, which changes seasonally, is also good.

MAP 2: 711 Lake St. W., Minneapolis, 612/259-7891, www.volsteads.com; Thurs.-Mon. 5pm-2am

### C.C. Club

Thousands, if not hundreds of thousands, of right-out-of-college Twin Cities youngsters have drunk through their aimless 20s right here in the C.C. Club. It's gritty. It was smoky as hell until the smoking ban went into effect (and that smell never goes away). But it's home. All the tattoos might make you feel a little out of place as you open the door, but order a pitcher of beer, put some Hüsker Dü on the jukebox, and let some 20-something pour his drunken heart out to you. And if you need the hair of the dog the next morning, the C.C. Club opens up bright and early for a greasy breakfast.

MAP 2: 2600 Lyndale Ave. S., Minneapolis, 612/874-7226, www.ccclubuptown.com; Mon.-Thurs. 11am-2am, Fri.-Sat. 8am-2am, Sun. 10am-2am

### Du Nord Cocktail Room

Beer lovers have their taprooms; now those who appreciate a properly mixed drink and small-batch spirits have cocktail rooms. And Du Nord is Minnesota's first. The team makes Fitzgerald gin and L'etoile vodka on-site and serves them up in seasonal cocktails. The vibe is light, bright, open, and casual, rather than lounge-y or luxurious.

MAP 2: 2610 32nd St. E., Minneapolis, 612/382-7236, http://dunordcraftspirits. com; Mon.-Thurs. 4pm-10pm, Fri. 4pm-midnight, Sat. noon-midnight

C.C. Club

## Moto-i

Moto-i takes the classic Japanese *iza-kaya* (pub) concept and runs with it. It brews its own sake on-site (and you may hear many times that this is the first sake brewery/restaurant outside Japan) and serves substantial snacks, some traditional and some not so, to go with it. Enough little plates will easily make a meal: spicy plum wings plus a pork bun and some sweet potato fries, for example. There are vocal partisans of Moto-i's ramen (with freshly made noodles) and equally loud critics.

MAP 2: 2940 Lyndale Ave. S., Minneapolis, 612/821-6262, www.moto-i.com; Mon.-Fri. noon-2am, Sat.-Sun. 11am-2am

## Pat's Tap

Pat's Tap has a strong local pedigree: Restaurateur Kim Bartmann is also behind Red Stag Supper Club and Barbette. She works her magic here with a beer list heavy on the local brews, bar snacks (and full meals) that celebrate the best of homey American cooking, and—this is key—Skee-Ball. The atmosphere is neighborhood-y and casual, and even, depending on your kids, family-friendly.

MAP 2: 3510 Nicollet Ave., Minneapolis, 612/822-8216, www.patstap.com; Mon.-Fri. 11am-2am, Sat.-Sun. 9am-3pm

## Stella's Fish Café & Prestige Oyster Bar

Stella's Fish Café is actually a seafood restaurant—a rare enough thing in Minnesota—but the hot young things lined up on Lake Street in skimpy blouses no matter the weather are not here for fish-and-chips (though the fish-and-chips are really pretty good). They're here because this is young Minneapolis's pickup joint of the moment. You can watch the scene unfold on the truly beautiful rooftop patio and avail yourself of fresh oysters at the same time.

MAP 2: 1400 Lake St. W., Minneapolis, 612/824-8862, www.stellasfishcafe. com; Sun.-Wed. 11:30am-11:45pm, Thurs. 11:30am-1am, Fri.-Sat. 11:30am-2am

## V.F.W. James Ballentine Post No. 246

Yes, the V.F.W. In the young professional paradise that is Uptown, the V.F.W. is among the hottest hot spots. Cheap beer, strong drinks, bingo, karaoke (put your name in early; the schedule fills up), and a veritable peaceable kingdom among patrons. Truckers, tourists, and Target marketing managers are all welcome here—as long as they don't try to snag two songs on the karaoke list. This is also the place to enjoy that quintessential Midwestern bar experience: the meat raffle. Buy your ticket, cross your fingers, and, if you're lucky, take home some steaks, pork chops, or ground meat.

MAP 2: 2916 Lyndale Ave. S., Minneapolis, 612/823-6233; Mon.-Wed. 11am-1am, Thurs.-Sat. 11am-2am, Sun. 11am-midnight

# WINE BARS
## Riverview

A neighborhood wine bar is a great concept, and the Riverview is a reflection of the warmth and class of the Longfellow neighborhood around it. (It's a family-oriented neighborhood, so the Riverview Café, right next door, is equipped with one of the best play areas in the Twin Cities.) Pick a wine flight off the menu or tell your server what sorts of wines you like and have him or her put one together just for you. Beer lovers can have just as much fun, with more than 40 bottles from around the world to choose from.

MAP 2: 3753 42nd Ave. S., Minneapolis, 612/722-7234, www.theriverview. net; Wed.-Thurs. 5pm-11pm, Fri.-Sat. 5pm-midnight, Sun. and Tues. 5pm-10pm

### Terzo Vino

Restaurateurs Tom and Molly Broder have been keeping locals happy with authentic pastas for a couple of decades. They decided to share their love of another Italian treasure—its wines—in a bar right across the street. The small space fills up fast with neighborhood fans enjoying 40 to 50 wines by the glass and more than 1,000 choices from the Broders' cellar. The menu, from antipasti to full plates, is brief and classic.

MAP 2: 2221 50th St. W., Minneapolis, 612/925-0330, http://broders.com/ terzo-vino-bar; Sun.-Mon. 4pm-9:30pm, Tues.-Sat. 4pm-10pm

## GAMES

### Bryant-Lake Bowl

There are a couple of reasons it's so crowded in here: For starters, this popular establishment in the Uptown neighborhood is working on its second generation of hip regulars. More importantly, it crams a lot into a small space: a bowling alley, restaurant, bar, and theater space. If you come for the food, think comfort food from around the world: burritos, pad Thai, smoked trout quesadillas, and the like. Locals swear by the carrot cake. Monday is cheap date night: dinner for two, bowling, and a bottle of wine for $28.

MAP 2: 810 Lake St. W., Minneapolis, 612/825-3737, www.bryantlakebowl.com; daily 8am-2am; no cover

### Tilt Pinball Bar

With two dozen pinball machines, from classic to brand-new, lining the walls, Tilt can feel a bit cozy, but you won't find a friendlier crowd. Nothing goes better with games than gourmet hot dogs and local brews, so that's what Tilt serves up. The venue is 21 and over after 9pm. Before that, anyone under 18 must be accompanied by an adult.

MAP 2: 113 26th St. E., Minneapolis, 612/236-4089, www.tiltpinballbar.com; daily 11am-2pm; no cover

### Up-Down Arcade

Treat your inner kid to the kind of time every kid dreams of: pizza for dinner and a handful of tokens that will keep you playing Donkey Kong, Mortal Kombat, and Mario Bros. all night long. (Actual kids are not allowed, because Up-Down is a bar with more than 60 beers on tap.) There are more than 50 games to choose from, plus Skee-Ball and a Nintendo.

MAP 2: 3012 Lyndale Ave. S., Minneapolis, 612/823-3487, www.updownmpls.com; Mon.-Fri. 3pm-2am, Sat.-Sun. 11am-2am; no cover

## COMEDY

### HUGE Theater

Improv can be more than one-off lines. Long-form improv performers pull off complex scenes, long monologues, and even whole, unscripted shows, sparked by a word or thought and spun by fast-thinking actors. By and large, that's the kind of improv you'll see at Huge, although every night of the week is dedicated to a different troupe or style. The space is bare and comfortably grungy, with folding chairs and a bar serving wine, beer, and coffee.

MAP 2: 3037 Lyndale Ave. S., Minneapolis, 612/412-4843, www.hugetheater.com; check calendar for hours; cost varies depending on event

# Nordeast and Dinkytown   Map 3

## LIVE MUSIC

### ✪ Cedar Cultural Center

This warehouse-like gutted former movie theater packs in serious music lovers for more than 150 shows a year: indie rock, folk, roots, jazz, blues, world music, and anything uncategorizable and out of the mainstream. One of the most anticipated events on the calendar each year is the late-September Nordic Roots Festival, when the quiet giants of the Scandinavian folk-rock movement bring their electric hurdy-gurdies to town and sell out shows. All ages at the Cedar means all ages: Kids and grandparents are welcome and likely to come.

MAP 3: 416 Cedar Ave. S., Minneapolis, 612/338-2674, www.thecedar.org; opening hours depend on show times, only open when there is a show; tickets vary, generally $15-30

### Honey

You never know what kind of music you might hear at this basement club.

Cedar Cultural Center

It might be a DJ playing hits from the 1990s for one of its popular dance parties, it might be live jazz, or it might be a band leaning more toward rock and roll or even house. But there is one constant: The crowd always comes ready to dance, filling up the small dance floor. If you need a break, you can seek out a low, lounge-y seat in the other room or snag a table. There's usually a $5-10 cover charge for live music. And the food is better than most bar food: sweet potato fries and fresh spring rolls from Ginger Hop, the restaurant upstairs, are always a hit.

MAP 3: 205 Hennepin Ave. E., Minneapolis, 612/746-0306, www.honeympls.com; daily 8pm-2am, varies with shows; cover varies, $5 most nights

### Kitty Cat Klub

By day a hip, low-key coffee shop. By night a swank lounge that attracts a slightly older crowd than you might expect right here in Dinkytown, practically on the campus of the University of Minnesota. Most nights a rock band plays, but if not, there's a DJ (expect a small cover). The layout, with lavishly furnished nook-like rooms, encourages conversation, socializing, and discreet people-watching.

MAP 3: 315 14th Ave. SE, Minneapolis, 612/331-9800, www.kittycatklub.net; daily 4pm-2am; cover varies

## BREWPUBS AND TAPROOMS

### Bauhaus Brewlabs

A big, bright, bold room designed for maximum enjoyment of big, bright, bold German-style lagers.

## PERSON-POWERED PUB CRAWL

You could go on a typical pub crawl—the working-class neighborhoods of Nordeast are great for that—or you could bring the pub crawling—er, rolling—right along with you. You and up to 15 friends can rent the one and only **Pedal Pub** (952/703-9000, www. pedalpub.com, $335 Sun.-Thurs., $395 Fri.-Sat., for a two-hour tour) and ride it from bar to bar or set up your own bar right on board. It's 100 percent BYOB and, yep, it's legal in Minnesota. Apparently, the mobile pub is based on a contraption known in Amsterdam as a *fietscafe*. Five people on each side pedal, while a company-provided driver steers. You can ride one of the Pedal Pub folks' seven routes in Minneapolis and St. Paul or one in Shakopee—all pretty flat—or you can customize your own for an extra fee. If you've got a hankering to tailgate at a Twins or Vikings game and lack a tailgate itself, the Pedal Pub is a great option.

The Bauhaus crew, in the old Crown Ironworks building, are the consummate hosts. They don't just sell beer, they host a full calendar of music and other amusements, including summertime night markets with local artisans, that make their Nordeast brewery a destination. Food trucks park outside, and you're also welcome to bring your own food to enjoy.

**MAP 3:** 1315 Tyler St. NE, Minneapolis, 612-276-6911, www.bauhausbrewlabs.com; Wed.-Thurs. 4pm-11pm, Fri. 3pm-11pm, Sat. noon-11pm

### Dangerous Man Brewing

Imagine a raucous—or, let's say, enthusiastic—crowd at a European beer hall, filling the long communal tables and all the spaces in between. That's Dangerous Man on a Friday night, a destination for serious beer drinkers who come for the innovative brews they can't get in any retail markets. They keep 12 beers on tap, including the beloved, indulgent chocolate milk stout, in addition to house-made sodas and kombuchas. There's no kitchen, but there are local takeout menus on the tables.

**MAP 3:** 1300 2nd St. NE, Minneapolis, 612-236-4087, www.dangerousmanbrewing. com; Tues.-Thurs. 4pm-10pm, Fri. 3pm-midnight, Sat. noon-midnight

### Indeed Brewing Company

A positive name (Indeed!), a positive outlook, a positive-feeling space—that's Indeed. With an atmosphere somewhere between a pub and a coffee shop, Indeed's taproom feels like a space where you can spend some time. Claim a spot at the long wooden bar or a table in the corner with friends. For people who like to try several different beers, Indeed offers two smaller sizes in addition to the traditional pint.

**MAP 3:** 711 15th Ave NE, Minneapolis, 612/843-5090, www.indeedbrewing.com; Wed.-Thurs. 3pm-11pm, Fri.-Sat. noon-11pm, Sun. noon-8pm

### Sociable Cider Werks

When your beer-loving friends have their hearts set on a night at a taproom, you can make everyone happy with a trip to the cidery. Choose among six prize-winning ciders (from dry to funky to fruity), two meads, and even four beers for the holdouts. There's almost always a food truck parked outside. The room is bare-bones but friendly and hosts occasional concerts, pop-up markets, and special events. Tours are at 12:30pm on Saturday (bring a donation to a food shelf).

MAP 3: 1500 Fillmore St. NE, Minneapolis, 612/758-0105, www.sociablecider.com; Wed. 4pm-10pm, Thurs. 4pm-11pm, Fri. 4pm-midnight, Sat. noon-midnight, Sun. 11am-9pm

## BARS

### Nye's Bar

Nye's is dead. Long live Nye's! Once a fixture—no, the fixture—on the Twin Cities bar scene, Nye's was nearly swallowed up by a condo development, but local protest brought it back. It's a little cleaner, a little slicker, and a lot better lit, but the tufted booths, round piano bar (made for impromptu sing-alongs), massive cocktails, and old-school atmosphere are 100 percent Nye's.

MAP 3: 112 Hennepin Ave. E., Minneapolis, 612/236-4854, www.nyesbar. com; Mon.-Thurs. 4pm-1am, Fri. 4pm-2am, Sat. 11am-2am, Sun. 11am-1am

### Nomad World Pub

It's a bar. It's a welcoming hangout in Minneapolis's most diverse neighborhood. It's a bocce club. It's a live music venue, with raucous hardcore and global folk bands a few nights a week. And, it's the official home for Tottenham Hotspur supporters (but they'll tune into just about any soccer match televised anywhere).

MAP 3: 501 Cedar Ave., Minneapolis, 612/338-6424, www.nomadpub.com; Mon.-Fri. 4pm-2am, Sat.-Sun. 8am-2am

### Psycho Suzi's Motor Lounge

No temple to kitsch in the history of kitsch worship has embraced the best of the lowbrow quite like Psycho Suzi's, with its year-round patio with palm-frond umbrellas and tiki-head drinking cups. The menu is like a spoiled 10-year-old's dream: beer-battered miniature hot dogs, tater tots, deviled eggs, massive deep-fried cheese curds, and Suzi's famous pizza. The drink menu is like that spoiled 10-year-old's dream after hitting legal drinking age: The Suffering Bastard is described as "Various blackberry-ish boozes, sour, spices, and 151 mixed into a tasty delight."

MAP 3: 1900 Marshall St. NE, Minneapolis, 612/788-9069, www.psychosuzis.com; Mon.-Fri. 11am-2am, Sat.-Sun. 10am-2am

### Stanley's

This, right here, is classic Nordeast Minneapolis. It's a neighborhood joint with a long menu of hearty burgers and sandwiches and an even longer bar, where locals watch football while the bartender just refills their "regular." It's a great place to start a bar crawl: Head south down University Avenue and then hook your way back north along 4th Street. (If you're eating outside, there's a menu just for dogs.)

MAP 3: 2500 University Ave. NE, Minneapolis, 612/788-2529, www. stanleysbarroom.com; Mon.-Fri. 11am-2am, Sat.-Sun. 9am-2am

Nye's Bar

## COCKTAIL ROOMS AND DISTILLERIES
### Norseman

Norseman brings a Scandinavian cleanliness to the usual scruffy distillery sensibility, adding white tiles and marble countertops. The most important addition might be the short menu of nibbles to go with your drinks (you're also welcome to bring in or order food). Cocktails are crafted from Norseman's own long and lauded list of spirits.

MAP 3: 451 Taft St. NE, Minneapolis, 612/568-6299, www.norsemandistillery.com; Tues.-Thurs. 4pm-11pm, Fri. 3pm-midnight, Sat. 1pm-midnight, Sun. noon-5pm

### Tattersall

Tattersall distills its own whiskey, gin, rum, vodka, and liqueurs (which, on their own, are a delightful Minnesota souvenir) and then conjures up pitch-perfect and creative cocktails. Invitingly tattered divans cozy up its industrial space, and the tables on the deck are ideal for whiling away a long Minnesota evening. For nibbles to go with your cocktail, there's usually a food truck outside.

MAP 3: 1620 Central Ave. NE #150, Minneapolis, 612/584-4152, www.tattersalldistilling.com; Wed.-Thurs. 4pm-11pm, Fri. 4pm-midnight, Sat. noon-midnight, Sun. 2pm-9pm

## GAY AND LESBIAN
### Lush

In an industrial-looking building on busy Central Avenue, Lush is as modern on the inside as it is on the outside, with techno colors to match the techno sounds. (People do dance, but it's not the only reason to go.) The massive patio with its attractive fire pit is a favorite hangout spot, and not a few people come to sing karaoke. The food at Lush will fuel a long night, with options including sandwiches and a long list of tacos. Drag brunch is de rigueur. Come for Drag Revolution on Thursdays and Saturdays or burlesque on Friday nights.

MAP 3: 990 Central Ave. NE, Minneapolis, 612/208-0358, www.lushmpls.com; Mon.-Wed. 4pm-midnight, Thurs.-Fri. 4pm-2am, Sat.-Sun. 10am-2am; typically no cover, $5 for drag and burlesque nights

# Downtown St. Paul and West Side

**Map 4**

## LIVE MUSIC
### Vieux Carre

As you open the nondescript doors in an otherwise dark side of the old Hamm building and head for the basement, you might feel like you're walking into a speakeasy. Well, you are. That's what this space was during Prohibition. Later it was the Artists' Quarter—the place to hear jazz in St. Paul. And now it has been revived by the team behind the Dakota in downtown Minneapolis—a team that knows food (the menu is New Orleans-style gumbo, po'boys, and Sazeracs), knows music (all jazz, with a heavy dose of NOLA acts), and knows hospitality. The joint is now jumping.

MAP 4: 408 St. Peter St., St. Paul, 651/291-2715, www.vieux-carre.com; Wed.-Thurs. 4pm-10pm, Fri. 3pm-11pm, Sat. noon-11pm, Sun. noon-5pm; $5-20

Vieux Carre

no bun). The authenticity feels just right in this stone building—the oldest commercial building in the Twin Cities, built as a brewery in 1857.

**MAP 4:** 445 Smith Ave. N., St. Paul, 651/222-1857, www.waldmannbrewery.com; Sun. and Tues.-Thurs. noon-9pm, Fri.-Sat. noon-10pm

## BARS
### ✪ St. Paul Grill

Feel like an old-time fat cat as you settle into the high-backed stools at the long, polished bar. Order a decades-old single malt, and strike up a conversation with the guy in the suit next to you. He might be a state senator. In truth, there are an awful lot of suits here, even though the jacket is not required. A classic shrimp cocktail or a bowl of lobster dip rounds out the whole living-large experience.

**MAP 4:** 350 Market St., St. Paul, 651/224-7455, www.stpaulgrill.com; Mon. 11am-midnight, Tues.-Sat. 11am-1am, Sun. 10:30am-midnight

### Amsterdam Bar and Hall

You know who does bar food right? The Dutch. You've got some of the cities' best fries, you've got *broodjes* (little sandwiches), you've got *bitterballen* (fried potato balls), and you've got plenty of other salty, crispy things. Add in two dozen draft beers (many Dutch and Belgian) and live music nearly every night, and that's Bar Amsterdam. It's a big, open, dark room and frequently hosts events.

**MAP 4:** 6 6th St. W., St. Paul, 612/285-3112, www.amsterdambarandhall.com; daily 11am-2am; cover varies, generally free

### The Commodore

F. Scott Fitzgerald himself used to knock on the door of the hidden bar at the old Commodore Hotel. Now

## BREWPUBS AND TAPROOMS
### Tin Whiskers Brewing Company

Both the beer and the aesthetic at Tin Whiskers (engineers will get the joke) were brewed up by some nerdy engineer friends who aim for technical perfection in the science of beer brewing. Alone as a taproom destination in the heart of downtown St. Paul, Tin Whiskers attracts convivial groups of friends and families (it's a particularly kid-friendly space) who gather to play games and watch the brewers at work. Order food from Black Sheep Pizza or Sawatdee, both in the same building.

**MAP 4:** 125 9th St. E., St. Paul, 651/330-4734, www.twbrewing.com; Wed.-Thurs. 4pm-10pm, Fri. 3pm-11pm, Sat. noon-11pm, Sun. noon-5pm

### Waldmann Brewery & Wurstery

This is what it means to stick to your principles: Waldmann brews traditional German lagers with traditional ingredients in traditional styles. It makes its own sausages, with crisp, crackling skins, and serves them German-style (i.e., knife and fork, reincarnated a couple of times, it plays up the Great Gatsby connections at every turn. You can certainly come to dine (the menu is upscale and old-school), but the real pleasure is in the lounge, where it feels like time has stopped, with un-fancy classic cocktails, a little ambient jazz, and crystal chandeliers hanging over low couches. **MAP 4:** 79 Western Ave. N., St. Paul, 651/330-5999, www.thecommodorebar. com; Tues.-Sat. 4pm-midnight;

# Summit-University and Mac-Groveland

**Map 5**

## LIVE MUSIC
### Turf Club

Ask about great dive bars in St. Paul and you're going to hear about the Turf Club. And this is a town that knows its dive bars. In recent years, this former 1940s music hall has left its country music, line dancing roots and become a rock-and-roll mecca. A young local band has made it—and is on its way to big things—when it plays the Turf Club. National acts swing through here, too, and you'll probably pay less to see them than you would anywhere else.
**MAP 5:** 1601 University Ave., St. Paul, 651/647-0486, www.turfclub.net; Tues.-Fri. 11am-1am, Sat.-Sun. 10am-1am; cover varies, generally $5-13

## BREWPUBS AND TAPROOMS
### Summit Brewing Company

Let's all take a moment to thank Summit for kicking off the revolution that brought us three dozen (and counting) local craft brews. Summit has been around since 1986, and although it was once a bold order in a bar, signaling you were in the know, a Summit IPA or Extra Pale Ale is now a safe, reliable local choice. At the taproom—which feels a bit like a cafeteria—you can try flights, $2 seven-ounce samples, and newly tapped casks. A food truck parks outside, and Summit hosts frequent movie and trivia nights.
**MAP 5:** 910 Montreal Circle, St. Paul, 651/265-7800, www.summitbrewing.com; Thurs.-Fri. 2pm-9pm, Sat. noon-9pm, Sun. noon-6pm

## BARS
### Happy Gnome

St. Paulites are so used to having a bar in this spot under some name or other that many have not noticed the subtle shift toward finer dining at the Happy Gnome. Chef Matthew Hinman came to helm the kitchen from the lauded Minneapolis bistro Lucia's and now offers dinner in the Firehouse Room upstairs. The Happy Gnome offers 44 beers on tap and more than 180 bottles, along with a first-rate selection of scotch. This is a bar with great food (try the bison burger).
**MAP 5:** 498 Selby Ave., St. Paul, 651/287-2018, www.thehappygnome.com; Sun. 10am-1am, Mon.-Sat. 11am-1am

### O'Gara's Bar and Grill

O'Gara's has been serving beer to thirsty St. Paulites since 1941. Since then, it has added the Shamrock Room, which hosts jazz and big band music;

the Garage, which attracts local and national rock acts; and the Brew Pub, where you can sample O'Gara's own house-made beer. The lunch and dinner menus are lengthy, and the atmosphere is warm. This is the place to be if you're in St. Paul on St. Patrick's Day.

**MAP 5:** 164 Snelling Ave. N., St. Paul, 651/644-3333, www.ogaras.com; daily 10am-2am

## GAY AND LESBIAN
### Town House
The operative word here is fun. Gay men and lesbians come to the clean, comfortable Town House, near the U of M campus, for a casual night of dancing. On Sunday and Thursday, the Pumps and Pearls Drag Revue performs. On other nights, you'll find raucous karaoke or live entertainment. Wednesday is the Original Cheapie Night, with $2 beers. For an even more mellow time, head to the piano bar in the back.

**MAP 5:** 1415 University Ave. W., St. Paul, 651/646-7087, www.townhousebar.com; Mon.-Tues. and Thurs. 3pm-1am, Wed. and Fri. 3pm-2am, Sat. noon-2am, Sun. noon-1am; no cover

# Como and St. Anthony — Map 6

## BREWPUBS AND TAPROOMS
### ✪ Surly Brewing Company
This is the mother ship. Although other taprooms opened their doors before Surly, it was the team behind the already beloved brewery who lobbied hardest for a law to allow brewers to sell pints and growlers for consumption on- or off-site. And this is what they built as a result: a massive beer hall, a spacious restaurant, a vast beer garden—you get the idea. This place is huge. It's a destination. It's a place to show off to out-of-towners. It's the perfect place to enjoy big-flavored beers like Furious and Bender.

**MAP 6:** 520 Malcolm Ave. NE, Minneapolis, 763/999-4040, www. surlybrewing.com; Sun.-Thurs. 11am-11pm, Fri.-Sat. 11am-midnight

## BARS
### Half Time Rec
St. Paul is an old Irish town at heart, and Half Time Rec is St. Paul's favorite old Irish bar. Although the music half of the layout has stopped booking exclusively Irish bands, it's still the best place to hear Irish music in the cities. And you can play bocce (Hey, is that Irish?) on the two courts in the basement. If that doesn't sufficiently tire your arms out, try *hammerschlagen*

Surly Brewing Company

Can Can Wonderland

(Again, Irish?): The point is to be the first to hammer a nail into a tree stump. What definitely is Irish is the warmth and energy of Half Time Rec's atmosphere and the way generations of serious drinkers come together for a good time.

**MAP 6:** 1013 Front Ave., St. Paul, 651/488-8245, www.halftimerec.com; daily 10am-2am

## GAMES
### ✪ Can Can Wonderland

At every step in Can Can Wonderland it feels like you might turn around and bump into Willy Wonka—maybe on the bright and fanciful 18-hole indoor golf course or under the "trees" in the arcade. For the grownups, there are boozy slushies and malts, and for the kid in everyone there are pizzas and sandwiches, along with fair favorites like cotton candy, mini donuts, and popcorn. Kids are welcome until 9pm, when Can Can goes 21-plus.

**MAP 6:** 755 Prior Ave. N., St. Paul, 651/925-2261, www.cancanwonderland. com; Thurs. 4pm-11pm, Fri. 11am-1am, Sat. 10am-1am, Sun. 10am-8pm; no cover

# Greater Twin Cities Map 7

## COMEDY

### Rick Bronson's House of Comedy

If you like your comedy club slick and you're looking for big national names, rather than local heroes, this is the venue for you. On the fourth floor of the Mall of America, the House of Comedy makes it easy to combine a night of stand-up with a day of shopping and sightseeing. Dine on pub-style food while you watch.

**MAP 7:** Mall of America, 408 E. Broadway, Bloomington, 952/858-8558, www.houseofcomedy.net; check calendar for hours; cost varies

# ARTS AND CULTURE

Come as you are: That's the attitude around arts and culture in the Twin Cities, whether you're exploring art galleries and museums or going out for a concert or the theater. Wear a suit, a designer dress, or jeans and a fleece—you will be welcomed.

And, while you're at it, bring the kids! Whether you see it as a pro or a con, you should know that, for the most part, arts institutions from museums to galleries to theaters are very accommodating of children, and you are likely to encounter plenty of families enjoying the arts together. (And, if I may say so myself, Minnesota children tend to know how to behave themselves in these situations.)

Another welcoming aspect is the price. Theater tickets, except for the big Broadway productions that blow through town, can usually be had for $20-40 (although the Guthrie can charge up to $80 for weekend shows). Museum admission—again, except for high-profile touring exhibits—is almost universally under $10, and some of the most worthwhile museums are free. And if you've got your

Frederick R. Weisman Art Museum

heart set on seeing a show but don't have tickets in hand, rush seats, especially at the Guthrie, are almost always available.

## HIGHLIGHTS

**✪ BEST INTRODUCTION TO MINNEAPOLIS HISTORY:**
Minneapolis built its early economy and reputation on flour. The **Mill City Museum,** in a rehabbed flour mill, makes that important history come alive (page 113).

**✪ MUST-SEE THEATER, EVEN WITHOUT A TICKET:** Seeing a show at the **Guthrie Theater** is almost guaranteed to be a great experience. But the modern building itself is open nearly all day, every day, and worth a visit to walk on the "endless bridge" cantilevered over the Mississippi (page 114).

**✪ MOST BEAUTIFUL BRIDGE BETWEEN PAST AND PRESENT:**
The **American Swedish Institute** brings together 100 years of Swedish history in Minnesota in two stunning buildings (page 118).

**✪ BEST ARTS DEAL IN TOWN:** The **Minneapolis Institute of Art** is a free, first-rate museum with a world-class Asian art collection (page 119).

**✪ MOST UNEXPECTED MUSEUM FIND:** Nobody comes to Minnesota expecting to find one of the finest collections of 20th-century Russian art, but **The Museum of Russian Art** is changing that (page 120).

**✪ TOP THEATER CHOICE FOR ANY AGE:** You don't have to be a kid or have one in tow to enjoy the award-winning, visually stunning, and smartly scripted shows at the **Children's Theatre Company** (page 122).

**✪ MOST ACCESSIBLE—AND STUNNING—ARCHITECTURAL LANDMARK:** Visitors to the **Landmark Center** can marvel at 20-foot ceilings and hand-carved mahogany as well as visit several museums (page 129).

**✪ BEST MUSEUM FOR THE WHOLE FAMILY:** Beautiful inside and out, the **Bell Museum of Natural History** is a trip through Minnesota, from its prehistoric past to its future (page 136).

**✪ BEST (AND ONLY) PLACE TO COMBINE DINNER AND A SHOW:** The dying art of dinner theater is alive and kicking (high-kicking) at the **Chanhassen Dinner Theatres,** where top local talent performs crowd-pleasers to sold-out houses (page 138).

**✪ BEST CELEBRATION OF THE COLD:** Enjoy the perks of snowy, icy weather throughout the month of January at the **Winter Carnival** (page 139).

**✪ BEST PLACE TO MEET ALL OF MINNESOTA AT ONCE:** Join upwards of 100,000 people on the midway, in line for fried foods, and, of course, gawking at the butter sculptures at the **Minnesota State Fair** (page 144).

## MUSEUMS

### ✪ Mill City Museum

Minneapolis's reputation as the mill city was cemented in the 1880s with the development of a revolutionary process for milling flour that maximized quality and output, and it held its place until the flour market shifted to Buffalo and Chicago in the 1930s. The Washburn A. Mill continued to produce flour until 1965, then sat empty on the waterfront until it was mostly destroyed by fire in 1991. The Minnesota Historical Society saw the beauty and potential in the ruins of the structure, transforming it into the Mill City Museum in 2003 but keeping much of the burned-out shell. The museum itself is small, but the two multimedia presentations are mustsees on your visit: the Flour Tower Tour and *Minneapolis in 19 Minutes Flat,* a humorous look at local history by beloved Minneapolis writer and comedian Kevin Kling. Kids will especially enjoy the interactive water exhibit, and the gift shop is an excellent place to find local souvenirs and books. Combine your visit with a walking tour organized by the Minnesota Historical Society, many of which leave from the museum itself.

MAP 1: 704 2nd St. S., Minneapolis, 612/341-7582, www.millcitymuseum.org; Tues.-Sat. 10am-5pm, Sun. noon-5pm; $12 adults, $10 seniors and college students, $6 children 6-17, free for children 5 and under

### Wells Fargo History Museum

The red-and-black Wells Fargo stagecoach in the lobby of the Wells Fargo tower is a landmark for downtown workers. The exhibits are on the skyway level of the stunning art deco building. Displays include the weather ball from the top of the Northwestern Bank (Wells Fargo's predecessor in the Midwest), which turned green to herald good weather and red when bad weather was coming. Posters, documents, and artifacts trace the bank's Midwestern history. Tiny kids can ride in a mini stagecoach. In June, July, and August, free half-hour tours are offered at 11am, noon, and 1pm twice per month. Groups can also book free tours.

MAP 1: 90 7th St. S., Minneapolis, 612/667-4210, www.wellsfargohistory.com; Mon.-Fri. 9am-5pm; free

## GALLERIES

### Gallery 13

Tucked into the most business-y corner of the downtown business district, Gallery 13 is a surprising little place to take a break, whether from your own workday or from watching other people go about their workdays.

Mill City Museum

The space itself is spare, the better to show off contemporary works, almost exclusively from Minnesota and the Upper Midwest. Exhibits change monthly, and you're just as likely to find colossal paintings as tiny mixed-media sculptures.

MAP 1: 811 Lasalle Ave., Minneapolis, 651/592-5503, www.gallery13.com; Tues.-Sat. noon-6pm; free

### Minnesota Center for Book Arts

Books are art. Books can be transformed into art. And the skills we use to construct books, like papermaking and binding, can be used in other arts. The Minnesota Center for Book Arts, which shares space with The Loft Literary Center, the independent press Milkweed Editions, and a coffee shop, is dedicated to all these things. There are studios, where you might find someone making paper or setting type, and exhibition spaces, where national and international book artists display their work. The center, open since 1983, is the largest of its kind in the country. Check its website for regular hands-on events.

MAP 1: 1011 Washington Ave. S., Ste. 100, Minneapolis, 612/215-2520, www.mnbookarts.org; Mon. and Wed.-Sat. 9:30am-6:30pm, Tues. 9:30am-9pm, Sun. noon-5pm; free

### Soap Factory

The Soap Factory is far more than just a venue. The space itself—three cavernous rooms totaling 40,000 square feet in the old National Purity Soap Company—informs the choice of artists and exhibits, as well as the work. The rooms are just as gritty and unfinished as they were when the gallery opened in 1988, so that a visit can feel like an intrepid spelunking trip into a semi-abandoned warehouse. To get around a lack of heating, the Soap Factory programs furiously between April and November and shuts down for the winter. Exhibitions often combine media and artists thematically, exploring questions of identity and perception. Many of the summer "exhibitions" are, in fact, artist-led tours of the surrounding area, with an eye toward its industrial and artistic past.

MAP 1: 518 2nd St. SE, Minneapolis, 612/623-9176, www.soapfactory.org; Apr.-Nov. Wed.-Fri. 1pm-7pm, Sun. noon-5pm; free

the Guthrie Theater's "endless bridge"

## THEATER
### ✪ Guthrie Theater

When Sir Tyrone Guthrie decided the country needed a resident repertory theater, Minneapolis won him over. The Guthrie opened in 1963 with *Hamlet* and has stayed true to its founder's artistic vision ever since. The company's bread and butter is classics, from Shakespeare to Noel Coward, but the Guthrie is also known for world premieres from leading contemporary playwrights.

In 2006, the Guthrie moved from digs it shared with the Walker Art Center into the striking blue building overlooking the Mississippi River. Three stages allow for a wide range of programming, from experimental works by new playwrights in

# LOCAL THEATER

On any given weekend night during the theater season—and even in the summer—somebody with an urge to see a play will have more than 40 shows to choose from. The metro area, in fact, is second only to New York City in per capita attendance at theater and arts events. Which means you'll find high-quality productions and enthusiastic audiences as well as just plain variety. Don't expect safe old chestnuts to dominate the playbills, either, with some theaters well known for presenting original scripts or regularly premiering works by internationally known playwrights. Here are some good places to start exploring the Twin Cities' theater scene:

Guthrie Theater

- **Guthrie Theater:** This is the crème de la crème of Minnesota theater, with top national performers in classics and contemporary favorites (page 114).

- **Children's Theatre Company:** See theatrical productions created for kids and teens but sophisticated enough to be enjoyed by anyone—even without a child in tow (page 122).

- **Mixed Blood Theatre:** Mixed Blood expands the boundaries of the theatrical canon, with plays by and about marginalized people, from immigrants to the elderly (page 126).

- **Penumbra Theatre:** The nation's largest African American theater launched the career of August Wilson, and continues to lead the way (page 135).

- **Chanhassen Dinner Theatres:** Enjoy your stuffed chicken breast with a side of high-quality musical theater—or vice versa (page 138).

the Dowling Lab to classics on the asymmetrical thrust stage and contemporary American works on the proscenium stage. In 2015, long-time beloved artistic director Joe Dowling stepped down, replaced by acclaimed young director Joe Hajj.

You don't need tickets to a show to enjoy the Guthrie. Come for some of the city's finest seafood at **Sea Change** or a casual bite at the Level Five restaurant, or walk out over the river on the "endless bridge." Take a free self-guided, downloadable audio tour (available at the website or on iPods you can rent) or take a backstage tour on Friday or Saturday at 10am ($12 adults, $7 students or seniors). Costume and architectural tours are also offered monthly or can be scheduled in advance for five or more people.

**MAP 1:** 818 2nd St. S., Minneapolis, 612/377-2224, www.guthrietheater.org; check calendar for hours; cost varies depending on event

### Brave New Workshop

The Brave New Workshop lays claim to the title of longest-running satirical theater company in the United States, with roots that go back to 1958. The

Brave New Workshop

Illusion's educational work in the community. Watch for shows in the Fresh Ink series. These are exciting works by Minnesota artists still in the development stage. And Miss Richfield 1981's holiday show (call it earnest drag) is a local tradition. The theater is on the top floor of the Hennepin Center for the Arts, which is also home to dozens of dance, theater, and education programs.

**MAP 1:** 528 Hennepin Ave., 8th Fl., Minneapolis, 612/339-4944, www. illusiontheater.org; check calendar for hours; cost varies depending on event

company moved to fancy new digs in downtown Minneapolis in 2011, after more than 40 years in a ramshackle storefront in Uptown. Now it's got a more flexible, sleeker space and occasionally hosts other troupes as well. Nationally known performers got their start here, including Al Franken, who took the political and social satire he learned on to *Saturday Night Live* and the political arena. Some of the show titles tell you this is a no-holds-barred place: *The Lion, the Witch, and the War Hero; or Is McCain Able?, Bushwhacked II: One Nation Under Stress,* and *Martha Stewart's Prison Jamboree*. In addition to the main shows, the BNW troupe does improv Fridays and Saturdays at 9:45pm ($5).

**MAP 1:** 824 Hennepin Ave., Minneapolis, 612/332-6620, www.bravenewworkshop. com; check calendar for hours; cost varies depending on event

### Illusion Theater

Illusion Theater is a kind of nesting ground for new plays and playwrights. It has launched more than 500 plays, developed for its very own stage, in its history and then sent them off into the world, often to find success nationally. Most of the shows tackle contemporary social issues, a complement to

## CONCERT VENUES
### The Armory

The Twin Cities' newest concert venue (2017) is an old Works Progress Administration gem: the National Guard Armory, still sporting its art deco style. After stints as a sporting arena and (yeah) a parking garage, the Armory now holds 8,400 concert-goers on a large general admission floor and two tiers of balconies. The size is just right for attracting mid-range touring acts that are too big or just not right for a sit-down theater. Watch for boxing bouts and other sporting events, as well. Be sure to leave extra time, because this 1930s building wasn't built for 21st-century security checks.

The Armory

MAP 1: 500 6th St. S., Minneapolis, 612/315-3965, www.armorymn.com; hours vary; cost varies depending on event

## The Cowles Center

In 1999, Minneapolis's oldest theater, the Shubert, was picked up and moved a full block to the north. All 3,000 tons of it. The city wanted to redevelop the land under the Shubert (where Mayo Clinic Square now sits), and the artistic community wanted to save the building. And there the theater sat for more than a decade. Finally, in late 2011, The Cowles Center for Dance and the Performing Arts opened, with a sleek glass atrium connecting the old Shubert to the equally historic Hennepin Center for the Arts.

The old Shubert Theater has been rechristened the **Goodale Theater** (but few Minneapolitans will know that, as old names tend to stick) and has been completely refitted. The 500-seat theater has a dramatic rake that allows for excellent sight lines for all ticket holders, and the stage has probably the best acoustics in the area. Whether it's a choral concert by **Cantus,** a performance by the **Zenon Dance Company,** or a visiting opera, it's worth getting tickets to anything at the Cowles. (It's pronounced "COALS," by the way.) The complex is also home to the black box-style JSB Tekbox stage, where the nationally recognized **James Sewell Ballet** performs, and the **Illusion Theater,** which hosts independent theater productions.

MAP 1: 528 Hennepin Ave., Minneapolis, 612/206-3636, www.thecowlescenter. org; check calendar for hours; cost varies depending on event

## Hennepin Theatre Trust

The Hennepin Theatre Trust comprises four theaters. **New Century Theatre** (615 Hennepin Ave.) is the place to see modern comedies—often bawdy. **The Orpheum** (910 Hennepin Ave.) hosts Broadway shows and big names in music, while the **Pantages** (710 Hennepin Ave.) is a popular concert and comedy venue and the **State Theatre** (805 Hennepin Ave.) does a little bit of everything. The four share a central box office at the State Theatre and an online booking system.

The Orpheum, Pantages, and State all share a rich history. In the 1910s and 1920s, Hennepin Avenue was the place to see vaudeville in lavish theaters. At the end of the 1920s, vaudeville's popularity had declined and the theaters embraced movies. By the 1970s, Hennepin Avenue was no longer a safe destination. The buildings sat empty for many years before being refurbished and revived by the Hennepin Theatre Trust. Public tours of the theaters are offered on the second Saturday of the month at 10am or the last Monday of the month at 1pm (612/455-9500, $5/person).

MAP 1: Hennepin Ave., Minneapolis, 612/673-0404, www.hennepintheatretrust. org; check calendar for hours; cost varies depending on event

## Orchestra Hall

With the **Minnesota Orchestra**, you are as likely to hear Copland and Bernstein as Mahler and Shostakovich. Since 1903 the orchestra has had a history of commissioning original pieces and nurturing new American composers. You're also likely to hear some Sibelius or other Nordic-influenced work, thanks to music director Osmo Vänskä, who hails from Finland and has found a very receptive audience for the sounds of his homeland here in the Twin Cities. Sommerfest in July and

August brings a particularly audience-friendly schedule.

The building itself, with its trademark blue pipes, is a landmark, anchoring the south end of Nicollet Mall. The two-story glass atrium that wraps around the building hosts glittering events and even some chamber music concerts. The seats in the hall are comfortable, and the renowned acoustics are beloved by musicians and audiences alike.

MAP 1: 1111 Nicollet Mall, Minneapolis, 612/371-5600, www.minnesotaorchestra.org; check calendar for hours; cost varies depending on event

### Target Center

Home to the **Minnesota Timberwolves** basketball team and the WNBA team the **Minnesota Lynx,** Target Center is a major landmark in downtown Minneapolis. When it opened in 1990, it was the first entirely nonsmoking arena in the country. Along with St. Paul's **Xcel Energy Center,** this is where you can expect to see major national and international tours when they come to town, including pop stars of all stripes, family shows, wrestling, and even the Cirque du Soleil. The arena seats about 20,000 for basketball games and 13,000-19,000 for concerts. Also in the building, which is connected to the skyway system, is a **Lifetime Fitness** gym. Call 612/673-1380 to find out if a parents room, where chaperones of event ticket holders can wait during shows, will be available.

MAP 1: 600 1st Ave. N., Minneapolis, 612/673-0900, www.targetcenter.com; check calendar for hours; cost varies depending on event

# South Minneapolis          Map 2

## MUSEUMS

### ✪ American Swedish Institute

In the late 1800s, waves of Swedish immigrants began making their homes in Minnesota, where the terrain, with its lakes, rivers, and gentle rolling fields and forests, reminded them of home. Among them was Swan Turnblad, who rose from typesetter to newspaper publisher and built the massive 33-room mansion (rumored at the time to cost $1 million to build) on Park Avenue. The building, with its turrets and stately portico, was completed in 1903, and in 1929, Turnblad revealed why he had built such a grand house for his small family: He had intended all along to create a museum of Swedish American culture. Today, several rooms display examples of early-20th-century furnishings, including a large and impressive collection of *kakelugnar* (Swedish tiled stoves), while others host traveling exhibits. The third floor is dedicated to the history of Swedish culture in the Twin Cities.

In 2012, the American Swedish Institute built a 21st-century addition to the 100-plus-year-old mansion. The Nelson Center, with its long, modern lines and weathered gray shingles, is a sharp contrast to the heavy Turnblad house, but together they represent two sides of the Swedish American experience. The Nelson Center houses a small exhibit space, large meeting rooms, a well-curated gift shop, and

American Swedish Institute

a café, **Fika** (Tues. and Thurs.-Sat. 8:30am-5pm, Wed. 8:30am-8pm, Sun. 11am-5pm). Fika, which means "coffee break" in Swedish, serves sweet and savory snacks and light meals in the Nordic tradition.

Most importantly, however, the Nelson Center addition opens up what was once a rather cramped museum, with soaring ceilings, white walls, a rooftop garden (open to the public), and natural light streaming in from every direction. It's worth a stop even if you don't have enough time to see the whole museum.

MAP 2: 2600 Park Ave., Minneapolis, 612/871-4907, www.asimn.org; Tues. and Thurs.-Fri. noon-5pm, Wed. noon-9pm, Sat. 10am-5pm, Sun. noon-5pm; $9 adults, $7 seniors, $5 children and full-time students, children 5 and under free

## ✪ Minneapolis Institute of Art
A neoclassical surprise in a gentrifying neighborhood, the MIA (say it "Mia" to sound like an insider) welcomes half a million people every year. The museum was founded in 1883 and moved into its present home in 1915. Two additions—a 1974 minimalist wing and a 2006 Michael Graves-designed wing—contrast with the main facade. While the main collection covers nearly every period and area of the globe, the MIA is particularly well known for its Asian art collection.

Families can take a break in the Family Center, where they can read a book, play a game, have a snack, and emerge ready for more art. One Sunday a month, the museum hosts special kid-oriented events. Grown-ups get the run of the museum on third Thursday evenings, with music and drinks (6pm-9pm). A fee is charged for some special exhibitions.

Perhaps the most unusual item in the MIA's collection is the **Purcell-Cutts House** (2328 Lake Pl., Minneapolis, 612/870-3000, $5 adults, $4 students and seniors), about a mile away on Lake of the Isles. Tours of the elegant Prairie

School home are offered the second weekend of every month.

MAP 2: 2400 3rd Ave. S., Minneapolis, 612/870-3000, www.artsmia.org; Tues.-Wed. and Sat. 10am-5pm, Thurs.-Fri. 10am-9pm, Sun. 11am-5pm; free

Minneapolis Institute of Art

## ✪ The Museum of Russian Art

What is one of the finest collections of Russian art doing in a renovated church in a mostly residential neighborhood of South Minneapolis? It all comes down to one man: Minnesota businessman and passionate art collector Ray Johnson, who was among the first Westerners to start poking around in attics, country homes, and artists' cluttered apartments as the Soviet Union began opening up under *glasnost* in the late 1980s. He found paintings—officially sanctioned and not—that reflected a side of Russian art most Western eyes would not recognize even today. Beyond Wassily Kandinsky and early Modernist propaganda posters, Soviet realism embraced and encouraged art that was meant to speak even to uneducated peasants. Villages, fields, forests, and other beloved icons of Russian culture are rendered realistically and sympathetically. The gallery space itself, while small, has excellent lighting and an inviting mezzanine.

MAP 2: 5500 Stevens Ave. S., Minneapolis, 612/821-9045, www.tmora.org; Mon.-Fri. 10am-5pm, Sat. 10am-4pm, Sun. 1pm-5pm; $10 adults, $8 seniors, $5 students and children, children 13 and under free

## The Bakken

At the Bakken, visitors can experience electricity in just about every form, starting in the front hall, where cranking a machine from the 1920s delivers a powerful jolt of electricity. Farther along in the museum's warren of small rooms and hallways, a theremin (one of the first electronic musical instruments) hums and whistles as visitors pass their hands around it, electric fish spark in dark aquariums, and the monster in Mary Shelley's *Frankenstein* lies on his inventor's table (the 15-minute Frankenstein show based on the novel—not later movie interpretations—is not to be missed). Visitors can even play Mindball, a game you win by moving a ball with your mind. In 1957, Earl Bakken invented the first wearable pacemaker. His company, Medtronic, went on to become one of Minnesota's most important companies and a major player in medical electronics. Medtronic's collection of devices and documents was opened to the public in its current location in 1976.

MAP 2: 3537 Zenith Ave. S., Minneapolis, 612/926-3878, www.thebakken.org; Tues.-Wed. and Fri.-Sat. 10am-5pm, Thurs. 10am-8pm; $10 adults, $8 seniors and ages 13-24, $5 ages 5-12, children under 4 free

## Hennepin History Museum

Sadly often overlooked, the Hennepin History Museum takes advantage of its under-the-radar status to put on creative exhibits that change frequently, drawing on its deep collection of costumes, household artifacts, toys, and Native American items. The permanent exhibit in this 1919 mansion mixes whimsy with some somber truth. The Century of the Child displays children's toys, books, clothes, and other artifacts from throughout the 20th century, but it also looks hard at darker subjects, like child labor and child trafficking. The museum's library and collections—with photographs, maps, government documents, and ephemera—are open to researchers and the curious public (Tues. 10am-2pm and Wed.-Sat. 1pm-5pm). The museum is not wheelchair-accessible.

MAP 2: 2303 3rd Ave. S., Minneapolis, 612/870-1329, www.hennepinhistory.org; Tues. 10am-2pm, Wed. 1pm-5pm, Thurs. 1pm-8pm, Fri.-Sun. 1pm-5pm; $5 adults, $3 seniors and students, children under 7 free

### Norway House

About 12 percent of Minnesota's population identifies as Norwegian, still the second-largest ethnic group in the state, even after a century and a half of continued migration by other groups. Norway House has long been the voice of the Norwegian population, but the organization opened its beautiful, modern new home in 2015. There's a small gallery space that celebrates traditional and modern Norwegian culture, art, and crafts, as well as a coffee shop, Also (Tues.-Sat. 10am-4pm, Sun. 11am-3pm), run in partnership with Ingebretsen's, the longtime shopping destination for those seeking Norwegian anything.

MAP 2: 913 Franklin Ave. E., Minneapolis, 612/871-2211, www.norwayhouse.org; Tues.-Sat. 10am-4pm, Sun. 11am-3pm; $6 adults, $5 seniors, $4 children

# GALLERIES
## Highpoint Center for Printmaking

Highpoint is an artistic oasis in the bustling Lyn-Lake neighborhood. Members of the printing cooperative make art in the studios, and the public is welcome to view their work—and more—in the inviting galleries. The annual summer exhibition features co-op members, while exhibitions throughout the year might highlight guest artists or fellows. Watch the schedule for Free Ink Days, when members of the public are invited into the studios to don aprons and start mixing and rolling inks to make their own prints.

MAP 2: 912 Lake St. W., Minneapolis, 612/871-1326, www.highpointprintmaking.org; Mon.-Fri. 9am-5pm, Sat. noon-4pm; free

## Minneapolis College of Art and Design

The MCAD Gallery is the place to see works by some of Minnesota's top art students, as well as their teachers—talented working artists themselves. While you're visiting the galleries, you also get a peek into life on this dynamic urban campus. Keep an eye out for the annual art sale and faculty exhibitions, in the late spring and early fall, respectively.

MAP 2: 2501 Stevens Ave. S., Minneapolis, 612/874-3700, www.mcad.edu; Mon.-Fri. 9am-8pm, Sat. 9am-5pm, Sun. noon-5pm; free

## Northern Clay Center

The Northern Clay Center celebrates pottery in every form, from functional to fantastical. Cool and inviting in blond wood tones, the two-room gallery hosts 10 exhibitions every year, drawing on works from local, national, and international artists.

Programming also includes popular classes and special events. The center's shop is a great place to find works of art as gifts and souvenirs, especially if you happen to come during the American Pottery Festival in the fall or in time for the special sale around the winter holidays.

**MAP 2:** 2424 Franklin Ave. E., Minneapolis, 612/339-8007, www.northernclaycenter.org; Tues.-Wed. and Fri.-Sat. 10am-6pm, Thurs. 10am-7pm, Sun. noon-4pm; free

### Soo Visual Arts Center

For more than a decade, Soovac, as some know it, has brought underrepresented artists—those from communities whose voices are rarely heard in artistic communities and those whose aesthetics many might feel are just too out there—to the fore. The shows are curated with both whimsy and seriousness, launching perhaps from a play on words or from a social mission. Watch for educational programs and performances, as well.

**MAP 2:** 2909 Bryant Ave. S., Minneapolis, 612/871-2263, www.soovac.org; Wed. 11am-5pm, Thurs.-Fri. 11am-7pm, Sat.-Sun. 11am-4pm; free

## THEATER

### ✪ Children's Theatre Company

The Children's Theatre Company was the first children's theater in the country to win a Regional Theatre Tony Award, in 2003, and that was even before its lush new wing opened to the public and attracted even larger audiences and greater loyalty among Twin Cities fans. No matter what your age, this is a great place to see theater (and there's no shame in buying a ticket for yourself without a kid in tow). The main proscenium stage holds lavish, sophisticated sets for the big musical productions, and the innovative, welcoming Cargill Stage is the perfect place to introduce the youngest kids to theater. In fact, the Children's Theatre is a leader in this area: Shows for preschoolers are expertly geared toward tiny attention spans, and actors always introduce themselves and then, like pied pipers, lead the kids personally into the theater. The theater is connected to the Minneapolis Institute of Art, making it easy to combine an afternoon of art with an evening at a show.

**MAP 2:** 2400 3rd Ave. S., Minneapolis, 612/874-0400, www.childrenstheatre. org; check calendar for hours; cost varies depending on event

Children's Theatre Company and Minneapolis Institute of Art

### Bryant-Lake Bowl

It's a restaurant! It's a bowling alley! It's a cabaret-style theater! Bryant-Lake Bowl is most definitely all three, as well as a South Minneapolis institution—and you never know what you'll find in the theater. It might be a family-friendly production on a weekend morning. It might be bawdy improv late in the evening. It might be sociopolitical commentary presented by Dykes in Drag. It might be a round-table discussion on environmental science. It might be hard to hear over the din of bowling balls and restaurant chatter. It might be so mesmerizing that even the bowlers and the diners stop to listen in.

**MAP 2:** 810 Lake St. W., Minneapolis, 612/825-8949, www.bryantlakebowl. com; check calendar for hours; cost varies depending on event

### In the Heart of the Beast Puppet and Mask Theatre

Towering, larger-than-life-size puppets, marionettes, hand puppets, and multi-actor dragons interact with live actors on fantastical folk art-inspired sets. In the Heart of the Beast takes social issues like water conservation, immigration—even the Holocaust and the Korean DMZ—and makes them understandable for the whole family. It also stages fun folk tales from around the world and an annual Nativity play. Housed in a 1930s art deco theater, In the Heart of the Beast has been around since 1973 and is also the force behind the annual May Day parade on the first Sunday of May, when massive puppets made and carried by community members wind down to Powderhorn Park.

**MAP 2:** 1500 Lake St. E., Minneapolis, 612/721-2535, www.hobt.org; check calendar for hours; cost varies depending on event

### Jungle Theater

The Jungle is a snug and intimate theater with just 150 seats and a reputation, since its very first season in 1991, for excellent contemporary plays. A season at the Jungle—which runs January through December, rather than September through June—might include new and commissioned works, revived classics from the early 20th century, and even a musical or two. Whether comedy or drama, you can expect a tight and emotionally charged production with some of the best set design in town. And you are allowed to bring your wine or coffee or cookie from the lobby concession stand into the theater—a friendly touch.

**MAP 2:** 2951 Lyndale Ave. S., Minneapolis, 612/822-7063, www.jungletheater.org; check calendar for hours; cost varies depending on event

### Open Eye Figure Theatre

The intimate Open Eye Theatre seats barely 100 people in a single room that doubles as the lobby, but what happens on the tiny stage seeks to reach beyond the confined space. Performers combine storytelling with music and puppetry, and some of the Twin Cities' most innovative playwrights and actors, including beloved NPR commentator Kevin Kling, have made Open Eye their local theater home.

**MAP 2:** 506 24th St. E., Minneapolis, 612/874-6338, www.openeyetheatre. org; check calendar for hours; cost varies depending on event

## CINEMA
### Riverview Theater

The lobby of the Riverview today looks much as it did when it was built in 1948, with mirrored and tiled walls, midcentury sofas and lamps, marble tabletops, and a copper fountain. The screening room is updated, but only for comfort, with modern stadium seating in front of the classic stage. This is one of the last places in the Twin Cities to see second-run Hollywood films for just $3. The theater is also a popular venue for film festivals and special showings.

MAP 2: 3800 42nd Ave. S., Minneapolis, 612/729-7369, www.riverviewtheater. com; check calendar for hours; cost varies depending on event

Trylon Microcinema

## Trylon Microcinema

Film nerds who can appreciate classic Robert Altman as much as the latest Danish auteur, who recognize the importance of schlocky sci-fi as much as films on gender and social issues, who believe in the enduring talent of Jeff Bridges, and who still care about 35mm film—these are the people who love the Trylon. There are just an intimate 50 seats in the theater, but they are posh. Most showings are Mondays and Tuesdays, and most of the time you have just one shot to see a film.
MAP 2: 3258 Minnehaha Ave., Minneapolis, 612/424-5468, www.trylon. org; check calendar for hours; cost varies depending on event

## Uptown Theatre

The Uptown Theatre's 50-foot-tall marquee is a landmark on Hennepin Avenue. The large single-screen theater—the largest screen in the Twin Cities—shows indie films, often of the lefty documentary sort, as well as fun Saturday midnight showings of cult classics. After a week or two at the Uptown, movies often move on to screens at the larger sister theaters **Lagoon Cinema** (1320 Lagoon Ave., 612/392-0402) and **Edina Cinema** (3911 50th St. W., 952/920-8796). The Lagoon and Edina, with five and four screens of their own, also show foreign, independent, and small studio films.
MAP 2: 2906 Hennepin Ave., Minneapolis, 612/823-3005, www.landmarktheatres. com; check calendar for hours; cost varies depending on event

# Nordeast and Dinkytown  Map 3

## MUSEUMS
### Frederick R. Weisman
### Art Museum

The silver curves and planes of architect Frank Gehry's Weisman Art Museum float high above the Mississippi River. The Weisman—Gehry's first and so far only museum design in the United States—looks familiar to those who know his design for the Guggenheim Museum in Bilbao, Spain. But, in fact, the 1993 Weisman predates the Guggenheim and was where Gehry first started working in this distinctive style. The interior galleries, ingeniously simple and functional, are both a contrast and a complement to the wild exterior, as well as a beautiful backdrop for art. The museum's permanent collection includes an impressive number of works of American Modernism, including Charles Biederman, Roy Lichtenstein, and Georgia O'Keeffe, as well as an unrivaled collection of traditional Korean furniture.

With more than half a dozen rooms in about 15,000 square feet of space, the Weisman hosts as many as three large exhibitions at a time, as well as pieces from its extensive permanent collection. One space, the Target Studio for Creative Collaboration, is dedicated to bringing together teams of artists from various disciplines to create new works.

MAP 3: 333 E. River Rd., Minneapolis, 612/625-9494, www.weisman.umn.edu; Tues. and Thurs.-Fri. 10am-5pm, Wed. 10am-8pm, Sat.-Sun. 11am-5pm; free

## GALLERIES

### House of Balls

Sculptor and House of Balls proprietor Allen Christian makes art out of everything he can get his hands on, from old typewriter parts to doll heads to alabaster. After three decades in downtown Minneapolis, Christian moved his collection and his workspace to a larger home, with outdoor space, right on the light rail. While you can't guarantee the artist will be around or the gallery will be open, it's worth stopping by and knocking on the door.

MAP 3: 1504 7th St. S., Minneapolis, 612/332-3992, www.houseofballs.com; hours change with the sculptor's whim; free

### Minneapolis Photo Center

The gorgeous renovated warehouse space of the Minneapolis Photo Center is worth a visit in itself. Galleries are located throughout the first and second floors, punctuated by exposed beams and other industrial details. Exhibits include works by Photo Center students and teachers, as well as visiting artists.

MAP 3: 2400 2nd St. N., Minneapolis, 612/643-3511, www.mplsphotocenter.com; daily 11:30am-5:30pm; free

### Northland Visions

This is a place to experience fine arts and native crafts by the indigenous peoples of the central plains and northern woodlands. Paintings, sculptures, jewelry, and baskets are for sale, along with supplies for crafters themselves, including a huge selection of beads. This is a great place to pick up the quintessential Minnesota souvenir: hand-harvested, true wild rice.

MAP 3: 861 Hennepin Ave. E., Minneapolis, 612872-0390, www. northlandvisions.com; Mon.-Fri. 10am-6:30pm, Sat. 10am-5pm; free

### Rogue Buddha Gallery

This storefront gallery in Nordeast Minneapolis regularly makes local and national lists of the best places to see and buy art. Owner and artist Nicholas Harper is self-taught and has been making art for more than two decades. As a rule, the artists displayed push the edges of visual arts, with raw images and unusual techniques. Harper himself takes traditional portraiture and distorts it, adding a disturbing emotionality. The gallery space is pure Nordeast: tin ceilings, rough floors, and an ersatz feel.

MAP 3: 357 13th Ave. NE, Minneapolis, 612/331-4266, www.roguebuddha.com; Wed.-Sat. 3pm-8pm; free

### Rosalux Gallery

Twenty well-established artists—including nationally recognized painters, photographers, and sculptors—make up the collective that runs and shares Rosalux. The spare space takes up several rooms in the Van Buren Building, in an industrial part of the city. Look for the "Luck" sign above the door.

MAP 3: 1400 Van Buren St. NE, Minneapolis, www.rosaluxgallery.com; Sat.-Sun. noon-4pm; free

### Textile Center

Originally a Ford dealership, the Textile Center has big, beautiful front windows and a wide-open gallery space for works by textile artists of all stripes: knitters, quilters, weavers, and those that defy description. There's also a small library with a collection of books and periodicals on all fabric arts (open to everyone; members can check books out). The Textile Center is also a great place to connect with its member organizations, such as the Weavers Guild of Minnesota and the Minnesota Quilters.

MAP 3: 3000 University Ave. SE, Minneapolis, 612/436-0464, www. textilecentermn.org; Mon.-Thurs. 10am-7pm, Fri.-Sat. 10am-5pm; free

## THEATER

### Mixed Blood Theatre

Founded in 1976 by 22-year-old Jack Reuler, Mixed Blood showcases works by and for groups that are often left out of traditional theater: immigrants, people of color, people with disabilities, the elderly, and more. The converted fire station in the Cedar-Riverside neighborhood—itself an ever-shifting portrait of the area's newest immigrant groups—is on the small side and a bit rickety, but the atmosphere is always one of shared discovery and pure joy in the theater. You may feel like everybody but you knows somebody, but grab a glass of wine in the lobby, strike up a conversation, and that will soon change.

MAP 3: 1501 4th St. S., Minneapolis, 612/338-6131, www.mixedblood.com; check calendar for hours; cost varies depending on event

Mixed Blood Theatre

### Ritz Theater/Theater Latte Da

Nearly two decades old, Theater Latte Da is not just a leader in musical theater in the Twin Cities, it is also an engine pulling the artistic community forward. Latte Da is in the midst of an ambitious plan to commission and stage 20 new musical works by local and national artists over the course of five years, while at the same time expanding and pushing the limits of its core season. Founder and director Peter Rothstein is renowned and beloved not just for ambition but for remarkable musical and creative talent as well. He is the mind behind the annual holiday show *All Is Calm*, a powerful musical rendition of the Christmas Truce of World War II. Latte Da is the owner and core tenant of Ritz Theater, which also hosts works by other theater troupes.

MAP 3: 345 13th Ave. NE, Minneapolis, 612/339-3003, www.latteda.com; check calendar for hours; cost varies depending on event

## Southern Theater

This spare, dramatic space showcases some of the most innovative music and dance programs in the area. Jazz, funk, modern, and Asian dance styles are all part of a typical season. The Southern doesn't have its own company; instead, it rents space to dance troupes and musical performers. Its history goes back to the early 20th century, when it was run by Minneapolis's Swedish community. Just over 200 seats look over a wide-open performance area with no stage.

MAP 3: 1420 Washington Ave. S., Minneapolis, 612/340-0155, www.southerntheater.org; check calendar for hours; cost varies depending on event

## Theatre in the Round

The words "community theater" don't have to have negative connotations. At the Theatre in the Round, you'll see some of the best community theater in the country, performed and staged almost entirely by volunteers. The theater is the second oldest in the Twin Cities, founded in 1952, but it moved into its current home in 1969. The stage, designed by acclaimed Modernist Ralph Rapson's firm, offers an experience unlike any other in the area: About 250 seats are arranged in a circle around the stage, and because the rows are only seven deep, no one is ever more than 30 feet from the stage.

MAP 3: 245 Cedar Ave., Minneapolis, 612/333-3010, www.theatreintheround. org; check calendar for hours; cost varies depending on event

# CONCERT VENUES
## Northrop Auditorium

When Northrop Auditorium was built in 1929 on the campus of the University of Minnesota, promoters called it "the Carnegie Hall of the Midwest." Today the building's soaring classical pillars are an iconic image. From the very early seasons, when Rachmaninoff, Stravinsky, and other luminaries made this their Midwest tour stop, the Northrop has attracted the top names in classical music, jazz, dance, and literature. The 4,800-seat auditorium looks much as it did more than eight decades ago, and the Northrop Organ has been recognized for the high quality of its preservation. The massive organ, Æolian-Skinner's Opus 892, has nearly 7,000 pipes, ranging from the size of a pencil to 32 feet tall. Members of the university community look forward to the free summer concerts on the lawn, held weekdays in June and July and featuring a wide range of music.

MAP 3: 84 Church St. SE, Minneapolis, 612/624-2345, www.northrop.umn.edu; check calendar for hours; cost varies depending on event

## Varsity Theater

This converted vaudeville theater has been called the best place to hear a concert in the Twin Cities, thanks to 20-foot ceilings, a nearly infinitely reconfigurable space, and a top-notch sound system. In fact, depending on the show, you may have a choice of seating that includes café tables, club chairs, and queen-size air mattresses. This isn't a music-every-night place, but it is where national touring indie acts, especially those just about to make it big, make their Twin Cities stops. Look for the art deco marquee and you'll know you're here.

MAP 3: 1308 4th St. SE, Minneapolis, 612/604-0222, www.varsitytheater.org; opening hours depend on events; tickets vary, generally $15-25

## CINEMA
### Heights Theater

The atmosphere is 100 percent classic—from the heavy velvet drapes to the chandeliers, orchestra pit, and Wurlitzer organ—but the shows are a mix of high-quality first-run Hollywood movies, foreign films, and unforgettable classics. You might even get to hear the organ on Friday and Saturday nights, sometimes before a show, sometimes accompanying a silent film. But don't expect the usual half-hour lead-up to the main attraction: The Heights shows no advertisements and just a few previews. This is the Twin Cities' oldest continually operated movie theater, in business since 1926.

MAP 3: 3951 Central Ave. NE, Minneapolis, 763/788-9079, www.heightstheater. com; check calendar for hours; cost varies depending on event

### St. Anthony Main Theatre

This slightly gritty two-screen theater is just as likely to show the latest

St. Anthony Main Theatre

Hollywood blockbuster as it is an Audrey Hepburn film, often on the same night. And that's the beauty of independent cinema. Conveniently located just across the river from downtown Minneapolis and in a row of decent pubs and restaurants, it's a good place for a night on the town. It's also the hub of the Minneapolis-St. Paul International Film Festival, held each spring.

MAP 3: 115 Main St. SE, Minneapolis, 612/331-4724, www.stanthonymaintheatre. com; check calendar for hours; cost varies depending on event

# Downtown St. Paul
# and West Side

Map 4

## MUSEUMS
### ✪ Landmark Center

The pink granite Landmark Center in downtown St. Paul's Rice Park is very much a local landmark. The 1902 Romanesque structure is also something of a one-stop shop for unique niche museums. The permanent exhibition, Uncle Sam Worked Here, tells the Landmark's own story: Built as a post office, it has also served as the federal courthouse where John Dillinger, his girlfriend Billie Frechette, and the St. Paul gangsters Machine Gun Kelly and Baby Face Nelson were tried. The Landmark Center Archive Gallery shows artifacts from 150 years of local postal history, and the Ramsey County Historical Society rotates exhibits, as well. (Those exhibits are all open during normal building hours.)

The **American Association of Woodturners Gallery** (651/484-9094, www.woodturners.org, Tues.-Fri. 11am-4pm, Sun. noon-3pm) features exhibitions of some of the nation's finest examples of woodturning. **The Schubert Club Museum** (651/292-3267, www.schubert.org, Sun.-Fri. noon-4pm) displays musical instruments in the basement gallery space and manuscripts on the second floor.

The Landmark Center's interior is worth a quick stop and look even if you don't have time to tour the museums. Concerts and special events are held in the building's five-story central atrium. Free public tours leave from the information desk by the 5th Street entrance on Thursday at 11am

and Sunday at noon. Or you can book the private Gangster Tour for $6 per person ($75 minimum) with two weeks' notice. Guides take on the personas of infamous gangsters tried in the courthouse.

**MAP 4:** 75 5th St. W., St. Paul, 651/292-3225 ext. 4, www.landmarkcenter. org; Mon.-Wed. and Fri. 8am-5pm, Thurs. 8am-8pm, Sat. 10am-5pm, Sun. noon-5pm; free

Landmark Center

### Alexander Ramsey House

Alexander Ramsey's elegant three-story home in St. Paul has been called one of the best-preserved Victorian houses in the country. Ramsey served as an appointed territorial governor of Minnesota and later as the state of Minnesota's second elected governor, and he held a host of other public offices. Costumed guides dressed as his wife, Anna, and servants lead tours through the home and offer insight into the upstairs/downstairs lives of the period.

MAP 4: 265 Exchange St. S., St. Paul, 651/296-8760, www.mnhs.org; public tours summer Sat. 10am-3pm on the hour, Christmas season tours Thurs.-Sat. 10am-4:30pm and Sun. noon-3pm every 15 min.; tours $10 adults, $8 seniors and college students, $6 ages 5-17, under 5 free (Christmas tours $8-12)

## James J. Hill House

Railroad baron James J. Hill personifies Minnesota's Gilded Age, when cities like Minneapolis and St. Paul were exploding in population and wealth, and grand stone homes lined St. Paul's Summit Avenue. His private home, now owned by the Minnesota Historical Society, is a shining example of the excesses of that time. Completed in 1891, the house cost nearly $1 million to build—all 36,000 square feet of it—with five floors and more than 40 rooms and intricate carving on nearly every wooden surface. It was also something of a technological marvel for its time, with modern conveniences like a security system and a telecom. Visitors need to take a 75-minute tour to see most of the house (tours leave on the half hour), but three rooms in the art gallery, with changing exhibitions, are open without a tour.

MAP 4: 240 Summit Ave., St. Paul, 651/297-2555, www.mnhs.org; summer and fall tours Wed.-Sat. 10am-3:30pm, Sun. 1pm-3:30pm; art gallery Mon.-Sat. 10am-4pm, Sun. 1pm-4pm; $10 adults, $8 seniors and students, $6 children, children 5 and under free

## Minnesota Children's Museum

Kids need room to move and to explore the world on their own terms— and that is exactly what the popular Minnesota Children's Museum gives them. The fun spreads across three floors that have a good mix of standing and traveling exhibits. The tiniest visitors can hang out in Sprouts, a soft environment where kids under four can climb, slide, and play with puppets. Kids can also climb four stories up through the Scramble, build their environment in Imaginopolis, run a play carwash, and do crafts in the Studio. Everything is built with children in mind, such as the kid-level handrail on the stairs. At midmorning and midafternoon, an announcement invites everyone to gather on the mezzanine for story time or Big Fun—when the parachutes, carpet skates, stilts, and other big-motor toys come out. The museum is closed Mondays Labor Day through Memorial Day.

MAP 4: 10 7th St. W., St. Paul, 651/225-6000, www.mcm.org; Sun.-Thurs. 9am-5pm, Fri.-Sat. 9am-8pm; $12.95

## Minnesota Museum of American Art

This mighty collection, with more than 4,500 works of American art from the 19th century on, has finally settled into a permanent home in the Pioneer Endicott Building. Its peripatetic existence, living in various historical buildings around St. Paul, kept the museum from getting the attention and accolades it deserves. The collection includes works by Native American artists, contemporary photographers, leaders in the crafts movement, and beloved American painters and sculptors. In particular, look for wooden pieces by George Morrison and photographs by Alec Soth, both Minnesotans.

MAP 4: 141 4th St. E., St. Paul, 651/797-2571, www.mmaa.org; Wed. 11am-5pm, Thurs. 11am-8pm, Fri.-Sun. 11am-5pm; free

## TWIN CITIES WITH KIDS

Minnesota Children's Museum

Minneapolis and St. Paul are, in general, very kid-friendly. Unless you've chosen one of the poshest restaurants in town, it's not hard to find booster seats, kids' menus, and crayons. Arts venues, too, welcome kids, although you should note that some, including the **Guthrie Theater,** have a minimum age for most of their shows.

The must-see list for families visiting the Twin Cities is long: The **Minnesota Children's Museum,** the **Science Museum of Minnesota,** the **Minnesota History Center,** the **Mill City Museum, Historic Fort Snelling,** and the **Minnesota Zoo** and **Como Park Zoo and Conservatory** are all good bets.

Keep an eye out for monthly special deals: Admission to the Minnesota Children's Museum is free on the third Sunday of the month. The **Walker Art Center and Sculpture Garden** hosts an all-out family-oriented bash on the first Saturday of the month, free of charge. The joint is hopping as families work on two crafts projects, rock out at the dance party in the auditorium, and watch offbeat films and live performances. (Note to those traveling without children: This is not a good day to try to enjoy the exhibits.) And admission to the **Minneapolis Institute of Art** is always free, but the museum hosts Target Family Day one Sunday a month, with art projects, performers, and special tours for families.

If you're traveling with toddlers, you need somewhere for them to get their wiggles out. You'll find great playgrounds in downtown Minneapolis's **Loring Park,** on the shores of **Bde Maka Ska (Lake Calhoun)** and **Lake Harriet** in South Minneapolis, and in St. Paul's **Como Park.** Inclement weather? Run the kids ragged in the empty hallways of the **Mall of America** in the hours after the doors open at 7am and before the stores open at 10am.

Got older kids who have to move, move, move all the time? Take them to **3rd Lair** skate park, rent them a board and a helmet, and say, "See you in three hours."

### Science Museum of Minnesota

Try your hand at piloting a river barge, see real human tissue through a microscope, handle dinosaur fossils, explore the science behind magnetism, whip up a tornado, and walk through a traditional Hmong house. These exhibits attract more than a million visitors a year (on weekends it can feel like they're all in line, waiting to buy tickets). A favorite exhibit includes the artifacts from Minneapolis's beloved Museum of Questionable Medical Devices, a small private museum that donated its collections when it closed. See a phrenology machine, which divines a person's personality from the bumps

Science Museum of Minnesota

on his or her head, and all manner of vibrating and electricity-conducting "medical cures." The museum is open extended hours during the summer, the winter holidays, and school vacation periods. It is closed Mondays during the fall.

The lobby is home to the **Mississippi River Visitor Center** (651/293-0200, www.nps.gov), where you can learn about the river, buy maps and souvenirs, and talk to National Park Service rangers about outdoor activities in the area. Check its website for the most current hours of operation.

And before you enter the museum itself, take in views of the Mississippi River—along with the Wabasha, Robert, and Smith street bridges—from the public patio directly to the left of the front door.

MAP 4: 120 Kellogg Blvd. W., St. Paul, 651/221-9444, www.smm.org; Tues.-Wed. 9:30am-5pm, Thurs.-Sat. 9:30am-9pm, Sun. 9:30am-5pm; museum $18.95 adults, $12.95 seniors and children; additional cost for Omnitheater and special exhibitions

# GALLERIES
## AZ Gallery

St. Paul's Lowertown is home to one of the highest concentrations of working artists in the country. And the AZ Gallery, which opened in 1997, is one of the area's longtime anchors. Ten Twin Cities artists are members of the cooperative, running the space and showing their work. They include photographers, painters, and sculptors at various stages of their careers. The wide-open warehouse space is well suited for exhibits of all types. Shows tend to change every month. Gifts@ AZ, the gallery's shop, sells works by 20 local artists, from jewelry to pottery and more.

MAP 4: 308 Prince St., St. Paul, 651/224-3757, www.theazgallery. org; Thurs.-Fri. 5pm-8pm., Sat.-Sun. 9am-3pm; free

# THEATER
## Minnesota History Theatre

The Minnesota History Theatre's bland name doesn't do it justice. Far from a high school field trip destination, the theater has built a nationwide reputation for supporting new work and staging world premieres. As the theater itself describes it, these are "real plays about real people": from the infamous Duluth lynchings to the founding of Minneapolis's Guthrie Theater to *Wellstone!*, about the late progressive senator from Minnesota. A single season might explore several decades or even centuries of Minnesota's past from the points of view of all of the state's myriad ethnic groups. A mix of newcomers and longtime stalwarts in the Twin Cities theater scene take on the roles, always admirably.

Park Square Theatre

**MAP 4:** 30 10th St. E., St. Paul, 651/292-4323, www.historytheatre.com; check calendar for hours; cost varies depending on event

### Park Square Theatre

When it was founded in 1974, the Park Square Theatre set out to bring the classics to St. Paul. But after a couple of decades of Shakespeare and Wilde, the theater decided to go bolder—and more professional at the same time—with more new and contemporary plays each season. The Park Square is still more staid and traditional than other theaters you might find in the Twin Cities, and the venue itself feels a little anonymous, but the draw is the extraordinary level of talent on stage. The majority of the cast in any show is likely to be made up of Actor's Equity members, many on a break from the Guthrie or bigger shows on the coasts. With a 350-seat proscenium stage and a 200-seat thrust stage, Park Square is able to put on more than a dozen shows every season.

**MAP 4:** 20 7th Pl. W., St. Paul, 651/291-7005, www.parksquaretheatre.org; check calendar for hours; cost varies depending on event

## CONCERT VENUES
### Fitzgerald Theater

The Fitz, as it's affectionately known, was once the home of the quintessentially Minnesotan radio show *A Prairie Home Companion*. Now operated by the talented and connected impresarios at First Avenue and 7th St. Entry, the well-preserved Gilded Age theater hosts musical and comedy acts, speakers, story slams, and other cultural events.

**MAP 4:** 10 Exchange St. E., St. Paul, 651/290-1200, http://fitzgeraldtheater.publicradio.org; check calendar for hours; cost varies depending on event

Fitzgerald Theater

### Ordway Center for the Performing Arts

On any given day on the Ordway stage, you're likely to find a nationally known modern dance troupe, the beloved local ensemble VocalEssence, a big Broadway show, or the musicians from one of the three major musical

organizations that make their home here (the Minnesota Opera, the St. Paul Chamber Orchestra, and the Schubert Club). In fact, the massive glass-fronted building facing St. Paul's lovely Rice Park hosts more than 500 varied performances a year in the 1,900-seat Music Theater and 1,100-seat Concert Hall, with acoustics especially designed for a chamber orchestra. Although the building, funded by local arts-lover Sally Ordway Irvine, opened in 1985, the plush two-story lobby with its thick carpet and dazzling chandeliers has a certain forgotten elegance.

MAP 4: 345 Washington St., St. Paul, 651/224-4222, www.ordway.org; check calendar for hours; cost varies depending on event

## Palace Theatre

A hundred years after it first opened as a vaudeville theater, in 1916, the Palace was given a second lease on life—and the neighborhood has welcomed it back with open arms. The venue hosts midsize touring acts in a restored hall that was purposefully left a little rough around the edges, to give it a little character. The space holds about 2,500 concert-goers, with the vast majority of these tickets being general admission on the open floor and the rest for seats in the balcony.

MAP 4: 17 7th Pl. W., St. Paul, 612/338-8388, www.palacestpaul.com; check calendar for hours, cost varies depending on event

## Xcel Energy Center

Home of the **Minnesota Wild** hockey team, the Xcel Energy Center opened in St. Paul in 2000 to give Minneapolis's Target Center a run for its money. And it has, selling out nearly every hockey game, snagging major international acts of all stripes, and attracting the 2008 Republican National Convention as well as 2008 Democratic presidential contender Barack Obama's first speech as the presumptive nominee. The arena seats around 20,000 and offers dozens of concession stands and two large restaurants. During some events, a family room is available, where chaperones of ticket holders can hang out for free. Call in advance to find out if this is the case.

MAP 4: 199 Kellogg Blvd. W., St. Paul, 651/265-4800, www.xcelenergycenter.com; check calendar for hours; cost varies depending on event

# Summit-University and Mac-Groveland

Map 5

ARTS AND CULTURE

SUMMIT-UNIVERSITY AND MAC-GROVELAND

## THEATER

### Penumbra Theatre

Penumbra Theatre, founded in 1976, is proud to be one of just three African American theaters in the United States to offer a full season of plays. The theater, founded by Twin Cities theater-scene stalwart Lou Bellamy, who passed the reins to his daughter Sarah Bellamy, helped launch the career of Pulitzer Prize-winning playwright August Wilson. In addition to plays and performances, Penumbra hosts regular community discussions—Let's Talk with Sarah Bellamy, and Reel Talk, inspired by films. Each December, the popular *Black Nativity* show combines gospel music, storytelling, and dance.

**MAP 5:** 270 Kent St. N., St. Paul, 651/224-3180, www.penumbratheatre. org; check calendar for hours; cost varies depending on event

### SteppingStone Theatre

SteppingStone, in a beautiful performance space in a converted neoclassical church, offers yet another superb place to introduce young audiences to theater. The theater seats 430 and offers an awe-inspiring first theater experience. The kids on stage may be young (actors are 8-18 years old), but their training, professionalism, and talent show in plays with themes from around the world. During the holiday season, watch for *The Best Christmas Pageant Ever.*

**MAP 5:** 55 Victoria St. N., St. Paul, 651/225-9265, www.steppingstonetheatre. org; check calendar for hours; cost varies depending on event

## CONCERT VENUES

### The O'Shaughnessy

The College of St. Catherine's impressive theater, fully overhauled in 2003, attracts big-name national acts in its Women of Substance Series (this is a respected women's college, after all). Over the past decade or so, Allison Kraus, Sweet Honey in the Rock, Maya Angelou, Madeleine Albright, and many, many more have played and addressed packed houses. The venue itself is conducive to a great show: Steeply raked, comfortable seats bring audience members even closer to the performers on stage.

**MAP 5:** 2004 Randolph Ave., St. Paul, 651/690-6700, www.oshag.stkate.edu; check calendar for hours; cost varies depending on event

## MUSEUMS

### ✪ Bell Museum of Natural History

The Bell Museum walks nature-lovers of all ages and scientific bents through the story of life, from its origins at the formation of the universe, through the evolutionary process, to today's complex ecosystems and into what tomorrow might look like, with and without human influence. In its stunning new home on the edge of the University of Minnesota's St. Paul campus, the Bell Museum combines classic dioramas (including the beloved wooly mammoth) with unique interactive exhibits. The planetarium hosts four shows a day.

**MAP 6:** 2088 Larpenteur Ave. W., St. Paul, 612/626-9660, www.bellmuseum.umn.edu; daily 10am-5pm; museum admission $12 adults, $10 seniors, $9 youth 21 and under, 2 and under free; planetarium shows $8 adults, $7 seniors, $6 youth 21 and under; discounts for combo tickets

### Gibbs Museum of Pioneer and Dakotah Life

Young newlyweds Jane and Herman Gibbs moved to this spot in 1849 and built a dugout sod hut. They later built a one-room cabin and then expanded it to an elegant Victorian farmhouse. Their Dakota neighbors, childhood friends of Jane, would often pass through the farm while traveling between their summer and winter homes. Because of this long and rich

Bell Museum of Natural History

history, the small Gibbs homestead offers a varied look at the lives of both the early pioneers and their Native American neighbors. Visitors are free to walk through the buildings—including the farmhouse, sod house, school, bark lodge, and tepees—without guides, but costumed interpreters are on hand to answer questions and tell stories.

**MAP 6:** 2097 Larpenteur Ave. W., St. Paul, 651/646-8629, www.rchs.com; Memorial Day-Oct. Sat.-Sun. 10am-4pm; $8 adults, $7 seniors, $5 children

## Goldstein Museum

A Christian LaCroix dress, an Eames chair, a high-concept magazine, a Turkish woven towel: All are examples of design and the way it interacts with our everyday life. This intersection of art and life was the passion of two sisters, Harriet and Vetta Goldstein, who taught at the University of Minnesota and built the foundation of what is now the Goldstein Museum. The permanent collection is not on display but can be viewed by appointment (call 612/625-2737). The museum's temporary exhibitions run the gamut from housing to fashion to surface design, and may focus on a single item—the chair—or a single designer—Russel Wright—or look boldly and broadly into the future. A smaller gallery with temporary exhibitions is also open in the lobby of **Rapson Hall,** on the East Bank of the Minneapolis campus (89 Church St., Minneapolis, Mon.-Thurs. 9am-9pm, Fri. 9am-6pm, Sat.-Sun. 1pm-5pm).

**MAP 6:** 364 McNeal Hall, 1985 Buford Ave., St. Paul, 612/624-7434, http://goldstein. design.umn.edu; Tues.-Fri. 10am-5pm, Sat.-Sun. 1:30pm-4:30pm; free

## Twin City Model Railroad Museum

Although the museum is small, it is situated in a wonderful and expansive old rail foundry building listed on the National Register of Historic Places. The O-scale layout will delight train buffs, history buffs, and kids. Volunteer train enthusiasts run up to six trains at a time on the scale two-mile track. The train table is expansive and easily viewed by kids as young as three years old. Trains from many eras, along with a few streetcars, run through a scaled historical Minneapolis riverfront, the Great Northern rail terminal, a fictitious rural town, and along the bluffs of the Mississippi (including a painstakingly detailed steamboat). The museum sells a full range of model train equipment, historical photos, and train paraphernalia—and is quite happy to let the littlest ones run wild on the toy train tables in front.

**MAP 6:** 668 Transfer Rd., St. Paul, 651/647-9628, www.tcmrm.org; Mon.-Tues. 10am-3pm, Fri. 10am-3pm, Sat. 10am-5pm, Sun. noon-5pm; $10, children 4 and under free

## MUSEUMS
### The Landing
In the tiny village of Eagle Creek, tucked in a bend in the Minnesota River, it is still 1890. A blacksmith shapes nails and door hinges, women in long dresses cook at woodstoves, and the village schoolteacher rings an enormous bell to call students to the one-room schoolhouse. Two draft horses bring a trolley full of guests to a small settlement of original 1840s cabins or all the way to Eagle Creek's town square, surrounded by houses, a church, and a general store. On weekends in the summer and in December, most of the buildings are open and staffed by costumed interpreters. On summer weekdays and throughout the week in the early fall, guided and self-tours are available, but without the interpreters to bring it to life. December weekends bring a merry re-creation of 19th-century Christmas traditions. A mile-long hiking trail hugs the river.

**MAP 7:** 2187 Hwy. 101 E., Shakopee, 763/694-7784, www.threeriversparkdistrict.org; Apr.-Oct. Mon.-Sat. 10am-5pm, Sun. noon-5pm; Nov.-Dec. Mon.-Sat. 10am-4pm, Sun. 11am-4pm; Jan.-Mar. Mon.-Fri. 10am-4pm; $8 adults, $5 seniors and children, children under 2 free, additional $5 for guided tours

### Pavek Museum of Broadcasting
As the story goes, Joe Pavek was an instructor at the Dunwoody College of Technology who couldn't bear to see his students tear up beautiful old radios. So he took one home. With the help of other radio enthusiasts, including the inventor of the implantable pacemaker, Earl Bakken, that one radio has now grown into a collection of broadcasting and recording equipment that fills more than 12,000 square feet. Visitors can create their own radio broadcasts in a 1960s studio, try their hand at operating a ham radio, and watch and listen to vintage television and radio programs.

**MAP 7:** 3517 Raleigh Ave., St. Louis Park, 952/926-8198, www.pavekmuseum.org; Wed.-Sat. 10am-5pm; $8 adults, $6 students

## THEATER
### ✪ Chanhassen Dinner Theatres
When was the last time you had a brandy Alexander or a grasshopper? When was the last time you had one while you applauded—or even clapped and sang along with—a show-stopping Broadway number? That's the kind of nearly lost pleasure the Chan is keeping alive. Minnesota's only true dinner theater stages two blockbuster shows per year on the main stage, with comedy and concerts on its two smaller stages. Chanhassen is also the home of the area's beloved **Stevie Ray's Comedy Cabaret** improv show. Dinner (or lunch) is served just before the curtain goes up, with a menu of classics like stuffed chicken breasts. The performers are among the area's best, and the shows are chosen to be crowd-pleasing commercial successes. Tables for two are in high demand, so bring a friendly foursome or expect to be seated with another couple.

MAP 7: 501 W. 78th St., Chanhassen, 952/314-5085, www.chanhassendt.com; check calendar for hours; cost varies depending on event

MAP 7: 5185 Meadville St., Greenwood, 952/474-5951, www.oldlog.com; check calendar for hours; cost varies depending on event

## Old Log Theatre

Seeing a show at the Old Log is a little like going to a classy summer camp. Near Lake Minnetonka, the grounds do in fact include an old log cabin. The season, which runs year-round, includes new comedies and musicals that appeal across generations, and the annual holiday show is especially popular. Arrive with plenty of time to enjoy the fireplace in the lobby and some time on the broad porch. Or combine your show with dinner beforehand at **Cast and Cru** (Wed. 4pm-10pm, Thurs.-Sat. 4pm-11pm, Sun. 10am-8:30pm), which serves upscale steaks and seafood. The restaurant is inside the theater.

## Stages Theatre

Children's literature staged by kids and for kids comes to life in Hopkins. While some of the plays are obvious choices for the stage (*Seussical, The Wizard of Oz*), others are delightful surprises, like children's classics *Goodnight Moon* and *The Paper Bag Princess*. Young audiences relate well to the actors on stage, all ages 10-21, and many will be inspired to join the Stages' theater classes.

MAP 7: 1111 Mainstreet, Hopkins, 952/979-1111, www.stagestheatre.org; check calendar for hours; cost varies depending on event

# Festivals and Events

## WINTER

**TOP** EXPERIENCE

### ✪ Winter Carnival

A fateful insult in the late 1800s launched a Winter Carnival that now draws about 350,000 visitors a year. That's when a New York newspaper reporter called St. Paul, then the fastest-growing city in America, "another Siberia, unfit for human habitation in the winter." St. Paulites took up the challenge and, since 1886, have spent much of the month of January thoroughly enjoying the winter weather. While the Ice Palace is the biggest draw, it isn't built every year, for economic and weather reasons. The entire city of St. Paul bustles with ice skating, ice-carving contests, and a 5K run and half marathon (yes, outside). Warm up in the Hotdish Tent with Minnesotans' favorite comfort food: hot dish (that's casserole to the rest of the country). Most of the action centers around Rice Park and the Landmark Center, but events are also held at other locations. **Downtown St. Paul and West Side:** Rice Park, St. Paul, 651/223-4700, www.winter-carnival.com; Jan.; free

### Rock the Cradle

One Sunday in January, a rocking party takes over the Minneapolis Institute of Art and the adjacent Children's Theatre. But, in this case, the raucous guests are toddling tots and their families, dancing at the kids' disco, going on air with DJs from Minnesota Public Radio's hip music station The Current, and exploring their musical future at the "instrument petting zoo." Rock the Cradle, sponsored by MPR, stretches from morning nap time to dinner, and given South Minneapolis's family-heavy demographics, it's wall-to-wall kids the whole time.

**South Minneapolis:** Minneapolis Institute of Art, 2400 3rd Ave. S., Minneapolis, 612/870-3000, www.mpr.org; Jan.; free

### Food and Wine Experience

For one long weekend in February, when nearly everyone is sick of winter's outdoor pursuits but nobody is yet ready to start dreaming of outdoor grilling and beachwear, the Minneapolis Convention Center becomes foodie central. Everyone connected with food in the Twin Cities—from restaurateurs to wine suppliers to critics to serious eaters—finds their way to the Food and Wine Experience. While eating, drinking, and socializing are the order of the day, seminars and learning lunches are also popular. Tickets to these and to the main event all sell out fast.

**Downtown Minneapolis:** Minneapolis Convention Center, 1301 2nd Ave. S., Minneapolis, 612/371-5800, www. foodwineshow.com; Feb.; $75, $80 at the door

# SPRING
## Minneapolis-St. Paul International Film Festival

When an 80-something curmudgeonly film buff puts together an international film festival for over two decades—not quite singlehandedly but certainly infusing his own unique spirit—you get a great depth of film choices and a whole lot of quirk. M-SPIFF, as it's known, has been curated by local fixture Al Milgrom for nearly as long as it's been around. This festival, which some years includes as many as 150 films from 50 countries, has a good mix of international Oscar nominees and long shots from obscure Baltic countries. (Actually, given Minnesota's history and the artistic proclivities of the audience, there's always a good selection from Scandinavia and the Baltics.)

The **Childish Film Festival,** which runs concurrently, is a refreshingly unexpected selection of films, many suited for children as young as preschoolers, showing a quieter, funnier, more independent sort of childhood.

**Nordeast and Dinkytown:** www. mspfilmfest.org; late Apr.; $14 per ticket

### Festival of Nations

The Latvian children's dance troupe takes the stage after the Japanese drums and sometime before the Karen dancers. Somebody wanders by with a Finnish rice pie in one hand and a Somali *sambusa* (savory triangular stuffed pastry) in the other. This is St. Paul's **Rivercentre** for four days in early May. And although the festival has changed and grown a great deal as Minnesota has grown and its ethnic makeup has changed, this happy fusion has been going on in some form since the first **Festival of Nations** in 1932, sponsored by the International Institute of Minnesota. More than 90 ethnic groups are represented, with food booths, dance and musical performances, and craft demonstrations. Come hungry and ready to see something you've never seen before, no matter where you're from.

**Downtown St. Paul and West Side:**
Rivercentre, 175 Kellogg Blvd. W., St. Paul, 651/647-0191, www.festivalofnations.com; early May; $11 adults, $8 children, children under 6 free

### Cinco de Mayo

The roots of the Latino population on St. Paul's West Side, an area also called District del Sol, go back well over 100 years, and a strong community is still centered on the area around **Cesar Chavez Street.** That is undoubtedly the place to be during the first weekend in May, when over 100,000 people show up to celebrate Cinco de Mayo, the historic celebration of the 1962 Battle of Puebla, when the Mexican army defeated the invading French. Music, art, sports, and children's activities fill Cesar Chavez between Wabasha and Anita Streets on Friday evening and all day Saturday during this decidedly family-oriented event. And food—of course there's food and plenty of it, from a salsa-tasting contest to street vendors.

**Downtown St. Paul and West Side:**
Cesar Chavez St., St. Paul, 651/222-6347, www.districtdelsol.com; first weekend in May; free

### Art-A-Whirl

If ever an art event could be said to fill a neighborhood, this is it. Art-A-Whirl, held the third weekend in May, takes over northeast Minneapolis, where much of the city's art scene fled after condo developers discovered downtown's Warehouse District. Each year, 500 artists—sculptors, painters, photographers, glass artists, and even musicians—open their studios and galleries to the public. Other local businesses get in on the fun, and area bars book local bands through much of the weekend. To get your bearings, start at the welcome booth at 13th and Marshall or on Quincy Street NE. Trolleys run periodically around the main sites.

**Nordeast and Dinkytown:**
612/788-1679, www.nemaa.org; third weekend in May; free

### Edina Art Fair

For some in South Minneapolis, the Edina Art Fair, generally held the first weekend of June, signals that, yes, summer really is coming and it is time to start shoehorning in all the outdoor activities, bratwurst, and kettle corn that the brief, intense warm weather demands. More than 400 artists bring their paintings, pottery, quilts, and more to the juried sale, squeezed onto the intersection of 50th Street and France Avenue in this decidedly upscale shopping district. Live music, cooking demonstrations, fashion shows, and food vendors help visitors make a real day of it, although there isn't much to keep antsy kids satisfied. This is a good time to watch for real deals at the 50th and France boutiques, many of which hold sidewalk sales.

**Greater Twin Cities:** 50th St. and France Ave., Edina, 952/922-1524, www.edinaartfair.com; first weekend in June; free

**TOP** EXPERIENCE

# SUMMER
### Grand Old Day

How much fun can one neighborhood pack into one day? On Grand Avenue, on a Saturday in early June, this neighborhood can pack in more than you ever thought possible: more than three dozen outdoor concerts on nine stages (some free, some for a nominal ticket price), four footraces, an art fair, a parade, and, oh, yeah, a quarter of a million people—all in the space of 20 city blocks. The beer flows freely on some blocks, while others are given over to petting zoos and bouncy castles. Devotees of the Grand Old Day plan far in advance to cope with the exhaustion that inevitably follows. Grand Avenue is known as St. Paul's favorite shopping district, and with the purchase of a $5 "grandee" button, you get discounts for most of the summer at retailers all up and down Grand Avenue.

**Summit-University and Mac-Groveland:** 651/699-0029, www. grandave.com/grandoldday; early June; free

### Twin Cities Jazz Festival

Outside of jazz circles, the Twin Cities Jazz Festival doesn't get a whole lot of attention—it competes with milk carton boat races, after all—but thousands of jazz lovers gather for free outdoor concerts at Mears Park in St. Paul, then hit the local clubs for more show.

**Downtown St. Paul:** www. twincitiesjazzfestival.com; June; free

### Twin Cities Pride

Every June, the Twin Cities Pride festival kicks off with a picnic in Como Park in St. Paul and culminates in a concert, daylong festival, and parade in Minneapolis. In the 10 days in between, look for a full schedule of concerts, readings, and get-togethers throughout the cities. Most of the activity is centered around Loring Park, where the Twin Cities' first LGBT march took place in 1972. Revelers fill downtown bars and nightclubs during the final weekend, so you're likely to get swept up in the celebration even if it's not what you came here for.

**Downtown Minneapolis:** 612/305-6900, www.tcpride.org; June; free

### Northern Spark

This weekend in mid-June is your chance to stay up all night and experience Minneapolis as you never see it during the day. Dancers, musicians, visual artists, and performers of all uncategorizable stripes take over the city. Some museums stay open into the wee hours, and unexpected experiences abound during the Northern Spark.

**Downtown Minneapolis:** www. northernspark.org; second Sat. June; free

### Stone Arch Bridge Festival

On Father's Day weekend, the Stone Arch Bridge Festival takes over the waterfront in downtown Minneapolis. The bridge itself is festival central, but it's grown to encompass St. Anthony Main and the park on the river's west side, with free concerts, artists from Minnesota and beyond, vendors, food, food, and more food.

**Downtown Minneapolis:** www. stonearchbridgefestival.com; mid-June; free

### Juneteenth

The day kicks off with a free community breakfast, followed by a parade with drum corps and community leaders, and then turns into something resembling the biggest family reunion you've ever seen. Theodore Wirth Park is filled with music, games, dancing, reminiscences, and the telling of shared histories as 60,000 people gather for the day. Juneteenth—June 19th—marks the day in 1865 when federal troops rode into Texas to enforce the emancipation of slaves, nearly three years after the Emancipation Proclamation. While it is primarily an African American celebration, all are welcome.

**Nordeast and Dinkytown:** 612-238-3733, www.juneteenthminnesota. org; June 19; free

## Aquatennial

This is how you know summer in Minnesota is at its peak: The Torchlight Parade winds through downtown Minneapolis, fireworks explode over the river, the River Rats perform feats of waterskiing derring-do on the Mississippi, and the Aquatennial crowns its royalty. The 75-year-old festival was long known as the 10 best days of summer. Now the fun is compacted into a third of that time, but it's still a landmark on the calendar.

**Various locations:** 612/376-7669, www.aquatennial.org; July; free

## Basilica Block Party

Party at the Catholic Church? You bet. This is one of the biggest parties of the summer. Every July, about 25,000 people pack into the area around the Basilica of St. Mary for two days of music. The good-natured crowds and party atmosphere—as well as the traffic and the music itself—spill over into the rest of downtown and even beyond. In the past, headliners have included Ziggy Marley and the Jayhawks. Buy your tickets early; they tend to sell out.

**Downtown Minneapolis:** Basilica of St. Mary, 88 17th St. N., Minneapolis, 612/317-3428, www.basilicablockparty.org; July; $50-125

## Uptown, Powderhorn, and Loring Park Art Fairs

Art lovers in the Twin Cities once faced a problem: art-fair fatigue. The **Uptown Art Fair** (Lake St. and Hennepin Ave., 612/823-4581, www.uptownartfair.com), by far the biggest of the summer, had its considerable charms. And they wanted to enjoy the edgier **Loring Park Art Fair** (Loring Park, 612/203-9911, www.loringparkartfestival.com) and the small, community-oriented **Powderhorn Art Fair** (Powderhorn Park, 612/722-4817, www.powderhornartfair.org). But three art-fair weekends in one summer was enough to put them off the experience of wandering from one pottery-filled booth to the next. The solution? Combine forces. Now all three art fairs are held the second weekend in July, although they remain separate events with separate identities. Metro Transit provides free bus service for all three art fairs. And art lovers can sate themselves on paintings, photographs, sculptures, and more, while cherry-picking the best of the musical offerings (probably Uptown) and food (definitely Loring Park).

**Various locations:** second weekend in July; free

## Dragon Festival

St. Paul's Phalen Regional Park is a beautiful backdrop for this annual pan-Asian celebration, which began in 1996 and now attracts more than 10,000 visitors. The highlight of the two-day Dragon Festival is the dragon boat races. Two dozen 20-person teams—many of which have never paddled a dragon boat before—race the long, skinny boats across the lake. Each boat is 40 feet long and just 4 feet wide and glides swiftly across the water, as dragon boats have done for two and a half millennia. The entire festival is free and includes Japanese *taiko* drumming, dragon dancing, martial arts, and plenty of children's activities.

**Greater Twin Cities:** Phalen Regional Park, St. Paul, www.dragonfestival.org; mid-July; free

## Minnesota Fringe Festival

The Minnesota Fringe Festival is among the largest of its kind in the nation. More than 150 productions in 14 locations go on during the 11-day festival. Up to 50,000 tickets sell each year. You'll find comedy, drama, and the truly uncategorizable, but keep in mind that this is potluck: Productions are chosen by lottery rather than jury, so to say you'll find some gems and some duds is a wild understatement. Die-hard Fringe fans hit dozens of shows, so don't be surprised if everybody waiting in line seems to know each other already. In recent years, a limited number of shows for kids and teens have been added.

**Various locations:** www.fringefestival. org; late July-early Aug.; $10-15

## ✪ Minnesota State Fair

If you are anywhere near St. Paul during the 12 days leading up to Labor Day, the Minnesota State Fair is not to be missed. The 320-acre fairgrounds becomes the third-largest city in Minnesota, with more than 100,000 visitors each day. What began as an agricultural fair in 1855 has evolved to include more than 100 musical acts, a massive midway, butter carving, daily marching band parades (at 2pm), and nightly fireworks (around 10pm). Fuel up with a gut-bedeviling array of foods, including more than 60 served on a stick.

With all that going on and only 9,000 parking spaces at the fair itself, driving and parking in the northwest corner of St. Paul is pretty tight. You're better off using one of the dozens of park-and-ride lots around the Twin Cities (many are free, and buses operate daily 8am-10pm). Call 651/603-6808 after August 1 for park-and-ride information.

In Minnesota, you know summer

Minnesota State Fair

is over when you have eaten your last deep-fried cheese curd.

**Como and St. Anthony:** State Fairgrounds, 1265 Snelling Ave. N., St. Paul, 651/288-4400, www.mnstatefair.org; late Aug.-early Sept. daily 6am-midnight, gate closes at 10pm; $14 adults, $12 seniors and children 5-12, children under 5 free

# FALL

## Minnesota Renaissance Festival

For a half dozen weekends a year, a medieval village emerges in the southern suburb of Shakopee. Minstrels and maidens wander the streets. Jugglers, clowns, and fire-eaters perform. Potters, jewelers, and tailors hawk their wares. Giant turkey legs and funnel cake are consumed. In fact, a lot of turkey legs are consumed: This is the largest Renaissance festival in the United States, and it attracts about 275,000 people every year. And, as medieval villages go, this is a pretty big one, with 275 craft booths, 120 food sellers, and about 700 costumed entertainers wandering around, most of them remarkably faithful to the festival's demands for period dress and staying in character. Watch for themed weekends each year celebrating Irish, Scottish, and Italian heritage, and more. The Minnesota Renaissance Festival is also open on Labor Day itself.

**Greater Twin Cities:** 12364 Chestnut Blvd., Shakopee, 952/445-7361, www. renaissancefest.com; late Aug.-Sept. Sat.-Sun. 9am-7pm, Labor Day 9am-7pm; $24.95 adults, $22.95 seniors, $15.95 children

## Medtronic Twin Cities Marathon

The Twin Cities Marathon has been called "the most beautiful urban marathon in America"—albeit by the organizers, who have a considerable stake in the matter. But there's undoubtedly something to the claim. The course starts on the eastern side downtown Minneapolis and then winds its way around four lakes in South Minneapolis before heading back north along the Mississippi to St. Paul, where it ends at the State Capitol. The flat and shady course attracts top runners from all over the world and is an Olympic qualifying race. Every year the race is booked to its full capacity of 10,500 runners, and a quarter million spectators cheer them on. Family events and 1-mile, 10-mile, and 5K races are also held. Out-of-towners shouldn't worry about the weather: Minnesota is beautiful in October, with highs in the mid-60s. Perfect for running. Or watching.

**Various locations:** www.tcmevents.org; Oct.; free

## Twin Cities Book Festival

For one day in October, 6,000 writers, publishers and booklovers take over the Minnesota State Fair Grounds (well, a couple of large exhibit halls, anyway). Shop, schmooze, attend readings and talks, get your stack of new books signed and generally revel in the company of others who love the printed page. Bring the kids for special story hours.

**Como and St. Anthony:** http://www. raintaxi.com/twin-cities-book-festival; Oct.; free

# RECREATION

Far from the 80-hour workweeks and hour-long commutes of the coasts, Twin Citians often find themselves with some time on their hands—but they are rarely at a loss as to what to do with it.

Grand Rounds National Scenic Byway

It may be an "idle hands do the devil's work" philosophy handed down subconsciously from the cities' largely German and Scandinavian ancestry. It may be an appreciation for nature that comes from being a generation or two off the farm. It may just be there's so darned much to do out here. For whatever reason, this is a population that rarely sits still. Minneapolis is frequently rated among the best cities to live for those who love outdoor activities.

Both cities make it easy to get outside, hit the water, find solitude in the woods, breathe clean air, and get pleasantly sweaty—without ever leaving the city itself. Each—but Minneapolis in particular—is known for having some of the best park systems in the country, with more per capita parkland than nearly anywhere else. And the region is rife with opportunities for water activities from swimming to kayaking and sailing, field games from horseshoes to golf, and trails for walking, biking, and more. Outdoor pursuits barely slow in the winter. Locals switch out their inline skates for cross-country skis and canoes for ice fishing houses.

## HIGHLIGHTS

✪ **THE WINNINGEST MINNESOTA SPORTS TEAM: Minnesota Lynx** fans are a proud, enthusiastic bunch—and they have good reason to be (page 152).

✪ **BEST OUTDOOR ACTIVITY:** Rent or borrow a bike and hit the **Grand Rounds National Scenic Byway**—the only urban national scenic byway (page 154).

✪ **THE CLOSEST YOU CAN GET TO THE MISSISSIPPI RIVER:** Rent a kayak with **Mississippi River Paddle Share** and make your way down the great body of water (page 156).

✪ **THE MOST FUN YOU'LL EVER HAVE AT A GAME, WHETHER YOU LIKE SPORTS OR NOT:** While the **St. Paul Saints** are pretty good, a game at CHS Field is all about the experience (page 160).

✪ **THE MOST MINNESOTAN THING YOU COULD EVER DO:** See the **Minnesota Wild** fly across the ice at the Xcel Energy Center (page 161).

kayaking via Mississippi River Paddle Share

## PARKS

### Central Mississippi Riverfront Regional Park

Locals may not know it, but one single name encompasses all of their favorite parks along the Mississippi River in downtown Minneapolis. This complex of urban parkland includes wooded pockets where you can ramble down to the river's edge, grassy fields, an interpretive walk, and the **Stone Arch Bridge** itself, where you can stand over the roaring St. Anthony Falls.

A hidden gem, **Water Power Park** is as close as you can possibly get to St. Anthony Falls: Standing on the viewing platform, you can sometimes feel the spray from one of the best natural sources of water power in the nation.

One of the country's first hydroelectric plants was built here on Hennepin Island more than 120 years ago, and to this day Xcel Energy operates a plant on the island that powers downtown Minneapolis. Water Power Park, with walking paths and interpretive signs, is owned by Xcel Energy and is open to the public as a provision of its license to operate here. You can enjoy a stroll and a picnic in the park on your own, but for a tour of the plant, call 800/895-4999.

Just a short stroll away is **Father Hennepin Bluffs Park,** where a wooden staircase leads deep into the river gorge. Within a few steps, you feel like you've left the city.

**Hennepin Island,** which is no longer a true island, is a popular spot

Loring Park

# LIFE ON TWO WHEELS

The Twin Cities have a well-deserved reputation for a vibrant cycling culture and a strong infrastructure for two-wheeled transportation. St. Paul maintains 101 miles of paved off-street trails, 24 miles of dirt trails, and 30 miles of dedicated bike lanes. Minneapolis has 81 miles of on-street bikeways and 85 miles of off-street bikeways.

According to the U.S. Census Bureau, of major cities, Minneapolis has the second-highest percentage of bike commuters: 4.6 percent. The Minneapolis Department of Public Works estimates that city bike lanes and trails see about 10,000 cyclists a day—and, yes, while some park their bikes for the winter, many more bike year-round. One thing that makes all this biking possible is that all Metro Transit buses have two bike racks in front available for use for no extra charge. On the light rail, cyclists can walk their bikes onto the trains and stand with them or hang them in designated areas.

biking on Stone Arch Bridge

Downloadable maps of bike paths are available for Minneapolis (www.minneapolismn.gov/bicycles) and St. Paul (www.ci.stpaul.mn.us). The Metropolitan Council has region-wide maps at www.metrotransit.org.

**Nice Ride** (877/551-6423, www.niceridemn.org) is a popular self-service, short-term bike rental service with 400 stations throughout the Twin Cities. Find a rack of bright green bikes (and some are now dock-less), swipe your credit card or use the app, take a bike, and return it to any other Nice Ride rack in the Twin Cities. You can get a subscription ($6 for 24 hours, $30 for 30 days, $75 a year), and you may need to pay trip fees (all of which can be taken care of right at the rack or on the app. It's a fantastic service for people who would rather get across town on their own power than by bus (which is what the locals use it for), but it's not so economical for a leisurely ride around the lakes. The only drawback: Helmets are not available. They're not required by law in Minnesota, but they are a darn good idea.

for weddings and outdoor concerts and movies in the summer. Boats launch from **Boom Island** (also connected to the mainland), which has a good playground. During a stroll of an hour or so, making a loop using the Stone Arch Bridge and the Hennepin Avenue Bridge (or, for a longer walk, the Lowry Avenue Bridge), you'll witness Minneapolis's past and present and see a remarkably varied urban landscape.

**MAP 1:** 204 Main St. SE, Minneapolis, 612/230-6400, www.minneapolisparks.org; daily 6am-10pm

## Gold Medal Park

A spiral pathway ascends a 32-foot grass-covered mound in the center of Gold Medal Park, which takes its name from a brand of flour once milled right here in the former mills district. From there, you get terrific views of the bridges across the Mississippi River, St. Anthony Falls, and downtown Minneapolis. The eight-acre park, created in 2007, is a popular lunch spot for office workers in the area and a welcome spot of green in downtown. The small plaza with 13 pillars next to the park commemorates the

## TARGET FIELD TOURS

In its first season in 2010, Target Field caught the eye of a ballpark-loving nation. *ESPN The Magazine* named it the country's best, and local fans made nearly every game a sellout. Tickets are easier to get these days, depending on how the Twins are doing. A behind-the-scenes tour, 90 minutes long, is available on most days April-December, although times vary based on game times. Check the schedule and buy tickets ($17 adults, $14 seniors, $12 students, $8 children 6-12, free for children under 5) at www.twinsbaseball.com or call 612/659-3875. Pregame tours are also available ($40), allowing guests to watch Twins staff prepare the field and stadium for the game.

13 people who died when the I-35W bridge across the Mississippi collapsed on August 1, 2007.

MAP 1: 2nd St. S. and 11th Ave. S., Minneapolis; daily 6am-10pm

### Loring Park

In the 1980s and '90s, Loring Park was the place suburban parents warned their kids against when they came into Minneapolis to see a show. Today it's a great place to recommend to visitors for a stroll around the lake, a game of shuffleboard or horseshoes, a moment to relax in the gardens, or some off-leash fun with their dogs. Loring Park, created in 1883 and named after one of the architects of Minneapolis's public park movement, is among the city's oldest parks. A footbridge connects it to the Walker Art Center and Sculpture Garden, and the Loring Greenway connects it to Nicollet Mall. On Monday nights in the summer, come for a concert and an outdoor movie at dusk.

MAP 1: 1382 Willow St. S., Minneapolis, www.minneapolisparks.org; daily 6am-10pm

### Mill Ruins Park

At the base of Stone Arch Bridge, on the banks of the Mississippi River, you can see several layers of Minneapolis history exposed. Archaeologists have been digging here since the 1980s, when several road construction projects were underway. When they found railway footings and extensive traces of the water-power and milling systems, they decided to preserve them for the public to explore. Today, interpretive signs lead from the wooden-plank section of West River Parkway down to the river and around catwalks that bring you close to the remains of the old mills.

MAP 1: 102 Portland Ave. S., Minneapolis, www.minneapolisparks.org; daily 6am-10pm

# BICYCLING
## TRAILS

Downtown Minneapolis is the hub for a system of "bike highways" popular with commuters and weekend pleasure riders alike. The **Cedar Lake Trail** heads southwest and connects, via the **Kenilworth Trail,** to the east-west **Midtown Greenway** as well as to the **Chain of Lakes.** The downtown portion of the **Grand Rounds National Scenic Byway** hugs the river, sharing West River Drive with

Mill Ruins Park

the cars (buckle up for some hills). And the Hiawatha LRT Trail heads southeast to hook up with the **Fort Snelling Trail.** In short, if you're coming into or out of downtown by bike, it's easy to do so from the south (not so easy from the underserved north, unless you're comfortable sharing the road).

## BIKE TOURS
### The Fit Tourist
The best way to see downtown Minneapolis is under your own power. The Fit Tourist leads 2- to 3-hour biking tours following three itineraries, including bike and helmet rental. They weave along the river and through downtown. If you'd like to end your bike rides with a cold beer, that's an option, too. Reserve online.

MAP 1; bike tours start from 125 Main St. SE, 952/888-9200, www.thefittourist.com; $50 per person

## WALKING TRAILS
### St. Anthony Falls Heritage Trail
Plenty of history is crammed into this 1.8-mile loop, which crosses the river at the Stone Arch and Hennepin Avenue Bridges and follows its banks along West River Parkway and Main Street. Be sure to leave ample time in your stroll to read about the geology and history of the area on the many interpretive signs. On the western end of the Hennepin Avenue Bridge, be sure to stop under the bridge in First Bridge Park and see some of the archaeological remains of the first bridge ever to cross the Mississippi.

MAP 1: Main St. SE, Minneapolis, 612/341-7552, www.mnhs.org/places/safhb

## SPECTATOR SPORTS
### BASEBALL
#### Minnesota Twins
The Minnesota Twins play at Target Field, on the west side of downtown Minneapolis. It features a beautiful downtown view, connections to bus and rail transit, and occasionally competitive baseball from the hometown team. Among the Twins' highlights are a pair of World Series wins in 1987 and 1991, spearheaded by local heroes Kirby Puckett, Kent Hrbek, Frank Viola, and Jack Morris, but more recent highlights are harder to find. The neighborhood features plenty of happy hour locales, and if you hold on until you get inside, you'll find a curated collection of locavore and standard ballpark fare, including local draft beers like Surly and Fulton. An afternoon in the outfield will set you back $11-13, with better seats topping out around $58, but it is a fine way to spend a summer day.

MAP 1: Target Field, 351-413 5th Ave. N., Minneapolis, 800/338-9467, www. minnesota.twins.mlb.com; tickets $11-58

The Minnesota Twins play at Target Field.

## FOOTBALL
### Minnesota Vikings

The Minnesota Vikings' U.S. Bank Stadium opened on the east side of downtown Minneapolis for the 2016 season. The hordes in Helga Hats (purple hats, white horns, yellow braids) holler for gridiron greatness. You can also take in a downtown view and check out the game-day goings-on at the Commons Park in front of the stadium and the Longhouse, a free, public

U.S. Bank Stadium is home to the Vikings

event space attached to the stadium. The Vikings' famed Purple People Eater defenses, anchored in the 1970s by retired Minnesota Supreme Court Justice Alan Page, are gone, as are trips to the Super Bowl (Minnesota has lost four of them). Minnesotans remain committed fans of the team and arch-enemies of neighboring Wisconsin's Green Bay Packers. Fans regularly spend up to $135 for tickets (the cheap seats can rarely be had for $25 but that's more luck than anything), with another $20-plus thrown in for parking—and that's before anyone decides to eat anything or buy a souvenir Helga Hat. The stadium is easily accessible by train if you want to park and ride.

**MAP 1:** U.S. Bank Stadium, 900 S. 5th St., Minneapolis 612/338-4537, www.vikings. com; tickets $25-135

## BASKETBALL
### ✪ Minnesota Lynx

During the NBA off-season, there are still plenty of chances to watch basketball at the Target Center. The Minnesota Lynx, the WNBA franchise attached to the Minnesota Timberwolves, play 34 games (17 at home) during the regular season, which runs May-August. The Lynx are Minnesota's most successful sports franchise and won the WNBA championship in 2011, 2013, 2015, and 2017. They are always competitive and feature a host of Olympians and All Stars. Games are affordable, fun, and a welcome option for mothers and fathers to show their kids that professional athletes aren't all men. Tickets are easy to come by: The crowd averages about 9,300 a game, about half of the arena's capacity.

**MAP 1:** Target Center, 600 1st Ave. N., Minneapolis, 612/673-8400, http://lynx. wnba.com; tickets $10-65

### Minnesota Timberwolves

Professional basketball returned to Minnesota in 1987—the Minneapolis Lakers having long ago become the oddly named Los Angeles Lakers. The Minnesota Timberwolves call Minneapolis's Target Center home, and from the rafters hangs a single division title (2004). From 1995 to 2007, the Timberwolves were synonymous with Kevin Garnett. The team peaked in 2004, losing in the conference finals. Garnett took home the league MVP and eventually left for Boston. He returned in 2014, mostly to retire. After more than a decade, the team finally returned to the playoffs in 2018. They can be both exciting and frustrating to watch. When the Wolves play one of the league's marquee teams, the Target Center sells out. Otherwise, tickets are not too hard to find. A few hours at the Target Center (on the west side of downtown Minneapolis) could be a nice way to cap off an evening downtown or begin the night before heading to the nearby bars and clubs.

**MAP 1:** Target Center, 600 1st Ave. N., Minneapolis, 612/673-1600, www.nba.com/timberwolves; tickets average $37 but range $9-250

# South Minneapolis                      Map 2

## PARKS

### Lyndale Park

Lyndale Park slopes gently down to the parkway circling Lake Harriet and contains several delightful gardens in its 60 acres. A favorite is the **Lyndale Park Rose Garden,** designed in 1907 by Theodore Wirth, an early and influential Minneapolis parks superintendent. Rose lovers can see 100 varieties of plants laid out in neat rows (sadly encircled by chain-link fencing). The best time to see the roses in bloom is mid-June through early September. The **Peace Garden** was created through the efforts of dedicated neighbors and combines some elements of a traditional Japanese garden and a formal rock garden. Two large stones in the garden were brought in from the cities of Nagasaki and Hiroshima, Japan.

**MAP 2:** 1300 42nd St. W., Minneapolis, 612/230-6400, www.minneapolisparks.org; daily 6am-10pm

### Minnehaha Falls

The 53-foot waterfall that inspired Henry Wadsworth Longfellow to write *The Song of Hiawatha* is the main attraction at this popular park, but there is so much else to do.

Wander the gardens in the upper park or take a slightly more strenuous hike through the wild lower park.

**Rent a bike** (Wheel Fun Rentals, 612/729-2660, www.wheelfunrentals.com, mid-May-Labor Day Mon.-Fri. 10am-9pm, Sat.-Sun. 9am-9pm; May, Sept., and Oct. weekends only; two-person surrey $26/hour, four-person surrey $36/hour, single-person recumbent bike $13/hour). Visit the historic **Princess Depot,** a small transport museum (4900 Minnehaha Park Dr. S., 612/230-6400, Memorial Day-Labor Day Sun. 1:30pm-5:30pm, free); the **John H. Stevens House** (4901 Minnehaha Park Dr. S., 612/722-2220, Memorial Day-mid-Sept., Sun. noon-4pm), the first wood-frame house built west of the Mississippi; or the replica of **Longfellow's home** (4800 Minnehaha Park Dr. S., 612/230-6540, Memorial Day-Labor Day Sat.-Sun. 10am-8pm), where you can learn about the history of Minneapolis's park system. Other park features include a disc golf course, a wading pool, and fish tacos at **Sea Salt.**

**MAP 2:** 4801 Minnehaha Park Dr. S., Minneapolis, 612/230-6400, www.minneapolisparks.org; daily 6am-10pm; rental costs vary; park admittance free

## FRISBEE GOLF

Frisbee of all sorts, from ultimate to disc golf, is well established in the Twin Cities. In fact, there are more than two dozen disc golf courses in the greater metro area. The best-known course, which is among the most highly rated in the Twin Cities, is in **Kaposia Park** (1028 Wilde Ave., South St. Paul, www.southstpaul.org), a beautiful park in its own right. 'Bee enthusiasts like the well-marked holes, which start in an open field and then wind through the woods. In the west metro area, **Bryant Lake Park's course** (6800 Rowland Rd., Eden Prairie, 763/694-7764, www.threeriversparks.org) is also highly regarded. Maintained by the Three Rivers Park District, it is groomed to a degree that will surprise DIY disc golfers, with wood chip "greens" around the baskets. A day pass costs $5, available online or by calling the park. Discs are available for rent.

# BICYCLING

## TRAILS

### ✪ Grand Rounds National Scenic Byway

One of the most beautiful and accessible rides—and a good way to see Minneapolis's leafy, green residential neighborhoods—is the Grand Rounds National Scenic Byway, a 50-mile ring of interconnected bike trails. It loops around the outer edges of the city, taking in Theodore Wirth Park, the Chain of Lakes in southwest Minneapolis, about 10 miles of riverfront on the Mississippi, downtown Minneapolis, and the parkways of North Minneapolis. The Grand Rounds, the only urban trail system designated as a National Scenic Byway, was part of the original vision for the Minneapolis Park System. That route has always had a 3-mile "hole" in it, north of I-94 and east of the Mississippi River. In 2008, the Minneapolis Park Board approved plans to acquire the rights-of-way to complete the circle, though it may be years before the funding and road improvements necessary are in place.

**MAP 2:** start at Minnehaha Park, Minneapolis, 612/230-6400, www.minneapolisparks.org

## Midtown Greenway

The Midtown Greenway, beloved by commuters, families, and recreational cyclists alike, crosses South Minneapolis from the lakes to the Mississippi River along a rail corridor (running alongside active rail lines in one stretch). Planners hope that the greenway will eventually cross the river, connecting cyclists to St. Paul. The easy, almost entirely flat 5.5-mile ride runs parallel to busy Lake Street, with plenty of opportunities to stop for a bite or a drink. One particularly recommended stop is the **Midtown Global Market.** There are about two dozen access points along the trail, many right at street level, and the path crosses the light rail line, making it a fun, car-free way to get into downtown Minneapolis. The western end of the greenway hooks up to the South Loop of the **Cedar Lake Trail,** if you want to extend your ride.

**MAP 2:** trail runs from Chowen Ave. to West River Pkwy., South Minneapolis, www.midtowngreenway.org

Grand Rounds National Scenic Byway

Wheel Fun Rentals

## BIKE SHOPS AND RENTALS
### Freewheel Midtown Bike Center
Right on the Midtown Greenway, which is a convenient place to start for just about any Twin Cities ride, Freewheel will set you up with a rental for $45 a day ($99 for high-end bikes), with some hourly rates available. But this is so much more than a rental shop. In addition to a full line of bikes and accessories available for sale, Freewheel does repairs, provides public shop space for a small fee if you want to do your own repairs, holds classes, rents bike lockers, and offers public showers for commuters. There's also a small café, all built directly into the hill right at the greenway level.

MAP 2: 2834 10th Ave. S., Minneapolis, 612/238-4447, www.freewheelbike.com; Mon.-Fri. 8am-8pm, Sat.-Sun. 9am-5pm

## WATER ACTIVITIES
### Lake Harriet Yacht Club
The Lake Harriet Yacht Club, based in the small sailing pavilion on the north side of the lake, organizes regattas and offers specialized clinics for new racers, women, and people who want more safety instruction. Also based in the sailing pavilion, the **Minneapolis Park Board** (www.minneapolisparks.org) offers multi-session classes for children and adults in the summer. Schedules are available at the website. The **Twin Cities Sailing Club** offers members access to a fleet of boats and informal instruction on Tuesday and Saturday mornings throughout the summer. While membership in the club is limited, those mornings are definitely the time to be hanging around the sailing pavilion if you're interested in getting to know the Twin Cities boating scene or picking up some tips.

MAP 2: Lake Harriet, Minneapolis, 612/920-9420, www.lhycsailing.com; costs vary for classes

### Wheel Fun Rentals
**Bde Maka Ska,** the largest of the four lakes in the Chain of Lakes at 3.2 miles around, is connected by a picturesque channel to Lake of the Isles, which is connected to Cedar Lake. You could spend an hour or half a day paddling and exploring Lake of the Isles, Bde Maka Ska, and Lake Harriet in a kayak, double kayak, paddleboat, stand-up paddleboard, or canoe from the Wheel Fun Rentals franchise on Bde Maka Ska. Keep in mind that while Lake of the Isles does, indeed, have two islands, they are both protected, and you are not allowed to land there. A separate Wheel Fun franchise (612/823-9226, early June-Labor Day Mon.-Fri. 10am-9pm, Sat.-Sun. 9am-9pm) is located on the north side of Lake Harriet, which is not connected by water to the other three lakes. The same equipment is available to rent.

MAP 2: 3000 Calhoun Pkwy. E., Minneapolis, 612/823-5765, www.wheelfunrentals.com; May Mon.-Fri. noon-7pm, Sat.-Sun. 10am-7pm; Memorial Day-Labor Day Mon.-Fri. 9am-9pm, Sat.-Sun. 8am-9pm; Sept.-mid-Oct. Mon.-Fri. 2pm-7pm, Sat. -Sun. 11am-7pm; bikes $12/hour, canoes and kayaks $14-22/hour

## U.S. POND HOCKEY CHAMPIONSHIPS

There's a difference between the hard-checking, high-stakes hockey of the NFL and hockey as nature intended it: outside, on any frozen body of water, with kids skating their hearts out in the freezing cold before the winter sun disappears.

That is the hockey celebrated at the U.S. Pond Hockey Championships (www. uspondhockey.com). Conceived by a couple of grown-up kids who had skated their hearts out on Minnesota's frozen lakes and ponds, the first tournament, in 2006, attracted 120 teams from across the country. It was an instant success: *Sports Illustrated*, ESPN, and even *Jeopardy!* have all taken notice.

The three-day tournament has grown to more than 200 games and moved from its original location on Bde Maka Ska to Lake Nokomis in South Minneapolis, where volunteers groom as many as 25 rinks.

## WINTER SPORTS

### ICE SKATING
#### Lake of the Isles

One of the most beautiful spots to skate in the Twin Cities is on Lake of the Isles. Minneapolis Parks maintains two separate rinks for figure skating and for hockey right out on the lake, along with a warming house. As you whoosh around the rink, you can enjoy the open sky, the quiet pace of traffic around the parkway, and the twinkling lights from the stately homes that ring the lake. Before you venture out, however, call the hotline to learn about ice conditions. Some loaner skates are available for free, but to be sure you get your size it's better to bring your own.

**MAP 2:** 2500 Lake of the Isles Pkwy. E., Minneapolis, ice hotline 612/313-7708; Dec. 15-Feb. 15 daily 6am-10pm; free

# Nordeast and Dinkytown   Map 3

TOP EXPERIENCE

## WATER ACTIVITIES

### ✪ Mississippi River Paddle Share

Perhaps the best way to experience the Mississippi River is by kayak, which is easy to do with a little planning: Paddle Share is a relatively new self-service that allows you to rent kayaks, paddles, and life jackets and cruise the Mississippi from six different starting spots, then drop your equipment in a designated custom-built kayak locker. A couple of convenient put-in spots are located on the Nordeast side of the Lowry Avenue Bridge and across the river further north at the North Mississippi Regional Park. Paired with Uber or Lyft, you've got a nice half-day activity with very little stress. Single and double kayaks are available and should be booked online at www. paddleshare.org.

**MAP 3:** 612/293-8436, www.paddleshare. org; $25-40

### Paradise Charter Cruises

The *Minneapolis Queen*, a retro paddleboat, leaves from Bohemian Flats Park, on the west side of the river, just south of St. Anthony Falls. The comfortable ship holds about 125 people, and the narrated cruise covers the natural and human history south of the falls. (Mississippi cruises no longer pass through the St. Anthony

kayaking on the Mississippi River

Falls lock, which has been permanently closed to prevent the spread of Asian carp.) Evening cruises include cocktails or dinner. Reservations are recommended for all tours and are required for dinner and brunch cruises. **MAP 3:** Bohemian Flats Park, 2150 West River Pkwy., Minneapolis, 952/474-8058, www.twincitiescruises.com; Mother's Day-Oct. Sun. brunch cruise 11am, other tours daily at noon, 2pm, 6pm, and 6:30pm, depending on the season; $18-48

# SPECTATOR SPORTS

## FOOTBALL
### Golden Gophers Football Team

The University of Minnesota Golden Gophers have not done much on the field to match the architectural glory of their 2009 on-campus horseshoe stadium, TCF Bank Stadium. The program hasn't won a conference championship since 1967 and, even though there are lovely downtown views and a letter-jacketed collegiate setting, if you want to see good college football, it is usually played by the visiting stalwarts of the Big 10 conference. The days of Bronko Nagurski are long gone, but fierce rivalries for Floyd of Rosedale

(the pig statue trophy awarded to the winner of the Minnesota-Iowa game) and for Paul Bunyan's Axe (awarded to the winner of the Minnesota-Wisconsin game) continue. The Battle of the Little Brown Jug (Minnesota-Michigan) has only gone to the Gophers three times since 1978. The hilarious trophies bespeak a fun, if collegiately drunken, afternoon. **MAP 3:** TCF Bank Stadium, 420 23rd Ave. SE, Minneapolis, 612/624-8080, www.mygophersports.com; tickets $40-149, plus package options

## BASKETBALL
### Golden Gophers
### Basketball Teams

The University of Minnesota Golden Gophers, men and women, provide an opportunity for the sports enthusiast to don maroon and gold and enjoy Big Ten basketball and the occasional run in March Madness (the women reached the Final Four in 2004). The teams play in Williams Arena (a.k.a. the Barn), located on the East Bank of the university, with its unique raised-floor architecture. Basketball is not a strong suit for either men or women, but 2004's Lindsay Whalen has now retired from the WNBA's Lynx to take the reins of the women's program, and at both games you can shout "ski-u-mah"—the Gopher's cheer—to your heart's content. **MAP 3:** Williams Arena, 1925 University Ave. SE, Minneapolis, 612/624-8080, www.gophersports.com; tickets for men's team $20-65; tickets for women's team $6-15

## HOCKEY
### Golden Gophers Hockey Teams

Mariucci Arena at the University of Minnesota, the only hockey facility to make *Sports Illustrated*'s list of top campus sporting venues, is home to top-shelf men's collegiate hockey.

Just across the street, the women's team plays in Ridder Arena, the first facility nationwide exclusively dedicated to women's hockey. The Golden Gophers are perpetual contenders, the men having brought home back-to-back trophies from the Frozen Four in 2002 and 2003, and the women doing the same in 2004, 2005, 2012, 2013, 2015, and 2016. Both teams feature, nearly exclusively, talent from the state of Minnesota, which instills an even greater sense of pride in the already rabid college hockey fan. The women's tickets are more affordable (topping out at $8 compared with $35), but the games are no less entertaining. Getting to a men's game requires more planning and a higher tolerance for alcohol-fueled spectators.

**MAP 3:** Mariucci Arena, 1901 4th St. SE, Minneapolis, 612/624-8080, www. gophersports.com; tickets for men's team $30-70; tickets for women's team $8

# Downtown St. Paul and West Side

## Map 4

## PARKS

### Harriet Island Regional Park

While the channel of the Mississippi River separating Harriet Island from the bank filled in long ago, the park retains the name. A stage and a wide-open lawn host public events, but even when there's nothing in particular going on, this is a popular place to stroll along the riverbank and boardwalk, looking up at the skyline of downtown St. Paul. The **Clarence W. Wigington Pavilion,** the beautiful limestone building combining art deco and classic elements at the center of the park, was designed by the nation's first African American municipal architect. Wigington (1883-1967) was a senior designer for the city of St. Paul for 34 years, and 60 of his buildings are extant today. Harriet Island is also the place to board **Padelford Cruises.**

The gathering area surrounded by flagpoles you see is known as the American Veterans Memorial-Plaza de Honor, dedicated in 2012. It honors all veterans, and particularly the Latino American vets from St. Paul's West Side (also called District del Sol).

**MAP 4:** Harriet Island, 200 Doctor Justus Ohage Blvd., St. Paul, www.stpaul.gov/harrietisland; Mon.-Thurs. 7am-10pm, Fri.-Sun. 9am-midnight; free

### Mears Park

Lowertown's quiet oasis is every office worker's favorite secret lunch spot, as well as a weekend gathering place for concerts, fairs, and other events. Instead of open fields and meadows, Mears Park is planted closely with birches and other native trees, making it feel like a patch of forest even bigger than its actual single-block size. Unique among Twin Cities parks, a manufactured stream burbles through the park, inviting little (and not so little) feet to splash.

**MAP 4:** 6th St.and Wacouta St., St. Paul; free

## BICYCLING

### TRAILS

Downtown St. Paul is a terrific place to kick off a bike ride along

bike trail

the Mississippi River. The **Sam Morgan Regional Trail** runs along the river's western side, which connects to the bike path on East River Road through Crosby Farm and Hidden Falls regional parks. (Stay with me: There's a big C curve in the river here, so St. Paul's west side of the river is the east side farther upstream in Minneapolis.) And the **Big Rivers Regional Trail** runs along the eastern side to the Mendota Bridge and Fort Snelling. Or head north on the **Vento Regional Trail** for a spin around Lake Phalen.

## Gateway State Trail

St. Paul's beloved rail-to-trail venture is the Gateway State Trail, which connects to Stillwater. The 18-mile ride starts 1 mile north of the Minnesota State Capitol. There is street parking at this location, as well as several lots along the trail. You can pick up a Nice Ride bike rental on Cayuga Street, right by the trail. Your ride passes through urban, suburban, then rural landscapes, rolling through the northeastern suburbs of Maplewood, North St. Paul, and Oakdale, ending at the eastern trailhead in Pine Point Regional Park. A horse path runs parallel to a 10-mile section of the trail, which follows the old Soo rail line. A nice stopping point for those who don't want to make the whole 36-mile round-trip is at **Lake Phalen Regional Park,** which has a pretty trail network of its own. Although the narrow paved trail can get crowded, riding through the woods feels like an instant escape from the city.

**MAP 4:** start at Cayuga Park, St. Paul, www.dnr.state.mn.us/state_trails/gateway

# WATER ACTIVITIES
## Padelford Cruises

Three large boats depart from Harriet Island in downtown St. Paul almost daily throughout the summer. Ride inside the cabin or on the open upper deck as the boat slips down the river under the St. Paul High Bridge, past the caves where St. Paul began, and beneath Fort Snelling. Tour guides share historical and geographical tidbits the whole way. The high bluffs of the river in this area are a beautiful sight no matter what the season, but especially during September and October, when Padelford runs longer fall-color cruises. Watch for other special cruises on the schedule, including Sunday brunch cruises, Mother's Day and Father's Day excursions, and more. On particularly busy days, the *Betsey Northrup,* a converted barge, is hooked up behind the riverboat *Anson Northrup,* and the two together carry more than 700 passengers.

**MAP 4:** 205 Doctor Justus Ohage Blvd., St. Paul, 651/227-1100, www.riverrides. com; June-Aug. Mon. departures at noon, 2:30pm, and 6pm, Tues.-Sat. departures at noon and 2:30pm, Sun. departures at noon, 1pm, and 2:30pm; $18 adults, $16 seniors, $10 children

**TOP** EXPERIENCE

# A LIFE ON SKATES

In hockey-mad Minnesota, skating is a way of life. The Minneapolis Park Board maintains 30 outdoor ice rinks in city parks, and St. Paul maintains 20. The temperature generally has to stay below 25°F for a week before it's possible to flood them and create a nice hard surface. Generally speaking, these are no-amenities spots: just a rink with some sideboards and overhead lights and a warming house if you're lucky. Many Minneapolis rinks also have a limited number of used skates available to borrow for free, usually in the park building near the rink. (For a list, go to www.minneapolisparks.org and search for "outdoor rinks.")

Some rinks are divided into designated areas for **hockey** and for **figure skating.** Be courteous—and safe—by staying out of the hockey players' way. Slower skaters stay to the outside of the rink. If you see teams of people out on the ice chasing a ball with sticks that look like giant Q-tips, that's **broomball.** Similar to hockey but played without pads, it's a quintessentially Minnesotan thing and a good way to get some really nice bruises to take home as a souvenir.

## WINTER SPORTS
### ICE SKATING
#### Landmark Center Rink

In downtown St. Paul, the Landmark Center Rink combines the beauty of outdoor skating with the convenience of (cheap! $4!) skate rental. There's truly a festival atmosphere, as locals and visitors enjoy skating among St. Paul's most beautiful buildings and drinking hot chocolate around a roaring fire. Skate rentals are limited and the rink does fill up, so be prepared to wait your turn.

**MAP 4:** 75 5th St. W., St. Paul, 651/749-0435, www.visitstpaul.com; late Nov.-early Feb. Mon.-Thurs. 11am-5pm, Fri.-Sat. 11am-10pm, Sun. 11am-9pm; free admission, skate rental $4

## SPECTATOR SPORTS
### BASEBALL
#### ✪ St. Paul Saints

The second-level league success of the Minneapolis Millers (who disbanded in 1960 but featured, at times, Ted Williams, Willie Mays, and Carl Yastrzemski) is still going strong with the St. Paul Saints. The Saints play at the beautiful, open, modern CHS Field in St. Paul's Lowertown. As soon as it opened in 2015, the field became a favorite

St. Paul Saints at CHS Field

destination for fans, families, and people who don't care a whit about baseball but love to spend a summer afternoon or evening surrounded by 7,000 other people in a remarkably good mood.

Owned by Mike Veeck, the son of legendary Major League Baseball showman Bill Veeck, the Saints play decent ball in the North Division and provide a tremendous amount of entertainment—from the usual (beer, sunny days) to the unusual (a mascot pig delivering game balls, children racing tires, fans in inflatable sumo suits), all the while embodying Veeck's mantra, "Fun Is Good." Tickets should be sought in advance.

**MAP 4:** CHS Field, 360 Broadway St., St. Paul, 651/644-6659, www.saintsbaseball.com and www.chsfield.com; tickets $5-17

## ROLLERGIRLS!

The sport of roller derby started in the 1930s, peaked in the 1970s, and flatlined soon thereafter. But a cohort of enthusiastic women brought it back to life in the Twin Cities in 2004 after seeing leagues in other U.S. cities. And it is alive and well today—even growing.

Nine teams compete in the all-volunteer, all-women **Minnesota Roller Girls** league in rowdy but good-natured and family-friendly bouts held at downtown St. Paul's **Roy Wilkins Auditorium** (next to the Xcel Energy Center). The track is flat (unlike the sloped tracks you may remember), the costumes and nicknames are bawdy, the music is good, and the energy is strong.

Tickets ($14-18, kids 9 and under free) are available at the Roy Wilkins box office (www.theroy.org), and more information can be found at www.mnrollergirls.com.

## HOCKEY
### ✪ Minnesota Wild

Minnesota's first NHL team was the beloved Minnesota Northstars, who hightailed it for Dallas (and became the Stars) in 1993. In 2000, the Minnesota Wild brought professional hockey back to Minnesota. The team now showcases winger Zach Parise (a Twin Cities native) and defenseman Ryan Suter (married to a Twin Cities native), who reignited fan support and are set to be here for a long time: The pair received matching 13-year $98 million contracts in the summer of 2012. While a 10-year sold-out streak was briefly interrupted in October 2010, tickets are still quite hard to come by.

The Xcel Energy Center ("The X" to locals) is also home to the boys' and girls' state high school hockey tournaments. There is hardly a better way to get a true Minnesota sports experience than to spend an evening watching teams from around the Twin Cities and from greater Minnesota duke it out for statewide supremacy for three days in March. Check out www.mhshl.org for current information.

**MAP 4:** Xcel Energy Center, 199 Kellogg Blvd. W., St. Paul, 651/602-6000, www.wild.nhl.com; tickets $28-100

## OTHER RECREATION
### Vertical Endeavors

Hard-core climbers and newbies both love Vertical Endeavors. The state-of-the-art facilities have climbing walls of all degrees of difficulty and bouldering caves with up to 60 degrees of overhang. The facilities are fastidiously maintained, friendly, and filled with climbing enthusiasts. If you're a novice climber, you're welcome as well, but you'll want to sign up in advance for one of the beginning classes. A day pass gives you access to the entire facility, including exercise equipment and showers. You can even leave, rest up, and come back for even more climbing. Equipment rental is $12. Vertical Endeavors is also in Minneapolis (2540 Nicollet Ave. S., Minneapolis, 612/436-1470, Mon.-Fri. 10am-11pm, Sat. 10am-10pm, Sun. 10am-6pm) and Bloomington (9601 James Ave. S., Bloomington, 952/881-1110, Mon.-Fri. 10am-11pm, Sat. 10am-10pm, Sun. 10am-6pm).

**MAP 4:** 845 Phalen Blvd., St. Paul, 651/776-1430, www.verticalendeavors.com; Mon.-Sat. 10am-10pm, Sun. 10am-6pm; day pass $18

# Summit-University and Mac-Groveland     Map 5

## PARKS

### Hidden Falls Park and Crosby Farm Park

These two wooded havens line the deep bend on the St. Paul side of the Mississippi for several miles and nearly connect where Highway 5 crosses the Mississippi. Nearly undeveloped except for miles of paved paths and shady picnic pavilions, both offer quiet, up-close-and-personal access to the Mississippi and its wildlife that's hard to find even in these two cities that hug the river so tightly. There is, in fact, a manufactured waterfall in Hidden Falls Park, as well as a convenient boat launch area for canoes.

**MAP 5:** 1415 Mississippi River Blvd. S., St. Paul, 651/632-5111, www.stpaul.gov; daily sunrise-10pm; free

## SOCCER

### Minnesota United FC

Minnesota United joined Major League Soccer in 2017 as the Loons, replete with scarf-waving fans chanting team songs (with lyrics nicely displayed on the in-stadium screens). Their home, Allianz Field, opened in the Midway neighborhood in St. Paul in 2019. The field offers convenient access to the light rail line. A dynamic 90 minutes of soccer, at a level consistent with American professional soccer, makes for a fun afternoon with a little international flair. Tickets are $30-189 during the February-October season.

**MAP 5:** Allianz Field, corner of University and Snelling Avenues, St. Paul, 763/476-2237, www.mnufc.com; $30-189

# Como and St. Anthony     Map 6

## PARKS

### Como Park

Como Park is the center of outdoor life in St. Paul, a beloved haven of nearly 400 varied and well-kept acres. More than 2.5 million people come every year to play tennis, soccer, baseball, football, golf, or mini golf; to swim in the outdoor pool or fish on Lake Como; or just explore the grounds, with sculptures, ponds, a waterfall, and a labyrinth. The Historic Streetcar Station (1224 Lexington Pkwy. N., Sun. noon-4pm) includes a small exhibit on the history of streetcars in the Twin Cities. Park visitors can bring picnics, use public grills, or get a Louisiana-inspired meal at Spring Cafe (1360 Lexington Pkwy. N., www.springcafestp.com). This is also where you can rent canoes and paddleboats for a ride on Lake Como and hear concerts several nights a week during the summer.

An expansive outdoor water park (1151 Wynne Ave., St. Paul, 651/489-0378, Mon.-Fri. noon-8pm, Sat.-Sun. 11am-7pm, $6 adults, $5 children) has a lazy river, a zipline over one pool, and a climbing wall rising out of the

Como Park

other (climb up, jump back down into the water). Combine your day at the park with a stop at the **Como Park Zoo and Conservatory** and **Como Town** amusement park.

MAP 6: 1199 Midway Pkwy, St. Paul, www. stpaul.gov; daily sunrise-11pm

## GOLF

### Les Bolstad University of Minnesota Golf Club

On the St. Paul campus of the University of Minnesota, this bit of University of Minnesota sports history could be described as the people's golf course. Thanks to the convenient location, low greens fees (just $25, with discounts for off-hours), and complete lack of pretension, the fairways can get pretty crowded. Opened in 1929 and home to the U of M's championship men's and women's golf teams, the course features tight fairways and rolling, shaded terrain over more than 6,000 yards. The 18-hole course has a par of 71.

MAP 6: 2275 Larpenteur Ave. W., St. Paul, 612/627-4000, http://recwell.umn.edu/golf; May-Oct. daily dawn-dusk

## WINTER SPORTS
### CROSS-COUNTRY SKIING
### Como Ski Center

The Como Ski Center in Como Park takes over the open, rolling terrain of the golf course as soon as the snow flies, with 3.5 miles of groomed classical and freestyle trails and a 1-mile loop for beginners. The beginner's loop stays lighted until 11pm. Equipment rental is available at the chalet for very reasonable fees (cross-country skis, poles, and boots for $12-15 for two hours). Group and private instruction is available for all levels, but preregistration is required. Call 651/266-6400 during business hours for trail conditions.

MAP 6: 1431 Lexington Pkwy. N., St. Paul, 651/488-9673, www.stpaul.gov; mid-Dec.-mid-Feb. Tues.-Wed. 3pm-9pm, Fri. 5pm-10pm, Sat. 8am-6pm (ski lessons only), Sun. 11am-6pm

# GET OUT YOUR SKINNY SKIS

The metro area is one of the most enthusiastic cross-country ski towns in the country. The **North Star Ski Touring Club** (www.north-stars.org) is the largest ski touring club in the United States outside of Alaska, with 800 members. And Minneapolis hosts the **City of Lakes Loppet Ski Festival** (www.loppet.org, late Jan./early Feb.), a beautiful race that attracts skiers from around the region.

If you've got your own skis with you, there are about four dozen trails right in the cities or the near suburbs, groomed and maintained by the city and state park systems. Three of the best trail networks—at **Como Park, Hyland Lake Park Preserve,** and **Theodore Wirth Park**—also rent skis. All skiers over the age of 16 on public trails (including within city, state, and regional parks) must purchase a ski pass: $6 for the day, $20 for the season, or $55 for three seasons, available online at www4.wildlifelicense.com/mn or by phone at 651/296-6157. Have your driver's license and credit card handy.

## DOWNHILL SKIING AND SNOWBOARDING
### Como Park
Como Park in St. Paul offers a very gentle downhill ski slope with a not-entirely-necessary rope tow back to the top in an easygoing family atmosphere. There are no show-offs swooshing down the slopes at Como, but there are plenty of kids learning to snowplow. The area has the added benefit of inexpensive equipment rental (just $12 for children and $15 for adults). Snowboards are allowed on the hill as well (snowboard equipment rental is $20). Private downhill ski and snowboard lessons are available for $25 (call ahead to schedule). Six-week group lessons at all levels are also available; preregistration is required.

**MAP 6:** 1431 Lexington Pkwy. N., St. Paul, 651/488-9673, www.stpaul.gov; mid-Dec.-mid-Feb. Tues.-Wed. 3pm-9pm, Sat. 9am-6pm, Sun. 11am-6pm; $15 adults, $12 children

# Greater Twin Cities          Map 7

## PARKS
### Theodore Wirth Park
Named for the father of the Minneapolis Park System, Theodore Wirth Park is the jewel in a very beautiful crown. By far the city's largest park at 759 acres, it's nearly as large as New York City's Central Park (843 acres). In addition to two golf courses, park visitors will find a small sandy beach for swimming on Wirth Lake and a quiet pier for boating and fishing on Birch Pond.

The real wonders of the park are things you'll find almost nowhere else: the 5-acre **Quaking Bog,** shaded by tall tamarack trees, and the 15-acre **Eloise Butler Wildflower Garden,** home to 500 plant species and 140 bird species.

Opened in 2018, the Trailhead building (1221 Theodore Wirth Pkwy., 612/355-7757, www.loppet. org; daily 7am-9pm) serves as a hub for all outdoors enthusiasts, with showers and lockers (a $20 day pass allows you to use both), a restaurant, and rentals including mountain bikes, skis, and snowshoes.

## GET OUT ON THE GREENS

The Minneapolis Park Board (www.minneapolisparks.org) maintains seven public golf courses, and the City of St. Paul (www.stpaul.gov) maintains four—which adds up to a lot of inexpensive golfing right in the city limits. The golf season in Minnesota runs a lot longer than you might expect: Avid golfers are out on the greens as soon as it's dry in the spring and have been known to putt in the snow well into November or December.

Call the winter recreation hotline (612/355-7757) for updates on trail conditions.

**MAP 7:** 1301 Theodore Wirth Pkwy., Minneapolis, 612/230-6400, www. minneapolisparks.org; daily 6am-10pm; rental costs vary; park admission free

# BICYCLING

## TRAILS

### Cedar Lake Trail

Heading west from Minneapolis, this wide paved trail is one of the most popular of the many maintained by the Three Rivers Park District. Hop on the South Loop of the trail at the Midtown Greenway, just off Lake Street in Minneapolis, and ride five miles to Hopkins, a nearby suburb. The trail also connects to the Luce Line Trail, the North Cedar Lake Regional Trail, and the Minnesota River Bluffs LRT Regional Trail.

**MAP 7:** trailhead off Lake St. W., Minneapolis, www.threeriversparks.org; free

### Luce Line Trail

For a more ambitious ride, set out on the 72-mile Luce Line Trail, which heads northwest to the small town of Cosmos, near Hutchinson. The first 9 miles of the trail, through the Minneapolis suburb of Plymouth, are paved. The remainder of the former railroad line is paved with crushed limestone for most of the way, then with a dirt surface in the last few miles. The trail is flat, owing to its past as a railroad bed and, of course, to

Minnesota's bicycle-friendly terrain. A path for horses runs alongside.

**MAP 7:** Theodore Wirth Golf Course, Minneapolis, 651/259-5841, www.luceline. com; free

## BIKE SHOPS AND RENTALS

### Gateway Cycle

If you're headed east, Gateway Cycle, right across from the entrance to the Gateway State Trail, is the place to go. It rents mountain bikes, road bikes, hybrids, tandems, recumbents, and trailers starting at $20 a day (prices go up on the weekends). Weekly and monthly rentals are also available at even lower daily rates. Gateway also sells a range of bikes and does repairs and tune-ups.

**MAP 7:** 6028 N. Hwy. 36, Oakdale, 651/777-0188, www.gatewaycycle.com; Mon.-Fri. 10am-8pm, Sat. 9am-5pm, Sun. noon-4pm

# GOLF

### Baker National Golf Course

The award-winning Baker National Golf Course, 20 miles outside of the cities proper, has been recognized by *Golf Digest* as a terrific deal. The Three Rivers Park District, which maintains the course in the heart of the Baker Park Preserve, keeps greens fees low. The bluegrass course totals nearly 7,000 yards, with a par of 72 on the 18-hole course and 30 on the 9-hole course. Practice areas, a driving range, a pro shop, snack cart, cart rental, and lessons are also available.

## CURLING

Curling is widely known as "chess on ice"—well, insofar as it's widely known as anything anywhere, and that's largely in Scotland, Canada, and Minnesota. In fact, Minnesotans regularly pack the U.S. Olympic curling team. The game looks a little odd to outsiders, but it is strangely addicting: One team member slides a large smooth stone with a handle down the lane toward a series of concentric circles, aiming to get it as close to the center as possible. Two sweepers hurry ahead of the stone, brushing the ice hard with their brooms to reduce friction and speed the stone on its way. The fourth team member, the "skip," stands down by the target (the "house"), giving directions. Rounds of play are scored like bocce: The team with the stone closest to the center gets to count toward its score all its stones that are closer than the opponents' closest stone.

St. Paul boasts the largest and one of the oldest curling clubs in the country, the **St. Paul Curling Club** (470 Selby Ave., St. Paul, 651/224-7408, www.stpaulcurlingclub.org). This storied club, founded in 1888, however, is not the right place to turn if you are a novice curler or even if you're a longtime pro looking to get some ice time. The membership rolls are so packed that there's no public ice time available, and even longtime members vie for good slots. Missing your curling night is just not done in Minnesota.

Thank goodness, then, that **Dakota Curling** (20775 Holt Ave., Lakeville, 952/479-0322, www.dakotacurling.com) is helping pick up some slack. It offers learn-to-curl classes and instructional leagues. Remember that curling is played in teams of four, so you'll want to bring some friends, along with some soft-soled, clean shoes. The club has some equipment (brooms and sliders, which fit over your shoes) to lend.

---

MAP 7: 2935 Parkview Dr., Medina, 763/694-7670, www.bakernational.com; daily 6:30am-sunset; greens fees $22-40

### Rush Creek Golf Club

In the northeastern suburb of Maple Grove, Rush Creek is the posh and pricey option (greens fees top out over $100). The clubhouse looks like the archetypal suburban golf chateau, with its gabled roofs rising above a sea of gently rolling green. Inside, the decorating style harks back to golf's Scottish origins. Even the restaurant, the Highlander, reaches for a little bit of Scottish cachet (although the menu is all-American). This 18-hole championship course with more than 7,000 yards of golf and a par of 72 has hosted three LPGA Tour events and has frequently been voted best public golf course in the Twin Cities.

MAP 7: 7801 County Rd. 101, Maple Grove, 763/494-8844, www.rushcreek.com; daily dawn-dusk weather permitting; greens fees $59-119

# WINTER SPORTS
## CROSS-COUNTRY SKIING
### Hyland Lake Park Preserve

South of Minneapolis, the Hyland Lake Park Preserve has six trails totaling 7 miles winding through beautiful wooded terrain. Skis and poles are available to rent at the visitors center. Unlit trails close at sunset. Two trails, Lake and Star, are lit 5am-sunrise and sunset-10pm daily. The Three Rivers Park District, which maintains the park, also operates seven other ski areas, with a total of 70 miles of groomed trails that see as many as 78,000 skiers annually. Minnesota Ski Passes are not required in the Three Rivers Park District system, but skiers must buy a ski pass from the park itself for $4 a day. If skiing isn't your thing, or if you want to try something new, the park also has two dedicated snowshoe trails. Snowshoes are available to rent at the Richardson Nature Center (763/694-7676) within the park.

MAP 7: 10145 Bush Lake Rd.,
Bloomington, 763/694-7687, www.
threeriversparks.org; daily in season
5am-10pm; $4

## Theodore Wirth Park

The seven-plus miles of groomed
cross-country ski trails in Theodore
Wirth Park snake throughout the
whole park, winding through the golf
course, the gardens, across the lake,
even through the Quaking Bog. They
also connect directly to trails on and
around Cedar Lake and Lake of the
Isles. Expert and practice loops near
the ski chalet are lit and have snowmaking abilities. Rentals are downright cheap at $10 for everything
you need. And you can drop in on
a Saturday or Sunday lesson (10am,
noon, 2pm, and 4pm) if you're lucky.
Preregistration is recommended because classes with fewer than four
students will be canceled. A 1.5-hour
lesson costs just $15, not including
rental fees. The views of downtown
Minneapolis as you emerge from
the woods make this a beautiful way
to see the city. A map of the trails
is available for download at www.
minneapolisparks.org; search for
"Theodore Wirth ski."
MAP 7: 1301 Theodore Wirth Pkwy.,
Minneapolis, 612/230-6400, www.
theodorewirth.org; ski rentals daily
7am-9pm

## DOWNHILL SKIING AND SNOWBOARDING

### Buck Hill

Where did Olympic skier Lindsey
Vonn get her start? Right here on
Buck Hill. Along with generations of
skiers, she hurled herself down a 950-
foot hill, looking for all the world like
she was headed straight for I-35. (The
skiers actually aren't in any danger of
hitting the highway; it just looks that
way from the road.) Buck Hill has nine
lifts and 16 runs, including a half-
pipe and freestyle terrain and a separate snow tubing area, spread over 45
acres. Equipment rental—ski or snowboard package—is $26. Skiing under
the lights at night is a quintessential
winter-in-the-Twin Cities experience.
MAP 7: 15400 Buck Hill Rd., Burnsville,
952/435-7174, www.buckhill.com; hours
vary depending on snowfall, daily
9am-10pm with snow

### Theodore Wirth Park

Theodore Wirth Park jumped on
the snowboarding bandwagon a few
years ago and has been a big hit. The
terrain changes every few weeks and
includes a 24-foot-long staircase and
a wall. Day passes ($10 Wed.-Fri., $13
weekends and holidays, equipment
rental $15) and lessons (Sat.-Sun.
10am, noon, 2pm, and 4pm, $15) are
reasonable. Families and those less
athletically inclined can rent a snow
tube ($12 adults, $8 children) and slide
down the hill without all that exertion.
There's even a rope tow to take you to
the top.
MAP 7: 1301 Theodore Wirth Pkwy.,
Minneapolis, 763/522-4584, www.
minneapolisparks.org; Mon.-Sat.
10am-8pm, Sun. 10am-6pm; day pass
$10-13

### Hyland Ski and Snowboard Center

Three chairlifts and three rope tows
carry skiers and snowboarders to the
tops of some genuinely challenging
slopes spread out over 35 acres, all
groomed and equipped for snowmaking. Skiers are treated to glimpses of
the Minneapolis skyline peeking out
over the pines. Alpine ski equipment
rental is $22; snowboarding equipment

## GO FISH!

Fishing is legal and convenient in nearly all of Minneapolis and St. Paul's urban lakes. Throwing a line in from a boat, a pier, or even a street overpass is common. The most common species are bluegill, crappie, muskellunge, walleye, and carp, many stocked by the Minnesota Department of Natural Resources. All anglers over the age of 16 need a license, which can be purchased over the phone at 888/665-4236 or online at www.dnr.state.mn.us. Nonresident licenses cost $14 for 24 hours, $36 for 72 hours, or $43 for a week.

The Minnesota Health Department (www.health.state.mn.us) tests fish from 1,000 lakes in Minnesota, including most of those in the metro area, and publishes a lake-by-lake and species-by-species list of guidelines on which fish to eat and which to throw back. Many species fall on the "limit consumption to once per week" list; the most common contaminants are mercury and perfluorocarbons. The full list is available on the website.

Minnesota is battling a handful of aquatic invasive species, notably the dreaded zebra mussel, and requires anyone who transports a boat to take an online course and display a decal. Current law requires all boaters to clean and thoroughly drain boats, leaving the drain plug open. Visit www.dnr.state.mn.us to learn more.

is $33. Private and group lessons are offered with preregistration.

Hyland Lake Park is also home to three alpine ski jumps run by the **Minneapolis Ski Club** (651/231-0779, www.facebook.com/mnskiclub). You must be a member to jump, but memberships cost just $25 and can be purchased on the spot from a coach. Call for exact directions or to arrange a time. The small jumps, where beginners must start, are open Tuesday and Thursday 7pm-9pm and Saturday 10am-noon. Equipment rental is $20, but you should bring your own helmet. **MAP 7:** 8800 Chalet Rd., Bloomington, 763/694-7800, www.hylandski.com; mid-Nov.-mid-Mar. Mon.-Fri. 9:30am-9pm, Sat.-Sun. 9am-9pm; $31 adults, $28 children

## SPECTATOR SPORTS
### HORSE RACING
#### Canterbury Park

From May through Labor Day, you can watch the ponies run at Canterbury Park in suburban comfort. Lacking much grit or history, the track will never be confused with Churchill Downs, but it still attracts both the dyed-in-the-wool racing fan and the

purely curious looking for a relaxing afternoon. In between races, you can grab a bite to eat at one of the four restaurants or play a round of Texas Hold 'em in the 34-table poker room. The track has hosted the Claiming Crown, known as the blue-collar Breeders' Cup for most of the race series' short history. Even when the horses aren't running, Canterbury Park's doors are open 24 hours for betting on simulcast horse racing and poker. Keep in mind that the legal gambling age for the track and the tables is 18. **MAP 7:** 1100 Canterbury Rd., Shakopee, 952/445-7223, www.canterburypark.com; daily 24 hours; live racing $6 adults, children under 17 free, otherwise free

### Running Aces Harness Park

Bet on the horses or at the poker tables here in the northern suburbs. This is a casual, family-friendly environment, not down and dirty or full of ladies in broad-brimmed fancy hats. Watch the calendar for live music, family meal deals, and other specials. The All-In Grill, the on-site restaurant, is affordable and a good way to get out of the sun and still watch the horses run.

MAP 7: 15201 Zurich St. NE, Columbus, 651/925-4600, www.runningacesharness.com; daily 24 hours; free

## OTHER RECREATION
### 3rd Lair Skate Park

Teenagers dominate the 25,000-square-foot indoor-outdoor facility full of pipes, walls, banks, rails, and pyramids, but people of all ages are welcome. The owners and staff are all skaters themselves who seem to have a special affinity for kids. New riders and kids 12 and under are encouraged to come to the park Saturday mornings before noon, when it's less busy and there are instructors on hand (classes cost $35 and walk-ins are welcome). All equipment is available to rent for very reasonable prices. You pay admission per three-hour session. First-time users must buy a $5 pass and bring a photo ID or have a parent sign for them. Hours vary with the school year. Parents can stay and watch for free, hang out in the parents' lounge, or leave their kids in the capable hands of the "lifeguards."

MAP 7: 850 Florida Ave. S., Golden Valley, 763/797-5283, www.3rdlair.com; Sun., Mon., Wed., and Fri. noon-6pm, Tues., Thurs., and Sat. noon-9pm; three-hour session $12, additional session same day $5

# SHOPS

It's hard to talk about shopping in the Twin Cities without mentioning the Mall of America.

downtown Minneapolis's North Loop

It's true; many locals have a love-hate relationship with the mall. But it sure is convenient to have all those national chains in one climate-controlled place. And all that parking! Right at the intersection of two major highways! Right next to IKEA! You'll find locals who sniff at the Mall of America, but you'll be hard-pressed to find one who doesn't visit on occasion.

But, while the Twin Cities have their fair share of big-box shopping (this is the home of our much-beloved Target Corporation, after all) and a ring of suburban malls known colloquially as the Dales (Southdale, Rosedale, Ridgedale), the "shop locally" ethos is alive and well. Local fashionistas would rather boast about a one-of-a-kind piece by a young, up-and-coming designer than a recognizable label.

There are a couple of other good reasons to keep your credit card close at hand in the Twin Cities: There's no sales tax on clothing here, shaving a few bucks off the expense, and this place is crawling with bookstores—new bookstores, used bookstores, specialty bookstores, and some of the country's best children's bookstores. In fact, Minneapolis sat at the top of the Most Literate Cities in the United States list in 2014, and St. Paul is always in the top 10.

## HIGHLIGHTS

✪ **INDIE BOOK-LOVERS' HEAVEN:** A local publisher of some renown, **Milkweed Books** also stocks carefully chosen titles from a wide range of other indies (page 174).

✪ **BEST SHOP TO READ TO THE KIDS:** The worn armchairs at **Wild Rumpus** are so inviting you won't be able to resist spending a few minutes, or longer, test-reading a children's book (page 177).

✪ **BEST PLACE TO BUY AN AUTHENTIC MINNESOTAN SOUVENIR:** Minnesota's Scandinavian roots are represented at **Ingebretsen's,** with hand-knit sweaters, painted Swedish Dala horses, and intricate rosemaling (page 179).

✪ **BEST PLACE TO BE A KID AGAIN:** Remember the joys of imaginative play at **Creative Kidstuff,** one of the Twin Cities' best toy stores for nearly three decades (page 181).

✪ **BEST PLACE TO FIND ABSOLUTELY ANYTHING FOR THE KITCHEN:** Serious cooks can find whatever they can dream up at **Cooks of Crocus Hill**'s three locations (page 184).

✪ **HOME OF YOUR NEW FAVORITE JEANS:** Find the denim of your dreams at **BlackBlue** in St. Paul (page 184).

✪ **ULTIMATE TRAIN FREAK HANGOUT:** Your Thomas-loving kiddo will play for hours at **Choo Choo Bob's,** while you pick up a few holiday gifts (page 186).

Choo Choo Bob's

# SHOPPING DISTRICTS

## DOWNTOWN MINNEAPOLIS

A bronze Mary Tyler Moore flings her tam in the air in front of Macy's (which die-hard Minnesotans may still refer to as Dayton's), and downtown office workers hurry down Nicollet Mall, squeezing in a little shopping during their lunch hour. With a little extra time to walk, they'll head to the corner of downtown known as the North Loop, where new loftlike construction cozies up to converted warehouses and factories and the ground floors are occupied by carefully curated hip clothing and housewares boutiques. While the residential population downtown is growing, the pace is still slow on Saturdays and barely alive on Sundays.

**MAP 1:** Nicollet Mall between 4th St. and 13th St., North Loop between the Mississippi River and N. 7th St.

## LINDEN HILLS

The neighborhood of Linden Hills has been called a small town in the middle of the city—the kind of place where everybody really might know your name. The shopping district is packed onto a single intersection (where Upton Avenue meets 43rd Street), but the variety could keep diehard shoppers busy all day. On weekdays you'll have plenty of parents pushing strollers to keep you company, and on weekends the whole neighborhood turns out.

**MAP 2:** intersection of Upton Ave. and 43rd St.

## UPTOWN

While chain stores have moved in on the onetime center of Twin Cities counterculture at the corner of Lake Street and Hennepin Avenue, the whole of the Uptown neighborhood is still a lively retail area with an independent bent. The two main north-south axes are Hennepin and Lyndale Avenues, with Lake Street connecting them east-west. Minneapolis's post-college crowd comes to Uptown to browse books and fashions.

**MAP 2:** Hennepin Ave. between Franklin Ave. and 31st St., Lake St. between Hennepin Ave. and Lyndale Ave.

## GRAND AVENUE

Grand Avenue stretches from the Mississippi River to downtown St. Paul, with pockets of retail and restaurants scattered along its length, but most of the action is at the intersection of Grand and Victoria Avenues. Here tasteful new construction mingles with converted stucco homes. Although the occasional chain pops up, mostly you'll find well-established, creative local shops, like the delicious Cooks of Crocus Hill, the irresistible Red Balloon Bookshop for kids, and the absolutely inimitable Golden Fig for handmade gourmet goods. Wear good walking shoes and head west to Grand and Lexington Avenues for even more unique boutiques.

**MAP 5:** Grand Ave. between Dunlap St. and Dale St.

## 50TH AND FRANCE

The shady crossroads of 50th and France, a roughly four-block shopping district on the border between South Minneapolis and the tony suburb of Edina, is the closest thing Minnesota has to Rodeo Drive, the sort of place where you'll find toned, fashionable women swinging shopping bags as they saunter from one boutique to another, and then sit down, exhausted, to a light and expensive lunch. National chains like Anthropologie and Athleta sit alongside local shops like Evereve. Those who know their way around a kitchen as well as a charity luncheon might spend hours shopping and then have a glass of wine at Beaujo's Wine Bar.

**MAP 7:** France Ave. between 49th St. and 50th St.

## HOPKINS MAINSTREET

Mainstreet in the family-oriented, first-ring suburb of Hopkins is the sort of thing newer suburbs try, unsuccessfully, to re-create with out-of-the-box storefronts and chains. But Hopkins is the real deal: a shady three- or four-block stretch of quaint buildings, some dating to the late 1800s. Antiques are the big draw, with 10 antiques stores within an easy stroll and sometimes right next to each other. Some dealers specialize in jewelry or trains, while others, like the Hopkins Antique Mall, represent multiple dealers. Just a few minutes from downtown Minneapolis, Hopkins feels like a whole different world.

**MAP 7:** Mainstreet between 7th Ave. and 12th Ave.

## MAIN STREET ANOKA

The northwestern suburb has a lively main street that stands as a reminder that it hasn't always been a suburb. Along five blocks you'll find more than a dozen independent stores, including a couple of antiques stores, bead and jewelry stores, and plenty of knickknacks. The Mad Hatter Tea Room is a good place to take a break for a little snack. The atmosphere isn't upscale like 50th and France, and it isn't overtly hip; instead it is small-town friendly and relaxed.

**MAP 7:** E. Main St. between 1st Ave. and 5th Ave.

## WAYZATA

Curled around a bay in Lake Minnetonka, Wayzata is a tony town with tony shops to match—a town that can support half a dozen jewelers. There are clothing boutiques with looks for those all along the age and hipness spectrums, along with antiques shops and toy stores. Combine this with lunch on the lake, whether it's a picnic in the park by the Wayzata Depot or at the upscale Sunsets. (And if you want to sound like a local, say it "why-ZETT-uh.")

**MAP 7:** Lake St. between Circle Dr. and Manitoba

# TO MARKET, TO MARKET

Nearly every neighborhood and every burb in the Twin Cities has its own little farmers market, a place where neighbors gather on weekend mornings or weekday evenings to shop a little, snack a little, hear a little music. They've become the new community centers, and there's no better place to get to know a city or a 'hood. The bigger, more established markets all have their own character and are spectacular places to see the real Minneapolis and St. Paul.

Serious shoppers go to the **Lyndale Market** (312 Lyndale Ave. E., Minneapolis, 612/333-1737, www.mplsfarmersmarket.com; mid-Apr.-mid-Nov. daily 6am-1pm, some vendors Sat. year-round), one of the biggest produce markets in the Midwest. On weekend mornings, you may need to throw some elbows or block with a bag of bok choy to make it down the crowded aisles, but the bargains and the quality of the produce make it worth it. Vendors sell bratwurst and other treats, and artisans sell jewelry and other handicrafts at the Farmers Market Annex (the three covered sheds to the south). Competition for parking spots under the I-94 overpass is fierce, but the market is just a short walk from Loring Park.

More than just a place to buy some local, organic beets, the **Mill City Farmers Market** (750 2nd St. S., Minneapolis, 612/341-7580, www.millcityfarmersmarket.org; May-Oct. Sat. 8am-1pm) is an all-in-one Saturday morning experience. Start with a cup of coffee and a fruit tart, watch demonstrations and cooking competitions by local chefs, pet the chickens

# Downtown Minneapolis   Map 1

## BOOKS

### ✪ Milkweed Books

Peek in the windows of Open Book, a building shared by Milkweed Editions, The Loft Literary Center, and the Minnesota Center for Book Arts, and we dare you not to be drawn inside. Milkweed Editions, one of the tenants, is an independent publisher and runs a bookstore in this building. It celebrates and sells books from its own authors and other indies and also hosts frequent author events and signings. Peruse the shelves, have a cup of coffee and a snack, then explore the gallery of book-related art in the Minnesota Center for Book Arts.

MAP 1: 1011 Washington Ave. S., Minneapolis, 612/215-2540, www.milkweed.org; Mon.-Sat. 10am-7pm, Sun. 11am-3pm

### James & Mary Laurie Bookseller

Sure, your intention might be just to browse, to see what a collection of more than 120,000 carefully chosen rare books looks like, to appreciate a collection of 30,000 vinyl records, to stare upward at floor-to-ceiling shelves and sniff that old-book smell. But we dare you not to fall in love with at least one volume, record, or botanical print. The Lauries have been in the business of books for nearly 50 years. While their inventory might seem inexhaustible, their knowledge actually is.

MAP 1: 250 3rd Ave. N., Minneapolis, 612/338-1114, www.lauriebooks. com; Mon.-Sat. 11am-6pm and by appointment and tip the musicians, then swing through again for vegetables, meats, cheeses, and breads to take home. By this time you're probably hungry again, so get a kebab or bratwurst to eat on the steps overlooking the river. All this (and more!) is crammed into the old train yard connected to the Mill City Museum, next to the Guthrie Theater on the riverfront.

One of the best ways to enjoy downtown Minneapolis is to join the river of people moving up and down Nicollet Mall during the **Nicollet Mall Market** (Nicollet Mall, between 5th St. and 12th St., Minneapolis, 612/333-1718, www.mplsfarmersmarket.com; May-Nov. Thurs. 6am-6pm) at lunchtime on Thursdays during the farmers market, picking up string beans at one stall, flowers at the next, and bread or tamales one block down. Although much of the produce is grown locally, vendors are allowed to bring fruits and vegetables from outside the area. That means you can grab a peach and a roll from the St. Agnes bakery stall and enjoy it in the sunshine on Peavey Plaza (Nicollet Mall and 12th Street).

In a town where people have their pick of farmers markets and often have very strong opinions about them, the **St. Paul Farmers' Market** (290 5th St. E., St. Paul, 651/227-8101, www.stpaulfarmersmarket.com; late Apr.-mid-Nov. Sat. 6am-1pm, Sun. 8am-1pm) in the Lowertown neighborhood is widely regarded to be the best. It's just big enough to bustle a bit and offer a fantastic selection of vegetables and treats—including hand-harvested wild rice—without the overwhelming oppression of large crowds. All products must be locally grown and sold directly from the producer to the consumer. Most days there is live music 9am-noon.

## GIFTS AND HOME
### Russell+Hazel

If you believe your personal organizing system is inseparable from your personal brand, you're in the right place. At the flagship store of Minnesota's own Russell+Hazel, makers of high-end notebooks and binders, you can build your own journal and accessorize it, then get a blowout and a makeup consultation.

MAP 1: 219 2nd St. N., Minneapolis, 612/353-4149, www.russellandhazel.com; Mon.-Sat. 10am-6pm, Sun. 11am-4pm

D.NOLO

## CLOTHING AND ACCESSORIES
### Askov Finlayson

The lifestyle Askov Finlayson is selling is a little bit old money and a lot Minnesota. Owned and curated by heirs to the Dayton's department store fortune, the store sells the sorts of higher-end, "Oh, this old thing?" stuff you might wear or bring to the family cabin or a South Minneapolis garden party, including **Faribault Woolen Mills** blankets and fir-scented candles (Where does the shop's ultra-Scandinavian name come from? Askov and Finlayson are towns north of the Twin Cities on the same exit off I-35 as you head to Duluth. As anyone with a family cabin up north would know.)

MAP 1: 204 1st St. N., Minneapolis, 612/206-3925, www.askovfinlayson.com; Mon.-Fri. 11am-7pm, Sat. 10am-7pm, Sun. 10am-5pm

### D.NOLO

D.NOLO is a collective of retailers with a seamlessly integrated take on fashion: It should be comfortable, contemporary, and cosmopolitan. While you'll mostly find womenswear from up-and-coming and indie designers, the shop also displays a few pieces of appropriately hip furniture and smaller gift-y household items.

**MAP 1:** 219 2nd St. N., Minneapolis, 612/584-3244, www.dnolo.com; Mon.-Sat. 11am-6pm, Sun. noon-4pm

### Grethen House

If it's walked the runways in New York, this is the place to look for it in the Twin Cities—from Comme des Garçons to Yigal Azrouel. Although Grethen House been around for more than six decades, the fashion here is au courant. Expect a truly personalized boutique shopping experience, with individual attention and plenty of honest advice. (Another location is at 4930 France Ave. S., Edina, 952/926-8725, www.grethenhouse.com; Mon.-Fri. 10am-6pm, Sat. 10am-5pm, Sun. 11am-5pm.)

**MAP 1:** 212 3rd Ave. N., Minneapolis, 612/339-5702, www.grethenhouse.com; Mon.-Fri. 10am-6pm, Sat. 10am-5pm, Sun. 11am-3pm

### MartinPatrick3

Don't be fooled by the storefront. As you open the door, you may feel like you're the first to discover this up-and-coming boutique. But MartinPatrick3 is a 15,000-square-foot powerhouse, a veritable department store gradually taking over this old warehouse. Regulars make appointments to try on $3,000 blazers and have them tailored in-house (along with complimentary whisky shots, we've heard). The rest of us make do with $100 sweatpants.

**MAP 1:** 212 3rd Ave. N., Minneapolis, 612/746-5329, www.martinpatrick3.com; Mon.-Sat. 10am-8pm, Sun. 10am-6pm

### Wilson & Willy's

This is what your loft would look like if you lived in the North Loop—or what you'd like it to look like. Your soap dispenser, accent candles, and favorite loungewear would all have that same careless, timeless, this-old-thing look. Wilson &Willy's carries spare collections of men's and women's clothing, along with household goods.

**MAP 1:** 211 Washington Ave. N., Minneapolis, 612/315-2280, www.wilsonandwillys.com; Tues.-Sat. 11am-7pm, Sun.-Mon. 11am-4pm

# KIDS' STORES
## Pacifier

If your baby's taste runs to contemporary styles with modern colors and clean lines, this is the store for you. You'll find everything you might ever need for baby (and plenty of stuff that never occurred to you), including strollers, bags, and other gear. A small selection of baby clothes includes favorites like Zutano and Tea Collection. Pacifier is also in City Center (skyway level, 40 7th St. S., Minneapolis, 612/767-6330; Mon. 10am-5pm, Tues.-Fri. 10am-6pm, Sat. 10am-3pm), St. Paul (714 Cleveland Ave. S., St. Paul, 651/330-8747; Mon.-Thurs. 10am-6pm, Fri. 10am-7pm, Sat. 10am-6pm, Sun. 11am-5pm), and Edina (4942 France Ave. S., Edina, 952/767-6565; Mon.-Sat. 10am-6pm, Sun. 11am-5pm).

**MAP 1:** 219 2nd S. N., 612/623-8123, www.pacifier.me; Mon. 10am-6pm, Tues.-Fri. 10am-7pm, Sat. 10am-6pm, Sun. 11am-5pm

## BEST SOUVENIRS

Sure, you could go to the Mall of America and grab a few things with a moose on them. Or you could get these real Minnesota souvenirs.

- **Hmong Arts and Crafts:** Look for intricate applique known as *paj ntaub* at **Hmong Village** or **Hmongtown Marketplace** (page 78).

- **Native American Art:** Native American artists from the plains and the prairies display at **Northland Visions** (page 125).

- **Books from Local Presses:** Support (and even meet) local authors at **Milkweed Books** (page 174).

- **Faribault Woolen Mills Blanket:** The classic, warm, wooly, striped Faribault blanket is to Minnesota what Pendleton is to Oregon. Get yours at **Askov Finlayson** (page 175) or **BlackBlue** (page 184).

- **Scandinavian Goods:** Bring back a piece of Minnesota's Scandinavian roots via **Ingebretsen's** (page 179), your go-to for everything from foods like Finnish licorice to authentic handicrafts including hand-painted Swedish wooden Dala horses.

- **Local Gourmet Goodies:** Local producers sell packaged foods of all kinds at the **Golden Fig** (page 185), from homemade jams to caramels and chocolates. You can also find true hand-harvested wild rice, a Minnesota treat, at a couple of vendors (try Birchberry Native Arts and Food) at the **St. Paul Farmers' Market** (page 175).

- **A Bundt Pan:** Invented and beloved here, Bundt pans (and other quality bakeware) can be found at a discount at the **Nordic Ware Factory Store** (page 189).

- **MN-Branded Clothing:** Get your MN beanie and hoodie at **Sota Clothing** (page 189).

# South Minneapolis      Map 2

## BOOKS
### ✪ Wild Rumpus

Yes, that is a chicken wandering around. And a cat. The Wild Rumpus's menagerie includes birds, rodents, and the occasional lizard and arachnid. Go ahead, sit on one of the worn, comfy armchairs and read something from the well-chosen selection—one of the best in the country. From classic board books to popular tween series and carefully selected adult titles for mature young adult readers, the staffers know books.

**MAP 2:** 2720 43rd St. W., Minneapolis, 612/920-5005, www.wildrumpusbooks. com; Mon. 10am-5pm, Tues.-Fri. 10am-8pm, Sat. 10am-5pm, Sun. noon-5pm

### Birchbark Books

Novelist Louise Erdrich has created a haven for book lovers in just 800 square feet of space on a quiet, tree-lined, mostly residential street. While there is a special focus on Native American books (including a few published by Birchbark), the other quirks of the staff's interest show through as well, including a fine selection of books on language. The store also features the work of Native American artisans, including baskets, silver, and dolls.

MAP 2: 2115 21st St. W., Minneapolis, 612/374-4023, www.birchbarkbooks.com; daily 10am-6pm

### Boneshaker Books

Boneshaker is not just a bookstore that builds community, but a bookstore that is built by the community. Not-for-profit and volunteer-run, Boneshaker stocks its shelves with progressive, social justice-focused books for kids and adults, with cozy reading nooks and friendly staff.

MAP 2: 2002 23rd Ave. S., Minneapolis, 612/871-7110, www.boneshakerbooks.com; daily 11am-8pm

### Magers and Quinn

It might say something about the people of Minneapolis that Magers and Quinn is a popular date destination. Or it might say something about Magers and Quinn. Books of all kinds (new and used, rare collectibles and discounted bestsellers, children's books and foreign philosophers) fill three floors, floor to ceiling. High ceilings, antique prints, glass-fronted display cases, and a general feeling of reverence make this, one of the Midwest's largest bookstores, feel as much like a museum as a shop.

MAP 2: 3038 Hennepin Ave. S., Minneapolis, 612/822-4611, www.magersandquinn.com; Sun.-Thurs. 10am-10pm, Fri.-Sat. 10am-11pm

### Moon Palace Books

Empowerment is the operative word here at Moon Palace: Shelves are filled with new and used titles for grown-ups and kids that say, "You go, girl! Or however you identify," from classics to current fiction and nonfiction to books for baby feminists. Stop for pizza and salads at the little Geek Love Café, inside the bookstore.

MAP 2: 3032 Minnehaha Ave., Minneapolis, 612/454-0455, www. moonpalacebooks.com; daily 9am-9pm

### Uncle Edgar's Mystery Bookstore & Uncle Hugo's Science Fiction Bookstore

Genre fiction fans will know they're in the right place when they nearly trip over the large cardboard box labeled "Nick Carter, box 3"—and it's stacked on top of boxes 4 and 5 of the popular detective series. Uncle Hugo's, founded in 1974, claims to be the oldest science fiction bookstore in America; Uncle Edgar, Hugo's Siamese twin, joined him six years later. Both are straight out of geeky bookstore central casting: musty, silent, with walls packed tight with bright paperback spines and the floor covered knee-high in boxes of new and used books.

MAP 2: 2864 Chicago Ave. S., Minneapolis, Uncle Hugo's 612/824-6347, Uncle Edgar's 612/824-9984, www.unclehugo.com; Mon.-Fri. 10am-8pm, Sat. 10am-6pm, Sun. noon-5pm

# MUSIC
### Electric Fetus

Five decades of Minneapolis music history have accreted on the creaky racks at the Electric Fetus (or maybe that's the accumulated grime from nearly 50 years of burning incense). In this time of niche marketing and specialization, the Fetus has survived by making musicheads of all stripes deliriously happy. Spend hours browsing rock, jazz, metal, hip-hop, and every permutation thereof. Then sidle over to the used, vinyl, and local sections. New locations have opened in Duluth and St. Cloud, but this, in its unlikely spot on a frontage road off I-35W, is the original.

MAP 2: 2000 4th Ave. S., Minneapolis, 612/870-9300, www.electricfetus.com; Mon.-Fri. 9am-9pm, Sat. 9am-8pm, Sun. 11am-6pm

### Hymie's Vintage Records

Hymie's is like a museum tracing the evolution of popular sound from 45s to 78s to 8-tracks to cassette tapes to CDs, even relevant books and videos. While Hymie himself, a stalwart in the vinyl collecting world, is gone, his successors are knowledgeable and passionate about music. Building a collection? Start here. Already have a collection and need accessories like sleeves? Here as well.

MAP 2: 3820 Lake St. E., Minneapolis, 612/729-8890, http://hymiesrecords.com; Mon.-Sat. 11am-7pm, Sun. 1pm-6pm

## GIFTS AND HOME

### ✪ Ingebretsen's

When a craving hits for Finnish licorice, Swedish *lefse* (a bland flatbread), or the universally Scandinavian lingonberry jam, folks in Minneapolis—whether descended from Scandinavian stock or not—head to Ingebretsen's. Half the store is given over to foodstuffs and the other half to exquisite and authentic handicrafts, including sweaters, rosemaling (Norwegian folk painting), and Swedish Dala horses (traditional hand-carved and hand-painted wooden horses). Knitters will find a treasure trove of high-end natural fibers in the annex next door.

MAP 2: 1601 Lake St. E., Minneapolis, 612/729-9333, www.ingebretsens.com; Mon.-Fri. 9am-5:30pm, Sat. 9am-5pm

### Forage Modern Workshop

This is where midcentury modern meets the Northwoods. Forage features furniture and gifts, heavy on the local designers, that combine clean lines with natural beauty. You might drop a couple of thousand dollars on a coffee table, or just a couple of twenties on a hand-printed poster by a local artist.

MAP 2: 4023 Lake St. E., Minneapolis, 612/886-3603, www.foragemodernworkshop.com; daily 10am-8pm

### The Foundry Home Goods

If you've ever thought very hard about the intersection of Japanese and Scandinavian aesthetics, you almost certainly unknowingly conjured a vision of the interior of the Foundry: shades of white, bone, and ecru on imponderably useful things like reed whisks, natural pot scrubbers, and the perfect linen hand towels. Beauty and utility are inextricable here.

MAP 1: 322 48th St. W., Minneapolis, 612/333-8484, www.thefoundryhomegoods.com; Mon.-Sat. 10am-7pm, Sun. 10am-6pm

### Patina

A little kitsch, a little humor, a little modern design, a little inspiration: There isn't a single object in a Patina store that anyone actually needs, but it takes just a few minutes to find something you never knew you wanted, or wanted very badly to give to a friend. A tape dispenser shaped like a frog, a cake server that looks like a high heel, a trout stapler. But not all is fun and games: You'll also find seriously beautiful bags, jewelry, and modern kitchen goods. Patina has four other locations, including two in St. Paul (2057 Ford Pkwy., 651/695-9955, and 1581 Selby Ave., 651/644-5444) and two more in Minneapolis (2305 18th Ave. NE, 612/788-8933, and 821 50th W., 612/821-9315), all open the same hours.

**MAP 2:** 1009 Franklin Ave. W., Minneapolis, 612/872-0880, www. patinastores.com; Mon.-Sat. 9:30am-9pm, Sun. 11am-6pm

## CLOTHING AND ACCESSORIES
### Local Motion

The look at Local Motion is grown-up, feminine, and a little boho, heavy on dresses, skirts, and feminine blouses in the colors and cuts of the moment. While the boutique started as a showcase for local designers—and you'll still find many here—the owners now keep a close eye on fashion in New York and LA, bringing the best of what they find to the Twin Cities. Come in serious shopping mode: The racks are packed, the aisles small, and the prices make these clothes indulgences.

**MAP 2:** 2813 Hennepin Ave., Minneapolis, 612/871-8436, www.localmotionmpls.com; Mon.-Thurs. 11am-7pm, Fri. 11am-8pm, Sat. 11am-7pm, Sun. noon-5pm

### MILLE

Start with small, women-owned brands, show them off in a space that feels like your girlfriend's chic, spacious walk-in closet, and throw in hyper-personal service: That's MILLE. The collection is feminine and practical, on trend and timeless, at slightly-higher-than-the-mall prices.

**MAP 2:** 4760 Grand Ave S., Minneapolis, 612/209-7364, www.shopmille.com; Mon.-Fri. 10am-4pm

### Via's Vintage

If your wardrobe comfortably accommodates ruffled Edwardian blouses, 1950s fur stoles, and mod shift dresses, you can outfit yourself very, very nicely at Via's—and have fun doing it, too. For a store featuring items that are 30 to 100 years old, Via's is bright, clean, and free of that musty used-clothes feeling. There's a smaller collection of men's clothes and a rack of kids' stuff, as well as vintage pieces reworked into one-of-a-kind couture artifacts.

**MAP 2:** 2408 Hennepin Ave. S., Minneapolis, 612/374-3649, www. viasvintage.com; Mon.-Sat. 11am-7pm, Sun. noon-5pm

## ANTIQUES
### Hunt & Gather

The farther you wander into Hunt & Gather, the farther it seems like there is to go. More than a dozen individual dealers, each with his or her own individual taste, fill the space. And we do mean fill it. In one corner you'll find vintage camping gear stacked to the ceiling, in another, huge barrels of keys, negatives, or printers' type, all there for you to explore.

**MAP 2:** 4944 Xerxes Ave. S., Minneapolis, 612/455-0250, www. huntandgatherantiques.com; Mon.-Sat. 10am-6pm, Sun. noon-6pm

MILLE

## KIDS' STORES
### ✪ Creative Kidstuff

Creative Kidstuff seems to know what the next hot toys will be before anybody else does. We're not talking about movie tie-ins or action figures (you won't find those here), but creative hands-on toys for babies right on up through the early teens. The stores also stock plenty of relative classics, like Playmobil, Brio, Ryan's Room, Groovy Girls, and Corolle dolls. Most of the friendly sales staff are parents themselves and eager to share their expertise. There are five other locations in the Twin Cities, including in St. Paul (1074 Grand Ave., 651/222-2472; Mon.-Wed. and Sat. 10am-6pm, Thurs.-Fri. 10am-8pm, Sun. 11am-4pm) and in the Galleria mall in the western suburb of Edina (3555 69th St., 952/926-4512; Mon.-Fri. 10am-9pm, Sat. 10am-8pm, Sun. 11am-6pm).

**MAP 2:** 4313 Upton Ave. S., Minneapolis, 612/927-0653, www.creativekidstuff.com; Mon.-Wed. and Sat. 10am-6pm, Thurs.-Fri. 10am-8pm, Sun. 11am-4pm

### Heartfelt

The Waldorf influences at Heartfelt are clear as soon as you walk through the door. Just about everything is made from a natural material, like wood or felt, and everything is geared toward sparking kids' creativity. There are plenty of art and craft materials for sale, and most Saturdays the store hosts a free craft activity.

**MAP 2:** 4306 Upton Ave. S., Minneapolis, 612/877-8090, www.heartfeltonline.com; Mon.-Sat. 10am-5pm, Sun. noon-4pm

# Nordeast and Dinkytown  Map 3

## GIFTS AND HOME
### Blu Dot Weekend Outlet Store

This darling of contemporary design, born in Minnesota but beloved around the country, sells scratch-and-dents, closeouts, floor models, and prototypes at its first and so far only outlet store. Blu Dot is known for a kind of perky, optimistic minimalism, with designs so simple they seem to float off the floor.

**MAP 3:** 1323 Tyler St. NE, Minneapolis, 612/354-7964, www.bludot.com; Sat. 10am-4pm, Sun. 11am-3pm

### I Like You

Imagine your super-talented sister or cousin, the one who always sends the cleverest homemade cards and baby gifts, got a little corner of retail space. This is where she would sell. I Like You takes handmade items, from buttons to aprons to baby bibs, on consignment from local crafters.

**MAP 3:** 501 1st Ave. NE, Minneapolis, 612/208-0249, www.ilikeyouonline.com; Tues.-Fri. 11am-7pm, Sat. 10am-6pm, Sun. 11am-4pm

## GOURMET GOODIES
### Surdyk's

What Surdyk's lacks in ambience it makes up for in so, so many other ways: history (theirs was reputedly the first liquor license issued in Minneapolis after Prohibition), selection (name a country, it's probably got a bottle from there), and price. (Under $12? No problem. Under $10? Still no problem.) Even better is that you can pick up your fabulous $9 bottle of wine, then head next door to Surdyk's unmissable gourmet shop and blow all your savings on imported cheeses and chocolates.

MAP 3: 303 Hennepin Ave. E., Minneapolis, 612/379-3232, www.surdyks. com; Mon.-Thurs. 9am-9pm, Fri.-Sat. 9am-10pm

## ANTIQUES
### Art and Architecture

Poking around the dim, crowded corners of Art and Architecture is like finding an enchanted attic, where the best architectural remnants of another time have come to rest from the very large (church pews, stained-glass windows, and solid wood doors) to the rather small (printing press blocks, doorknobs, boxes of brass hinges). Nearly every decade and major design era is represented, and everything is sorted almost compulsively, so you don't have to go digging in the bathroom fixtures for that perfect chandelier.

MAP 3: 3338 University Ave. SE, Minneapolis, 612/904-1776, www.artandarc. com; Mon.-Sat. 10am-5pm, Sun. noon-5pm

## BATH AND BEAUTY
### Intelligent Nutrients

When the founder of the internationally known Aveda line of styling products needed a new challenge, he decided to turn himself to the care of the entire body, inside and out. Horst Rechelbacher, Austrian transplant and longtime Twin Citian, created the Intelligent Nutrients line of aromatherapy oils, dietary supplements, hair care, chocolate bars, and teas—all organic. While those products are distributed in salons throughout the country, here at the national headquarters you will find a lush retail showroom, extraordinarily enthusiastic staff, and a small café serving healthful sandwiches, soups, and salads for lunch.

MAP 3: 983 Hennepin Ave. E., Minneapolis, 612/617-2000, www. intelligentnutrients.com; Mon.-Fri. 10am-8pm, Sat. 9am-5pm

# Downtown St. Paul and West Side
Map 4

## BOOKS
### Subtext Books

Downtown St. Paul offers many ways to while away the hours, but for 10 years, it had no bookstore. Thank goodness the long-established Subtext Books decided to pull up stakes from Cathedral Hill and make a new home in a beautiful 19th-century building near Rice Park. As much a salon and a community as a store, Subtext is both serious and welcoming, both literary and contemporary. Browse new and used books and be ready to settle in for long chats with the staff.

MAP 4: 6 5th St. W., St. Paul, 651/493-2791, www.subtextbooks.com; Mon.-Sat. 9am-9pm, Sun. 9am-6pm

## CLOTHING AND ACCESSORIES
### Heimie's Haberdashery

Men get the high-end tailoring experience at Heimie's. Choose just the right

trendy boutiques in St. Paul

off-the-rack suit, or get the full-on bespoke treatment. Shirts, ties, shoes, hats, and luggage, all carefully chosen, are also available. And, while you're waiting for the tailor to finish up, you can get an old-fashioned straight-razor shave. While this particular store opened in 2004, its roots go back to the Russian Revolution, when owner Anthony Andler's grandfather Heimie came to St. Paul and opened a tailor shop.
**MAP 4:** 400 St. Peter St., St. Paul, 651/224-2354, www.heimies.com; Mon.-Fri. 10am-7pm, Sat. 10am-5pm

### Scout Handsome Apparel and Gifts

Huggable lumberjack chic? That might best describe the goods at Scout. You'll find lots of plaid and soft cottons, all gender-neutral and in a wide range of sizes. The owners care about the planet as much as they do about wearable clothes for real people, so they buy as much environmentally friendly stuff as they can.
**MAP 4:** 327 7th St. W., St. Paul, 612/272-1682, www.scoutstyleshop. com; Sun. and Tues.-Fri. 11am-7pm, Sat. 10am-8pm

# Summit-University and Mac-Groveland       Map 5

## BOOKS
### Common Good Books

Here you can pick up a book by a local writer, hear a speaker, or buy some Quality Trash—that's how the shelf is labeled—to read on vacation.
**MAP 5:** 38 Snelling Ave. S., St. Paul, 651/225-8989, www.commongoodbooks. com; Mon.-Sat. 9am-9pm, Sun. 10am-7pm

### Red Balloon Bookshop

For book-loving families, the Red Balloon is a regular pilgrimage. While the shop specializes in children's books, there's a small selection of titles just for adults, with a preference for new voices, indie booksellers' faves, and local nonfiction. There's plenty of room on the carpeted floor to give your purchases a test run, and a knowledgeable staff will gladly introduce you to the latest releases.
**MAP 5:** 891 Grand Ave., St. Paul, 651/224-8320, www.redballoonbookshop. com; Mon.-Fri. 10am-8pm, Sat. 10am-6pm, Sun. noon-5pm

### Uncle Sven's Comic Shoppe

A favorite with kids and seasoned comic book-lovers alike, Uncle Sven's is about as friendly as it gets. The store itself is tiny, but packed with the kind of character that comes with nearly four decades of enthusiasm for comic books and strategy games.

MAP 5: 1838 St. Clair Ave., St. Paul, 651/699-3409; Wed.-Sat. 11am-8pm, Sun. noon-5pm

## GIFTS AND HOME
### ✪ Cooks of Crocus Hill

Both expert and aspiring home cooks will find what they're looking for at Cooks of Crocus Hill, from Le Creuset and All-Clad cookware to shelves of cookbooks and a small collection of pantry wares. The staff all know their way around a kitchen and are more than happy to answer questions. If you're looking to improve your cooking chops yourself, see if there's room in an upcoming cooking class, held in professional kitchens at all locations. Cooks of Crocus Hill also has locations in in downtown Minneapolis (208 1st St. N., Minneapolis, 612/223-8167; daily 10am-7pm) and Stillwater (324 S. Main St., Stillwater, 651/351-1144; Mon.-Wed. 10am-7pm, Thurs. 10am-9pm, Sat. 10am-8pm, Sun. 11am-5pm).

MAP 5: 877 Grand Ave., St. Paul, 651/228-1333, www.cooksofcrocushill.com; Mon.-Fri. 10am-9pm, Sat. 10am-7pm, Sun. noon-5pm

Cooks of Crocus Hill

### Corazon

Corazon is stocked floor to ceiling with the bright, colorful, and unexpected: mostly trinkets and baubles, some books and paper goods, and a small selection of fun-to-wear clothes. Corazon is also in Minneapolis (4646 Lake St. E., Minneapolis, 612/276-0198; Mon.-Fri. 10am-8pm, Sat. 9am-8pm, Sun. 9am-5pm).

MAP 5: 526 Selby Ave., St. Paul, 651/219-4589, www.corazononline.com; Tues.-Fri. 10am-7pm, Sat. 9am-7pm, Sun. 11am-3pm

### The Grand Hand

This is where craft meets art meets great shopping. Pottery, jewelry, silk scarves, wrought iron, glasswork, and more—all made by hand and much, but not all, by artists from the Upper Midwest. The atmosphere is somewhere between a gallery and a boutique: Come to look—especially in the River Gallery attached to the shop, where there are regular exhibitions of fine art—but you may find buying irresistible.

MAP 5: 619 Grand Ave., St. Paul, 651/312-1122, www.thegrandhand.com; Mon.-Wed. and Fri.-Sat. 10am-6pm, Thurs. 10am-7pm, Sun. noon-5pm

## CLOTHING AND ACCESSORIES
### ✪ BlackBlue

When you put function and quality over fashion and still end up looking super-fashionable—that's BlackBlue, with high-quality denim (including lots of raw denim) and kicks, mostly for men, but with a small selection for women. This is a great place to pick up Minnesota brands like J. W. Hulme and Faribault Woolen Mills.

MAP 5: 614 Selby Ave., St. Paul, 651/260-5340, www.blkblu.com; Tues.-Sat. 11am-7pm, Sun. 11am-4pm

### Idun

With minimalist style in a minimalist boutique (lots of white walls and exposed brick), Idun (say it "EE-den") brings edgier brands you won't find in too many other Minnesota shops, like Trademark, Jesse Kamm, and Stutterheim. Prices are high, but so is the quality and the level of customer service.

**MAP 5:** 495 Selby Ave., St. Paul, 651/348-6104, www.shopidun.com; Mon.-Fri. 11am-6pm, Sat. 10am-5pm

### Lula's Vintage Wear

Feminine dresses (many of them handmade by skilled seamstresses) from the 1950s through the 1980s fill two walls, and costume jewelry from all eras fills the display case. Men get more rack space here than they do in most vintage stores: a solid collection of sports coats, weekend button-downs, and ties. Be prepared to enjoy the hunt—most racks aren't arranged by size—and don't be afraid to ask the incredibly friendly staff for help.

**MAP 5:** 1587 Selby Ave., St. Paul, 651/644-4110, www.lulavintagemn.com; Mon.-Thurs. 11am-7pm, Fri.-Sat. 11am-6pm, Sun. noon-5pm

### Poppy

Poppy specializes in bright casual basics—the kind of knit dresses and tops that make weekends even more fun and can help pull you through the end of a workweek. While the pieces are bold, the prices are the sort that allow experimentation. You can also find Poppy apparel in Linden Hills (4301 Upton Ave. S., Minneapolis, 612/719-7636), open the same hours.

**MAP 5:** 251 Snelling Ave. S., St. Paul, 651/728-1694, www.poppytogsandclogs. com; Mon.-Fri. 10am-7pm, Sat. 10am-6pm, Sun. 11am-5pm

### Primp

"Cheap chic": Primp puts its motto right on its walls—as well as on every rack. Everything is up-to-the-minute trendy and priced under $100, but so much more fun to shop than mall fast-fashion. (And it's definitely not just for teens.) Primp now has eight locations, including in Minneapolis (4755 Chicago Ave. S., 612/259-7609; Mon.-Thurs. 11am-8pm, Fri. 10am-8pm, Sat. 10am-6pm, Sun. noon-5pm).

**MAP 5:** 618 Selby Ave., St. Paul, 651/414-0091, www.primpyourself.com; Mon.-Sat. 10am-8pm, Sun. 11am-5pm

### Quince

Bold, bright, fun fashion for big girls and little girls (in fact, the panties and ruffled undies are on the opposite side of the display of baby onesies with sassy sayings and ballerina skirts). College kids and those who can still carry off a college look will find pieces that stand out, including accessories and trinkets. And who doesn't know a little girl who needs purple cowboy boots? Mixed in with the clothes are artsy gifts of the sort no one actually knows they want until you give it to them, like sock monkeys and joke books.

**MAP 5:** 850 Grand Ave., St. Paul, 651/225-9900, www.quincegifts.com; Mon.-Sat. 11am-6pm, Sun. noon-3pm, may vary by season

## GOURMET GOODIES
### Golden Fig

Jars of homemade jams, pickles, and chutneys. Cruets of flavored vinegars. Infused sugars, spice mixes, compound butters. Homemade caramels and marshmallows. All of it made in small batches, by hand, mostly right here in Minnesota. The Golden Fig is like a food lover's dream pantry. There is no way to walk into this small, friendly shop and not put together a fabulous gourmet snack. This is a great place to find a local favorite, B. T. McElrath chocolates.

MAP 5: 790 Grand Ave., St. Paul, 651/602-0144, http://goldenfig.com; Mon.-Sat. 10am-8pm, Sun. 11am-6pm

### Solo Vino

If you're the kind of person who likes to duck into a wine shop, grab a familiar label, and check out as quickly as possible, Solo Vino probably isn't for you. It's a shop run by and for people who are passionate about wines—particularly, but not solely, Spanish and Portuguese bottles—and everything about it encourages exploration and conversation.

MAP 5: 517 Selby Ave., St. Paul, 651/602-9515, www.solovinowines.com; Mon.-Thurs. 10am-8pm, Fri.-Sat. 10am-9pm

## BATH AND BEAUTY
### Garden of Eden

Garden of Eden's own line of natural beauty products, which has been available since 1972, is totally customizable. Pick your product (shower gel, lotion, and more) and pick your scents, and have them mixed up right there. The store, in a small mall at the corner of Victoria and Grand, also offers a huge line of essential oils and products from Thymes and Caldrea (both Minnesota companies), Kiehl's, and Burt's Bees.

MAP 5: 867 Grand Ave., St. Paul, 651/293-1300, www.gardenofedenstores.com; Mon.-Sat. 10am-6pm

## KIDS' STORES
### ✪ Choo Choo Bob's

Choo Choo Bob's is more than just a store; it's a hangout for the Thomas the Tank Engine-obsessed set, where they can play, hear stories, and maybe even meet their hero, Engineer Paul, from the local *Choo Choo Bob* TV show. The kids can watch the model train sets and play at the wooden train tables as long as they want—or as long as you can take it.

MAP 5: 2050 Marshall Ave., St. Paul, 651/646-5252, www.choochoobobs.com; Mon.-Thurs. 9am-6pm, Fri. 9am-8pm, Sat. 8:30am-8pm, Sun. 9:30am-6pm

### Baby Grand

This converted single-family home on St. Paul's hottest shopping street is like the Mary Poppins bag of baby stores: It holds far more than it ever looks like it could from the outside. From cribs and gliders to onesies and burp cloths, from high-end brands like Stokke and Inglesina to more everyday stuff like Chicco, it's all packed tightly in here. Baby Grand's second store opened in the western suburb of Hopkins in 2008 (1010 Mainstreet, 952/912-1010, Mon.-Fri. 10am-8pm, Sat. 10am-6pm, Sun. 11am-5pm).

MAP 5: 1137 Grand Ave., St. Paul, 651/224-4414, www.babyongrand.com; Mon.-Fri. 10am-8pm, Sat. 10am-6pm, Sun. noon-5pm

## ARTS AND CRAFTS
### Treadle Yard Goods

You might walk right by Treadle's plain-Jane storefront without even noticing. But inside it's a different story. Are those the latest Japanese import fabrics (very big in the crafting world) on that modest stand? Are those full fabric lines from hot designers Amy Butler and Joel Dewberry? Why, yes, they are. Treadle feels as much like a welcoming community as a shop, with home garment makers (that's the focus here, rather than quilting or other crafts) stopping by to chat about projects and even help out a newcomer.

**MAP 5:** 1338 Grand Ave., St. Paul, 651/698-9690, www.treadleyardgoods.com; Mon.-Thurs. 10am-8pm, Fri. 10am-6pm, Sat. 10am-5pm, Sun. 1pm-5pm

### The Yarnery

Before knitting was hip—before there was the Yarn Harlot or a Stitch and Bitch Nation—there was the Yarnery, a cozy bungalow stuffed to the rafters with yarn. You will invariably find a table of women (and maybe men) knitting—very likely winter clothes for a local organization or squares for a blanket raffle. This is a community-minded place with a particular penchant for supporting local designers. Clinics are free and classes are inexpensive.

**MAP 5:** 840 Grand Ave., St. Paul, 651/222-5793, www.yarnery.com; Mon.-Thurs. 10am-8pm, Fri.-Sat. 10am-6pm, Sun. noon-5pm

# Como and St. Anthony    Map 6

## BOOKS

### Micawber's Books

Anyone who has ever passed through Micawber's quaint half-timbered door more than once knows it is more a book club than a bookstore. The passionate owners and staff are ready not only to share their recommendations, but also to really listen to what their customers say they love to read. Come with an open mind about what you're looking for. Bestselling books aren't automatically disqualified, but being on the bestseller list is not enough to guarantee a spot on the rigorously edited shelves at Micawber's.

**MAP 6:** 2238 Carter Ave., St. Paul, 651/646-5506; Mon.-Fri. 10am-8pm, Sat. 10am-6pm, Sun. 11am-5pm

# Greater Twin Cities    Map 7

## SHOPPING CENTERS

### Albertville Premium Outlets

With more than 100 stores, Albertville is worth the 45-minute drive from the Twin Cities. You'll find the usual suspects, from Ann Taylor and the Gap to Van Heusen and Tommy Hilfiger, and some rarer treats in the outlet world: Le Creuset cast-iron cookware and Hanna Andersson clothing from Sweden. Aside from a small Dunn Bros. coffee shop, it's hard to find much in the way of a decent lunch near the outlets, so plan accordingly or be prepared for fast food. Watch for live music on summer weekend afternoons.

**MAP 7:** 6415 Labeaux Ave. NE, Albertville, 763/497-1911, www.premiumoutlets.com; Mon.-Sat. 10am-9pm, Sun. 10am-7pm

## MINNESOTA SOUVENIRS AT THE MALL OF AMERICA

There's no need to be intimidated by the **Mall of America** (60 E. Broadway, Bloomington, 952/883-8800, www.mallofamerica.com, Mon.-Fri. 10am-9:30pm, Sat. 9:30am-9:30pm, Sun. 11am-7pm). In a lot of ways, it's just like your local mall. Well, okay, four or five local malls put together, with an amusement park in the middle and a shark tank underneath. But, aside from its sheer size, the shopping experience—from the chain stores to the food court—will be familiar to anyone who's spent time in any mall in the country. There's a good reason, however, for visitors to make a side trip to the mall, beyond just being able to say they've seen it: It's a great place to pick up Minnesota-themed souvenirs and gifts for family and friends.

A note about store addresses: The letter in front indicates the side of the mall the store is on (E for east, and so on), and the first of the three digits indicates the floor, so E350 is on the east end of the third floor.

A handful of specialty stores, tucked in among the Gap and Long John Silver's, make the mall a one-stop shopping destination for mugs, T-shirts, and key chains, as well as more specialized gifts.

The mall itself sells souvenirs at the **Mall of America Gift Store** (N128, 952/883-8918, www.mallofamericagifts.com), and two separate stores sell the typical sort of destination gear you might find in a college bookstore or airport gift shop: **Love from Minnesota** (W380, 952/854-7319, www.lovefrommn.com) and **Minnesot-ah!** (E157, 952/858-8531, www.lovefrommn.com).

During the holidays and other key shopping seasons, **RAAS** (www.raas.co) hosts a market-like experience with Minnesota brands both large and small.

### The Galleria

The Galleria, in the tony western suburb of Edina, is where you go in the Twin Cities if you want to have breakfast at Tiffany's. The other upscale stores arrayed along the mall's long central corridor (an oddly gloomy one, strangely enough) include the perfumery L'Occitane, Coach, the French children's clothier Oililly, and gardening great Smith and Hawken, to name just a few. When the ladies who shop and lunch get tired of the former, they have a healthy sandwich at the **Good Earth Restaurant and Bakery** (952/925-1001, Mon.-Sat. 7am-10pm, Sun. 7am-9pm) or a big steak at **Pittsburgh Blue** (952/567-2700, Mon.-Thurs. 11am-10pm, Fri.-Sat. 11am-11pm, Sun. 10am-10pm).

**MAP 7:** 3510 70th St. W., Edina, 952/925-4321, www.galleriaedina.com; Mon.-Fri. 10am-9pm, Sat. 10am-8pm, Sun. 11am-6pm

### The Shoppes at Arbor Lakes

The sheer size of the Arbor Lakes shopping center is the draw, along with the piazzas and fountains that add a pleasant touch of fantasy to your suburban shopping experience. There are more than 75 stores and restaurants in this complex and well over two dozen in the nearby Fountains shopping area. You'll find nearly every major national chain and some local gems like Evereve. During the summer, you might run into an outdoor music performance.

**MAP 7:** I-94 and I-694 at Hemlock Ln., Maple Grove, 763/424-0504, www.shoppesatarborlakes.com; Mon.-Sat. 10am-9pm, Sun. noon-6pm

## GIFTS AND HOME

### Golden Rule Collective

Handmade and heartfelt, every print, every painting, every piece of jewelry, and every darling little child's apron at Golden Rule is an individual piece of art. Local artisans and national indie designers share the space and show off their designs in a charming little white house on Lake Minnetonka. The tiny carriage house in back houses **Ace General Store** (356 Water St., Excelsior, 952/217-3217, Mon. 11am-4pm, Tues.-Sat. 10am-5pm, Sun. noon-5pm), which offers a collection of wood and leather goods and tools.

MAP 7: 350 Water St., Excelsior, 612/598-2098, www.goldenrulecollective. com; Mon.-Wed. and Fri.-Sat. 10am-5pm, Thurs. 10am-7pm, Sun. noon-5pm

### GRAY Home + Lifestyle
With home goods and clothing in soothing palettes and high-end materials, Gray is where you come to imagine yourself living an artfully comfortable lifestyle. Your cropped sweater can match your throw pillow, and it can all smell of the same lovely soap.

MAP 7: 366 Water St., Excelsior, 952/474-9150, www.grayhomeandlifestyle. com; Mon. 11am-4pm, Tues.-Sat. 10am-5pm, Sun. noon-5pm

### Nordic Ware Factory Store
The Bundt pan was invented here in Minneapolis, in the first-ring suburb of St. Louis Park, to be more precise, when a group of ladies from a local synagogue asked for a pan they could use to bake the coffee cakes they remembered from Germany. Nordic Ware obliged and a classic was born. Nordic Ware, however, is so much more than one pan. The factory store stocks the brand's full line of bakeware, pans, cooking gadgets, and more. Not everything is discounted, but there are some great deals to be had on seconds and discontinued lines.

MAP 7: 4925 Hwy. 7, St. Louis Park, 952/924-9672, www.nordicware.com; Mon.-Sat. 10am-5pm

# CLOTHING AND ACCESSORIES
### Evereve
The folks at Evereve are dedicated to making expecting and no-longer-expecting mothers feel at least as hot as they did pre-baby. And they are enthusiastic about it: Don't be surprised to find your arms draped with $150 pairs of jeans and $35 tanks as you walk in the door. For all the high prices and chic atmosphere, this is a kid-friendly space: Park the kids at the train table and they'll most likely have plenty of company. This is the original, but there's a sister store on Grand Avenue in St. Paul (867 Grand Ave., 651/209-0222, Mon.-Sat. 10am-8pm, Sun. 11am-6pm).

MAP 7: 3914 50th St. W., Edina, 952/746-8255, http://evereve.com; Mon.-Sat. 10am-8pm, Sun. 11am-5pm

### Sota Clothing
Minnesotans wear their love for their home state on their sleeves. And their T-shirts. And their hats. And their bags. On the mugs they carry around. And Sota Clothing thinks you should, too. There's no better souvenir from your time in Minnesota than a pair of MN socks.

MAP 7: 6518 Walker St., St. Louis Park, www.sotaclothing.com; Wed.-Fri. 11am-8pm, Sat. 10am-pm, Sun. noon-5pm

# ANTIQUES
### Hopkins Antique Mall
This is one-stop shopping for antiques aficionados, with more than 60 dealers showing their wares, from furniture to jewelry, Tiffany lamps to collectible lunch boxes, kitchenware to books. Just when you think you've seen it all, there's another level to explore. Many

dealers are eager to buy as well. Be sure to stroll up and down Mainstreet, where there are nearly a dozen other antiques dealers, though none as big as this.

MAP 7: 1008 Mainstreet, Hopkins, 952/931-9748, www.hopkinsantiquemall. com; Mon.-Sat. 11am-6pm, Sun. 11am-5pm

## KIDS' STORES
### Kiddywampus

You've never seen a toy store like this. Spare, open, and modern, Kiddywampus lets the toys—and the kids—take center stage. You probably haven't seen most of these toys before, either. Owner Amy Saldanha hunts down the kind of high-design, high-concept building blocks, art sets, children's furniture, and more that a modern parent might not mind seeing scattered all over the living room. (Kids can test-drive many of the toys to be sure that fun hasn't been sacrificed to design.) Make art with your kids in the art studio (Mon. and Fri. 10 a.m.-4:30 p.m., Tues.-Thurs. 12:30-4:30 p.m., $8).

MAP 7: 1023 Main St., Hopkins, 952/926-7871, www.kiddywampus.com; Tues.-Sat. 10am-6pm, Sun. noon-4pm

# WHERE TO STAY

After new hotels were completed just in time for the cities to host the Super Bowl in 2018, Twin Cities visitors have more choices than ever (and a little more purchasing power), but most of the 40,000-plus hotel rooms are still clustered in two regions.

In downtown Minneapolis, you'll find high-end chains, many of which do a fine job of masquerading as stand-alone hotels with an individual flair to suit the area. While, in general, downtown is your most expensive accommodation choice, there are also one or two surprising bargains. Keep in mind that because downtown hotels cater to business travelers, prices tend to go down, rather than up, on the weekends, sometimes remarkably so. Because it's so easily navigable on foot and is the hub for much of the area's public transportation, including light rail to and from the airport and Mall of America, downtown is a good choice if you're arriving without your own transportation.

Nicollet Island Inn

In the southern suburbs, clustered around the Mall of America and the Minneapolis-St. Paul Airport, you'll find just about every chain hotel you can name—upwards of 30, as a matter of fact. Nearly all of these offer shuttle service to and from the mall (and two options are connected to the mall itself)—convenient not only if shopping is your primary reason for visiting the Twin Cities, but also because the light rail trains depart from the mall to downtown Minneapolis and the airport. You won't, however, find very much charm in the generic concrete jungle.

# HIGHLIGHTS

⭐ **WHERE TO STAY FOR LOCAL LUXURY:** A true Minnesota experience in a land of national chains, the **Hewing Hotel** is a treat from the moment you walk in the door (page 194).

⭐ **BEST HOTEL FOR ART LOVERS: Le Meridien Chambers Minneapolis** prides itself on its multimillion-dollar art collection and also opens a small gallery space to the public (page 194).

⭐ **BEST WAY TO RELIVE THE GILDED AGE:** The **W Minneapolis—The Foshay** is where 1920s verve meets 21st-century swank (page 194).

⭐ **BEST DOWNTOWN VALUE:** In an expense-account world, the **Hotel Minneapolis** offers value and oodles of style for guests paying their own way and watching their budget (page 195).

⭐ **MOST ROMANTIC HOTEL IN VIEW OF CITY SKYSCRAPERS:** It's easy to forget that the **Nicollet Island Inn,** on an island in the Mississippi, is within an easy walk of the central business district (page 195).

⭐ **BEST PLACE TO IMPRESS YOUR GUESTS:** One of the oldest hotels in Minnesota, the **St. Paul Hotel** is the classic embodiment of all that a high-end hotel should be (page 200).

⭐ **BEST PLACE TO SEE THE MISSISSIPPI:** The best place to see the river is right on it, from the floating **Covington Inn Bed and Breakfast** (page 200).

⭐ **BEST HOTEL FOR FAMILIES:** The **Marriott Residence Inn, Edinborough** in Minneapolis's southern suburb of Edina comes with the best amenity of all: a three-story indoor play structure (page 204).

## PRICE KEY

| | |
|---|---|
| **$** | Less than $100 per night |
| **$ $** | $100-200 per night |
| **$ $ $** | More than $200 per night |

## WHERE TO STAY IF...

**YOU'RE ONLY HERE FOR A FEW DAYS:**
Staying in **downtown Minneapolis** makes it easy to take in much of the best of the Twin Cities, from sports to plays to restaurants and nightlife.

**YOU'RE FEELING HIP:**
Settle into your Uptown digs in **South Minneapolis** and embrace life as a hipster. While choices for traditional accommodations here are few, the range of Airbnb options is growing.

**YOU LOVE STUDENT LIFE:**
University of Minnesota student life sprawls well beyond the campus confines into all of **Dinkytown,** where a number of hotels cater to visiting parents and professionals, as well as people who want to be close to downtown Minneapolis without feeling too stuffy.

**YOU LIKE QUIET EVENINGS:**
**Downtown St. Paul** is known for being quiet of an evening, and some people truly like it that way.

**YOU'RE HERE JUST FOR THE MALL OF AMERICA:**
The area's not picturesque, but the string of hotels along the I-494 corridor in the suburb of **Bloomington** are all terrifically convenient to the mall and airport.

Downtown St. Paul offers a couple of reasonably priced chain options, as well as two that are truly unique and tempting: the grand St. Paul Hotel and the floating Covington Inn.

The Dinkytown neighborhood around the University of Minnesota, more or less directly between Minneapolis and St. Paul, also offers a couple of less expensive chain hotel options catering to university guests (meaning that graduation, homecoming, and move-in weekends tend to be booked full), along with homey inns.

When you look to accommodations outside of Minneapolis and St. Paul proper, be sure to pay attention to which "side" of things you'll be staying on: The metro area sprawls, and while the town of Afton, for example, is very convenient for visitors to St. Paul and the east metro, it is quite a trek for those with business in Minneapolis or the west metro.

The reverse is true of the cities of Chanhassen and Chaska.

While prices in general will pleasantly surprise guests used to paying for hotels on the coasts, there aren't a lot of truly low-budget options.

## ALTERNATIVE LODGING

In the Twin Cities, where independent boutique hotels are few and even the chains limit your options, a short-term home rental can be the solution. Alternative lodging sites like Airbnb, Homeaway, and VRBO haven't caused the kind of uproar and disruption here that they have in other cities. About 3,000-4,000 homes and apartments are listed on the various sites, most flying under the radar in quiet neighborhoods and condo buildings. In downtown Minneapolis, most listings are higher-end condos and similar to or higher than hotel prices. Outside of downtown and in St. Paul, you'll find better prices and a homier variety.

# Downtown Minneapolis   **Map 1**

### ✪ Hewing Hotel  $$$

This former warehouse in the hippest part of downtown has been done up in refined cabin chic with delightful local touches, like Faribault Woolen Mills blankets on the luxurious beds. The lobby bar, with its cozy nooks and couches, is a favorite place to spend time, and the rooftop sauna and pool are reason enough to book a room here. Pets are not only welcomed, they are doted on. The Hewing's restaurant, **Tullibee** (Mon.-Fri. 11am-2pm and 5pm-10pm, Sat.-Sun. 10am-2pm and 5pm-10pm), serves updated, high-end Scandinavian fare.

**MAP 1:** 300 Washington Ave. N., Minneapolis, 651/468-0400, www. hewinghotel.com

Hewing Hotel

### ✪ Le Meridien Chambers Minneapolis  $$$

By the time you get to your room, you will have passed about $30 million worth of contemporary art displayed in the lobby. The contemporary rooms themselves show a careful attention to aesthetics (including valuable oil canvases), with clean, comfortable furnishings, two plasma TVs, and an iPod deck in every room. **Mercy** (Sun.-Thurs. 6:30am-11pm, Fri.-Sat. 6:30am-1am), the restaurant on the ground floor, is good for comfort food on an expense-account budget.

**MAP 1:** 901 Hennepin Ave. S., Minneapolis, 612/767-6900, www.lemeridienchambers. com

### ✪ W Minneapolis—The Foshay  $$$

Wilbur Foshay's tribute to the Roaring '20s barely saw the glories of that high-flying decade: It was completed just weeks before the stock market crashed in 1929. Nearly 80 years later, the building's rebirth as one of Minneapolis's poshest hotels is at least as showy as Foshay's original dream, if not more so. The original ceiling was restored at enormous cost, but the opulent furnishings and forward-thinking lighting are entirely 21st century. Wilbur's own office, notoriously extravagant, is now a bar called Prohibition, and his boardroom is available to rent for private events.

**MAP 1:** 821 Marquette Ave., Minneapolis, 612/215-3700, www.wminneapolishotel.com

### Elliot Park Hotel  $$$

Homey luxury with a Scandinavian vibe has moved into this gentrifying corner of downtown Minneapolis. Sip cider or hot chocolate on artfully mismatched chairs in front of an open fireplace in the lounge or the outdoor courtyard. This is a Marriott

Autograph Collection property, with all the little luxuries that come with it: premium linens and products, as well as a docking station and Amazon Alexa in every room.

MAP 1: 823 S. 5th Ave., Minneapolis, 866/376-8604, www.elliotparkhotel.com

### Hotel Ivy $$$

Comfortable, unfussy luxury is the Hotel Ivy's signature, from the cream-and-ivy color scheme to the elegant limestone bathrooms and the 400-thread-count sheets. (A nice touch: All guest rooms feature both a tub and a separate shower.) Part of the Starwood chain, it offers an accommodation option just off the skyway system and convenient to Orchestra Hall and the Minneapolis Convention Center. The Ivy Spa Club, right on the premises, offers top-of-the-line fitness facilities and spa services.

MAP 1: 201 11th St. S., Minneapolis, 612/746-4600, www.thehotelivy.com

Hotel Minneapolis

### ✪ Hotel Minneapolis $$

The Hotel Minneapolis hits some magical sweet spot, combining up-to-the-minute style and good value for a downtown hotel. While it is part of the Marriott chain, the furnishings and design are entirely unique and rooted in local history. Originally built as a bank in 1906, the building kept

W Minneapolis—The Foshay

its original vaults and commanding marble arches as conversation pieces in the lobby and in Restaurant Max.

MAP 1: 215 4th St. S., Minneapolis, 612/340-2000, www.thehotelminneapolis. com

### ✪ Nicollet Island Inn $$

Would you like the river side, the park side, the city side, or the bridge side? The Nicollet Island Inn sits smack in the middle of the island from which it takes its name, so all of its 24 rooms offer distinctive views. The furnishings are distinctive as well, from the modern comfort of Sleep Number beds to the Victorian chairs and damask wallpaper. There's no pool or workout room—but who needs it when some of the most inviting walking paths in the city are right out the front door?

MAP 1: 95 Merriam St. S., Minneapolis, 612/331-1800, www.nicolletislandinn.com

### AC Hotel Minneapolis Downtown $$

Stylish and modern, this is one of the newest additions to downtown Minneapolis. That means you get the freshest take on amenities and hospitality: wooden floors in the guest rooms, outlets and charging ports where you want them, walk-in showers, and a hotel lounge where you actually want to spend your happy hour.

MAP 1: 401 Hennepin Ave., Minneapolis, 612/338-0700, www.marriott.com

The Depot

### The Depot  $$

The Depot is actually two hotels in one, both by Marriott: The Depot Minneapolis, a Renaissance Hotel, and, for extended stays, Residence Inn at The Depot. Both offer Marriott-level services in a fantastic location—just a block or so off the river on one side and a short walk to the skyway system on the other. Rates go way, way down on the weekends, when The Depot transforms from a business hotel to a comfortable family retreat (look for affordable packages including water park passes).

MAP 1: 225 3rd Ave. S., Minneapolis, 612/375-1700, www.thedepotminneapolis. com

### Hampton Inn & Suites Minneapolis/Downtown  $$

The Hampton Inn couldn't have a better location. Connected directly to the skyway system, it's convenient for conference-goers, business travelers, and anyone here to see a show or a game at Target Center or Target Field. Expect plenty of thoughtful amenities, including free Wi-Fi, lap desks that roll over the bed, and weekday breakfast to go. Suites with kitchenettes are available.

MAP 1: 19 8th St. N., Minneapolis, 612/341-3333, www.hamptoninn.com

### Hilton Minneapolis  $$

The Hilton makes a show-stopping first impression—all marble and mirrored columns, with chandeliers and bronze statues in the lobby. The lobby's always a lively place, too, with frequent events in the ballrooms upstairs and a large, popular bar. The 800-plus guest rooms aren't quite so lavishly appointed, but with carved oak furniture and up-to-date fabrics they go beyond the typical hotel room.

MAP 1: 1001 Marquette Ave. S., Minneapolis, 612/376-1000, www.hilton.com

### Hyatt Regency Minneapolis  $$

On the outside this downtown stalwart looks like a giant white cruise ship docked on the end of Nicollet Mall, but on the inside it is both welcoming and modern. A small handful of the 500-plus rooms have balconies, a fun amenity on the upper floors. Ask about hypoallergenic rooms. The Hyatt is conveniently located, only three blocks away from the nearest skyway entrance.

MAP 1: 1300 Nicollet Mall, Minneapolis, 612/370-1234, www.minneapolis.hyatt.com

## Grand Hotel Minneapolis  $$

From the red-coated doorman to the ornate furnishings to the Godiva chocolate on your pillow at night, Kimpton's Grand Hotel harks back to a time of great luxury and service. Guests appreciate the full range of business services and the direct connection to the skyway system, as well as complimentary access to the Lifetime Fitness Center, with a full-size pool and indoor running track.

MAP 1: 615 2nd Ave. S.,
Minneapolis, 612/373-0407, www.
grandhotelminneapolis.com

## Loews Minneapolis  $$

Loews offers a softer version of modern sophistication, after a design overhaul (this building was, for a long time, the Graves 601 hotel). The wood is blonder, the lobby lighter, and the art more accessible. But it's still a place that attracts local diners with modern American cuisine at Cosmos and a one-of-a-kind champagne bar at Releve. Loews is connected to the skyway system and one block from the light rail. Ask for an upper-level room with a view of the skyline.

MAP 1: 601 1st Ave. N., Minneapolis,
612/677-1100, www.loewshotels.com

## LuMINN Hotel Minneapolis  $$

Sleek and *Star Trek* chic, this boutique hotel is decorated with hard lines, bright whites, and neon colors (in fact, you get to choose the color of the lighting in your room). Every room is a suite, with kitchen facilities and amazingly deep, soft beds. Most rooms don't have great views, but otherwise its location in the heart of downtown, right off the light rail, is ideal, especially for people planning to explore the city's nightlife.

MAP 1: 219 S. 4th St.,
Minneapolis, 612/338-3500, www.
luminnhotelminneapolis.com

## The Marquette Hotel  $$

The Marquette has consistently been one of the area's best travel values. Located in the IDS Center, Minneapolis's tallest building, it's been around long enough to have mastered the art of customer service. Rooms are extra large and comfortably appointed for business travelers. Many rooms look out on the elegant obelisk that was the city's tallest until the IDS surpassed it: the Foshay Tower.

MAP 1: 710 Marquette Ave., Minneapolis,
612/333-4545, www.themarquettehotel.
com

## Marriott City Center  $$

The fifth-floor lobby of the Marriott City Center is like Grand Central Station: a popular meeting spot not only for guests of the hotel but for travelers and businesspeople of all sorts. The rooms, however, are serene and welcoming, with tasteful modern decor. The top floors of this 31-story hotel have stunning views (and higher prices to match). The Marriott is connected directly to the skyway and located right in the heart of downtown's shopping and business district.

MAP 1: 30 7th St. S., Minneapolis,
612/349-4000, www.marriott.com

## Radisson RED Minneapolis  $$

One of the newest additions to downtown's hotel scene, Radisson RED brings all the artsy hipness the brand promises, with big, bold murals on the walls, wood floors in the rooms, an app for ordering from the kitchen, and a bring-your-pooch policy. On the north end of downtown and right off the light rail, this is a prime location for bar hopping.

MAP 1: 609 3rd St. S., Minneapolis,
612/252-5400, www.radissonred.com

### 300 Clifton  $$

Here's a taste of how the lumber and flour barons of Minneapolis once lived, in a renovated 1887 mansion just a short walk from the heart of downtown. Choose one of five unique rooms, including the renovated former blacksmith's forge, with its own private garden. Guests have full use of the fitness center and spa at the Hotel Ivy, about a mile away.

MAP 1: 300 Clifton Ave., Minneapolis, 612/281-1550, www.300clifton.com

### Aloft  $

Just like your much cooler friend's loft-like home: nine-foot ceilings, platform beds, huge walk-in showers, and funky furnishings (love the faux cowhide on the walls) feel very downtown and of-the-moment, as do the Euro-inspired lobby lounge and bar. You can't beat Aloft's location, a block from the river and right across from the Guthrie Theater.

MAP 1: 900 Washington Ave. S., Minneapolis, 612/455-8400, www. alofthotels.com

# South Minneapolis                Map 2

### Moxy Minneapolis Uptown  $$

Three words that tell you this is an Uptown hotel: "vinyl listening lounge." Also: "shuffleboard," "foosball," and "hammocks." The amenities, the atmosphere, and the location are all chosen to welcome a very specific, young, hipster demographic. While rooms are small, common areas are designed like a club that never wants you to leave. It's on the Greenway bike path and in walking distance from restaurants and nightlife.

MAP 2: 1121 Lake St. W., Minneapolis, 612/822-5020, www.marriott.com

### Sheraton Minneapolis Midtown  $$

The Sheraton Midtown fills a need for lodging in a neighborhood where there really aren't many choices. The hotel is connected to the Midtown Global Market, a shopping and dining destination, and right on the Midtown Greenway, a popular bike path. It's also about two miles south of downtown and convenient to major highways. It's not,

however, an area where you are likely to feel comfortable on your own after dark. The rooms are comfortable, up-to-date, and good-sized.

MAP 2: 2901 Chicago Ave. S., Minneapolis, 612/821-7600, www. sheratonminneapolismidtown

### Minneapolis International Hostel  $

This 1909 mansion in a gentrifying section of South Minneapolis is a short walk from both downtown and Uptown, making it perfect for younger and cash-strapped travelers. There are 30 beds in five dormitory-style rooms segregated by gender, as well as eight private rooms: three singles, four doubles, and a triple. Dorm guests get a storage locker, and linens and towels are provided. All guests share the spacious and inviting sitting room and porch, as well as the fully equipped kitchen.

MAP 2: 2400 Stevens Ave. S., Minneapolis, 612/522-5000, www.minneapolishostel. com

## Graduate Minneapolis $$

The most convenient lodging option for anyone visiting the University of Minnesota is, in fact, right on the campus itself, surrounded by academic buildings and, of course, student traffic. A renovation has brought an inviting Northwoods feel to both the rooms and the large common areas. Zip around campus on a complimentary bike.

MAP 3: 615 Washington Ave. SE, Minneapolis, 612/379-8888, www. graduatehotels.com/minneapolis

## Hotel Alma $$

This tiny, seven-room hotel is the dream of chef Alex Roberts, who is known for keeping customers very happy for over a decade at Alma, the restaurant downstairs. Each room is exquisitely appointed with custom furnishings, high ceilings, and a certain indescribable air of relaxation. Hotel Alma is near the Mississippi River and convenient to both the University of Minnesota and downtown Minneapolis.

MAP 3: 528 University Ave. SE, Minneapolis, 612/379-4909, www. almampls.com

## Wales House $

The Carver family makes guests at Wales House feel like family. On the edge of the University of Minnesota's East Bank, the inn is on a very quiet residential street, giving guests, many of whom are visiting the university from overseas, a taste of authentic neighborhood life. Guests gather for an organic continental breakfast each morning and have the use of the well-stocked kitchen and three common areas.

MAP 3: 1115 5th St. SE, Minneapolis, 612/331-3931, www.waleshouse.com

# Downtown St. Paul and West Side

## Map 4

### ❂ St. Paul Hotel  $$$

Old-school elegance is the rule at the St. Paul Hotel. The current building was built in 1910, but a hotel has operated on this spot in the heart of downtown St. Paul almost continuously since 1856. From the sweeping curved drive to the uniformed doormen in the grand lobby to the four-poster beds in the rooms, it almost feels like you're stepping back into that Gilded Age yourself. Guests should be sure to pack their gym shoes: The fitness center, open 24 hours, is on the roof of the hotel and commands stunning views of St. Paul.

**MAP 4:** 350 Market St., St. Paul, 651/292-9292, www.saintpaulhotel.com

### ❂ Covington Inn Bed and Breakfast  $$

This is the closest you'll ever get to the Mississippi without getting in and swimming. The Covington is a 1946 tugboat permanently moored at Harriet Island, right in downtown St. Paul. The four suites are remarkably spacious for having been carved out of the tight decks of a small ship. In fact, you won't have to give up any of the comforts of home while staying on the boat, from private bathrooms and air conditioning to a working fireplace. The only thing missing is a television, which your hosts chose to leave out on purpose.

**MAP 4:** 100 Harriet Island Rd., St. Paul, 651/292-1411, www.covingtoninn.com

### DoubleTree by Hilton  $$

Convenience, value, and familiarity are all good reasons to choose the Doubletree when you're staying in downtown St. Paul. It's right on the skyway system and offers a shuttle to the Xcel Energy Center for those here for large conferences or concerts. The fitness center is more extensive than most hotel gyms—which you might need to work off those famous Doubletree cookies.

**MAP 4:** 411 Minnesota St., St. Paul, 651/291-8800, www.doubletree.hilton.com

### Embassy Suites  $$

While downtown St. Paul is quaint and serene enough, hotel guests who need an escape can enjoy the quiet interior courtyard with its own family of ducks. Every room at the Embassy Suites has a separate sitting area with a pullout sofa, and the hotel lives up to its brand with an extensive breakfast and happy hour.

**MAP 4:** 175 10th St. E., St. Paul, 651/224-5400, www.embassysuites.hilton.com

St. Paul Hotel

### Hyatt Place St. Paul Downtown $$

St. Paul's Lowertown district is the place to be, and the Hyatt is right at the heart of it, built in a post office from the early 20th century. Most of the historic charm has been preserved on the outside, while the inside feels like a fresh, modern hotel. Rooms are large and the amenities are up to date.

MAP 4: 180 Kellogg Blvd. E., St. Paul, 651/647-5000, www.hyatt.com

### Intercontinental St. Paul Riverfront $$

A change of hands has remade this accommodation into a hotel worthy of the spectacular views of the skyline and the river (22 stories up, if you wish). Expect the style and service that make the Intercontinental brand, including amenities focused on the needs of the business traveler.

MAP 4: 11 Kellogg Blvd. E., St. Paul, 651/292-1900, www.intercontinental.com

### Hotel 340 $

St. Paul's only boutique hotel is a real gem. The 35 rooms take up the top

Hotel 340

floors of the St. Paul Athletic Club, a storied building with opulent turn-of-the-20th-century details. Rooms are all equipped with kitchenettes and have (so unusual in any hotel) lovely hardwood floors and ample windows. Many have views of the Minnesota State Capitol. Guests also get to use the athletic facilities at the St. Paul Club's Summit Avenue building, about a mile away.

MAP 4: 340 Cedar St., St. Paul, 651/280-4120, www.hotel340.com

# Greater Twin Cities          Map 7

### The Hotel Landing $$$

The Landing fits right in in tony downtown Wayzata, a charming lakeside town with a certain boat-shoes-and-polo-shirt vibe. From the outside it looks like a seaside resort. On the inside it feels like a tony club. It's great for a spa getaway (at the in-house Läka Spa) or doing business in the western suburbs.

MAP 7: 925 Lake St. E., Wayzata, 952/777-7900, www.thehotellanding.com

### Intercontinental St. Paul-Minneapolis Airport $$$

Business travelers, say it with me: Finally the Twin Cities has an airport hotel. The Intercontinental is connected directly to Terminal 1 and has its own security checkpoint. It has everything you need without ever leaving the grounds (although, of course, we don't recommend that): two restaurants, a spa, meeting rooms, and a glassed-in rooftop bar that will give you a view of the Twin Cities that few get to see, besides air traffic controllers.

MAP 7: 5005 Glumack Dr., Minneapolis, 612/725-0500, www.intercontinentalmsp.com

### Radisson Blu Mall of America $$$

While there are plenty of hotels near the Mall of America, the Radisson Blu was the first connected directly to it—and by far the ritziest in the area. Completed in 2013, this was the second Radisson Blu in North America (the first is in Chicago) and represents the top of the upscale chain's range. The 500 rooms are decorated in three modern styles, designated "urban," "naturally cool," and "mansion house." Every amenity you can think of is on-site, up to and including a spa. If there's anything else you need, the mall is right next door.

MAP 7: 2100 Killebrew Dr., Bloomington, 952/881-5258, www.radissonblu.com

### Afton House Inn $$

When you need a getaway in the midst of your getaway, the Afton House Inn is a good choice. Located 20 miles east of St. Paul, it's convenient to everything in the eastern metro area, and yet the quiet river town of Afton can be a destination in itself. With two dozen individually decorated rooms of all sizes, the inn has the charm of a bed-and-breakfast with the convenience of a small hotel. The Afton House Inn also offers riverboat cruises and is well known in the Twin Cities for the high quality of its restaurant.

MAP 7: 3291 St. Croix Tr. S., Afton, 651/436-8883, www.aftonhouseinn.com

### Bird House Inn $$

Make yourself at home, borrow the kind innkeepers' bikes, check out their extensive DVD collection— that's the ethos here at Bird House Inn, about 20 miles from downtown Minneapolis. The Victorian house with the wide wraparound porch and second-story deck sits three blocks from the parks and public docks on the shores of Lake Minnetonka. The living and dining rooms are prim and formal, but the seven guest rooms are more relaxed (the Garden Room, in particular, is unique with its themed murals).

MAP 7: 371 Water St., Excelsior, 952/474-0196, www.birdhouseinn.com

### Crowne Plaza Bloomington $$

The Crowne Plaza is one of a host of chain hotels convenient to the Mall of America and the Minneapolis-St. Paul Airport, but a few things set it apart. One is its Olympic-size indoor swimming pool, pleasantly surrounded by lounge chairs in a space that—unlike many hotel pools—actually invites lounging. It's also just one block away from the Hyland Lake Park Preserve, an oasis here in concrete-covered suburbia. While at other suburban hotels, you might not even be able to walk around the block, while here you can walk, jog, or even ski in the 1,000-acre preserve.

MAP 7: 5401 Green Valley Dr., Bloomington, 952/831-8000, www.cpmsp.com

### Great Wolf Lodge $$

Here you'll find Minnesota's largest water park and a family-friendly hotel all in one. Passes to all the slipping and sliding and lazy river-riding you wish come included with a stay, along with a full calendar of family

# CAMPING OUT

You have to get pretty far outside of the central cities to pitch a tent or park an RV, but it's still possible to combine a trip to the Twin Cities with some good old-fashioned camping.

The **Three Rivers Park District** (www.threeriversparkdistrict.org) maintains three campgrounds within easy driving distance of Minneapolis. Call 763/559-6700 to make reservations at any of the campgrounds. A $7.50 fee per reservation will be charged. Campgrounds are open May-October. The campground in **Baker Park Reserve** (763/694-7662, $20-28 per night) is 20 miles west of Minneapolis and has 203 sites, about half with electricity. The 54 sites at **Lake Auburn Campground** (952/443-2911, $16-19) near Victoria, about 25 miles west of Minneapolis, are more rustic, with no electric or water hookups and no showers. The sites at **Red Pine Family Camping Area** (763/694-7777, $16) near Prior Lake, about 26 miles south of Minneapolis, are hike-in only, with no amenities beyond pit latrines.

Two **Minnesota State Park** campgrounds are within easy driving distance of the metro area. Make reservations for campsites up to one year in advance at 866/857-2757 or www.stayatmnparks.com. The reservation fee is $8.50. Campsite fees are $12-20 per night. In the far east metro area, **Afton State Park** (6959 Peller Ave., South Hastings, 651/436-5391, www.dnr.state.mn.us) is about 20 miles southeast of St. Paul and open year-round. There are 24 tenting sites located about 1 mile from the parking lot, with wood and water available there. Flush toilets are located in the camp office, with vault toilets near the camping area. **Minnesota Valley State Park** (19825 Park Blvd., Jordan, 651/259-5774, www.dnr.state.mn.us) is about 40 miles southwest of Minneapolis, with 25 drive-in sites (good for car camping or RVs up to 50 feet long), 8 hike-in sites, and 3 sites that can accommodate horses. The campground is open mid-May through Labor Day.

The nationwide chain of RV parks, KOA, has two campgrounds (or is that "kampgrounds?") in the metro area. **Minneapolis Northwest KOA** (10410 Brockton Ln. N., Maple Grove, 763/420-2255, www.koa.com) is 20 miles north of Minneapolis. **Minneapolis Southwest KOA** (3315 166th St. W., Jordan, 952/492-6440, www.koa.org) is about 35 miles south of Minneapolis. Both are open May-October and have RV and tent sites and cabins available, as well as a swimming pool and a mini-golf course on-site.

activities. Parents are not forgotten: yoga classes and wine and cheese trays are also available. Ask about family rooms with bunkbeds that sleep up to four kids.
MAP 7: 1700 American Blvd., Bloomington, 952/851-9653, www. greatwolf.com

### JW Marriott Mall of America  $$

Walk out of your hotel room, down to the lobby, and right into America's shopping mecca, the Mall of America. A 2015 expansion added the 342-room JW Marriott along with the MOA's new grand entrance, a sweeping front door for the mall. The Marriott is sleek and up to date, with contemporary lines and all the modern amenities.

MAP 7: 2141 Lindau Ln., Bloomington, 612/615-0100, www.marriott.com

### Westin Edina Galleria  $$

Cool, modern class is the Westin's style, and it suits this location well: directly attached to the small, upscale Galleria mall. Just south of Minneapolis and convenient to major highways on the west side of the metro, the Westin is a good choice for business travelers who don't necessarily have business to do downtown. In addition to high-end shopping, there are also great dining options right in the Galleria, as well as a McCormick and Schmick's seafood restaurant in the hotel itself.

MAP 7: 3201 Galleria, Edina, 952/567-5000, www.westinedinagalleria

## ✪ Marriott Residence Inn, Edinborough  $

All Residence Inn hotels offer affordable suites with kitchenettes. This one, however, also comes with an indoor park. Edinborough, maintained by the city of Edina, is a one-acre indoor park with flowers, trees, a small waterfall, and a concert stage, along with an indoor pool, a gym, and a three-story children's climbing structure called Adventure Peak. It's all attached to the hotel—along with a child-care center and senior citizens residence—and guests get free entry. The park itself can be deafeningly loud, but the hotel is completely insulated from the noise.

MAP 7: 3400 Edinborough Way, Edina, 952/893-9300, www.marriott.com

## Oak Ridge Hotel and Conference Center  $

Oak Ridge is a massive complex that feels like a little city unto itself out in the western suburbs. It's especially popular with large corporate groups but accommodates families and vacation travelers as well. The rooms feel particularly anonymous, even for a hotel, but they are freshly decorated and sizable (many suites are available). Visitors can walk the trails on the hotel's 130-acre grounds or just enjoy the view of the small lake and woods right outside their windows.

MAP 7: 1 Oak Ridge Dr., Chaska, 952/368-3100, www.oakridgeminneapolis. com

# DAY TRIPS

As blessed as they are with ready access to lakes and trails, residents of the Twin Cities have a time-honored tradition of getting the heck out of town whenever they possibly can.

They go "up north" or "to the cabin"—vague answers to the question "What did you do this weekend?" that are as evocative to a native Minnesotan as a full description of the destination and the route. They tend to do this, en masse, on summer Fridays, when the highways headed out of town (especially going north and east) clog up in the early afternoon.

Even if you don't have a family cabin in Minnesota, you can enjoy a little bit of the "up north" lifestyle with a weekend in Duluth, on the shore of Lake Superior. Or you can spend a day in one of Minnesota's most charming small towns: shopping for antiques in Stillwater, hiking up the bluffs of Red Wing, or soaking up the college-town atmosphere in Northfield. When you head out of the cities, the transformation is dramatic. You can leave behind the skyscrapers and mild congestion

Split Rock Lighthouse

of either downtown in a matter of minutes and find yourself in a compact grid of single-family homes. You can put the straight urban streets behind you and find the curvy lanes of suburbia in another easy quarter of an hour, and then a few moments later you're driving through farmland. Stick to the two-lane rural highways and you'll come upon two-intersection towns in a steady rhythm, the sort with a church, a coffee shop, and a hardware store.

Minnesota's flat prairie is a stunning sight for natives of the hillier, woodsier, more crowded coasts, who may never have seen the horizon over land. Watching lightning strike where the land meets the sky, miles away, during

## HIGHLIGHTS

 **BEST ANTIQUES SHOPPING IN MINNESOTA:** With a half dozen large antiques stores and antiquarian booksellers within easy walking distance, Stillwater's **Historic Main Street** takes the prize, hands down (page 209).

 **MOST JAW-DROPPING VIEW OF THE MISSISSIPPI RIVER:** Near Red Wing, the great river broadens into the stunning Lake Pepin, easily viewed from a 20-mile stretch of the **Great River Road** (page 215).

 **BEST BIRDING, EVEN FOR NON-BIRDERS:** Eagles and other raptors congregate around Lake Pepin's warm waters on the Mississippi River and are easily spotted from the **National Eagle Center** (page 215).

 **BEST PLACE TO ENJOY THE STUDENT LIFESTYLE:** In the quiet college town of Northfield, students have long enjoyed the pleasure of hiking and running in **Carleton College**'s 880-acre Cowling Arboretum (page 220).

 **BEST TREAT FOR SHIPPING BUFFS:** With a copy of the *Duluth Shipping News* in hand, you can be sure to time your stop in **Maritime Duluth** at the aerial lift bridge in **Canal Park** to see it allow a massive freighter to pass through to the docks (page 224).

 **BEST WAY TO GO BACK IN TIME:** The railroad helped transform Duluth from a swamp to a major shipping port. Now you can enjoy pleasure rides along the North Shore of Lake Superior or the wooded St. Louis River, leaving from the **Duluth Union Depot** (page 227).

 **MOST ICONIC MINNESOTA SIGHT:** The **Split Rock Lighthouse** looks impressive on a postcard or Minnesota Historical Society brochure, but that's nothing compared to marveling at the building in person and staring straight down the bluff at Lake Superior 600 feet below (page 229).

# Day Trips

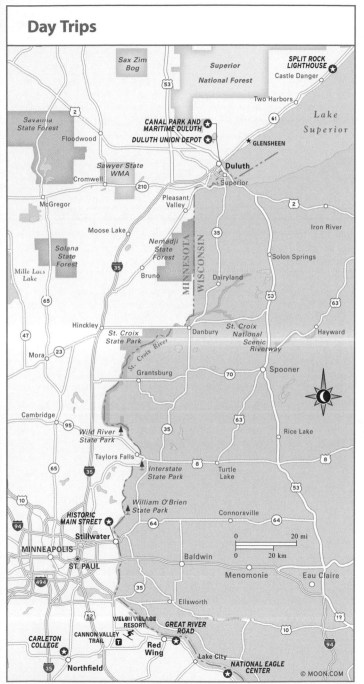

© MOON.COM

early-summer thunderstorms is simply unforgettable (if a little ill-advised, unless you're familiar with the local weather patterns). As you head south and east toward Red Wing and the bluff country, the prairie starts to roll and then spike into majestic hills with a downward slant that drops you right at the Mississippi River. North of the Twin Cities, the ancient mountains of the Iron Range touch down lightly at Duluth, a city built between the foothills and *gitchigami* (great water), as the Ojibwe call Lake Superior. And all along the way, there are lakes—well more than the advertised 10,000—and the Minnesota landscape that calls Twin Citians inexorably to head up north and to the cabin.

## PLANNING YOUR TIME

If you have an extra day or two in the Twin Cities, it's easy enough to head for the small towns and farmland that surround them—easy, that is, if you have your own transportation. Stillwater, just 20 miles from St. Paul, is close enough to be considered a commuting suburb, but it has enough history and personality of its own to make it worth exploring. This is our top pick if you've got limited time. It's a very comfortable day trip, but the huge selection of bed-and-breakfasts and the great dining options could easily tempt you to stay longer.

Two of Minnesota's most charming small towns, Red Wing and Northfield, are also within short driving distance, to the southeast and south of the cities, respectively. An ambitious sightseer could combine the two trips into one day but would lose out on the whole point of a relaxing, laid-back southern Minnesota jaunt.

Duluth is both a popular weekend getaway and a good place to kick off a more outdoorsy expedition on the North Shore. While you could certainly get a taste of the city in a day of wandering Canal Park, the 300-mile round-trip drive (straight north and then back south on I-35) might take the joy out of it. A better idea would be to plan at least one overnight, preferably in a homey bed-and-breakfast, and make sure you have enough time to drive up the stunning shore of Lake Superior, at least as far as the Split Rock Lighthouse.

Summer brings out the boating crowd and the T-shirt-buying hordes, but Duluth's famous "air conditioning" (the lake keeps the center of town as much as 10-20°F cooler than the surrounding area) can make braving the crowds worth it. The North Shore, like much of Minnesota, truly shines in September and October. (Fall foliage typically peaks in early October.)

Any expedition outside the Twin Cities requires a car, with a couple of possible exceptions: An Amtrak train makes one trip a day each way to Red Wing, and Greyhound services Duluth.

# Stillwater

Stillwater is where Twin Citians go to relax. Just half an hour from St. Paul, the small town on the St. Croix River is close enough to be a commuting suburb but distinct enough in its history to be an easy escape from the daily grind. May-October, tourists fill the historic downtown on the riverfront, an all-in-one stop for shopping, boating, fine dining, and drinking beer on a long summer evening on a deck overlooking the river. In the off-season—Minnesota's beautiful autumn and fleeting spring, even the cold winter—the crowds are smaller, but all of Stillwater's delights are still open and available. Stillwater can easily be enjoyed in a day—or even just a long evening.

## SIGHTS
### ✪ HISTORIC MAIN STREET

A trip to Stillwater can start and end quite satisfactorily on historic Main Street, which stretches along the riverfront. Storefronts dating to the mid-19th century crowd the sidewalk, now occupied by bookstores, candy shops, and tchotchke boutiques as well as antiques stores, antiques stores, and more antiques stores. Start at the south end, where Nelson Street crosses Main Street, and stroll north about half a mile until the shopping district ends abruptly in a bluff. How long it takes you will depend on how avid a shopper you are. At either end of your trip, long, steep flights of steps (the steps at the south end are known as the **Stillwater Steps**) will take you to the top of the

Stillwater's Historic Main Street

bluff for spectacular views of the St. Croix and the still green and undeveloped Wisconsin side of the river.

## HISTORIC WASHINGTON COUNTY COURTHOUSE

When the Washington County Courthouse (101 Pine St. W., Stillwater; 651/275-7075, www.co.washington.mn.us; Mon.-Wed. 9am-4:30pm, Thurs.-Fri. 9am-6pm, Sat. 10am-4:30pm; free, donations accepted) opened in 1870, Stillwater was a boomtown, flush with logging money. While government functions have moved to a more modern building, the grand structure—the oldest existing courthouse in Minnesota—stands proudly on the bluffs overlooking the St. Croix. Several guided tours are available each day. Visiting kids can do scavenger hunts and try on period costumes.

## STILLWATER AERIAL LIFT BRIDGE

The Stillwater aerial lift bridge, built in 1931, is one of only two of its type left in Minnesota (the other is in Duluth). The central part of the bridge lifts straight up, rather than tilt, to let boats pass through. The bridge is of tremendous sentimental value to locals and visitors alike, and to save it, they had to close it—to vehicles, that is. Because it has serious structural issues, it was replaced by a much larger bridge downstream in 2016 and is now open to pedestrians and bicycles only.

## WARDEN'S HOUSE MUSEUM

At the north end of Main Street, the Washington County Historical Society displays another piece of Stillwater's history in the Warden's House Museum (602 Main St. N., Stillwater, 651/439-5956; May-Oct.

lift bridge in Stillwater

Thurs.-Sun. 1pm-5pm; $5 adults, $1 children 17 and under). From the time it was completed in 1853 until 1914, the building housed 13 wardens who presided over the Minnesota Territorial (and later State) Penitentiary in Stillwater. Most of its 14 rooms are decorated in late-19th-century period style. Others house exhibits on the lumbering industry and some famous residents of the prison, including Jesse James's partners in crime, Jim, Bob, and Cole Younger.

## RESTAURANTS

The best Texas-style barbecue in Minnesota is just a few miles south of Stillwater in Bayport at the Bayport BBQ (328 5th Ave. N., Bayport, 651/955-6337, www.bayportbbq.com; Thurs.-Sun. 11am-2pm and 5pm-8pm; $7-13). Order your brisket, smoked chicken, ribs, house-made hot links, and sides by the pound, and it all comes to the table on a giant commercial half-sheet metal tray covered in wax paper. Don't miss Bayport's own vinegary barbecue sauce. Live blues acts play most evenings, and there may be a cover charge.

Even natives of the Twin Cities, who are now spoiled for choices when it comes to fine dining, have been known to drive to Stillwater for a memorable meal—or even a memorable glass of wine. **Domacin Wine Bar** (102 2nd St. S. #1, Stillwater, 651/439-1352, www. domacinwinebar.com; Mon.-Tues. 4pm-10pm, Wed.-Thurs. 4pm-11pm, Fri.-Sat. 4pm-midnight, Sun. 4pm-10pm; $20-38) serves both. Whether you want a flight with some Marcona almonds and carpaccio on the side, or a full dinner (the menu changes seasonally) with the perfect glass, you'll feel right at home. Come on Sunday evenings for the chef's tasting menu.

A luxurious meal can also be had at the **Dock Café** (425 Nelson St. E., Stillwater, 651/430-3770, www. dockcafe.com; Mon.-Thurs. 11am-8pm, Fri.-Sat. 11am-9:30pm, Sun. 11am-8pm; $15-30), with the added bonus of a broad, shaded patio right on the river. Although none of the fish comes from the St. Croix River, the location calls for a menu heavy on fish and seafood, from the local favorite walleye to scallops, shrimp, tuna, and salmon. Non-fish lovers can enjoy chicken, steaks, and burgers, but vegetarians will have a tough time filling up.

Built right into the bluffs along Main Street, **Feller** (402 Main St. S., Stillwater, 651/571-3501, www. fellerrestaurant.com, daily 11am-midnight; $16-35) pays homage to the wild flavors of the Upper Midwest. The brief menu changes frequently, but look for local cheeses, wild mushrooms, rye berries, quail, trout, and bison. Sharing space with Feller in the Lora Hotel, **The Long Goodbye** (daily 11am-2pm) and **Made** (Sun.-Thurs., 7am-3pm, Fri.-Sat. 7am-5pm) are your top choices along Main Street for cocktails and coffee, respectively.

**Phil's Tara Hideaway** (15021 60th St. N., Stillwater, 651/439-9850, www. tarahideaway.com; Tues.-Fri. 11am-10pm, Sat. 4pm-10pm, Sun. 4pm-9pm; $16-30) is a jumble of histories and influences: Originally a speakeasy and then a roadhouse, it now serves the Greek cuisine of current owner Phil Barbaitsis in a tiny log cabin. It's known for some of the best steak around. Come early or make reservations, because it gets crowded—and loud.

## RECREATION

While you can have a terrific time in Stillwater without ever getting on the water, the St. Croix River is an obvious attraction. The **St. Croix Riverboat and Packet Co.** (525 Main St. S., Stillwater, 651/430-1234, www. stillwaterriverboats.com; $19-33) offers two or three cruises a day, most with a meal included. Six boats, with capacities of 50 to 675, make the tours north up the picturesque St. Croix, passing under the lift bridge.

You can also ride smaller—much smaller—boats on the river, namely the two-passenger gondolas of **Gondola Romantica** (Nelson St. on the riverfront, Stillwater, 651/439-1783, www.gondolaromantica.com; May-Oct. daily noon-midnight by appointment). Rides on the Venetian-style boats poled by burly men in striped sailor shirts start at $95 for 45 minutes. Make an appointment; walk-ups are only available as the company's

gondola passing under the lift bridge

schedule allows. Packages combining a ride with a meal at the Dock Café are also available.

If you want to be in control of your own craft, rent a stand-up paddleboard from 45 Degrees (229 Main St. S., Stillwater, 651/430-3609, www.45-degrees.com; Sun.-Mon. noon-5pm, Tues.-Sat. 10am-7pm; $25 half-day, $50 full-day).

To see Stillwater from the land, hop on the Stillwater Trolley (400 Nelson St. E., 651/430-0352, www.stillwatertrolley.com; $13.50 adults, $12.50 seniors, $7.50 children) for a 45-minute narrated tour. This is a great way to get up on the bluffs above Stillwater for a view of the St. Croix valley, and to learn about the lumber barons' mansions, many of which are now B&Bs.

To see the town on foot—and learn why so many Twin Citians come here to enjoy the food—sign up for a tour with Foodies on Foot (855/236-6343, www.foodiesonfootmn.com; $70-75). From a bloody Mary brunch tour to a progressive beer dinner, these guides have the days covered. Be prepared to walk as much as you eat and to keep going despite the weather.

## SHOPS

Shopping is a pastime and a passion for many visitors to Stillwater, many drawn specifically by the well more than half a dozen antiques shops and antiquarian booksellers downtown. You'll encounter rare finds but not too many deals. One of the largest antiques shops is Staples Mill Antiques (410 Main St. N., Stillwater, 888/489-6682, www.staplesmillantiques.com; daily 10am-5pm), located in the old mill building at the north end of Main Street. As many as 30 dealers sell in the store's three levels, on more than 10,000 square feet of sales floor. You'll find pieces large and small, including furniture, Depression glass, jewelry, and old magazines.

Shop for deliciously exquisite paper goods and baubles at Mara Mi (201 Main St. S., Stillwater, 651/689-1730, www.mara-mi.com; Mon.-Thurs. 8am-6pm, Fri. 8am-7pm, Sat. 9am-7pm, Sun. 10am-6pm), then stop at the in-store café for exquisitely delicious cupcakes.

Midtown Antiques (301 Main St. S., Stillwater, 651/430-0808, www.midtownantiques.com; Mon.-Thurs. 10am-5pm, Fri.-Sat. 10am-7pm, Sun. 11am-6pm; during summer Mon.-Thurs. until 6pm, Fri.-Sat. until 8pm) is even larger than Staples Mill Antiques, with 100 dealers in an overwhelming 30,000 square feet. With so much on offer, you could stumble across virtually anything on one of the three floors. Appropriate to the setting, many dealers specialize in Victorian pieces, others in modern or Middle Eastern. A particularly nice selection of old advertisements is available.

Valley Bookseller (217 Main St. N., Stillwater, 651/430-3385, www.valleybookseller.com; Mon.-Sat. 9am-8pm, Sun. 9am-5pm) is an independent bookseller with a serious independent streak, right down to the birds living in a beautiful glass house in the middle of the store. While most of the selection is new books, a few good bargains on used are mixed in. Free Wi-Fi is available, too.

## WHERE TO STAY

Stillwater is known for its historical inns and bed-and-breakfast options. The Stillwater Bed and Breakfast Association (www.stillwaterbb.com) represents seven of them, all within easy walking distance of Main Street and the waterfront. High-season weekend rates are given here. Prices drop considerably in the winter and on weekdays. Some inns have a two-night minimum on the weekends.

Among the best known is the **Elephant Walk Inn** (801 Pine St. W., Stillwater, 651/430-0359, www. elephantwalkbb.com; $149-289 d). Proprietors Rita and Jon Graybill have filled the Victorian mansion with mementos from their diplomatic tours in Europe and Asia, and each of the four rooms reflects the flavor of one of their favorite countries. The house and owners are both filled to bursting with charm, right down to a complimentary bottle of wine and the four-course breakfast that comes with each night's stay.

Particularly convenient to downtown, the **Rivertown Inn** (306 Olive St. W., Stillwater, 651/430-2955, www. rivertowninn.com; $175-545 d) has nine rooms, each decorated in the style of a favorite author, from Agatha Christie to Oscar Wilde to Lewis Carroll. The mansion, with its broad, comfortable porch, and the carriage house are surrounded by fantastical gardens with fountains and a gazebo. The large professional kitchen offers cooking classes about once a month. Plan ahead if you want to include one in your trip: These sell out fast.

High above the southern end of downtown, the **Ann Bean Mansion** (319 Pine St. W., Stillwater, 651/430-0355 or 877/837-4400, www. annbeanmansion.com; $159-289 d) represents a lumberman's wife's determination to show up her neighbors with a grand house. The five rooms are all comfortably, though not sumptuously, furnished. The fourth-floor tower room is as cozy as a tree house and has one of the best views in Stillwater. The mansion does have a resident cat, but guests may ask that it be kept in the innkeeper's residence.

**Lora Hotel** (402 Main St. S., Stillwater, 651/571-3500, www. lorahotel.com; $150-500 d) combines the best of Stillwater's past and present. Modern furnishings and conveniences set off the original limestone walls of the old Joseph Wolf Brewery. Most of the 40 rooms have lovely views of the St. Croix River and historic Main Street.

## PRACTICALITIES

### GETTING THERE

While, in theory, there is a Metro Transit bus, it runs from St. Paul to Stillwater 3:40pm-5:40pm and from Stillwater to St. Paul 5:40am-6:50am. In other words, you need your own wheels for the 20-mile drive. Highway 36 east from Minneapolis or St. Paul (it runs across the northern half of the metro area) will drop you directly on Main Street. If you prefer two wheels to four, take the **Gateway State Trail** from St. Paul to the Brown's Creek State Trail, which leads straight into Stillwater.

### GETTING AROUND

Once you're in Stillwater, navigating on foot is very easy, as everything is within a block or two of the main half-mile stretch of Main Street.

# Red Wing and the Mississippi Bluffs

The city of Red Wing began on the site of a Dakota farming village. White missionaries and settlers began arriving in 1837, but the city saw a huge boom in population in the 1860s and 1870s, when this became a key— and even for a time the *most* important—shipping point in the world for wheat. When the wheat trade shifted elsewhere, Red Wing became an important manufacturing city, most notably (and this is where you've heard the name before, in case you've been wondering) for shoes and pottery.

Red Wing work boots and Red Wing pottery are still a big draw for tourists, who come for good prices and to see the famous products at their source. The city itself is compact and can be enjoyed in a single full day, including a trip to the **Red Wing Stoneware Factory.** But if you want to enjoy the other wonders of the bluffland, including the glistening **Lake Pepin** and charming small river towns like **Wabasha,** add in an overnight.

## SIGHTS

### RED WING'S HISTORIC DOWNTOWN

Red Wing's historic downtown district is a well-preserved and welcoming area of a half dozen blocks just steps from the Mississippi River. While tourists will find plenty to do, this is a modern business district, where barbers,

view of Red Wing from Barn Bluff

Lake Pepin area of the Mississippi River

hardware stores, and appliance stores sit in among the gift shops. A perfect example of the mix of old and new is the **Sheldon Theatre** (443 3rd St. W., Red Wing, 651/388-8700, www. sheldontheatre.org). A landmark since 1905, the playhouse, with its ornate interior restored to its original splendor, now shows a thoroughly modern mix of comedies, children's shows, concerts, and lectures.

Just four miles north of downtown, you can get a taste of Red Wing's manufacturing past and present. The **Red Wing Stoneware Factory** (4909 Moundview Dr., Red Wing, 651/388-4610, www.redwingstoneware.com) offers 20-minute tours weekdays at 1pm ($3 adults, $2 children 12-17, 11 and under free). Watch potters and painters at work on the distinctive, heavy gray and blue crocks, butter churns, bowls, and more.

The river bluffs that make this area unique are another draw in Red Wing. The easiest way to get a panoramic view of the city is to take the short but winding drive to the top of Sorin's Bluff in **Memorial Park** (entrance at 542 E. 7th St., Red Wing). You'll also find hiking trails and disc golf. For a more rewarding but much harder-won view, head to **Barn Bluff** (steps at 500 E. 5th St., Red Wing). The steps to the top of the 350-foot limestone cliff may leave you huffing and puffing, but you'll have a nearly 360-degree view of Red Wing.

## ✪ GREAT RIVER ROAD

Minnesota's Great River Road follows the Mississippi River from the headwaters in Itasca State Park to the Iowa border. In bluff country, the Great River Road curves along **Lake Pepin**, one of Minnesota's most popular destinations, for most of the lake's 22-mile length. Lake Pepin is the name given to the widest part of the Mississippi River from Red Wing to Reads Landing. It was formed by sediment carried down by the much narrower and steeper Chippewa River and dumped at the confluence of the two rivers, blocking the flow of the water upstream in the Mississippi. Spectacular views can be had from the road, especially on sunny summer days, when the wide smooth water glistens on one side and 450-foot bluffs soar on the other. There are several opportunities to pull off the highway at observation points and rest stops.

## ✪ NATIONAL EAGLE CENTER

The stretch of the Mississippi River below Lake Pepin doesn't freeze over in the winter, thanks to the warm water pouring down from the lake and the turbulence that forms at the confluence with the Chippewa River. This attracts, among other hungry species, bald eagles, who feed in the ice-free water. While hundreds of eagles live here year-round, peak eagle-viewing time comes when the cold weather hits, mid-November to mid-March. As many as 700 eagles have been counted in the area on a single day, according to the **National Eagle Center** (50 Pembroke Ave., Wabasha, 651/565-4989, www.nationaleaglecenter.org;

daily 10am-5pm; $10 adults, $9 seniors, $7 students, children 3 and under free). The Eagle Center, a modern building among century-old storefronts in the tiny historic town of Wabasha, sits directly on the river, with a small observation deck and spotting scopes aimed at the highway stretching over the river into Wisconsin. That's where eagles and other birds like to congregate. The center itself is home to four bald eagles that were injured in the wild and now live in the exhibit hall, where visitors can get up close and personal without glass or fencing in the way. After visiting the eagles, it's worth sparing some time to wander down Wabasha's Main Street to **Beach Park** and the marina, passing the **tourist information office** (137 Main St. W., Wabasha, 651/565-4158; Mon.-Fri. 9am-5pm, Sat. 9am-3pm) along the way.

## LARK TOYS

Farther south down Highway 62 (about 35 miles from Red Wing), the focus shifts from natural wonders to the wonder of childhood. **LARK Toys** (63604 170th Ave., Kellogg, 507/767-3387, www.larktoys.com; June-Labor Day daily 10am-6pm, Sept.-Dec. and Mar.-Memorial Day daily 9:30am-5pm, Jan.-Feb. Fri.-Sun. 10am-5pm) grew up in this off-the-beaten-path location thanks to one family's passion for wooden toys. LARK stands for Lost Arts Revival by Kreofsky. Now the 20,000-square-foot store sells original LARK designs (including rockers, dollhouses, and puzzles) as well as carefully selected toys, art supplies, science kits, and books in seven showrooms. While the 85-mile trip from the Twin Cities may seem like an awful lot for a toy store, even a truly great one, LARK

is much more than a toy store: An 18-hole mini-golf course (May-Oct., $7 adults, $5 children) stays open until 6pm on warm summer nights daily, and, almost worth the trip in itself, a fantastical carousel with carved moose, beavers, flamingos, and ostriches operates right in the middle of the café. Like any good children's fantasy, the café serves hamburgers, hot dogs, onion rings, ice cream, and fudge. In January and February, LARK Toys takes a little break, staying open only on Friday, Saturday, and Sunday.

## RESTAURANTS

Even the most upscale restaurants in Red Wing have a casual, resort-town air to them in the summer. The swankiest hotel in town, the **St. James Hotel** (406 Main St., Red Wing, 800/252-1875, www.st-james-hotel.com) has two restaurants and a pub where it's definitely no jackets required. **The Veranda** (Mon.-Thurs. 6:30am-8pm, Fri.-Sat. 6:30am-9pm, Sun. 7:30am-8pm; $10-25) serves breakfast (try the Sturdiwheat pancakes with maple-vanilla sauce), lunch, and a light dinner (hearty batter-fried walleye or a lighter sandwich) on the patio or inside, both with a great view of Levee Park and the Mississippi. Downstairs, **Port** (Tues.-Sat. 5pm-9pm; $22-34) serves steak and seafood in a former bank vault. **Jimmy's Pub** (Sun.-Thurs. 4pm-11pm, Fri.-Sat. 4pm-midnight; $12-13) offers pub fare, a long list of tap beers, and small-town camaraderie.

For a solid meal and a little bit of old-time diner attitude, you can't beat **Bev's Cafe** (221 Bush St., Red Wing, 651/388-5227, www.bevscafe.com, Mon.-Thurs. 5am-3pm, Fri. 5am-8pm, Sat. 6am-2pm, Sun. 8am-1pm; $5-11). The hand-formed burgers are served smashed, crispy, and delicious, perfect with a side of funnel cake "fries."

Check out the **Staghead Gastropub** (219 Bush St., Red Wing, 651/212-6494, www.thestaghead.com; Tues.-Thurs. 11am-8:30pm, Fri.-Sat. 11am-9pm; $18-30) for hearty fare that goes several steps beyond the usual pub burgers. Think bouillabaisse, cassoulet, and pot roast sandwiches dripping with local blue cheese. Live music and a lively atmosphere.

## RECREATION

One of the most popular ways to experience the natural beauty of southeastern Minnesota is on the **Cannon Valley Trail** (trail office: 825 Cannon River Ave., Cannon Falls, 507/263-0508, www.cannonvalleytrail.com). Nearly 100,000 cyclists, hikers, skaters, and skiers traverse the trail every year between the cities of Cannon Falls and Red Wing. The 20-mile paved trail follows the Chicago Great Western rail right of way along the Cannon River. Anybody on wheels—whether bike, skates, skateboard, or scooter—needs a wheel pass, available for $3 from the trail office and a variety of local businesses, including the **St. James Hotel** and the **Red Wing Visitors Center.** You can buy your pass and rent your bike at **Cannon Falls Canoe, Kayak and Bike Rental** (615 5th St. N., Cannon Falls, 507/407-4111; Mon.-Thurs. 10am-4pm, Fri.-Sun. 8am-4pm). A full-day rental is $25 and a half day is $20.

If you want to get in or on the water, **Lake City,** more or less halfway down the Minnesota side of the lake, is the place to be. **Hok-Si-La Municipal Park and Campground** (2500 Hwy. 61 N., Lake City, 651/345-3855, www.hoksilapark.org) is a convenient swimming spot, with a shady park and a broad sandy beach, as well as 41 tent-camping sites. There's also a big public beach at the **Lake City Marina** in the center of town. To rent speedboats, pontoons, and sailboats, head to **Hansen's Harbor** (35853 Hwy. 61 Blvd., Lake City, 651/345-3022). If you happened to bring your own boat, there's convenient public water access at **Roschen Park,** just south of the Lake City Marina.

Popular with skiers and snowboarders from around the region, **Welch Village Resort** (26685 County 7 Blvd., Welch, 651/258-4567, www.welchvillage.com) covers 120 acres of skiable terrain, with two dozen trails and eight lifts. The average annual snowfall in this area is 45 inches, but Welch Village is prepared to supplement that with plenty of snowmaking equipment to make sure the season lasts from November to March. A day pass costs $47, and hours vary throughout the season.

Some may say there is no better recreation than drinking a $3 beer on a lingering summer evening at a small-town baseball game. The whole town turns out to cheer and the sun sets over the cornfield. That's exactly what you can find at a **Miesville Mudhens** game, 15 miles northwest of Red Wing along Highway 61 and just a 30-minute drive from the Twin Cities. The Mudhens play at **Jack Ruhr Field** (Hwy. 61, center of Miesville, www.miesvillemudhens.com). Their regular season is in the Classic Cannon Valley League against teams like the Dundas Dukes, the Red Wing Aces, and the Northfield Knights.

For recreation of an altogether different sort, the Mdewakanton Sioux of Prairie Island, a band of Dakota, own and operate **Treasure Island Resort and Casino** (5734 Sturgeon

Lake Rd., Welch, 800/222-7077, www. treasureisland.com). The complex includes half a dozen restaurants, slots and gaming tables, a bowling alley, 18-hole golf course overlooking Lake Pepin, a massive hotel, marina, and RV park.

## SHOPS

A dedicated shopper in Red Wing can easily fill half a day or more exploring the shops downtown.

The **Red Wing Shoe Company** (315 Main St., Red Wing, 651/388-6233, www.redwing.redwingshoestore. com; Mon.-Fri. 9am-8pm, Sat. 9am-6pm, Sun. 11am-5pm) occupies most of the Riverfront Centre block. The company, which has been making work boots since 1905 (the first pair sold for $1.75), keeps its corporate offices here, along with an extensive display of its history and a store selling all its brands (watch for terrific semiannual sales).

"Uffda" is what a Minnesotan says when confronted with disappointment, consternation, or mild pain. It's a quiet, characteristically stoic two syllables, usually said under one's breath. At the **Uffda Shop** (202 Bush St., Red Wing, 651/388-8436; Mon.-Fri. 10am-7pm, Sat. 9am-6pm, Sun. noon-5pm, longer weekday hours Sept.-Dec. and shortened hours Jan.-Apr.), you can experience a little more of the Scandinavian national character—and a lot of the aesthetic. The Norwegian, Swedish, Finnish, and Icelandic wares are typically spare and elegant, and the extensive Christmas selection is a nice change from other schlocky and sentimental holiday stuff.

## WHERE TO STAY

The **St. James Hotel** (406 Main St., Red Wing, 800/252-1875, www.

st-james-hotel.com; $189 s, $239 d) has been a landmark in Red Wing since 1875. Today the hotel is like a one-stop getaway for weary Twin Citians, especially those who take advantage of the weekend meals-included packages. The Victorian ambience of the lobby extends to the 60-plus guest rooms, all individually decorated with period furniture and quilts. On the mezzanine level, take a quick break to see the artifacts in the **American Ski Jumping Hall of Fame,** or look for monthly book signings with Minnesota authors at Clara's Coffee in the main lobby.

A few miles outside of downtown Red Wing, you'll find the more intimate **Round Barn Farm** (28650 Wildwood Ln., Red Wing, 651/385-9250, www.roundbarnfarm.com; $159-249 d), which calls itself a B&B&B—or bed-and-breakfast-and-bread, after the sourdough bread the proprietors bake in the wood-fired stone oven. Five double rooms with feather beds, massage tubs, and fireplaces make this a welcoming retreat, and with extensive hiking trails on the farm itself, you may never feel the need to explore much farther.

For something a little different on longer trips, rent a houseboat from **Great River Houseboats** (125 Beach Harbor Rd, Alma, WI, 800/982-8410, www.greatriverhouseboats. com). The family-owned company nine miles south of the Minnesota border rents boats sleeping 2-4 people for a minimum of two nights ($725-930 for two nights), or 10 people for the long weekend ($1,655-2,490) or the week ($2,965-4,425). The boats are fully equipped and—provided you're ready to pilot a 48-foot boat—can move up and down the river within a 70-mile range.

## PRACTICALITIES
### VISITORS CENTERS
The Red Wing **Tourist Information Office** (420 Levee St., Red Wing, 651/385-5934, www.redwing.org; Mon.-Fri. 8am-5pm, Sat. 10am-3pm, Sun. 11am-3pm) is inside the historic train station, built in 1904 and modeled, like many buildings of the time, after the neoclassical revival style made popular by the 1893 Colombian Exposition. Even outside of regular hours, when the information office is staffed, the main lobby of the train station is stocked with brochures and information and has some historical photos on display.

### GETTING THERE
Train travel is rarely a convenient option in Minnesota, but the Twin Cities' only passenger train is, in fact, timed for a nice day trip to Red Wing. The Empire Builder, Amtrak's most popular long-distance train, carries half a million passengers a year between Chicago and Seattle, passing through both Red Wing and St. Paul. One train a day passes in each direction, leaving St. Paul at 8am and arriving in Red Wing about 9am, then departing Red Wing at 8:49pm and arriving in St. Paul about 10pm. The train, however, is notoriously unpredictable and is often delayed for hours in the Rocky Mountains.

If you want to explore the area outside of the historic downtown district, you'll want your own transportation. From the Twin Cities, many roads lead to Red Wing, each more picturesque than the last. Taking Highway 55 south to Highway 52 to Highway 61 will take you through small towns and rolling farmland. For a few more glimpses of the river, take I-94 to Highway 61, then cross into Wisconsin at Prescott and take Highway 55 south, crossing back into Minnesota at Red Wing.

### GETTING AROUND
Red Wing's historic downtown district is easily navigated on foot, from the train station on the riverfront park to the small shops in the area. But if you want to appreciate the rest of Lake Pepin or tour the Red Wing Stoneware Factory, you'll need your own transportation. Bus service in Red Wing is very limited.

# Northfield

When the city of Northfield tried to replace its longtime slogan, "Cows, colleges, and contentment," the good citizens led a quiet rebellion, and the phrase simply refused to go away, eventually returning to a place of honor on a sign on the main road into town. Apparently this happy agricultural city of 17,000, 20 percent of whom are students, wants the world to know it just that way.

History buffs are more likely to know Northfield as the end of the road for the James-Younger gang, which tried to rob the First National Bank in 1876 and was thwarted by an angry mob of citizens. Visitors can absorb Northfield's college-town charms in a morning or an afternoon, stretching it out to a full day by adding a trek through Carleton College's 880-acre arboretum.

# SIGHTS
## ✪ CARLETON COLLEGE

Two colleges, Carleton and St. Olaf, together help shape much of life in town, from attracting professors and staff members as residents to supporting arts and cultural life. Both colleges were founded by Protestant organizations (Carleton by Congregationalists in 1866 and St. Olaf by Lutherans in 1874), but only St. Olaf has retained the religious tie. Both schools rank highly among small liberal arts schools and were coeducational from the very first class. In local lore, a great rivalry rages, but in truth, the rivalry comes down to an annual football game—a sport neither school is known to play all that well—and a few ribald chants in an otherwise peaceful coexistence, with neither side paying the other much attention. **Carleton** (1 N. College St., Northfield, 507/222-4000, www. carleton.edu) sits immediately adjacent to downtown Northfield, along the river. Most of the school's historical buildings are arranged around a quadrangle known as the Bald Spot, where students play Frisbee in all sorts of weather and skate and play broomball in the winter. On the west side of the Bald Spot is Willis Hall, the campus's oldest building. Like the iconic "Old Main" at many schools, Willis was once a classroom building, dormitory, chapel, and cafeteria all in one. Today it houses several social science departments.

To the north and east of the Bald Spot is the historic **Goodsell Observatory,** built in 1887 and given to the school by the railroad magnate James J. Hill. For many years it sent daily time signals to railroads around the country. Goodsell has two domes: the larger with a 16-inch refractor (one of the largest in the world when it was installed in 1890) and the smaller with an 8-inch refractor. The telescopes are open to the public for about two hours on the first Friday of every month, starting at dusk.

The college's public art gallery, the **Carleton College Perlman Teaching Museum** (507/222-4469; Mon.-Wed. 11am-6pm, Thurs.-Fri. 11am-9pm, Sat.-Sun. noon-4pm, open during academic terms only; free) is in the Weitz Center for Creativity, an enormous building next to Northfield's Central Park that you couldn't miss if you tried.

The gem of the Carleton campus is the **Cowling Arboretum,** 880 acres of natural beauty originally dubbed "Cowling's Folly" by those who disagreed with then-president Donald Cowling's investment. But like so many so-called follies in history, the Arb, as it is known, has been vindicated and is now central to campus life. The Upper Arb, the area closest to the main campus, includes playing fields and is crisscrossed by paved and unpaved paths for running and biking. The much larger portion, the Lower Arb, is less developed and a lovely

chapel at Carleton College

place for more solitary hiking and running (but no biking is allowed). The easiest place to access the Lower Arb is behind **West Gymnasium** (321 Division St. N., Northfield). Cross Division Street and walk north a few hundred yards to access the Upper Arb. (Note that the Lower Arb, so named because it lies low in the Cannon River valley, actually lies to the north of the Upper Arb.)

## DEFEAT OF JESSE JAMES

Northfield's claim to fame is the 1876 bank robbery that proved the downfall of the James-Younger gang. Five men held up the First National Bank of Northfield with guns and bowie knives but were thwarted by a brave cashier and quick-acting local citizenry. The bank itself has moved up the street, and the **Northfield Historical Society** (408 Division St., Northfield, 507/645-9268, www.northfieldhistory. org; Mon.-Sat. 10am-5pm, Sun. 1pm-5pm) has restored the original location to its 1870s appearance. Visitors can see the cashier's booth and safe, as well as some of the weapons used in the raid. Rumor has it a skeleton of one of the Younger brothers was once on display in the museum but has now been moved into storage.

Drop by Northfield during the first weekend of September for Defeat of Jesse James Days (www.djjd.org). A small carnival atmosphere takes over the town, with games, rides, parades, food, and music, as well as more than a half a dozen chances to see reenactments of the famous raid.

## ST. OLAF COLLEGE

**St. Olaf** (1520 St. Olaf Ave., Northfield, 507/786-2222, www. stolaf.edu) sits on a hill overlooking Northfield's compact downtown. Strolling through the shady campus, one can enjoy the beautifully unified architecture, much of it in the Norman Gothic style. **Rølvaag Memorial Library** (1510 St. Olaf Ave.) is a good example of this. Built in 1942, it is named for Ole Edvart Rølvaag, an Olaf alum and author of the 1927 best-selling immigrant epic *Giants in the Earth*. Next door, **Holland Hall,** completed 20 years earlier, is like a brotherly bookend to the library, and the pair make a familiar Northfield sight.

St. Olaf is well known for its musical programs, including the annual **St. Olaf Christmas Festival** concert, broadcast nationally. About one-third of the school's roughly 3,000 students are involved in music somehow, many of them in the 17 instrumental ensembles and 10 vocal groups. The college also rates some pop-culture references, at times because its name sounds humorous to non-Midwesterners. Jay Gatsby, in F. Scott Fitzgerald's *The Great Gatsby,* attended the school.

## RESTAURANTS

For years Northfield residents had to drive to the Twin Cities for any cuisine other than American. But now Twin Citians have been known to drive to Northfield for **Chapati** (214 Division St. S., Northfield, 507/645-2462, www. chapati.us; Sun.-Thurs. 11:30am-2pm and 5pm-9pm, Fri.-Sat. 11:30am-2pm and 5pm-10pm, $8-17). Located inside the Archer House building, along with a host of small shops, the Archer House hotel, and a couple of other restaurants, Chapati offers fresh, authentic Indian cuisine, including excellent tandoori dishes and *biryani* (similar to rice pilaf). The daily lunch buffet includes as many as eight curries, plus rice and side dishes.

In a college town like Northfield,

academic types need a place to gather over a pint or a meal. The **Contented Cow** (302 Division St., Northfield, 507/663-1351, www.contentedcow. com; daily 3pm-late; $8-16) offers just that, informally and formally, with its Politics and a Pint gab fests on Sunday nights starting at 6pm. The pub also hosts live music on Sundays and Tuesdays, as well as frequent poetry readings, and it makes good use of its riverside deck with outdoor barbecues when the weather permits. The menu is lighter in the summer (salads and sandwiches) and heavier in the winter (with the addition of dishes like shepherd's pie and pork stew), and there are 13 beers on tap (also changing seasonally) to wash it down.

Another pub with a great riverside view is **Froggy Bottoms** (307 Water St. S., Northfield, 507/301-3611, www. froggybottoms.com; Mon.-Wed. 11am-10pm, Thurs.-Sat. 11am-1am, Sun. 11am-9pm; $10-13). Owned by a St. Olaf graduate who, no doubt, had noted the long-famous dearth of bars in this college town, Froggy Bottoms has a cozy, stone-walled main dining room and a small, flower-filled patio right on the river. The menu includes filling sandwiches, pizzas, and pasta dishes and a long list of goofily named cocktails (Sex on the Cannon, anyone?). Karaoke is on Thursday nights during the school year.

On the St. Olaf side of town, **The Ole Store** (1011 St. Olaf Ave., Northfield, 507/786-9400, www. olestorerestaurant.com; Mon.-Thurs. 11am-9pm, Fri. 11am-10pm, Sat. 7am-10pm, Sun. 7am-1pm) offers a little college town sophistication in a homey old farmhouse. For dinner ($20-26), it's classics like steaks, lamb chops, and mahi mahi. For brunch ($7-13) it's thick, orange-glazed French toast and,

of course, the famous Ole rolls. Expect a wait for weekend brunch.

## NIGHTLIFE

The very active **Northfield Arts Guild** (304 Division St., Northfield, 507/645-8877, www.northfieldartsguild.org; Tues.-Fri. noon-6pm, Sat. 11am-3pm) hosts visual arts exhibitions, concerts, and readings, and also produces six plays a year, including some for children, at the **NAG Theater** (411 3rd St. W.).

There is usually something interesting going on at **Carleton College** (1 College St. N., Northfield, 507/646-4000, www.carleton.edu) and **St. Olaf** (1520 St. Olaf Ave., Northfield, 507/786-2222, www.stolaf.edu), and the public is welcome.

Two wonderful basement pubs face each other across the river. While both the **Contented Cow** (302 Division St., Northfield, 507/663-1351, www.contentedcow.com; daily 3pm-late) and **Froggy Bottoms** (307 Water St. S., Northfield, 507/301-3611, www.froggybottoms.com; Mon. 4pm-10pm, Tues.-Wed. 11am-10pm, Thurs.-Sat. 11am-1am, Sun. 11am-9pm) have their own personal faunal theme, they have much in common, including riverside patios, live music, and smoke-free air. **Hogan Brothers' Acoustic Café** (415 Division St. S., Northfield, 507/645-6653, www. hoganbros.com; Sun.-Thurs. 11am-8pm, Fri.-Sat. 11am-9pm) also has live music on weekends.

## WHERE TO STAY

Rooms in and around Northfield fill up fast—as in four years in advance—for St. Olaf and Carleton graduation and homecoming weekends. During the Defeat of Jesse James Days festival (the weekend after Labor Day) and the St. Olaf Christmas Festival, rooms are also hard to come by. During those special events, many hotels may have higher rates and minimum stays.

The number of both chain hotels and B&Bs in and around Northfield is growing. An independent option right on the Cannon River in the center of town is the charmingly old-fashioned Archer House (212 Division St., Northfield, 507/645-5661, www.archerhouse.com, $90-240 d). The Archer House was built as a hotel in 1877 and has been welcoming visitors to town ever since (even through a couple of decades of relative disrepute and decrepitude during the 1960s and 1970s). Rooms are on the small side and individually decorated in a sweet country style. Many have old-timey details like sleigh beds, four-posters, and claw-foot tubs. Be sure to specify whether you want a full or a queen bed, and ask for a river view. Rates are higher on weekends and during special events.

For longer stays, or for more convenience during a single overnight, the Froggy Bottoms River Suites (309 Water St. S., Northfield, 507/650-0039, www.froggybottomsriversuites.com), next door to the pub of the same name, is a unique independent option. The one- and two-bedroom suites sleep 4-6 people and come with fully equipped kitchens and on-site laundry facilities. The price is the same no matter how many in your party: $100-150 for a weekday overnight, more on weekends and during special events, with weekly and monthly rates available. The suites are casually decorated, like spare, comfortable student apartments, with a goofy frog theme throughout. Several have decks directly overlooking the river.

## PRACTICALITIES
### VISITORS CENTERS
The Northfield Convention and Visitors Bureau (205 3rd St. W., Northfield, 507/645-5604, www.visitingnorthfield.com, brochures available daily 24 hours, staff available Mon.-Fri. 8am-4:30pm) doesn't see all that many drop-in visitors, but staff will happily answer questions and supply you with materials.

### GETTING THERE
Northfield is about 45 minutes to an hour's drive south of the Twin Cities. Take I-35 to exit 69. State Highway 19 will take you straight past the Malt-O-Meal factory to the center of town. Northfield Lines buses (www.northfieldlines.com) travel from key points in the Twin Cities (the airport, the Mall of America, both downtowns) to the Carleton and St. Olaf campuses six times a day on weekdays and three times on weekends (see website for schedule). Tickets are $15 online in advance or $25 from the driver.

### GETTING AROUND
Once you're in Northfield, the main drag, Division Street, is easy to navigate on foot and immediately adjacent to Carleton College. If you want to head the couple of miles up the hill to St. Olaf, you'll want to be able to get there on your own power. Northfield's single taxi is notoriously difficult to summon.

# Duluth and the North Shore

Duluth was once the definition of a boomtown: After financier Jay Cooke convinced the Lake Superior and Mississippi Railroad to open a line to Duluth in 1869, the population ballooned from practically 0 to 3,500 in a matter of months. By the early 20th century, the rail, timber, mining, and shipping industries were exploding, the port of Duluth handled more freight than any other port in the United States, and Duluth was home to more millionaires per capita than anywhere else in the world.

Some shadows of those boom times are still visible in the steep neighborhoods of Duluth, where today tourism easily surpasses shipping as the city's major industry. Grand mansions are now inns, and the railroads offer nostalgic pleasure rides. But one thing remains: Here at the westernmost edge of the Great Lakes, where the St. Louis River opens out into Lake Superior, *gitchigami* (great water, as the Ojibwe call the lake) shapes everything, from the food to the weather to the economy.

## SIGHTS
### ✪ CANAL PARK AND MARITIME DULUTH

A great way to get acquainted with Duluth is to walk along the three-mile **Lakewalk** from the **Bayfront Park Pavilion** through Canal Park and then north beyond the **Fitger's Brewery Complex.** You'll pass Duluth's iconic **aerial lift bridge,** which connects Canal Park with a narrow peninsula

aerial lift bridge in Duluth

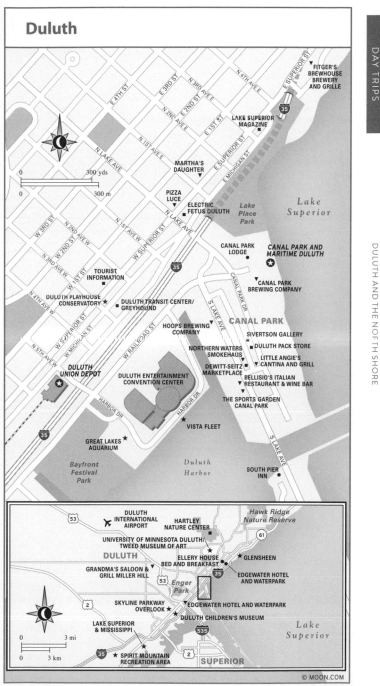

# Duluth

E 4TH ST
E 3RD ST
N 3RD AVE E
N 2ND AVE E
E 2ND ST
N 4TH AVE E
N 1ST AVE E
E SUPERIOR ST
FITGER'S BREWHOUSE BREWERY AND GRILLE
35
LAKE SUPERIOR MAGAZINE
E SUPERIOR ST
E MICHIGAN ST
N LAKE AVE
MARTHA'S DAUGHTER
PIZZA LUCE
ELECTRIC FETUS DULUTH
N 1ST AVE E
N LAKE AVE
W SUPERIOR ST
Lake Place Park
Lake Superior

0    300 yds
0    300 m

N 3RD ST
N 2ND ST
W 3RD ST
W 2ND ST
W 1ST ST
W 1ST AVE W
CANAL PARK LODGE
CANAL PARK AND MARITIME DULUTH
35
N 3RD AVE W
N 4TH AVE W
W SUPERIOR ST
TOURIST INFORMATION
CANAL PARK DR
CANAL PARK BREWING COMPANY
DULUTH PLAYHOUSE CONSERVATORY
DULUTH TRANSIT CENTER/ GREYHOUND
S LAKE AVE
CANAL PARK
N 5TH AVE W
W MICHIGAN ST
HOOPS BREWING COMPANY
SIVERTSON GALLERY
DULUTH PACK STORE
NORTHERN WATERS SMOKEHAUS
LITTLE ANGIE'S CANTINA AND GRILL
DEWITT-SEITZ MARKETPLACE
BELLISIO'S ITALIAN RESTAURANT & WINE BAR
DULUTH UNION DEPOT
DULUTH ENTERTAINMENT CONVENTION CENTER
THE SPORTS GARDEN CANAL PARK
W RAILROAD ST
HARBOR DR
HARBOR DR
VISTA FLEET
S LAKE AVE
35
GREAT LAKES AQUARIUM
Bayfront Festival Park
Duluth Harbor
SOUTH PIER INN

53
DULUTH INTERNATIONAL AIRPORT
HARTLEY NATURE CENTER
Hawk Ridge Nature Reserve
61
UNIVERSITY OF MINNESOTA DULUTH/ TWEED MUSEUM OF ART
DULUTH
ELLERY HOUSE BED AND BREAKFAST
GLENSHEEN
GRANDMA'S SALOON & GRILL MILLER HILL
53
35
EDGEWATER HOTEL AND WATERPARK
2
Enger Park
SKYLINE PARKWAY OVERLOOK
EDGEWATER HOTEL AND WATERPARK
LAKE SUPERIOR & MISSISSIPPI
DULUTH CHILDREN'S MUSEUM
535
Lake Superior
0    3 mi
0    3 km
35
SPIRIT MOUNTAIN RECREATION AREA
2
SUPERIOR

© MOON.COM

## FITGER'S

......................................................................

You could wander into the deceptively compact **Fitger's complex** (600 Superior St. E., Duluth, www.fitgers.com; shops open Mon.-Sat. 10am-9pm, Sun. 11am-5pm) and wander out blurry-eyed hours—or even days—later, fully satisfied. The former brewery, which operated on this site from 1859 to 1972, now houses four restaurants, a hotel, modern lounge, museum, wine shop, brewing shop, bookstore, fitness center, and more than a half dozen high-end clothing and gift shops. They even roast their own brand of coffee. And, oh yeah—since 1995, beer is again being made in the brewery. The whole thing is right on a beautiful patch of the Lakewalk, overlooking Lake Superior, with a high platform for watching the sailboats, the aerial lift bridge, and the trains that run along the lake.

The **Brewhouse** (218/279-2739, www.brewhouse.net, Tues.-Sat. 11am-11pm, Sun.-Mon. 11am-10pm; $11-15) is a great place to grab a burger in a classic brewpub atmosphere. But for a white-tablecloth experience and a steak, **The Boat Club** (218/727-4880, www.boatclubrestaurant.com; Sun.-Thurs. 6am-10pm, Fri.-Sat. 6am-11pm; $24-36) is the place to be. Follow with drinks and dancing on the lower level, **Rex Nightclub** (218/733-3090; Sun. 6pm-2am, Mon.-Sat. 4pm-2am). Take your cocktails to the lakefront patio for the ultimate Duluth night.

known as Park Point. The central portion of the bridge rises straight up (rather than at an angle) to let boats pass underneath. The bridge can make it all the way to the top in about three minutes and lifts about 40 times a day during peak shipping season. You can pick up a copy of the *Duluth Shipping News* (www.duluthshippingnews.com) to find out when ships are expected to pass through, or listen for the long-short-long-short series of horn blows that signals a request to raise the bridge. The bridge is an especially beautiful sight at night, when it is fully illuminated.

At the base of the bridge, the surprisingly diminutive tugboat *Essayons,* which takes its name from the Army Corps of Engineers motto "Let us try," stands outside the **Lake Superior Maritime Visitor Center** (south end of Canal Park Dr., Duluth, 218/720-5260, www.lsmma.com; summer daily 10am-9pm, fall daily 10am-4:30pm, winter Fri.-Sun. 10am-4:30pm, spring Sun.-Thurs. 10am-4:30pm, Fri.-Sat. 10am-6pm; free). Inside, you can get a good look at the tug's engine and learn more about the 1908 boat's history. Like

any good ship, the visitors center crams more than you would think possible into a small space: exhibits on shipwrecks in Lake Superior, the history of shipping on the lake, and early passenger travel conditions, as well as a working radar and marine radio. You can even try your hand at steering a large ship. Serious shipping buffs can call the **Boatwatcher's Hotline** at 218/722-6489 for news on which ships are expected to dock or leave port that day. This information is also listed on the *Duluth Shipping News*, a one-sheet publication distributed free at the visitor centers around town daily during the summer and occasionally during the spring and fall. The center's staff is small, and the center may close earlier between Labor Day and Memorial Day.

You can get even closer to Lake Superior's maritime past and present aboard a ship docked just off Canal Park. A ticket gets you access to the **SS *William A. Irvin*** (350 Harbor Dr., Duluth, 218/722-7876, www.decc.org; May daily 10am-4pm, Memorial Day-Labor Day daily 9am-6pm; adults $12, students and seniors $8, children 10 and under free). The *William A. Irvin,* built in 1937, carried both serious cargo and serious dignitaries, which means the one-hour tour will give you a look at a 2,000-horsepower engine and lavishly furnished staterooms. In October, the ghosts of Halloweens past come aboard for Haunted Ship Tours.

## ✪ DULUTH UNION DEPOT

Built in 1892, the Duluth Union Depot was accommodating seven different rail lines and 5,000 passengers daily by 1910 and served as an important hub for the transport of logs and iron ore for decades. In 1971, the building was placed on the National Register of Historic Places, and **The Depot** complex (507 Michigan St. W., www.duluthdepot.org, $12 adults, $6 children) now houses the Duluth Playhouse, the Duluth Art Institute, the St. Louis County Historical Society, and the Lake Superior Railroad Museum. One ticket offers admissions to the whole building.

The **Duluth Art Institute** (Union Depot, 506 Michigan St. W., Duluth, 218/733-7560, and 2229 2nd St. W., Duluth, 218/723-1310, www.duluthartinstitute.org; Memorial Day-Labor Day daily 9:30am-6pm, Labor Day-Memorial Day Mon.-Sat. 10am-5pm, Sun. 1pm-5pm) is a quintessentially accessible contemporary art museum. Its family programming

and hands-on training for artists make it an important part of the local arts community. The rooms are small and friendly, showcasing artists from Duluth and Minnesota's Arrowhead region in changing exhibitions.

The **Lake Superior Railroad Museum** is housed at the lowest level, where the old rails run. In addition to plenty of rail cars to clamber through, the history of the rails is on display, from the earliest of engines used in the area to specialty designs like huge rotary snowplows, converted autos that could run on tracks, and an odd-looking log loader that was important for the logging industry throughout the Upper Midwest. Re-created dining cars, model railroads, and an actual train operation simulator round out a fine afternoon.

In the warmer months, the **Duluth Zephyr** makes two 90-minute runs a day on the **North Shore Scenic Railroad** (12:30pm and 3pm, 218/722-1273, www.northshorescenicrailroad.org; $16 adults, $8 children), up the North Shore to the Lester River. On Friday, Saturday, and Sunday, the all-day Two Harbors Turn takes you up to Two Harbors and allows you enough time to shop and dine. Specialty trips include fall color tours, music, and pizza dinners on the train.

## GREAT LAKES AQUARIUM

The **Great Lakes Aquarium** (353 Harbor Dr., Duluth, 218/740-3474, www.glaquarium.org; daily 10am-6pm; $18 adults, $14 seniors, $13 youth, $12 children) is 120,000 gallons of freshwater, focusing on fish found in the Great Lakes. Some 70 species of freshwater fish, birds, amphibians, and reptiles are spread out over two floors, along a self-guided tour. The aquarium is fairly well curated and includes

Great Lakes Aquarium

## THE DULUTH LYNCHINGS

In June 1920, four black men were falsely accused of rape. Three were lynched by a mob of nearly 3,000, and the fourth was convicted in a mockery of a court trial. At the time, the lynchings earned headlines in newspapers across the country. But memories receded to the point where most Minnesotans were unaware of the crime. Court records were burned and the Duluth Historical Society discouraged research into the event. In 1992, the play *The Last Minstrel Show* premiered at Penumbra Theater and helped resurrect the tragedy. Since then, the play has been reprised, the Minnesota Historical Society Press published Michael Fedo's *The Lynchings in Duluth* and Warren Read's *The Lyncher in Me*, and Duluth has erected a memorial to Elias Clayton, Elmer Jackson, and Isaac McGhie, the three men who were murdered.

some historical perspective on lake life. Lake fish, by and large, lack the color and flash of the more commonly exhibited tropical species, but that in no way diminishes the appealing oddity of the paddlefish, the sturgeon, and the catfish on display in carefully chosen habitats, the most impressive of which re-creates the base of a waterfall. There are plenty of interactive exhibits, a touch pool, a wave maker, and an expansive model of the Great Lakes, where you can pilot a plastic boat from Duluth to the Atlantic Ocean and gain a working understanding of the lock and dam systems along the way.

### ST. LOUIS RIVER RAILROAD

The other scenic rail option in town, **St. Louis River Railroad** (6930 Fremont St., Duluth, 218/624-7549, www.lsmrr.org; $17 adults, $8 children) heads south instead of north, also for 90 minutes. On nice days, the open safari car is the place to be, as the tracks run through the Duluth area's varied terrain. Trains run from mid-June to early October (Sat.-Sun. 10:30am and 1:30pm).

### SKYLINE DRIVE

This scenic 25-mile drive stretches right across the top of the city. The marked route roughly follows the ancient Lake Superior shoreline some 600 feet above today's lake surface.

Though the central portion of the drive passes through the city, most of the parkway leads through forest and past rushing rivers and waterfalls. You can access the east end from Superior Street at Lester Park and the west end at Becks Road near Gary-New Duluth. The popular eastern section is known as **Seven Bridges Road,** a narrow unpaved route with not seven but nine stone-arch bridges and the most scenic of the road's many scenic overlooks.

Also along the eastern portion is the **Hawk Ridge Nature Reserve** (Skyline E. and 52nd Ave. E., 218/428-6209, www.hawkridge.org; daily 9am-4pm; free, donations accepted), a 315-acre hilltop natural area. People flock from all over the country beginning in mid-August, when tens of thousands of migrating raptors follow the air currents along the Lake Superior shoreline on their way south for the winter. Over 100,000 broadwinged hawks were once counted in a single day. The best viewing is usually early September through October between 9am and 4pm, and some hawks still pass by as late as December. During the migration, Hawk Ridge naturalists conduct research and offer free educational programs for the general public. The rest of the year, it's still a worthwhile destination for the 2.5 miles of hiking trails.

**Enger Park** (16th Ave. W. and

Skyline Dr.), near the middle of the parkway at 16th Avenue West, should also not be missed. A historic rock observation tower rises five stories from the city's highest point, and a Japanese garden, picnic area, and several secluded overlooks surround it.

## GLENSHEEN

In the early 1900s, Chester and Clara Congdon raised seven children in **Glensheen** mansion (3300 London Rd., Duluth, 218/726-8910, www. glensheen.org; summer daily 9am-4pm, late Oct.-mid-May Mon.-Fri. 1pm-3pm, Sat.-Sun. 10am-3pm; $15 adults, $7 children, expanded tour options $26-35), and much of the elaborate decor is still in place for the public to view. But that is not necessarily what draws Minnesotans to the house and grounds. In 1977, one of Chester and Clara's children, Elisabeth Congdon, was murdered, along with her nurse, Velma Pietila, by Elisabeth's son-in-law, in one of Minnesota's most notorious crimes.

## ✪ SPLIT ROCK LIGHTHOUSE

While it lies nearly 30 miles north of Duluth along scenic North Shore Drive, the **Split Rock Lighthouse** (3713 Split Rock Lighthouse Rd., Two Harbors, 218/226-6372, www.mnhs. org; mid-May-mid-Oct. daily 10am-6pm, mid-Oct.-mid-May Thurs.-Mon. 11am-4pm; $10 adults, $8 seniors and students, $6 children 6-17) is an iconic Minnesota sight and worth the drive for anyone who has time. It stands a full 600 feet above the surface of Lake Superior, built here after a 1905 storm damaged 29 ships. The Minnesota Historical Society has restored the lighthouse to its 1920s appearance and leads tours that focus on the lonely life of a lighthouse keeper. It is no longer operational, but the beacon

Split Rock Lighthouse

shines across the water once a year on November 10 to commemorate the wreck of the *Edmund Fitzgerald*. Call for winter hours.

## OTHER SIGHTS

On the campus of the University of Minnesota Duluth, the **Tweed Museum of Art** (1201 Ordean Ct., Duluth, 218/726-8222, www.d.umn.edu/tma; Tues. 9am-8pm, Wed.-Fri. 9am-4:30pm, Sat.-Sun. 1pm-5pm, $5 suggested donation) houses more than 6,000 works of art in its own dedicated building. Its core is a collection of 600 works of early-20th-century American art donated by a Duluth couple in 1950. The permanent collection now reaches across eras and cultures.

The **Duluth Children's Museum** (115 N. 29th Ave. W., Duluth, 218/733-7543, www.duluthchildrensmuseum.org; Mon.-Sat. 9am-5pm, Sun. noon-5pm, $12.50) aims to spark imaginative play through science, theater, history, and crafts. Kids can climb through the Old Woman's eponymous shoe, dig for dinosaurs, explore with magnifying glasses, and more.

## RESTAURANTS

Grandma's (www.grandmasrestaurants.com) is an unavoidable institution in Duluth, a Canal Park empire including four restaurants, all within a block of each other. **Grandma's Saloon and Grill** (522 Lake Ave. S., Duluth, 218/727-4192; Sun. 11am-10pm, Mon.-Thurs. 11:30am-10pm, Fri. 11:30am-11:30pm, Sat. 11am-11:30pm; $10-16) is the sort of authentic good-feeling place fast-casual restaurants should model themselves after, with towering burgers and mountainous fries, along with enough beer to fill Lake Superior and a large variety of shakes and malts. **Grandma's Sports Garden** (425 Lake Ave. S., Duluth,

218/722-4724, Memorial Day-Labor Day daily 11:30am-10pm, later on weekends, $8-12) is more of the same, with more television, even more beer, and live music or a DJ nearly every night.

**Bellisio's** (405 Lake Ave. S., Duluth, 218/727-4921; daily 11:30am-2pm and 5pm-10pm; $18-44) brings white-tablecloth Italian to the mix with entrées like chicken marsala and fennel-roasted rack of pork. And **Little Angie's Cantina and Grill** (11 Buchanan St. E., Duluth, 218/727-6117; Mon.-Fri. 11:30am-1am, Sat.-Sun. 11am-1am; $10-15) is young, south-of-the-border fun, heavy on the fajitas and margaritas.

A classic Duluth eatery has its roots in the Twin Cities: **Pizza Luce** (11 Superior St. E., Duluth, 218/727-7400, www.pizzaluce.com; Mon.-Thurs. 10:30am-2am, Fri. 10:30am-2:30am, Sat. 8am-2:30am, Sun. 8am-2am) serves the same quirky, thick-crust pizza you can get in Minneapolis and St. Paul (topped with mashed potatoes or mock duck, if you like). But it also serves breakfast: pesto Benedict, Cajun hash browns, vegan sausage, and more. A pizza serving 3-5 people is about $22; breakfast ranges $8-12.

Cozy little **Martha's Daughter** (107 Superior St. E., Duluth, 218/481-7887, http://marthasdaughterrestaurant.net; Fri. 4:30pm-1am, Sat.-Sun. 10:30am-2pm and 4:30pm-1am; $9-12) contains a whole world of cuisines, from chicken and waffles to dumplings to *mapo tofu* (tofu in a spicy sauce). What it all has in common is comfort.

Inside the Dewitt-Seitz Marketplace in Canal Park, **Northern Waters Smokehaus** (394 Lake Ave. S., Duluth, 218/724-7307, www.northernwaterssmokehaus.com; Sun. 10am-6pm, Mon.-Sat. 10am-9pm) sells house-smoked meat and local fish by the pound, along with other picnicables and a menu of deluxe sandwiches.

The best dining by far in Duluth is actually about eight miles north of town. The **New Scenic Café** (5461 North Shore Dr., Duluth, 218/525-6274, www.sceniccafe.com; Sun.-Thurs. 11am-9pm, Fri.-Sat. 11am-10pm) is a critics' darling and a destination for those seeking an up-to-date take on fresh, local cuisine. The restaurant itself is unaffected, comfortable, and subtly elegant, as is the menu, which changes seasonally and will likely include herbs from the garden out front. Expect to spend about $26 for an entrée or $13 for a sandwich.

## BREWPUBS AND TAPROOMS

It should surprise no one that casual, outdoorsy, beer-loving Duluth has joined the brewery boom that swept across Minnesota, with nearly a dozen local taprooms where you can stop for a pint or fill a growler.

Ales and lagers from **Bent Paddle Brewing** (1832 Michigan St. W., Duluth, 218/279-2722, www.bentpaddlebrewing. com; Tues.-Thurs. noon-10pm, Fri.-Sat. noon-11pm, Sun. noon-9pm) are on nearly every menu on the North Shore. At the brewery, you can try beers that are still in the experimental phase and take a tour (Sat.-Sun. 11am). There's no food menu, but you can order delivery from local restaurants.

Hang out, play lawn games, sit by the fire pit, enjoy the unbeatable views of Lake Superior. **Canal Park Brewing** (300 Canal Park Dr., Duluth, 218/464-4790, www.canalparkbrewery.com; Sun.-Thurs. 11am-11pm, Fri.-Sat. 11am-midnight) has a long menu of beer snacks and hearty sandwiches, in addition to the brews.

**Hoops Brewing** (325 Lake Ave. S., Duluth, 218/606-1666, www. hoopsbrewing.com; daily 11am-noon) is no spare, concrete-floored afterthought of a the brewery; it's a vast, beautiful beer hall with wide wood timbers. Your non-beer-drinking friends can enjoy cocktails and other drinks in the bar area, officially (but not really) separate from the brewery.

## ARTS AND CULTURE
### PERFORMING ARTS

Duluth has a reputation as an arts-loving community and supports several theaters and musical groups. The **Duluth Playhouse** (506 Michigan St. W., Duluth, 218/733-7555, www. duluthplayhouse.org) was among the first community theaters in the United States when it was founded in 1914 and among the first to include children's productions in its season. It moved to its current home in the Union Depot in 1977. The year-round season includes about seven plays for all generations, heavy on the musicals, and three children's productions.

The **Duluth Superior Symphony Orchestra** (350 Harbor Dr., Duluth, 218/623-3776, http://dsso.com) performs at the **Duluth Entertainment Convention Center** (350 Harbor Dr., Duluth, 218/722-5573), on the harbor. The season, which runs September-May, mixes well-known classical music and pops, including an annual performance by the youth orchestra and a popular December holiday concert. The Duluth-based **Minnesota Ballet** (218/529-3742, www.minnesotaballet.org) also puts on a few performances at the Duluth Entertainment Convention Center each year. The **Lake Superior Chamber Orchestra** (218/525-4076, www.lakesuperiorchamberorchestra.

org) holds 4-5 weeknight concerts at the University of Minnesota Duluth and the College of St. Scholastica each summer.

## FESTIVALS AND EVENTS

Unless you're a runner with a room booked a year in advance, the third weekend of June is not the time to visit Duluth. That's when more than 9,000 runners come to run **Grandma's Marathon** (www. grandmasmarathon.com), named for the restaurant, which was a major sponsor when the race started in 1977. Runners start near Two Harbors and continue along Scenic Route 61, finishing in Canal Park outside the namesake restaurant—you can see the finish line year-round. The race, a Boston Marathon qualifier, registers runners on a first-come, first-served basis. The men's record is 2:09:06 and the women's is 2:26:31.

A slightly smaller crowd (an estimated 4,000 spectators) converges on Duluth on the last Sunday in January for the **John Beargrease Sled Dog Marathon** (218/722-7631, www. beargrease.com). Run since 1981, the marathon is the longest sled dog race in the lower 48 and is an Iditarod qualifier race. Mushers race north from Duluth almost to the Canadian border and back. The mid-distance race, about 100 miles, starts in Duluth and finishes on the shore of Lake Superior in Tofte. The race is named for the son of an Ojibwe chief who helped the communities of the North Shore survive and grow by delivering mail by dogsled in the late 19th century.

More than 4,000 skaters follow the same route as Grandma's in September during the **Northshore Inline Marathon** (www. northshoreinline.com), the largest

inline race in the country and an official World Cup event.

The **Bayfront Blues Festival** (www.bayfrontblues.com) has the whole town swinging the second weekend in August. Dozens of acts perform on three stages in Bayfront Festival Park, and many area clubs get in on the action as well. Headliners have included Shemekia Copeland and Robert Cray.

## RECREATION

If a brisk walk on the **Lakewalk** isn't enough for you, the **Hartley Nature Center** (3001 Woodland Ave., Duluth, 218/724-6735, www.hartleynature.org; Mon.-Fri. 9am-5pm, Sat. 10am-5pm; free, donations accepted) is a great place to satisfy a craving for nature and recreation. The urban park, with a wide variety of natural environments and about a mile across at its widest point, has trails for hiking, biking, cross-country skiing, and snowshoeing, as well as docks for canoeing and fishing. The beautiful modern park building is also a model of sustainable building techniques and houses a small exhibit on green building.

During the winter, skiers can get their fix on the dozen ski and snowboard trails at **Spirit Mountain** (9500 Spirit Mountain Pl., Duluth, 800/642-6377, www.spiritmt.com; Sun.-Thurs. 9am-8pm, Fri.-Sat. 9am-9pm; ski pass $55 adults, $44 seniors and children). In the warmer months, the park is full of other kinds of adventure: mini golf, ziplines, and a coaster track that zips down the mountain through the trees.

With up to seven departures a day, **Vista Fleet** (DECC Dock and Harbor Dr., Duluth, 218/722-6218, www.vistafleet.com, $16-44) makes it easy to get out on the water and see Duluth's beautiful shoreline from the same vantage point as the shipping vessels that built the city. Sightseeing cruises run 90 minutes, while some meal cruises (including brunch, lunch, pizza, or dinner) run the same or a little longer. The fleet includes two boats, with capacities from 80 to 225 passengers. Both have both open observation decks and enclosed seating areas.

## SHOPS

A wander through the Canal Park area will turn up plenty of touristy T-shirt shops. Souvenirs of a different kind can be found at the Lake Superior Magazine Outlet Store (310 Superior St. E., Duluth, 888/244-5253, www.lakesuperior.com; Mon.-Fri. 8am-5:30pm, Sat. 9am-4pm), which sells wall maps, nautical maps, books, gear, and furnishings all related to the lake.

A "Duluth Pack," in regional parlance, is a heavy-duty rectangular canvas backpack with a fold-over top. The original 1882 design was known as a Poirier pack, named after the inventor. Duluth Pack still makes the bags, along with school bags and heavy-duty luggage, and sells them at its only retail outlet (365 Canal Park Dr., Duluth, 218/722-1707, www.duluthpack.com; Mon.-Sat. 9am-9pm, Sun. 10am-8pm), along with other high-quality outdoor gear.

For one-stop, less Duluth-oriented shopping, head to the Dewitt-Seitz Building in Canal Park (394 Lake Ave. S., Duluth, 218/722-0047, www.dewittseitz.com; Mon.-Fri. 10am-9pm, Sat. 10am-8pm, Sun. 10am-5pm). The renovated warehouse is home to the excellent toy shop J. Skylark (218/722-3794) and Hepzibah's Sweet Shoppe (218/722-5049). Across the street, Waters of Superior (395 Lake Ave. S., Duluth, 218/786-0233, www.watersofsuperior.com, daily 10am-7pm) combines high-end, contemporary women's clothing with Scandinavian-influenced art in a spare gallery setting.

A little piece of a particular era in Minnesota musical history—when the Minneapolis sound was on the rise in the 1980s—can be found at Electric Fetus (12 Superior St. E., Duluth, 218/722-9970; Mon.-Fri. 9am-9pm, Sat. 9am-8pm, Sun. 11am-6pm), a sister store to the original in Minneapolis, which sells music, clothing, books, and candles.

For fine art with a true Northland touch, check out Sivertson Gallery (361 Canal Park Dr., Duluth, 218/723-7877 or 888/815-5814, www.sivertson.com, Thurs.-Sat. 9am-7pm, Sun.-Wed. 9am-6pm). You'll find photos by *National Geographic* photographer Jim Brandenburg and works by many Native Americans.

## WHERE TO STAY

Duluth is a popular getaway for Minnesotans as well as visitors from farther afield, so its 5,000 hotel rooms fill up fast and reservations are always recommended. The downtown business district offers plenty of convenient chain options, but the mansion district east of downtown, where shipping and railroad tycoons once built grand homes, offers a different taste of Duluth. Six of these Victorian homes are now beautiful bed-and-breakfasts (find them all at www.duluthbandb.com), with 5-7 rooms each and both romantic and practical details. The neighborhood itself, a quiet area inviting leisurely walks, is a perk. Ellery House (28 S. 21st Ave. E., Duluth, 218/724-7639, www.elleryhouse.com, $119-199 d) is one of these hospitable homes, with a broad porch, delicious breakfasts, and welcoming, unobtrusive hosts.

No hotel is better situated than the **South Pier Inn** (701 Lake Ave. S., Duluth, 218/786-9007 or 800/430-7437, www.southpierinn.com, $150-285), on Park Point just across from Canal Park. Most rooms look up at the lift bridge, and you can watch ships pass through the harbor from a private balcony. Most of the 29 rooms are whirlpool suites, and there is a two-night minimum on weekends.

In Canal Park, four large hotels line the Lakewalk, overlooking Lake Superior. **Canal Park Lodge** (250 Canal Park Dr., Duluth, 218/279-6000, www.canalparklodge.com, $200-350 d) is charmingly rustic with a resort-like atmosphere and a high-ceilinged, comfortable lounge in the lobby. Breakfast and high-quality coffee are included in the cost of the rooms, which feature large HD TVs and—if you're lucky—a balcony facing the lake.

Two doors down, also on the Lakewalk, **The Inn on Lake Superior** (350 Canal Park Dr., Duluth, 218/726-1111, www.theinnonlakesuperior.com, $200-285 d) is a little older and less flashy but no less comfortable. The inn focuses on making families comfortable—from offering long, leisurely breakfasts in its café to evening story time and s'mores on the lakeside patio. In a nice Minnesota touch, a large sauna is available for guests to use.

Arguably the most elegant hotel in Duluth is located in a brewery. Well, the building was built in 1885 as a brewery, and now, after handsome renovations, it houses not only a much smaller brewing operation but also **Fitger's Inn** (600 Superior St. E., Duluth, 218/722-8826, www.fitgers.com, $170-380 d), along with a host of other businesses. The 62 rooms (including 20 suites) are, like all of the Fitger's complex's many charms, carved creatively out of the old brewery space. Many have exposed brick walls, raised separate seating areas, and other touches to remind you of the building's history. Luxury suites have fireplaces, balconies, and whirlpools. Be sure to request a lakeside room.

The **Edgewater Resort & Waterpark** (2400 London Rd., Duluth, 218/728-3601 or 800/777-7925, www.duluthwaterpark.com, $180-320) features a 30,000-square-foot water park with water slides, a kiddie play area, and more. The 297-room hotel also has a pool, whirlpool, sauna, arcade, miniature golf course, free bikes, and nicely appointed rooms. It's not directly on the shore, but it has easy access to the Lakewalk and great views from lakeside rooms.

# PRACTICALITIES
## VISITORS CENTERS

The **Visit Duluth tourist information center** (225 W. Superior St. W., Duluth, 800/438-5884, www.visitduluth.com; Mon.-Fri. 8:30am-5pm; waterfront info center at the Vista Fleet office summer daily 9:30am-6:30pm) is operated by the Duluth Convention and Visitors Bureau.

## GETTING THERE

From the Twin Cities, take I-35 straight north for 150 miles and you will find yourself in the middle of downtown Duluth. Delta schedules several flights a day between **Duluth International Airport** (www.duluthairport.com) and Minneapolis-St. Paul (and seasonally to Detroit as well), but the cost of these tickets almost never compares favorably to a rental car and a tank of gas. United Airlines flies daily to Chicago O'Hare. Two **Greyhound buses** a day run between the Twin Cities and Duluth, dropping passengers at two locations in the city: the Greyhound bus terminal (4426 Grand Ave., Duluth, 218/722-5591) and Kirby Student Center at the University of Minnesota Duluth (1120 Kirby Dr., Duluth, 218/762-8520).

## GETTING AROUND

If you plan to stay in downtown Duluth and forgo exploring the coast, it's possible to get by without your own car. The city is very walkable: The stretch of Superior Street where you're likely to spend the most time, from Fitger's to the Depot, is only about 1.5 miles long. The **skywalk** system (daily, hours vary) helps pedestrians when the weather's bad and makes it easier to get across I-35, which cuts the lakefront off from downtown. The skywalks are sadly underused compared to the lively Minneapolis and St. Paul systems.

From June through Labor Day, the free **Port Town Trolley** carries passengers in a loop through Canal Park and downtown Duluth, running along Lake Avenue and Superior Street. Pick up the trolley at eight locations (the Holiday Center, Radisson Hotel, Duluth Union Depot, Great Lakes Aquarium, Excursion Dock, SS *William A. Irvin,* Lake Superior Maritime Visitor Center, and Fitger's) once every 30 minutes 11:30am-7pm.

The Duluth Transit Authority runs 20 city bus routes, which run every 10 minutes to every hour during the day, with reduced service on the weekends. Route 5 runs between downtown and the bus station and airport. Route 8 runs up and down Superior, stopping at the Fitger's complex. Pick up schedules (and any bus) at the **Duluth Transit Center** (214 Superior St. W., 218/722-7283). Fares are $1.50 during peak hours (Mon.-Fri. 7am-9am and 2:30pm-6pm) and $0.75 otherwise.

# BACKGROUND

# The Landscape

The Mississippi River passes through Minneapolis.

The Twin Cities sit where the last bit of eastern deciduous forest touches the edge of the great tallgrass prairie that sweeps south and west. It is a city on the edge—not quite within the great American Heartland but opening the door to it. Minneapolis is known as the "first city of the West" and St. Paul as the "last city of the East." The Mississippi River, which divides the two, does not do so cleanly. Instead, its north-south course makes a giant sideways S as it passes through the area, cradling neighborhoods of St. Paul that are bounded by the river on three sides. It also divides both cities and the suburbs into rough north and south areas, with much of the wealth and most of the professional opportunities concentrated in the south.

## GEOGRAPHY

The Twin Cities are located almost precisely in the middle between the East and West Coasts and also lie right on top of the 45th parallel, exactly halfway between the North Pole and the Equator. A plaque in Minneapolis's Theodore Wirth Park (look for it near the intersection of Wirth Parkway and Golden Valley Road) marks this point.

True to its flatland reputation, Minneapolis sits at 830 feet above sea level and St. Paul at 702 feet.

Three rivers pass through the Twin Cities. The Minnesota River meets the Mississippi just south of St. Paul at Fort Snelling, and the St. Croix River flows south from Lake Superior, forming the border with Wisconsin for much of its length before meeting the Mississippi southeast of the cities near Hastings.

Retreating glaciers left the area a tremendous gift: nearly 1,000 lakes within the metropolitan area. And when Lake Agassiz, the massive glacial lake that covered much of northern Minnesota and the Dakotas, drained about 13,000 years ago, the water spilling out of it cut the Minnesota and St. Croix River valleys even deeper.

Historically, the Twin Cities' most important geologic feature is St. Anthony Falls, the only waterfall along the length of the Mississippi River. The falls originated well downstream of its present location near downtown Minneapolis and moved upstream, first slowly then more quickly, as the soft underlying sandstone eroded and the limestone overlayer collapsed. The waterfall was fixed in place in the late 1800s when, after the city had come to rely on its considerable waterpower, engineers built a massive wood apron (later replaced by concrete) to protect it. Had it moved a short distance farther upstream, the falls would have disappeared altogether.

## CLIMATE

Minnesota's climate is characterized by warm, wet summers and cold, dry winters, with some of the greatest temperature variations in the country. While the Twin Cities have the coldest average annual temperature of any major U.S. metropolitan area (45°F), they also on occasion see record-setting temperatures even higher than those in far more southerly parts of the country.

The Twin Cities are usually just a smidge warmer than the rest of the state, thanks to the warming effect created by all those paved streets and tall buildings trapping heat. January is the coldest month, with an average high of 22°F, and July is the warmest,

with an average high of 83°F. The first frost tends to come in early October, the last frost in early May. Below-zero temperatures have been seen in the Twin Cities as early as November 4, on one record-setting occasion in 1991, although that is not common at all.

During the winter, especially, temperatures can swing wildly. On one memorable day in 1996, the low temperature was -32°F. A week later, the high was 39°F. While Minneapolis averages just four nights below zero each year, in the winter of 2013-2014, the cities endured 53 below-zero nights.

Snow does fly in October and November, but it rarely sticks on the ground. A "permanent" winter snow cover of an inch or more tends to form in December and lasts, on average, three months. An average year sees about 60 inches of snow. To the surprise of some out-of-towners who associate March with spring, March is the snowiest month, averaging 13.5 inches—and damp, heavy stuff at that. (The explanation locals give for this strikes fear in the hearts of many: January and February are often just "too cold for it to snow." Meteorologists quibble, saying it's never actually too cold for snow to form, but colder air does hold less water vapor than warmer air, making large snowfalls less likely.) The infamous Halloween Blizzard of 1991 set the record for the largest single snowfall, with 28.4 inches falling on the Twin Cities over the course of two days.

The Twin Cities get about two-thirds of their annual precipitation in the summer, with much of it coming in the form of torrential summer storms, rather than slow drizzles. June, the rainiest month with 4.34 inches of rain, sees an average eight days of thunderstorms. Total average rainfall is about 30 inches a year.

# History

Although they were not the first humans to inhabit the area that is now the Twin Cities, people of the Hopewell tradition, a flourishing culture that spread across much of eastern North America between 200 BC and AD 500, left the most visible mark on the area: clusters of massive burial mounds that now make up Indian Mounds Park near downtown St. Paul.

The Hopewell peoples disappeared, but the Dakota people, who were here when the first European settlers arrived, are very likely the descendants of another ancient culture, the Mississippian, which reached into the southeast corner of what is now Minnesota.

The Dakota are also sometimes known as the Sioux, a shortened form of the Ojibwe word *nadouessioux* (poisonous snake). The Dakota and Ojibwe (sometimes known as Chippewa) have been fierce rivals, often fighting bloody battles, since the Ojibwe first began arriving in the area around 1700. European settlers' westward expansion pushed the Ojibwe out of their homes in the east. The rough and volatile line dividing the territories of the two groups settled more or less across the present-day Twin Cities, and the area saw its share of skirmishes.

What is now St. Anthony Falls, in downtown Minneapolis, was an important landmark for both the Dakota and Ojibwe people. Because they had to portage their canoes there as they came up- or downstream, it was a natural spot for a campground. The Dakota called the falls *mnirara* (curling waters), and the Ojibwe called it *kakabikah* (severed rock).

The first European to see the falls was Father Louis Hennepin in 1680. Hennepin, a Belgian-born Franciscan priest, had been dispatched along with a band of explorers to seek out the headwaters of the Mississippi by the French government. (Many others would be sent on this errand before the American geographer Henry Schoolcraft fixed the source of the river at modern-day Itasca, well northwest of the Twin Cities, in 1832.) Hennepin was captured by the Dakota and spent several months with them before escaping. He headed downriver and came upon the waterfall, which he named after his patron saint, St. Anthony of Padua. While the waterfall was indeed impressive—about 16 feet—in his enthusiasm he exaggerated its size to a massive 40 or 50 feet high.

Word of the falls spread, attracting explorers and even early tourists, but the U.S. government didn't show much interest in the area until well after the Revolutionary War. After the Louisiana Purchase brought what is now Minnesota—along with all the land from the Mississippi River to the Rocky Mountains—into U.S. territory in 1803, the U.S. government sent army lieutenant Zebulon Pike out to explore the northern reaches of it. Pike himself identified the promontory at the junction of the Minnesota and Mississippi Rivers, just south of the two present-day downtowns, as the perfect spot for a military fort. Pike bought a large tract of land from the Dakota in exchange for promises of better prices on furs, 60 gallons of whiskey, and $200 in trade goods.

In 1819, looking for a way to protect the upper Mississippi River area from

British and French fur traders, the U.S. Army ordered a fort built on the spot Pike had chosen. Soldiers and their families arrived to build Fort Snelling, a limestone fortress high above the Mississippi. Out in the hinterlands, far from the cities of the East Coast, the new settlers were largely on their own when it came to meeting their basic needs. They built the first sawmills and cultivated fields alongside the Mississippi.

By August 1848, fewer than 4,000 Europeans lived in what is now Minnesota, far below what the law required for territorial status. But the lumber companies were eager for Minnesota to have some sort of official status after Wisconsin had achieved statehood and left them in limbo, no longer part of the Wisconsin Territory. A group of settlers met in Stillwater, chose Henry Sibley as their representative, and sent him off to Congress, essentially with their fingers crossed that he would be seated. He was, and in March 1849, President Zachary Taylor named Alexander Ramsey the first territorial governor.

Minnesota would become a state in very short order, but in the meantime, affairs needed to be settled with the large Native American tribes in the area. The Treaty of Traverse des Sioux in 1851 would be one of the darker days in the history of Minnesota's native peoples. At a gathering place in the southwest corner of the present-day metropolitan area, 35 chiefs signed a treaty giving up 24 million acres to the United States. Immediately after signing, each sat down at a separate table and signed another paper giving up the rights to the annuity payments they had just been promised to repay debts to white traders. The tribes would get little or nothing in return for their land.

## STATEHOOD

When Minnesota became a territory, St. Paul was named as its capital. In 1857, there was a drive to move the capital to the town of St. Peter, which was a little more centrally located. The law passed the territorial legislature and only needed the governor's signature. But an opposing legislator, Joseph Rolette, decided to take matters into his own hands. He absconded with the bill and then hid in a hotel drinking and playing cards until the clock ran out on the legislative session and the bill expired, leaving the capital in St. Paul.

Minnesota became a state in 1858 and quickly found itself embroiled in two wars. When the Civil War broke out in 1861, Governor Alexander Ramsey happened to be in Washington, D.C., and responded immediately to President Lincoln's call for troops. Thanks to some new technology—the telegraph—the nation's first volunteers were lined up at Fort Snelling within days. About 1 in 10 Minnesota men fought in the Civil War, in battles from Bull Run to Gettysburg.

Within the year, Minnesota had another war on its hands, this time right at home. The harvests had been bad for several years, and the U.S. government had not been paying its annuities to the Dakota. Unrest grew and the situation exploded in the summer of 1862, when four young Dakota men killed a farming family. Brutal battles raged for two months, with horrors committed on both sides. After the Dakota surrendered, thousands of men, women, and children were imprisoned in a camp outside Fort Snelling, where nearly all perished from disease or starvation. More than 300 men were sentenced to hang. President Lincoln

## MINNESOTA STATE SYMBOLS

- **State bird:** Common loon (*Gavia immer*)

- **State butterfly:** Monarch (*Danaus plexippus*)

- **State drink:** Milk

- **State fish:** Walleye (*Sander vitreus*)

- **State flower:** Pink-and-white lady's slipper (*Cypripedium reginae*)

- **State fruit:** Honeycrisp apple (*Malus pumila*)

- **State gemstone:** Lake Superior agate

- **State grain:** Wild rice (*Zizania aquatica*)

- **State motto:** L'Etoile du Nord (*Star of the North*)

- **State muffin:** Blueberry

- **State mushroom:** Morel (*Morchella esculenta*)

- **State photo:** "Grace," by Eric Enstrom, 1918

- **State song:** "Hail Minnesota"

- **State tree:** Red or Norway pine (*Pinus resinosa*)

personally reviewed the cases and reduced most of the sentences, but the settlers were calling out for blood and 39 Dakota men were hanged.

# THE MINNESOTA MIRACLE

After the Civil War, the nation looked westward again and the Twin Cities boomed. It became a center for the lumber industry and then the flour industry, connected to the rest of the country by "the Empire Builder" James J. Hill's railroads. All this growth was fueled by immigration not just from the rest of the country, but from Scandinavia, Germany, Ireland, and Eastern Europe as well. By the late 1870s, well more than one-third of Minnesota's population had been born in another country.

Minneapolis rode the milling wave until 1930, when production dropped off sharply and the city of Buffalo took over as the leading producer. But by that time, other industries were already on the rise. Minnesota Mining and Manufacturing (3M) introduced a wide range of industrial, military, and consumer products (including Scotch tape) that helped it thrive through the war years. Medtronic rose to the top of the biotech field with the first implantable pacemaker. And a number of growing companies in a variety of fields kept Minnesota's diversified economy strong: Honeywell in defense manufacturing, Cargill in grain trading, Control Data and IBM in computers, and General Mills and Land O'Lakes in food production. An enterprising developer built the nation's first indoor shopping mall, Southdale, in the first-ring suburb of Edina in 1956.

By the 1970s, Minnesota had a reputation for a sound economy, a strong education, and a high quality of life. Minnesota governor Wendell Anderson, grinning and holding a walleye on a fishing hook, was featured on the cover of *Time* magazine in 1973, under the title "The Good Life in Minnesota." Anderson is largely credited with the successful restructuring of funding for municipalities and public schools that helped bring about the Minnesota Miracle.

Anderson, however, left the governor's office in 1976 when he appointed himself to fill the U.S. Senate seat vacated by Walter Mondale, who had been elected vice president. This didn't go over well with Minnesotans, who punished the Democratic-Farmer-Labor Party in subsequent elections and helped usher in an era of moderate Republican leadership in Minnesota, including governors Al Quie and Arne Carlson, U.S. Senator Dave Durenburger, and, later, U.S. Representative Jim Ramstad.

The governor most famous to those outside of Minnesota was surely Jesse Ventura, who was elected on a wave of disgust with the two major parties (or, possibly, in a massive public game of chicken) in 1999. Ventura made himself a reputation for antagonizing both the press and Minnesota's bicameral legislature—and for governing fairly effectively simply by getting out of the way. He left office in 2003 and was replaced by Republican Tim Pawlenty, a more conservative model of Republican than previous Minnesota leaders. Democrat Mark Dayton, local department store heir and former U.S. senator, was elected the state's 40th governor in 2010 and reelected in 2014.

In recent years, Minnesota (and the Twin Cities in particular) has been shaped by new waves of immigrants, as the Latin American, South Asian, and East African communities have grown. St. Paul sent the nation's first Hmong American to a state legislature in 2002, when Mee Moua was elected to the Minnesota Senate, and Minneapolis elected the first Somali-American legislator in 2018, sending Ilhan Omar to the state House of Representatives. Although the percentage of foreign-born citizens is at 7 percent, rather than around 40 percent as it was in the late 1800s, there are shades of that earlier turbulent time of change and growth.

# Government and Economy

## GOVERNMENT

Both Minneapolis and St. Paul are strongholds of the Democratic Party—or the Democratic-Farmer-Labor Party, as it is known here. Minneapolis has not elected a Republican mayor since 1973, and St. Paul hasn't since 1952 (although Norm Coleman switched to the Republican Party in the middle of his term as St. Paul mayor in 1996). Both the 13-member Minneapolis City Council and the 7-member St. Paul City Council are typically made up almost entirely of DFLers, with a Green Party member or independent or two thrown in for variety.

Another characteristic the cities share is strong neighborhood control. St. Paul's 17 districts are governed by independent district councils. Each has control over its own budget and has a say in vital land-use questions. Minneapolis's neighborhood councils also control significant budgets used for neighborhood revitalization programs, from housing to scholarships to landscaping and more.

## METROPOLITAN COUNCIL

With two major cities sitting cheek by jowl, not to mention the surrounding suburban areas, there's bound to be some redundancy in government functions. In the seven-county Minneapolis-St. Paul metropolitan area (including Hennepin County, which contains Minneapolis, and Ramsey County, which contains St. Paul), there are as many as 182 cities, from tiny New Trier, population 113, to Minneapolis, population 400,000.

The Minnesota State Legislature

foresaw the problems this could cause as disparities grew and municipalities battled for ever scarcer resources as early as 1967. Lawmakers created the Metropolitan Council to centralize planning and coordinating powers in one body. The council is charged with creating an evolving framework for growth and vetting the growth plans of member communities to be sure they fit that framework.

Today the powerful Met Council (390 Robert St. N., St. Paul, 651/602-1000, www.metropolitancouncil.org) has an annual budget of about $1 billion and a staff of 3,700. It is governed by a board of 17 members appointed by the governor and approved by the Minnesota Senate. Each member represents a geographic district within the seven-county area.

In its five-decade history, the council has taken on operating responsibilities beyond its original role as planner and coordinator. It operates the Metro Transit bus system, serving Minneapolis, St. Paul, and the surrounding communities, as well as the light rail systems between the Mall of America and downtown Minneapolis and connecting the two downtowns. It also operates the sewer and wastewater treatment programs for 100 communities and funds a system of 49 regional parks.

While the bulk of the council's budget comes from legislative funding, sewer treatment fees, and transit fares, it also serves another important function in the area: redistributing the wealth. Communities have given the council 40 percent of the growth in their commercial-industrial tax base

Ever wonder where the Bundt pan came from? Right here in St. Louis Park, Minnesota, a product of local company Nordic Ware. Some other notable Twin Cities inventions: the implantable pacemaker, Magnetic Poetry, the Milky Way candy bar, Post-Its, Rollerblades, Spam (well, Spam comes from a little farther afield, in Austin, Minnesota), and Zubaz (those wide-legged pants from the 1980s).

since 1971. That money is then redistributed to member communities based on population and the market value of homes.

## DEMOCRATIC-FARMER-LABOR PARTY

One of Minnesota's most telling political quirks is the existence of the Democratic-Farmer-Labor Party, the DFL. That's right, Minnesota doesn't have just any old Democratic Party; it has its very own. The DFL was formed in 1944, when Minnesota's Democrats merged with the Farmer-Labor Party. The Farmer-Labor Party had a presence in other states but had been particularly strong in Minnesota, producing three governors and four U.S. senators between its founding in 1918 and the merger. Two national Democratic nominees for president, Hubert H. Humphrey in 1968 and Walter Mondale in 1984, have been DFLers, though both lost to their Republican opponents.

## ECONOMY

The Mississippi River drove the early economic development of Minneapolis and St. Paul. Long before the railroad reached the new West, waterways tied the new cities to the whole of the eastern seaboard and the burgeoning frontier. St. Anthony Falls powered two boom times in

Minneapolis in particular: From 1848 to 1887, Minneapolis sawmills turned out more boards than in any other city in the nation. And from 1884 to 1930, Minneapolis led the world in flour production.

Today the Twin Cities area is a hub for biotechnology, and Minnesota has 19 Fortune 500 companies, more per capita than any other state. The metro area had a gross metropolitan product of nearly $250 billion in 2016, representing about two-thirds of Minnesota's gross state product (and about the same proportion of the state's population).

The Twin Cities also rank first in the nation among major metropolitan areas in labor force participation (82 percent of working-age adults) and employment (77 percent). Minnesota has the country's highest labor-force participation rate for women (72 percent). Unemployment falls below the national average, at 3.3 percent in 2018. Workers enjoy a median household income of $66,000 and relatively short average commute times (25 minutes in 2015). The cost of living sits just above the national average, with a median home price of $246,000.

These factors—and, of course, the cultural amenities—no doubt are some of the reasons that the Twin Cities regularly land on national lists of best places to live.

# Local Culture

Minnesota has the fastest-growing population in the Midwest, and much of that growth is happening in the Twin Cities metro area, if not in the central cities themselves. The seven-county metro area had a population of 3.03 million in 2016—about two-thirds of Minnesota's total population—with just over 400,000 people in Minneapolis, the state's largest city, and roughly 300,000 in St. Paul, the capital. The metro area includes 182 cities, many of which are growing at a faster rate than both Minneapolis and St. Paul, while the two central cities' share of the region's population continues to shrink. The Metropolitan Council, which oversees planning for the area, predicts that the population will reach 3.7 million by 2030.

Residents of the Twin Cities are, on average, well-educated middle-class people. Thirty-six percent of adults in the metro area have bachelor's degrees, putting Minneapolis-St. Paul fourth among U.S. metropolitan areas. The metro area ranks first in the percentage of population in the middle-income bracket (at 46 percent).

Minnesota has a reputation as a pretty white place. And, according to statewide statistics, yes, it is. But the picture changes depending on where you look. In the central cities (Minneapolis and St. Paul proper), 66 percent of the population is white, while in the first-ring suburbs that number is 89 percent, and in the outer burbs it's 95 percent. Seven percent of residents in the metro area are foreign-born. Many visitors are surprised to learn that the Twin Cities are home to large Hmong, Somali, Ethiopian, Eritrean, and Liberian populations.

About 50,000 Hmong live in Minnesota, immigrants and the children and grandchildren of immigrants from Vietnam, Thailand, and Laos. The largest number—more than half—live in St. Paul. Outside of Asia, only California's Hmong population is larger. The Hmong started arriving in Minnesota after the Vietnam War, where many had fought on the United States side in the "secret war" against the communists in Laos. The population grew again in 2004 when thousands of Hmong refugees from the Wat Tham Krabok camp in Thailand arrived.

Minnesota's Somali population, the largest in the United States, is estimated by some at 74,000, by others much higher than that. The population grew explosively in the 1990s, after the civil war in Somalia resulted in the total dissolution of a functioning government there. Most of the Somali population is centered in Minneapolis, where Somali-owned businesses and cultural centers are flourishing.

## EDUCATION

The University of Minnesota predates the state of Minnesota itself. It was chartered in 1851 and began enrolling students in 1857, the year before Minnesota became a state. It became a post-secondary institution in 1869. Today it is the fourth-largest in the nation, with more than 50,000 students, and boasts a number of top-ranked graduate programs, including chemical engineering, health-care administration, geography, applied economics, psychology, and more.

The Twin Cities metro area, in fact, is home to about two dozen colleges and universities. St. Paul alone ranks second in the nation in the number of higher-education institutions per capita. A number of them, including the University of Minnesota itself, attract many students from out of state who stick around to join the local workforce after they finish their education.

Minnesota has long had a reputation for excellence and innovation in public education. It was the first state to mandate full interdistrict school choice (any student can enroll in any school anywhere in the state, as long as there's room) and the first to introduce charter schools, in 1991.

## THE ARTS

It goes against all the stereotypes—the hardworking, no-nonsense Scandinavian ancestors; the cold weather; its location smack dab in between two coasts that both view themselves as the center of the universe—but the Twin Cities are a place where serious artists do serious art: on stage, on the page, and in their studios. More importantly, this is a place full of happy amateur artists: those who do for the love of doing and love living in a culture that supports that.

### ARTS, CRAFTS, AND FOLK TRADITIONS

Several organizations are working to keep alive some of the Scandinavian folk art traditions that came to Minnesota over a hundred years ago. The **American Swedish Institute** (www.asimn.org) hosts exhibits and offers classes in woodcarving, bobbin winding, the traditional painting technique known as rosemaling, and other crafts. **Ingebretsen's** (www.ingebretsens.com) is a store specializing in Scandinavian foods and crafts and a mini cultural center. Look on its website for classes in cooking, knitting, weaving, carving, and other crafts. Enterprising citizens also teach classes in a very wide range of crafts through Minneapolis Community Education (http://commed.mpls.k12.mn.us) and its St. Paul counterpart (www.commed.spps.org).

Another folk tradition that you are likely to see—one newer to the Twin Cities—is *pa ndau,* intricate Hmong appliqué work, characterized by concentric squares, often on purses, wall hangings, and pillow covers. A good place to look for *pa ndau* is at the **Nicollet Mall Market,** a Thursday farmers market. Keep your eyes out, as well, for the more modern cousin of *pa ndau:* story cloths, which are appliquéd works of art that tell a story. The style originated in the refugee camps of Thailand in the 1970s.

The **Textile Center** (www.textilecentermn.org) is a national umbrella organization for textile arts of all kinds that span centuries and cultures, with member organizations dedicated to needlepoint, sewing, spinning, knitting, and more. The center hosts exhibits and has a public library collection. In a similar vein, the **Northern Clay Center** (www.northernclaycenter.org) is a national organization based here in the Twin Cities that supports ceramicists through grants, exhibitions, publications, and more.

For arts of all sorts, from writing to photography, painting, fabric design, and more, the **Split Rock Arts Center** (http://cce.umn.edu/splitrockarts) at the University of Minnesota hosts summer workshops in the Twin Cities and retreats at its location in Cloquet, in northern Minnesota.

## LITERATURE

There's just something in the water here—that's sometimes the only explanation people can come up with to explain the Twin Cities' remarkable literary culture. The two cities regularly appear at the top of the list of America's most literate cities (as ranked by Central Connecticut State University, which tracks these things based on libraries, bookstores, publishers, and so on). In 2007, Minneapolis was number one and St. Paul number three.

But there's more to it than mysterious waterborne substances. A strong history of supporting the arts financially, top-notch educational institutions, and generations of immigrants from book-loving cultures all contribute, along with the snowball effect: A great literary culture attracts more people to contribute to it.

The area is home to a one-of-a-kind literary incubator, Open Book (www.openbookmn.org), where you'll find the Minnesota Center for Book Arts (www.mnbookarts.org), The Loft Literary Center (www.loft.org), and one of the country's most successful small nonprofit publishers, Milkweed Editions (www.milkweed.org), all under one roof.

The Twin Cities have also been called a hub of small-scale publishers, comparable to New York's status as the hub for mega-scale publishing. In addition to Milkweed, several other small presses survive and thrive here, including Coffee House Press (www.coffeehousepress.org) and Graywolf Publishing (www.graywolfpress.org).

Another pillar of the literary community in the Twin Cities is *Rain Taxi* (www.raintaxi.com), a scrappy quarterly nonprofit literary journal that reviews books nobody else is reviewing but everybody else should be. The folks behind *Rain Taxi* also organize the annual Twin Cities Book Festival, a well-attended day of readings, talks, and exhibits.

The Twin Cities literary calendar includes another much anticipated event: the announcement of the Minnesota Book Awards, which honor Minnesota-related authors and illustrators in eight categories and often feature writers who get attention on the national scene as well.

## THEATER

When Sir Tyrone Guthrie had a vision of a new sort of theater—one with a resident professional company dedicated to the classics—he looked all over the country for a good home for it. And he settled on Minneapolis. That was in 1963. What drew Guthrie to the Twin Cities—the strong cultural community, the many colleges and universities, the enthusiasm for theater—is still characteristic of the area today.

At any given time during the season, there are as many as four dozen shows running in the Twin Cities, and several theaters run summer shows or have year-round seasons. And the future looks good for theater in the Twin Cities: Younger generations are well-represented among both audiences and theater movers and shakers. The highlight of the year for many adventurous theatergoers, young and old, is the Minnesota Fringe Festival, the largest unjuried theater festival in the United States, with attendance at more than 150 shows topping 40,000.

## FAMOUS TWIN CITIANS

These are a few of the famous folks to come out of the Minneapolis and St. Paul area.

- **In literature:** Mary Casanova, Kate DiCamillo, Louise Erdrich, F. Scott Fitzgerald, Thomas Friedman, Garrison Keillor, Chuck Klosterman, Sinclair Lewis, Charles Schulz, August Wilson

- **In movies and television:** Loni Anderson, Richard Dean Anderson, Diablo Cody, Joel and Ethan Coen, Josh Hartnett, Tippi Hedren, Craig Kilborn, Peter Krause, Jessica Lange, Mystery Science Theater 3000, Cheryl Tiegs, Lizz Winstead

- **In music:** The Andrews Sisters, Atmosphere, Babes in Toyland, Brother Ali, Eddie Cochran, Morris Day and the Time, Bob Dylan, Jimmy Jam, The Jayhawks, Mason Jennings, Bob Mould, Prince, The Replacements, Semisonic, Soul Asylum, The Suburbs

- **In politics:** Kofi Annan (graduated from Macalester College in St. Paul), Al Franken, Hubert H. Humphrey, Eugene McCarthy, Walter Mondale, Paul Wellstone, Jesse Ventura

- **In sports:** The 1980 Olympic hockey team (11 of the 20 players and coach Herb Brooks), Greg LeMond, John Madden, Kevin McHale, Bronko Nagorski, Alan Page, Kirby Puckett

- **In law:** Harry Blackmun, Warren Burger, Pierce Butler, William Douglas

- **Explorers:** Ann Bancroft, Dan Buettner, Charles Lindbergh, Will Steger

- **Fictional characters:** Betty Crocker, Jolly Green Giant, Mary Tyler Moore, Pillsbury Doughboy, Rocky and Bullwinkle

- **Others:** Norman Borlaug, Jean Paul Getty, Billy Graham, Robert Mondavi, Thorstein Veblen, Roy Wilkins

In addition to the high-profile **Guthrie Theater,** the Twin Cities have a reputation for strong support of out-of-the-mainstream theaters. **Penumbra Theater** is one of only three African American theaters in the United States to produce a full season of plays. Penumbra premiered several of playwright August Wilson's plays when he lived and wrote here in the 1980s. And shows at **Mixed Blood Theatre,** which is dedicated to diversity of all kinds, regularly fill all the seats.

Supporting all this enthusiasm for the theater is another critical component of healthy cultural life: arts criticism. While grousing about the lack of arts criticism is a popular pastime in the Twin Cities, the truth is both major daily newspapers employ full-time theater critics, a good thing in a time of slashed media budgets.

## TELEVISION AND FILM

Some might argue that the best television to come out of the Twin Cities is the cult classic *Mystery Science Theater 3000*, which ran on Comedy Central and the Sci-Fi channel for 11 years in the 1980s and 1990s, even spawning a feature film. Silhouettes—voiced by local comedians and visible at the bottom of the screen as if they were watching the movie themselves—riffed on science fiction B movies. The series ended in 1999.

People of a certain age will remember that Brandon and Brendan of the 1980s TV hit *Beverly Hills 90210* moved from Minnesota to Beverly Hills at the start of the series. Minnesotans of a certain age will remember that the filmmakers apparently threw a dart at the Midwestern portion of the map, looking for an

## MINNESOTA ON-SCREEN

The Twin Cities have served as the backdrop for a number of movies, including:

- *Airport* (1970)

- *Purple Rain* (1984)

- *Mighty Ducks* (1992)

- *Grumpy Old Men* (1993)

- *Mallrats* (1995)

- *Fargo* (1996)

- *Drop Dead Gorgeous* (1999)

- *North Country* (2005)

- *A Prairie Home Companion* (2006)

- *A Serious Man* (2009)

appropriate foil to the Beverly Hills lifestyle. Most mentions of Minnesota places, including Wayzata and the University of Minnesota, were somehow mangled. That's a big turnaround from the 1970s *The Mary Tyler Moore Show,* in which Minneapolis got to play the part of the big city.

The Twin Cities and Minnesota are often played for laughs in the movies as well. *The Mighty Ducks* and *Grumpy Old Men* series were both set in and around the Twin Cities and partially filmed here. The Coen brothers' 2009 film *A Serious Man* was filmed in a local synagogue and seemed to use the whole of the local Jewish community as extras. In 1995's *Mallrats,* Eden Prairie Center mall, south of Minneapolis, stood in for the locus of universal teenage ennui. And the Minneapolis-St. Paul International Airport was a Midwestern airport in distress in the filming of the 1970 disaster movie *Airport.* And who could forget how Prince burst onto the scene in the 1984 iconic hit *Purple Rain*? It was filmed almost entirely on location in the Twin Cities and is virtually a cinematographic tour of many Minnesotans' young adulthood.

# ESSENTIALS

# Transportation

Exactly halfway between the two coasts, with the largest airport in the Upper Midwest, Minneapolis is easy to get to and, once you're here, easy to get around.

## GETTING THERE

### AIR

**Minneapolis-St. Paul Airport (MSP)** (612/726-5555, www.mspairport.com, daily 24 hours) is the country's 17th busiest airport by passenger boardings and is frequently ranked among the best airports in the country, based on a reader survey focused on amenities and service. It is 16 miles southeast of downtown Minneapolis and 12 miles southwest of downtown St. Paul, in the Fort Snelling unincorporated area. Once you're on the main concourse, shopping and dining and listening to the piano player, it's easy to understand why. (Fun trivia: The Minneapolis-St. Paul Airport was the set for parts of the 1970 film *Airport*.)

downtown Minneapolis highway

MSP is **Delta Air Lines**' third-largest hub, and the airline (www.delta.com) dominates most of the gates in the main terminal, formerly the Lindbergh Terminal and now uninspiringly known as Terminal 1. The other carrier that uses MSP as its main hub, **Sun Country** (www.suncountry.com), takes up much of the considerably smaller Terminal 2, formerly the Humphrey Terminal. In all, 14 domestic airlines and two international airlines serve the airport.

Make sure you know which terminal you're flying to or from. Check your paper ticket or itinerary for "Terminal 1" or "Terminal 2." If you need to travel between the two terminals, the best way to go is via the light rail, which runs 24 hours and is free of charge on this portion of the track alone. The trains run every 7-15 minutes. The light-rail station at Terminal 1 is underground, between the blue and red parking ramps. Get on the free people-mover tram one level below the baggage claim and ride it to the light rail station. The light-rail station at Terminal 2 is on the north side of the orange parking ramp. Take the skyway from level 2 and follow the signs.

### Airport Transportation

The light rail is the easiest way to get into downtown Minneapolis. Trains run nearly 24 hours a day (with just a couple of runs in the wee hours between midnight and 3:30am), and the comfortable trip takes just 25 minutes. Buy a ticket ($3.25 during rush hours, $2.50 at other times) from the machine on the platform before you board the train. There are no fare boxes on the trains.

Metro Transit buses from the airport serve St. Paul and other parts of Minneapolis. Buses leave from level 1 of the blue and red parking ramps at Terminal 1. If you land at Terminal 2 and need to catch a bus, you have to take the light rail to Terminal 1.

Airport taxis leave from the tram level at Terminal 1 (follow signs to Ground Transportation) and from the Terminal 2 parking ramp on level 1. Fares are metered at $2.75 per mile with a $2.75 flag drop and an additional $4.25 airport fee. The fare to downtown Minneapolis will run between $38 and $49 and to downtown St. Paul between $30 and $37. The

Super Shuttle (612/827-7777, www. supershuttle.com) will take you to either downtown for between $18 and $89, depending on whether you want a shared shuttle or a private car. Book online or by phone or catch a last-minute ride at the Super Shuttle service desk on the ground transportation level of Terminal 1. The shuttle also stops at Terminal 2, on the ground level of the parking lot.

Both Uber (www.uber.com) and Lyft (www.lyft.com) now serve the airport. To meet your ride at Terminal 1, go to level 2 of the green parking ramp. Signs pointing to App-Based Ride Services will get you there. At Terminal 2, go to the ground transportation center, on the ground level of the purple parking ramp. Prices are roughly comparable to taxis.

## TRAIN

Since 2012, Amtrak trains once again pull in and out of the refurbished Union Depot (214 4th St. E., St. Paul, www.amtrak.com), which hadn't seen train traffic since 1971.

One route, the Empire Builder, passes through here, a single train in each direction. The Empire Builder travels between Chicago and Seattle, arriving in St. Paul around 10:30pm headed westbound and around 7am headed east. That is, those are the scheduled times. The train is notoriously unpredictable, often held up by bad weather in the Rocky Mountains or other issues near Chicago.

Upon arriving in St. Paul, you can board a St. Paul city bus or a Greyhound or regional bus, such as Jefferson Lines. The light rail Green Line connects Union Depot with Target Field in downtown Minneapolis.

## BUS

Greyhound buses stop at **Hawthorne Transportation Center** (950 Hawthorne Ave., Minneapolis, 612/371-3325, www.greyhound.com) on the western edge of downtown Minneapolis, convenient to many Metro Transit bus routes and a short walk from the light-rail lines.

Jefferson Lines buses, which serve outstate Minnesota and much of the Midwest, also use the Hawthorne Transportation Center, with additional stops at the University of Minnesota campus, the Mall of America, the airport, and Union Depot.

## GETTING AROUND
### PUBLIC TRANSPORTATION

Metro Transit operates city buses and two light-rail lines within Minneapolis and St. Paul and the surrounding suburbs. The route coverage is good, but anyone planning to rely on public transportation outside of the downtown areas should remember to plan extra time for changing buses and for longer waits during off-peak hours.

Full fare is $3.25 during peak hours (Mon.-Fri. 6am-9am and 3pm-6:30pm) and $2.50 otherwise, with discounts for seniors and people with disabilities with proper ID. Kids under 6 ride free. Within the designated downtown zones in both Minneapolis and St. Paul, the fare is just $0.50. Drop exact change into the box; the driver can't make change. If you ask the driver for a transfer as you board, he or she will give you a ticket good on any other bus or train within the next 2.5 hours.

For fare passes, route maps, and any other information, go to Metro Transit stores in downtown Minneapolis (719 Marquette Ave., Minneapolis, Mon.-Fri. 7:30am-5pm), downtown St. Paul (101 5th St. E., skyway level, St. Paul, Mon.-Fri. 7:30am-4:45pm), and at the Mall of America (60 E. Broadway, Bloomington, Tues.-Fri. 3pm-6:30pm, Sat. noon-2pm and 3pm-6:30pm). There's a convenient trip planner at www.metrotransit.org: Enter your starting point, destination, and the time, and the website will generate a handful of itineraries, complete with maps and walking directions.

The light-rail Blue Line runs between Target Field in downtown Minneapolis and the Mall of America, stopping at the Minneapolis-St. Paul Airport. The Green Line connects Target Field with Union Depot in downtown St. Paul. Fares are the same as on the buses. Buy tickets from the vending kiosks on the platforms (cash and credit cards accepted). Ticketing is on the honor system, but conductors do check frequently and fines are hefty. Trains run mostly around the clock, with just a few trains between midnight and 3:30am. Wait times are about 7-8 minutes during peak times and more than 30 minutes in the wee hours.

The Twin Cities' first commuter rail line, **Northstar** (www.metrotransit.org/northstar), carries passengers from downtown Minneapolis, also by Target Field, to Big Lake, about 45 miles to the north, via Fridley, Coon Rapids, Anoka, and Elk River. Five departures in each direction serve morning commuters (between 6:30 and 8:45), and five serve evening commuters (between 3:30 and 5:30) for the 50-minute trip. The ride from Minneapolis to Big Lake costs $6.25, and rides between other stations cost $3.25.

## DRIVING

If you'd like more flexibility and freedom in your travel than you might get from public transportation, you'll need a car. In theory, navigating the cities is fairly straightforward, as both are laid out primarily in a grid system. But nature throws up enough surprises, from rivers to creeks to lakes and major highways, that you'll want to invest in a good road map. When you're at the bookstore perusing maps, make sure you find one that gives you the level of detail you need. Many map publishers cover the whole metro area but without any detail anywhere except in insets of downtown Minneapolis and St. Paul. The AAA Headquarters just south of Minneapolis (5400 Auto Club Way, 952/927-2600, Mon.-Thurs. 8am-7pm, Fri. 8am-6pm, Sat. 9am-5pm) is a great place to get maps of all sorts.

Every major rental car company has an outlet at the airport. Avis Rent A Car (www.avis.com) has locations in both downtown Minneapolis (829 3rd Ave. S., Minneapolis, 612/332-6321) and downtown St. Paul (411 Minnesota St., St. Paul, 651/917-9955).

Street parking in downtown Minneapolis and St. Paul is metered, and meters now accept credit cards and bills. Ramps and lots, which are also well signed and easy to find, cost $8-20 a day. In residential neighborhoods, pay attention to signs restricting parking to a single side of the street during certain times. At city parks, watch for signs restricting parking to those with prepurchased parking passes.

## TAXIS

Outside of downtown Minneapolis and St. Paul, forget trying to hail a cab. In fact, forget trying to hail a cab downtown, too. Instead, head for the nearest major hotel and look for the taxis parked at the rank outside. Minneapolis has created late-night taxi stands in the downtown Warehouse District and at Lake Street and Hennepin.

Fares are standardized: $2.75 flag drop plus $2.75 per mile. An additional fee of $4.25 is added to airport trips. Trips originating at the airport are metered at $2.50 per mile.

Rather than trying to hail a cab, call one—as far in advance as you can, if possible. There are dozens of small companies; in Minneapolis, try Yellow Taxi (800/829-4222) or Blue & White Taxi (612/333-3333). St. Paul companies include City Wide Cab Co. (651/489-1111) and Diamond Cab (651/642-1188). There may be a $5 minimum fare. If you're traveling between downtown Minneapolis and downtown St. Paul, expect to pay about $30; from downtown Minneapolis to the Mall of America it's about $34.

Like most American cities, the Twin Cities are now well served by Uber and Lyft.

## BICYCLING

Both Minneapolis and St. Paul are terrific cities to navigate by bike. In fact, each city maintains well over 100 miles of dedicated bike lanes and paved off-road trails. Bike racks are common throughout the cities.

All Metro Transit buses are equipped with bike racks for use at no extra charge, and bikes are allowed on light rail trains.

Purchase the comprehensive Twin Cities Bike Map online at www.bikeverywhere.com. It's compiled by avid local cyclists, updated every three years, and printed on heavy water- and tear-resistant paper. It is also available at bookstores and bike shops in the Twin Cities. Map PDFs are available online from the Metropolitan Council (www.metrocouncil.org), the City of Minneapolis (www.ci.minneapolis.mn.us/bicycles), and St. Paul (www.stpaul.gov).

**Nice Ride** (877/551-6423, www.nicceridemn.org; $6 for 24 hours, $30 for 30 days) is a popular self-service, short-term bike rental service. Find more information on renting bikes in the *Recreation* chapter.

## SCOOTERS

Another way to take advantage of the city's bike paths is via scooter, though the culture around scooter use is still developing. Note also that scooters are not yet so prevalent that you can rely on drivers to be aware of them. Both of the national app-and-drop scooter rental companies, **Bird** (www.bird.co) and **Lime** (www.li.me), operate in the

Twin Cities, and their black or bright green products—respectively—are getting easier to find. Download either app and you're good to go. For both companies, scooters cost $1 to unlock and $0.15 per minute. Lime also has bike rentals that cost $1 to unlock and $0.05 per minute.

## ACCESS FOR TRAVELERS WITH DISABILITIES

All Metro Transit buses are equipped with wheelchair lifts. All light-rail trains have areas set aside for wheelchair customers and offer step-free access so riders in wheelchairs can roll right on. All platforms are wheelchair accessible. For more information, call 612/373-3333 or ask for an *Accessible Transit* brochure at Metro Transit stores.

# Travel Tips

## WHEN TO GO

Take a tip from Minnesota brides: October, not June, is the most popular month for weddings in Minnesota. That's when the Twin Cities are at their best: after the sticky summer and before the snow flies. May and June are a close second, although spring is an elusive thing here, lasting just a week or two. Summer is high season, when you'll see longer hours at venues, slightly higher hotel prices (except downtown), and venues packed with music and festivals. In late June, the sun sets at around 9pm and dusk lingers until around 10pm. But don't count out the winter! Yes, the snow and cold can add a bit of hassle, but these cities know how to deal with it,

even how to revel in it (case in point: late January's Winter Carnival).

## WHAT TO PACK

If you're accustomed to looking smart and spiffy, by all means pack those trendy or formal clothes. But if your inclination is toward jeans and casual wear, you'll blend right in here. If you're so inclined, you should absolutely bring walking or running shoes or biking gear. Winter visitors will need a heavy coat, gloves, and a good scarf and hat. A possible exception can be made for business travelers and conventioneers staying in hotels connected to the skyways. In June, July, and August, rainstorms can be sudden and severe, calling for an umbrella and jacket.

## TOURIST INFORMATION

Nicollet Mall includes a very large **Visitor Information Center** (505 Nicollet Mall, Minneapolis, 612/466-7170, open Mon.-Sat. 10am-7pm, Sun. noon-5pm) with city-themed retail space. You can contact **Meet Minneapolis** (888/676-6757, www.minneapolis.org), the city's convention and visitors association, to request information or go to its well-organized and attractive website. The **Minneapolis Convention Center** (1301 2nd Ave. S., Minneapolis, 612/335-6000, www.minneapolisconventioncenter.org) is right on the southern edge of downtown Minneapolis and connected to the skyway system. If you see someone in a neon-green top with a DID (Downtown Improvement District) logo, say hi. These are "ambassadors," and their job is to keep downtown looking good, to be welcoming and answer questions, and to be an extra pair of eyes and ears keeping people safe.

St. Paul's **Visitor Information Center** is in the Landmark Center (75 5th St. W., St. Paul, 651/292-3225). You can also get help by contacting the **St. Paul Convention and Visitors Association** (800/627-6101, www.stpaulcvb.org). St. Paul's convention center is the **RiverCentre** (199 Kellogg Blvd. W., St. Paul, 651/265-4800, www.rivercentre.org).

## HOURS

Minneapolis and St. Paul are both early-to-bed, early-to-rise places. Coffee shops open at 6am or 6:30am. Office workers start their day at 8am or even before. Favorite spots for a leisurely weekend breakfast or brunch start to fill up at the not-so-leisurely hour of 9am. And, having gotten started so early, many people are ready to pack it in early. You're unlikely to get an office worker on the phone after 5pm. Dinner at 6pm is a common reservation request. And it's hard to find a restaurant still serving after 9pm on weekdays and 10pm on weekends. Last call in Minneapolis and St. Paul bars is 2am—and even then they don't have to kick a lot of people out the door.

"Summer hours" is another interesting Minnesota phenomenon: Many workplaces shift employees' schedules during the tantalizing months of June, July, and August so that they work an extra hour Monday through Thursday and leave at noon on Friday, presumably to head to the family cabin. Even at workplaces that don't officially observe summer hours, trying to get hold of a professional on a summer Friday afternoon is a fool's errand.

## TIPPING

As in most other areas of the United States, 15-20 percent is a standard tip for good service at restaurants, salons, valet parking, and other service establishments. Taxi drivers, too, expect a tip. If you're paying cash, it's easiest to hand over exactly what you'd like to pay in total and say, "No change, thanks!" or to specify the amount of change you'd like back.

Baggers at grocery stores do not work for tips and at some establishments cannot accept them.

Tipping your hotel concierge $5-10 per service is standard, as is, at fancier hotels, leaving $2-10 per day for the housekeeping staff.

At the airport, if you check your bag with a skycap at the curb, be prepared to tip about $3-5 per bag, plus a little more if they go out of their way for you. The courtesy cart drivers do not expect tips but do appreciate them, especially if they go above and beyond.

## SMOKING

Smoking is on the decline in Minnesota, as it is throughout the country. About 14 percent of adult Minnesotans smoke, compared to about 18 percent of Americans nationwide.

The Freedom to Breathe Act, enacted in 2007, prohibits smoking in any indoor public space. This means all Minnesota restaurants, bars, bowling alleys, coffee shops, and office buildings are entirely smoke-free. Smoking is prohibited in the common areas of hotels, but hotel management may choose to allow it in hotel rooms themselves.

Smoking is also permitted on outdoor patios of bars and restaurants, so long as they aren't closed in under a tent. Both the smoker and the owner of the establishment can be charged with a misdemeanor in case of a violation. The law is enforced on a complaint basis only—which means police officers aren't patrolling bars and restaurants looking for illicit ashtrays—but Minnesotans in general are a compliant people, and you are unlikely to see anyone violating the ban.

## MAJOR BANKS

The largest banks in the Twin Cities are **Wells Fargo** (www.wellsfargo.com) and **TCF Bank** (www.tcfbank.com). You'll find ATMs for both banks all over town. You'll also encounter **Bank of America** (www.bankofamerica.com), **Bremer Bank** (www.bremer.com), **Franklin Bank** (www.franklinbank.com), and **U.S. Bank** (www.usbank.com).

# MEDIA AND COMMUNICATIONS
## PHONES AND AREA CODES

Until 1998, the area code for the whole of the Twin Cities area was 612. That area has subdivided twice since then. Minneapolis (and a small portion of the southern suburb of Richfield) retained the 612 code. St. Paul and the eastern suburbs got 651. The northeastern suburbs took 763 and the southeastern suburbs 952. All calls within all four area codes are local calls, as are calls from the Twin Cities to parts of the 507 area code to the south and to parts of the 320 area code to the north.

### INTERNET SERVICES

All **Hennepin County Library** branches (www.hclib.org), which include Minneapolis libraries, and all **St. Paul Public Library** branches (www.stpaul.lib.mn.us) offer free public wireless Internet access. You do not need to have a library card to bring your own computer and work in the library. Library computer stations are reserved for library cardholders. Hennepin County Library does not issue cards to out-of-state residents, and St. Paul Public Library charges non-Minnesotans $45 a year.

Nearly all independent coffee shops in town, including all **Dunn Bros.** locations, offer free Wi-Fi (though they do ask that you be courteous to customers who have come to, you know, drink coffee), and many have terminals for customer use (generally limited to 15 minutes). **Panera Bread** and **Bruegger's Bagels** are two chains that commonly offer free Wi-Fi for unlimited use.

## MAIL AND MESSENGER SERVICES

There are five post office locations in downtown Minneapolis: the **main post office** (100 1st St. S., Minneapolis, 612/349-4715, Mon.-Fri. 7am-8pm, Sat. 9am-1pm), inside the **Butler Square** building (100 6th St. N., Ste. 120B, Minneapolis, 612/333-3688, Mon.-Fri. 9am-1:15pm and 2:30pm-5pm), a few blocks from **Loring Park** (18 12th St. N., Minneapolis, 612/333-6213, Mon.-Fri. 8:30am-5pm, Sat. 9am-1pm), in an office building on the north end of town (307 4th Ave. S., Minneapolis, 612/333-3153, Mon.-Fri. 9am-5pm), and in an office building a little to the south (110 8th St. S., Minneapolis, 612/333-2574, Mon.-Fri. 7:30am-5pm).

There are two post offices in downtown St. Paul: the **main post office** (180 Kellogg Blvd. E., St. Paul, 651/293-6035, Mon.-Fri. 8:30am-5:30pm, Sat. 9:30am-noon) and the **Uptown branch** (408 St. Peter St., St. Paul, 651/889-2457, Mon.-Fri. 8:30am-5pm). Go to www.usps.com to find one of the dozens of other post offices in the metro area.

The **UPS Store** is an alternative to the U.S. Postal Service and a good place to pick up packing supplies. There's one in downtown Minneapolis (40 7th St. S., Ste. 212, Minneapolis, 612/332-4117, Mon.-Thurs. 7am-7pm, Fri. 7am-6pm, Sat. 10am-4pm) and—convenient if you've just done a lot of shopping—one on Grand Avenue in St. Paul (1043 Grand Ave., St. Paul, 651/222-2019, Mon.-Fri. 8:30am-7pm, Sat. 9am-5pm, Sun. 11am-4pm). Go to www.ups.com to find other UPS Stores in the area.

There are FedEx drop boxes all over the central business districts in downtown Minneapolis and St. Paul (check the skyway levels of buildings as well as the lobbies). To talk to an actual human being when you FedEx your package, you'll have to go to the **FedEx Kinko's,** with branches in the IDS Center (80 8th St. S., Ste. 180, Minneapolis, 612/343-8000, daily 24 hours), in South Minneapolis (1430 Lake St. W., Minneapolis, 612/822-7700, daily 24 hours), and in the Summit-University neighborhood of St. Paul (58 Snelling Ave. S., St. Paul, 651/699-9671, daily 24 hours).

If you need to have a package or papers delivered within the Twin Cities right away, two large and well-reputed messenger services are **Street Fleet** (612/623-9999, www.streetfleet.com) and **Quicksilver Express** (651/484-1111, www.qec.com).

## MAGAZINES AND NEWSPAPERS

Two major daily newspapers serve the Twin Cities. The *Minneapolis Star Tribune* (www.startribune.com) was part of the McClatchy chain until 2006, when McClatchy sold it to a private equity firm. The *Strib,* as it is known, gets a lot of guff locally for its supposed liberal leanings, but we will leave that to readers to discern. It has a daily print circulation of 240,000. The *Minneapolis Tribune,* one of the two papers that merged to form the *Star Tribune,* dates back to 1867.

The *St. Paul Pioneer Press* (www.twincities.com) is a descendant of the area's oldest daily newspaper, the *St. Paul Pioneer,* founded in 1849, and it serves the east metro area. (It's fairly easy to find a *Star Tribune* in St. Paul but not so easy to find a *Pioneer Press* in Minneapolis.) The *PiPress,* as it is known, has a daily print circulation of about 130,000.

The Twin Cities are now down to

one alternative weekly, *City Pages* (www.citypages.com)—not so alternative now that it is owned by the *Star Tribune*. *City Pages* and the now-defunct *Twin Cities Reader* egged each other on to scoops and admirable reporting until Stern Publishing (now Village Voice Media) purchased both in 1997 and shut down the *Reader*. There are, however, robust neighborhood newspapers in the area, including the *Downtown Journal* (www.dtjournal.com), a biweekly freebie serving downtown Minneapolis, and its sister the *Southwest Journal* (www.swjournal.com), serving southwest Minneapolis. In St. Paul, the biweekly *Villager* (www.myvillager.com) serves the Summit-University neighborhood and, to some extent, downtown St. Paul.

The University of Minnesota's student newspaper, the *Minnesota Daily* (www.mndaily.com), is one of the largest student-run newspapers in the country, with a daily circulation of 24,000. It is published every weekday during the school year and twice weekly during the summer. The paper is entirely student-run and -staffed and is supported largely by (student-sold) advertising. *Daily* alumni can be found in nearly every newsroom in the Twin Cities, if not throughout Minnesota. You can find it free on racks in and around the U of M campus.

Also free to pick up on many newsstands are several papers serving individual ethnic communities in the Twin Cities. *Insight News* (www.insightnews.com) has covered the African American community since 1974. It hits newsstands every Monday. The weekly *Asian American Press* (www.aapress.com) also publishes in English, covering the Asian American

and Pacific Islander communities. *La Prensa de Minnesota* (www.laprensademn.com) is published in both English and Spanish (in a single edition). Latino Communications Network publishes both Spanish-language newspapers and the weekly entertainment tabloid *Vida y Sabor* (www.vidaysabor.net), aimed at a younger audience.

The Twin Cities also have two big, glossy lifestyle magazines. *Mpls. St.Paul Magazine* (www.mspmag.com) and *Minnesota Monthly* (www.minnesotamonthly.com) are the two established publications, with a moneyed, slightly older readership. *Twin Cities Business* (www.tcbmag.com) and *Minnesota Business* (www.minnesotabusiness.com) are both full-color, glossy monthlies serving the business community, while *Finance and Commerce* (www.finance-commerce.com) is a must-read for movers and shakers.

Two more free magazines that are worth picking up are the ubiquitous and remarkably thick biweekly *Lavender* (www.lavendermagazine), serving the GLBT community, and the quarterly literary journal with a national reputation, *Rain Taxi* (www.raintaxi.com).

## RADIO AND TV

Corporate radio has the same stranglehold on the Twin Cities market as it does everywhere else. But, as you spin the dial, a few unique frequencies will stand out. **KNOW 91.1** is the home of Minnesota Public Radio (www.mpr.org), where several nationally syndicated programs originate, including *Live from Here with Chris Thile*. MPR's music station, **The Current 89.3** (www.mpr.org), plays a truly innovative mix of new and time-tested alternative music. **Cities 97.1** (www. cities97.com) reaches a grown-up audience whose beloved 1980s hits are veering toward easy listening.

For slick right-wing talk, tune to **KTLK 1003** (www.ktlkfm.com). For community-access lefty talk (including news from Democracy Now) and world music, tune to **KFAI 90.3** (www.kfai.org). Minneapolis Public School students staff the jazz station **KBEM 88.5** (www.jazz88fm.com) 35 hours a week, with professional announcers and syndicated programming filling out the rest of the schedule. **FM 107.1** (www.fm1071. com) fills the day with chatter geared toward a female audience.

On the AM dial, **WCCO 830** (www.wccoradio.com), "The Good Neighbor," has kept Minnesotans informed for generations. **KLBB 1220** (www.klbbradio.com) plays nostalgic hits, heavy on the Frank Sinatra. You never know what you're going to get with student DJs spinning the tunes at the University of Minnesota's **KUOM 770 AM** (www.radiok.org).

It's all sports all the time at **KFAN 1130** (www.kfan.com). **KSTP 1500** (www.am1500.com) covers the waterfront with news and sports, including Twins baseball games. **KTNF 950** (www.am950.com) broadcasts lifestyle chat and left-wing politics. **AM 1280 The Patriot** (www. am1280thepatriot.com) covers the other end of the political spectrum. **La Invasora 1400** (www. lainvasora1400.com) broadcasts music, news, and talk in Spanish.

All the major television networks have affiliates in the Twin Cities. **Twin Cities Public Television** (www. tpt.org) runs four channels, including tpt 2, its main channel; tpt MN for Minnesota-focused original programming; tpt Life for cooking and home improvement; and a weather channel.

Of the numerous public access stations in the Twin Cities, **Minneapolis Television Network** (www.mtn.org), **Metro Cable Network** (www.mcn6.org), and **St. Paul Neighborhood Network** (www.spnn.org) are the biggest.

# Health and Safety

Some travelers will remember the "Murderapolis" headlines of the 1990s, when the titillating combination of Minneapolis's high murder rate and its staid Midwestern reputation proved too much for the national media to resist. Those days are past, and as a visitor, especially in the two downtowns and in the residential neighborhoods of southwest Minneapolis, St. Anthony, and south of I-94 in St. Paul, you are unlikely to experience even a hint of trouble. Some visitors to downtown

Minneapolis, however, are surprised by the number of panhandlers they encounter on Hennepin Avenue and Nicollet Mall. Panhandling is not illegal unless it is aggressive. The city defines "aggressive panhandling" as asking repetitively for money after a person has said no, or asking for money in a confined or intimidating place (for example, in a bus shelter or on a bus, near an ATM, or at a sidewalk café). If this bothers you, the city advises you to call 911 or tell a cop.

There are a few areas where you want to be careful. Much of the city's crime takes place in North Minneapolis, which is north of downtown and west of the Mississippi River. This is an almost entirely residential area, so there isn't much to attract visitors, in any case. In downtown Minneapolis, stay alert as you bar-hop along 1st Avenue after dark. In South Minneapolis, be cautious and stick with a friend on and around Lake Street in the evenings. If you're the sort to stand on the light rail platform obliviously scrolling through your phone, you should know that there's a class of criminal watching for people just like you. Be aware of your surroundings.

St. Paul's crime rate is significantly lower than Minneapolis's, but there are caveats here, as well. Downtown St. Paul isn't statistically a dangerous place to be, even after dark, but it is deserted, which is a good signal that you don't want to be wandering about alone. Use the buddy system around the Xcel Energy Center and around the bars along West 7th Street. And University Avenue, especially the east end of it, just northwest of the Minnesota State Capitol, is a place where you want to keep your wits about you.

## HOSPITALS

Both downtown Minneapolis and downtown St. Paul have excellent hospitals. Hennepin County Medical Center (701 Park Ave., Minneapolis, 612/873-3000, www.hcmc.org) is in downtown Minneapolis. Also convenient to downtown, in South Minneapolis, are Abbott Northwestern Hospital (800 28th St. E., Minneapolis, 612/863-4000, www.abbottnorthwestern.com) and Children's Hospitals and Clinics (2525 Chicago Ave. S., Minneapolis, 612/813-6000, www.childrensmn.org).

Clustered around downtown St. Paul, you'll find Bethesda Hospital (559 Capitol Blvd., St. Paul, 651/232-2000, www.bethesdahospital.org), Regions Hospital (640 Jackson St., St. Paul, 651/254-3456, www.regionshospital.com), St. Joseph's Hospital (69 Exchange St. W., St. Paul, 651/232-3000, www.stjosephs-stpaul.org), United Hospital (333 Smith Ave. N., St. Paul, 651/241-8000, www.unitedhospital.com), and Children's Hospitals and Clinics (345 Smith Ave. N., St. Paul, 651/220-6000, www.childrensmn.org). Gillette Children's (200 University Ave. E., St. Paul, 651/291-2848, www.gillettechildrens.org) is also in downtown St. Paul, but it offers specialized pediatric services and wouldn't be your first stop for an emergency.

Roughly halfway between the two downtowns are the two campuses of the University of Minnesota Medical Center: University of Minnesota Medical Center/Children's Hospital, Fairview Riverside campus (2450 Riverside Ave., Minneapolis, 612/273-3000, www.university.fairview.org) and University of Minnesota Medical Center/Children's Hospital, Fairview University campus (500 Harvard St., Minneapolis, 612/273-3000, www.university.fairview.org).

In the southern suburbs, head to Fairview Southdale Hospital (6401 France Ave. S., Edina, 952/924-5000, www.southdale.fairview.org). The most convenient hospital in the western suburbs is Methodist Hospital (6500 Excelsior Blvd., St. Louis Park, 952/993-5000, www.parknicollet.com/

methodist). In the northern and eastern suburbs, **St. John's Hospital** (1575 Beam Ave., Maplewood, 651/232-7000, www.stjohnshospital-mn.org) is convenient.

The Twin Cities Veterans Administration hospital is **Minneapolis VA Medical Center** (1 Veterans Dr., Minneapolis, 612/725-2000, www.va.gov/minneapolis).

## CLINICS AND PHARMACIES

If the emergency room isn't the appropriate option but you can't wait to get an appointment, try urgent care.

Park Nicollet maintains six urgent care clinics. Two convenient ones in the west metro area are **Park Nicollet Clinic-St. Louis Park** (3800 Park Nicollet Blvd., St. Louis Park, 952/993-1000, www.parknicollet.com, Mon.-Fri. 8am-8pm, Sat.-Sun. 8am-5pm) and **Park Nicollet Clinic-Maple Grove** (15800 95th Ave. N., Maple Grove, 952/993-1440, www.parknicollet.com). Approximate wait times are updated in real time on their website.

HealthPartners has eight urgent care clinics. The three in Minneapolis and St. Paul proper are **HealthPartners St. Paul** (205 Wabasha St., St. Paul, 952/853-8800, www.healthpartners. com, Mon.-Fri. 5pm-9pm, Sat.-Sun. 9am-8pm), **HealthPartners Como** (2500 Como Ave., St. Paul, 952/853-8800, www.healthpartners.com, Mon.-Fri. 1pm-9pm, Sat. 9am-8pm), and **HealthPartners Riverside** (2220 Riverside Ave., Minneapolis, 952/853-8800, www.healthpartners.com, Mon.-Fri. 5pm-9pm, Sat. 9am-5pm, Sun. noon-5pm).

Several **Target** stores operate clinics for diagnosing and treating common minor ailments such as strep and pinkeye. The Target in downtown Minneapolis (900 Nicollet Mall, Minneapolis, 612/338-0085, www.target.com, Mon.-Fri. 8am-6pm, Sat. 9am-4pm) and the one in North St. Paul (2199 Hwy. 36E, North St. Paul, 651/779-5986, www.target.com, Mon.-Fri. 8am-8pm, Sat.-Sun. 9am-4pm) are two that have clinics.

Most Targets also have full-service pharmacies (and you truly can't throw . . . well, anything you can actually throw . . . without hitting a Target in the Twin Cities).

## EMERGENCY SERVICES

For police and fire emergencies in the Twin Cities, dial 911.

The nonemergency number for the St. Paul Police Department is 651/291-1111.

To report nonemergency crimes in Minneapolis, call 311. This is also the number you use to contact any department in the City of Minneapolis. The helpful folks who answer the phone will connect you to the right people. For information about a crime in Minneapolis, call the Tip Line at 612/692-8477.

# RESOURCES

## Suggested Reading

### HISTORY AND GENERAL INFORMATION

Atkins, Annette. *Creating Minnesota: A History from the Inside Out.* St. Paul: Minnesota Historical Society Press, 2007. A uniquely textured history book, *Creating Minnesota* pieces together the story of Minnesota and Minnesotans through the eyes of individuals, from a mixed-blood interpreter at Fort Snelling to a state congresswoman. Atkins's writing is both dense and readable.

Diers, John, and Aaron Isaacs. *Twin Cities by Trolley.* Minneapolis: University of Minnesota Press, 2007. The story of the streetcars in the Twin Cities—first used in the late 1800s and finally pulled out of service in the 1950s—is the story of a growing metropolis hungry for modernity and eager to travel faster and farther than ever before. Diers and Isaacs, who have both been instrumental in preserving the history of the streetcars through the Minnesota Streetcar Museum, have put together a very readable and relevant history.

Diffley, Atina. *Turn Here, Sweet Corn.* Minneapolis: University of Minnesota Press, 2012. Minnesota was at the forefront of the community-supported agriculture (CSA) and organic movements, and one of the state's pioneering small organic farms was Diffley's farm, Gardens of Eagan. Her memoir is a compelling story of urban agriculture, hard work, and Minnesotan stick-to-it-iveness.

Dregni, Eric. *Vikings in the Attic: In Search of Nordic America.* Minneapolis: University of Minnesota Press, 2011. Dregni traveled the length and breadth of Minnesota and its neighboring states, digging into tales of its recent past (and even its present). And he found out what many Minnesota transplants have long suspected: Scandinavians can be kind of weird. We knew about the lutefisk and the *lefse,* but what's with the eggs in the coffee and the trolls?

King, Tim, and Alice Tanghe. *The Minnesota Homegrown Cookbook.* Osceola, Wisconsin: Voyageur Press, 2008. Through the stories of dozens of beloved restaurants and chefs and more than 100 recipes, the authors paint a picture of Minnesota's remarkable food landscape. It's not all lutefisk and *lefse* here!

Koutsky, Kathryn Strand, and Linda Koutsky. *Minnesota State Fair: An Illustrated History.* Minneapolis: Coffee House Press, 2007. This mother-daughter team dug deep to find the history and lore behind this most beloved Minnesota institution, along with a fascinating collection of historical photos. Their previous endeavors, *Minnesota Eats Out* and *Minnesota Vacation Days,* also tell important Minnesota stories with humor and depth.

Millett, Larry. *Once There Were Castles: Lost Mansions and Estates of the Twin Cities.* Minneapolis: University of Minnesota Press, 2011. Many of Minneapolis's and St. Paul's Gilded Age homes—whole neighborhoods, in fact—were razed long ago. Millett, an architectural historian, digs up stories and photos of nearly 100 of them. Millett is also the author of *Lost Twin Cities, Twin Cities Then and Now,* and several guides to Minnesota architecture.

Roberts, Kate. *Minnesota 150: The People, Places, and Things that Shape Our State.* St. Paul: Minnesota Historical Society Press, 2007. In preparation for Minnesota's sesquicentennial in 2008, the Minnesota Historical Society asked people all over the state to nominate people, places, objects, organizations, and phenomena that were uniquely Minnesotan. The flood of responses was culled to 150 and organized into a uniquely illustrative exhibit at the Minnesota History Center and published in this beautifully written and illustrated book.

Seeley, Mark. *Minnesota Weather Almanac.* St. Paul: Minnesota Historical Society Press, 2006. What's more Minnesotan than talking about the weather? Not much. Climatologist and radio commentator Mark Seeley combines weather lore and history, biographies of weather-related figures in local history, and answers to burning weather questions, such as:

What's the record number of consecutive below-freezing days in the Twin Cities? Answer: 66.

Treuer, Anton. *Everything You Wanted to Know About Indians but Were Afraid to Ask.* St. Paul: Minnesota Historical Society Press, 2012. Treuer is a professor of the Ojibwe languages at Bemidji State University and is of Ojibwe descent, but he answers more than 100 questions about Native Americans in general—including, "Is it okay to use the word 'Indians'?" Treuer has also written eight other books about Ojibwe culture and history, including the excellent *Assassination of Hole in the Day.*

Walsh, Jim. *The Replacements: All Over but the Shouting.* Osceola, Wisconsin: Voyageur Press, 2007. When the Replacements crashed their way onto the Minneapolis music scene in the late 1970s, disaffected teens from around the country sat up and took notice—not only of the 'Mats, as they were known—but of Minnesota itself. Jim Walsh was there, opening for the Replacements many times, and has been a fixture in Twin Cities journalism since.

Westerman, Gwen, and Bruce White. *Mni Sota Makoce: Land of the Dakota.* St. Paul: Minnesota Historical Society Press, 2012. While this very readable history was published to coincide with the 150th anniversary of the 1862 Dakota War, it examines the stories of the Dakota people in Minnesota in the centuries leading up to that tragic conflict. The word "Minnesota" comes from the Dakota phrase in the title, meaning "land where the water reflects the clouds."

White, Bruce. *We Are at Home: Pictures of the Ojibwe People.* St. Paul: Minnesota Historical Society Press, 2007. Historian Bruce White digs for the stories behind a remarkable collection of photographs of Ojibwe people, from the earliest daguerreotypes to prints from the 1950s. The book tells stories not only of the Ojibwe people but also of their interaction with the growing population of whites.

## LITERATURE AND FICTION

Bly, Carol. *Letters from the Country.* New York: Harper & Row, 1981. In the 1970s, Carol Bly wrote monthly essays for a Minnesota Public Radio feature called *A Letter from the Country.* Those essays became Bly's first book, to be followed by five more books of essays, five novels, and two books on the craft of writing. While Bly's writing evokes what she, following F. Scott Fitzgerald, called "the lost Swede towns," it reflects the natural world and ethical systems that shaped the cultures of Minnesota's city dwellers as well. Carol Bly, who died in 2007 at the age of 77, was married to the poet and men's movement leader Robert Bly.

Erdrich, Louise. *Love Medicine.* New York: Henry Holt & Co., 1984. Minnesotan Louise Erdrich won the National Book Critics' Circle Award for her first novel, *Love Medicine,* which tells a tangle of stories centered around a Native American reservation in North Dakota. While this novel and later ones, including the acclaimed *Tracks,* explore her Ojibwe heritage, Erdrich draws on her German-American side for other novels, including *The Beet Queen* and *The Master Butcher's Singing Club.* Erdrich owns Birch Bark Books in Minneapolis.

Fitzgerald, F. Scott. *The Great Gatsby.* New York: Penguin Popular Classics, 2007. While Fitzgerald's 1925 novel is set in Long Island and Manhattan, the Midwestern values of the narrator, Nick, and of Jay Gatsby's father, Henry Gatz, are a constant presence in the story, as the flip side of the lush and amoral lifestyle of the main characters. Fitzgerald was born in St. Paul's Cathedral Hill neighborhood and raised there and in East Coast boarding schools.

Keillor, Garrison. *Lake Wobegon Days.* New York: Viking, 1985. Former host of the *A Prairie Home Companion* radio show, Keillor is almost audible right off the page in these stories of small-town Midwestern life.

Kling, Kevin. *The Dog Says How.* St. Paul: Borealis Books, 2007. Playwright, performer, and essayist Kevin Kling is a gifted storyteller who is often heard on National Public Radio. His tales of growing up in suburban Minnesota and his recovery after a serious motorcycle accident are both uniquely Minnesotan and fascinatingly universal.

Landvik, Lorna. *The View from Mount Joy.* New York: Ballantine, 2007. Minnesotan Lorna Landvik mixes humor and a peculiar knack for plot in her novels, many set in Minnesota. *The View from Mount Joy* takes readers back to high school in Minneapolis circa 1972. Her earlier novels include *Angry Housewives Eating Bon Bons, Patty Jane's House of Curl, Tall Pine Polka, Your Oasis on Flame Lake,* and *Welcome to the Great Mysterious.*

Lewis, Sinclair. *Babbitt.* New York: Signet Classics, 2007. Sinclair Lewis's satirical take on conformity and boosterism in the Midwest hit especially hard in Minneapolis, where Lewis no doubt drew some of his inspiration (he has said that his city of Zenith could have been any midsized Midwestern city). Lewis's equally well-known earlier novel, *Main Street,* tells the story of a strong-willed Minneapolis woman who marries and moves to the small town of Gopher Prairie, a thinly disguised Sauk Centre, Minnesota, Lewis's hometown.

Longfellow, Henry Wadsworth. *Song of Hiawatha.* Minneola, New York: Dover Publications, 2006. Longfellow had never visited Minnesota or seen Minnehaha Falls when he wrote his 1855 epic poem set there, but the work became an instant smash hit in its day and attracted many tourists to the falls. Longfellow based his work on the retellings of Ojibwe legend and history by other writers and explorers. Generations of Minnesota schoolchildren have memorized the lines "By the shores of Gitche Gumee / By the shining Big-Sea-Water / Stood the wigwam of Nokomis."

Rølvaag, Ole Edvart. *Giants in the Earth.* New York: Harper, 1927. Norwegian immigrant O. E. Rølvaag (1876-1931) was the first to chronicle the hardships faced by the pioneers on the prairie, from snowstorms to hunger and loneliness, and even the infamous locust plague of 1873-1877. *Giants in the Earth* is the first in a trilogy, followed by *Peder Victorious* and *Their Father's God.* Rølvaag graduated from St. Olaf College in Northfield and taught there for many years. The Rølvaag Memorial Library is named in his honor.

Swensson, Andrea. *Got to Be Something Here: The Rise of the Minneapolis Sound.* Minneapolis: University of Minnesota Press, 2017. The Minneapolis sound, a mix of funk and soul and a little something from the Upper Midwest, started seeping up from the cities' clubs and bars in the late 1960s, becoming a wave ridden by favorite son Prince.

# CHILDREN'S LITERATURE

Lovelace, Maud Hart. *Betsy-Tacy.* New York: Thomas Y. Crowell Company, 1940. Maud Hart Lovelace told her daughter Merian stories about growing up in Mankato, Minnesota, then wrote them down in a series of beloved children's books. The series began in 1940 with *Betsy-Tacy* and culminated in 1955 with *Betsy's Wedding.*

Wargin, Kathy-Jo. *V Is for Viking: A Minnesota Alphabet.* Chelsea, Michigan: Sleeping Bear Press, 2003. G is for gopher. L is for loon. M is for Mall of America, on through all 26 letters of the alphabet in this beautifully illustrated children's book, part of a series that covers all 50 states.

Wilder, Laura Ingalls. *Little House on the Prairie.* New York: Harper

Collins, 1953 (revised). Generations of children have grown up reading about the adventures of Laura and Ma and Pa and the rest of the families, but Minnesotans have always felt a special connection to the stories, knowing that the real-life Walnut Grove and Plum Creek are a few miles down the road in southern Minnesota.

# Internet Resources

## E-Democracy
www.e-democracy.org
This moderated online forum now has discussion groups for 10 cities in the United States, United Kingdom, and New Zealand, but it started right here in the Twin Cities. Users are required to post under their real, full names and give their neighborhood of residence, a policy that has fostered some of the most thoughtful and civil discourse you'll see on the Internet. They're also limited to two posts a day, so you'll find long, thought-out posts rather than sniping and one-liners. This is a great place to find out what's on the minds of ordinary Twin Citians.

## Hennepin County Public Library Photo Collection
www.hclib.org/browse/digital-collections
More than 10,000 historical photos are available to search online. Look up trolleys or blizzards or political figures or whatever else interests you. You can also order reproductions.

## Minnesota Bookstore
www.comm.media.state.mn.us/bookstore
Want your own copy of the local building codes, the Minnesota state accounting statutes, a Minnesota mug, or a state hiking map? It's all here in this eclectic online store run by the State of Minnesota.

## Minnesota Historical Society
www.mnhs.org
The Minnesota Historical Society's rich website offers resources for serious researchers and the casually curious. The society's enormous photo collection is online and fully searchable, as are extensive birth and death certificate databases.

## Minnesota Reflections
http://reflections.mndigital.org
More than 75 organizations from around the state have pooled their image and document archives into one online searchable database including almost 20,000 images.

## MinnPost
www.minnpost.com
After a serious shake-up in Twin Cities journalism in 2007, respected editor Joel Kramer decided to take excellent journalism online. And many of the cities' best reporters and writers followed him. Find in-depth coverage of news, education, business, arts, and more.

## MNopedia
www.mnopedia.org
A project of the Minnesota Historical Society, MNopedia is an encyclopedic

source for local history buffs, searchable by maps, general topic, and keyword. Individual entries cover the people, places, and events that continue to shape Minnesota.

### Secrets of the City
www.secretsofthecity.com

From fashion shows to gallery openings to bingo, Secrets of the City covers the hipper side of Twin Cities culture. It's a great place to look for something out of the ordinary to do on any given night and to read about area arts news. Listen to its podcast, *The Weekend Starts Now,* for even more up-to-the-minute local color.

### Twin Cities Daily Planet
www.tcdailyplanet.net

A consortium of small and specialized news sources in the Twin Cities feed into the Twin Cities Daily Planet, which also includes a few originally reported stories as well. It's a great place to catch the news that the bigger news outlets will overlook.

### The Uptake
www.theuptake.org

"Will journalism be done by you or to you?" asks The Uptake. This is citizen journalism in the hands of some talented folks with a video camera. Much of the video is uploaded live as it is being shot.

# Index

## WXYZ

# Restaurants Index

# Nightlife Index

# Shops Index

# Hotels Index

# Photo Credits

Title page photo: kathrine martin | dreamstime.com;

page 2 © joshua wanyama | dreamstime.com; sophiejames | dreamstime.com; tricia cornell; page 4 © (top left) stevengaertner | dreamstime.com; (top right) wengewood | dreamstime.com; (left middle)jim roberts | dreamstime.com; (right middle)tricia cornell; (bottom) tricia cornell; page 5 © tricia cornell; page 6 © aliaksandr nikitsin | dreamstime.com; page 8 © (top) jacob boomsma | dreamstime.com; (bottom) ken wolter | dreamstime.com; page 9 © (bottom) tricia cornell; page 10 © nikitsin | dreamstime.com; page 11 © (top) master1305 | dreamstime.com; (bottom) wengewood | dreamstime. com; page 13 © (top) yinyang/istock.com; page 14 © (bottom) jon bilous | dreamstime. com; page 15 © joshua wanyama | dreamstime.com; page 16 © andreykr | dreamstime. com; page 17 © tricia cornell; page 18 © vladimir daragan/123rf.com; page 19 © (bottom) sophiejames | dreamstime.com; page 20 © tricia cornell; boscophotos1 | dreamstime. com; page 21 © (top) spease | dreamstime.com; page 22 © ffooter | dreamstime.com; page 24 © (bottom) randall runtsch | dreamstime.com; page 26 © bill5md | dreamstime. com; page 27 © bruce manning; page 28 © bruce manning; page 29 © bruce manning; page 31 © (bottom) jzhu0930 | dreamstime.com; page 32 © tricia cornell; page 33 © tricia cornell; page 35 © cupertino10 | dreamstime.com; page 36 © joe ferrer | dreamstime. com; page 38 © (top) benkrut | dreamstime.com; page 39 © tricia cornell; page 40 © tricia cornell; page 41 © tricia cornell; page 42 © ferrerphoto | dreamstime.com; page 43 © tricia cornell; page 44 © yanmingzhang | dreamstime.com; page 46 © (top) wolterk | dreamstime. com; page 51 © tricia cornell; page 53 © tricia cornell; page 54 © (bottom) tricia cornell; page 58 © tricia cornell; page 60 © tricia cornell; page 62 © tricia cornell; page 67 © tricia cornell; page 68 © tricia cornell; (top) tricia cornell; page 69 © tricia cornell; page 70 © tricia cornell; page 71 © tricia cornell; page 73 © tricia cornell; tricia cornell; page 80 © tricia cornell; page 82 © tricia cornell; page 83 © tricia cornell; page 87 © tricia cornell; page 89 © tricia cornell; page 91 © (bottom) joe christensen/istock; page 92 © tricia cornell; page 93 © aaronrayburnphotography | dreamstime.com; page 95 © tricia cornell; page 99 © tricia cornell; page 102 © tricia cornell; page 104 © tricia cornell; page 106 © tricia cornell; page 108 © tricia cornell; page 109 © (top) tricia cornell; page 111 © sophiejames | dreamstime.com; page 113 © bruce manning; page 114 © bruce manning; page 115 © ken wolter | dreamstime.com; page 116 © bruce manning; tricia cornell; page 119 © (top) tricia cornell; page 120 © tricia cornell; page 122 © tricia cornell; page 124 © tricia cornell; page 126 © tricia cornell; page 128 © tricia cornell; page 129 © tricia cornell; page 131 © tricia cornell; page 132 © tricia cornell; page 133 © tricia cornell; tricia cornell; page 136 © (bottom) tricia cornell; page 144 © (bottom) mkopka | dreamstime.com; page 146 © tricia cornell; page 147 © tricia cornell; page 148 © (bottom) tricia cornell; page 150 © tricia cornell; page 151 © tricia cornell; page 152 © bruce manning; page 154 © tricia cornell; page 155 © tricia cornell; page 157 © bruce manning; page 159 © tricia cornell; page 160 © ron hoff | dreamstime.com; page 163 © (top) daniel thornberg | dreamstime. com; page 170 © tricia cornell; page 171 © tricia cornell; page 175 © tricia cornell; page 180 © tricia cornell; page 182 © tricia cornell; page 184 © tricia cornell; page 191 © tricia cornell; page 194 © bruce manning; page 195 © tricia cornell; yanmingzhang | dreamstime.com; page 196 © tricia cornell; page 200 © tricia cornell; page 201 © tricia cornell; page 205 © johnsroad7 | dreamstime.com; page 209 © (bottom) giuseppe tozzo | dreamstime.com; page 210 © daniel reiner | dreamstime.com; page 211 © sequential5 | dreamstime.com; page 214 © (bottom) joe ferrer | dreamstime.com; page 215 © johnsroad7 | dreamstime. com; page 220 © chris graff | dreamstime.com; page 224 © (bottom) alkerk | dreamstime. com; page 227 © candyce herman | dreamstime.com; page 229 © (bottom) kaye e | dreamstime.com; page 236 © rudi1976 | dreamstime.com; page 249 © mark herreid | dreamstime.com.

**SIGHTS**

| | | |
|---|---|---|
| 28 | B4 | Hennepin Avenue Bridge |
| 46 | C3 | Minneapolis Central Library |
| 53 | C5 | St. Anthony Falls |
| 58 | C6 | Stone Arch Bridge |
| 67 | D3 | Nicollet Mall |
| 73 | D3 | Foshay Tower |
| 78 | D4 | Minneapolis City Hall and Hennepin County Courthouse |
| 89 | E1 | Basilica of St. Mary |
| 103 | F1 | Walker Art Center and Sculpture Garden |

**RESTAURANTS**

| | | |
|---|---|---|
| 1 | A2 | Bar La Grassa |
| 3 | A2 | Jun |
| 4 | A2 | Borough |
| 7 | A2 | Black Sheep Pizza |
| 9 | B2 | Smack Shack |
| 23 | B3 | Spoon and Stable |
| 25 | B3 | The Bachelor Farmer |
| 27 | B4 | Kado no Mise |
| 42 | C3 | Pizza Lucé |
| 44 | C3 | 112 Eatery |
| 51 | C3 | Murray's |
| 57 | C5 | Spoonriver |
| 64 | D2 | Butcher and the Boar |
| 71 | D3 | Zelo |
| 72 | D3 | Hell's Kitchen |
| 81 | D5 | Zen Box Izakaya |
| 82 | D5 | Sea Change |
| 90 | E1 | Bar and Café Lurcat |
| 99 | E3 | Monello |

**NIGHTLIFE**

| | | | | | |
|---|---|---|---|---|---|
| 2 | A2 | Bunker's | 43 | C3 | Fine Line Music Café |
| 5 | A2 | Parlour | 45 | C3 | Aqua |
| 6 | A2 | Freehouse | 47 | C3 | Gay 90s |
| 8 | A3 | Acme Comedy Company | 62 | D2 | The Saloon |
| 10 | B2 | Inbound BrewCo | 77 | D4 | The Eagle/The Bolt |
| 11 | B2 | Fulton Beer | 87 | D5 | Day Block Brewing Company |
| 12 | B3 | Dalton and Wade | 91 | E1 | Bar Lurcat |
| 13 | B3 | Bev's Wine Bar | 94 | E2 | Brit's Pub |
| 19 | B3 | Monte Carlo | 96 | E2 | Dakota Jazz Club and Restaurant |
| 26 | B3 | Marvel Bar | 97 | E3 | The Local |
| 37 | C2 | First Avenue and 7th St. Entry | 105 | F2 | Lakes & Legends |
| 39 | C3 | Kieran's Irish Pub | 106 | F2 | 19 Bar |
| 40 | C3 | Music Hall MPLS | | | |
| 41 | C3 | Rouge at The Lounge | | | |

**DISTANCE ACROSS MAP**
Approximate: 2.1 mi or 3.4 km

0 — 200 yds
0 — 200 m

Hennepin Avenue Bridge **28**

MARCY HOLMES

Nicollet Island

River

**29** **30** **31** **32**

3RD AVE BRIDGE

Pillsbury Park

**53** St. Anthony Falls **54**

Hennepin Bluffs Park

**52**

DOWNTOWN WEST

**55** Mill Ruins Park

**58** Stone Arch Bridge

Lower Dam

**76** Minneapolis City Hall and Hennepin County **78** Courthouse

Government Plaza

**77** **81** **82 83**

**56** **57**

**79** **84** **88**

**80**

U.S. Bank Stadium

**85 66** **87**

SEE MAP 3

**102** U.S. Bank Stadium

DOWNTOWN EAST

**101** **35W**

**4** Franklin Ave

SEE MAP 1

**5**

FRANKLIN AVE E

22ND ST E

**6** 94

Mississippi River

SEE MAP 6

Midtown Greenway

EAST PHILLIPS

LONGFELLOW

Lake St Midtown

CORCORAN

Powderhorn Lake

Powderhorn Park

To **72** Northbound Smokehouse and Brewpub

## SIGHTS

| | | | |
|---|---|---|---|
| **A1** | Chain of Lakes | **91 D1** | Como-Harriet Streetcar Line |

## RESTAURANTS

| | | | | | | | | |
|---|---|---|---|---|---|---|---|---|
| **A1** | Kenwood | **32 B1** | Rustica | **73 C2** | Victor's 1959 Café | **90 D1** | Harriet Brasserie |
| **A2** | Burch | **35 B1** | Barbette | **74 C2** | Grand Cafe | **94 D2** | Tenant |
| **A2** | Sebastian Joe's | **38 B2** | Chino Latino | **76 C3** | Hola Arepa | **95 D3** | Revival |
| **A2** | Common Roots | **46 B2** | World Street Kitchen | **77 C3** | Kyatchi | **97 E1** | Broder's Pasta Bar |
| **A2** | French Meadow Bakery and Café | **54 B2** | Fuji Ya | **78 C3** | Blackbird | **99 E2** | St. Genevieve |
| **A2** | The Lynhall | **56 B4** | Taqueria Los Ocampo | **82 D1** | Naviya's Thai Brasserie | **100 E2** | Patisserie 46 |
| **A3** | Jasmine Deli | **65 B5** | Manny's Tortas | **83 D1** | The Zumbro | **103 E3** | Sun Street Breads |
| **A3** | Quang | **67 B5** | Himalayan Restaurant | **84 D1** | Rose Street Patisserie | **104 E3** | Corner Table |
| **A3** | Fika | **68 B6** | Sonora Grill | **85 D1** | Martina | **107 F1** | Pizzeria Lola |
| **A4** | Maria's Café | **72 C2** | Sonny's Café | **88 D1** | Tilia | **108 F3** | Wise Acre Eatery |
| **A6** | Birchwood | | | | | | |

## NIGHTLIFE

| | | | | | | | | |
|---|---|---|---|---|---|---|---|---|
| **A2** | C.C. Club | **47 B2** | V.F.W. James Ballentine Post No. 246 | **52 B2** | Volstead's Emporium | **75 C3** | Pat's Tap |
| **A3** | Icehouse | | | **53 B2** | Up-Down Arcade | **79 C5** | Northbound Smokehouse and Brewpub |
| **A3** | Tilt Pinball Bar | **48 B2** | The Herkimer | **55 B2** | HUGE Theater | | |
| **B2** | Stella's Fish Café & Prestige Oyster Bar | **50 B2** | LynLake Brewery | **62 B5** | Du Nord Cocktail Room | **81 C6** | Riverview |
| | | **51 B2** | Moto-i | | | **98 E1** | Terzo Vino |
| **B2** | Famous Dave's | | | **66 B5** | El Nuevo Rodeo | | |
| **B2** | Bryant-Lake Bowl | | | | | | |

## ARTS AND CULTURE

| | | | | | | | | |
|---|---|---|---|---|---|---|---|---|
| **A2** | Soo Visual Arts Center | **22 A3** | Hennepin History Museum | **37 B2** | Uptown Theatre | **63 B5** | Trylon Microcinema |
| **A3** | Minneapolis College of Art and Design | **24 A3** | Open Eye Figure Theatre | **43 B2** | Highpoint Center for Printmaking | **71 C1** | The Bakken |
| | | **26 A3** | American Swedish Institute | **45 B2** | Bryant-Lake Bowl | **80 C6** | Riverview Theater |
| **A3** | Children's Theatre Company | **27 A4** | Norway House | **49 B2** | Jungle Theater | **109 F3** | The Museum of Russian Art |
| **A3** | Minneapolis Institute of Art | **30 A5** | Northern Clay Center | **60 B4** | In the Heart of the Beast Puppet and Mask Theatre | | |

## RECREATION

| | | | | | | | | |
|---|---|---|---|---|---|---|---|---|
| **A1** | Lake of the Isles | **59 B4** | Freewheel Midtown Bike Center | **93 D2** | Lyndale Park | **106 E6** | Minnehaha Falls |
| **B1** | Midtown Greenway | **92 D1** | Lake Harriet Yacht Club | **105 E6** | Grand Rounds National Scenic Byway | | |
| **B1** | Wheel Fun Rentals | | | | | | |

## SHOPS

| | | | | | | | | |
|---|---|---|---|---|---|---|---|---|
| **A1** | Birchbark Books | **39 B2** | Magers and Quinn | **64 B5** | Moon Palace Books | **87 D1** | Creative Kidstuff |
| **A2** | Patina | **57 B4** | Uncle Edgar's Mystery Bookstore & Uncle Hugo's Science Fiction Bookstore | **69 B6** | Hymie's Vintage Records | **89 D1** | Wild Rumpus |
| **A2** | Via's Vintage | | | **70 B6** | Forage Modern Workshop | **96 E1** | Hunt & Gather |
| **A3** | Electric Fetus | | | **86 D1** | Heartfelt | **101 E2** | MILLE |
| **A5** | Boneshaker Books | **61 B4** | Ingebretsen's | | | **102 E2** | The Foundry Home Goods |
| **B2** | Local Motion | | | | | | |

## HOTELS

| | | | | | | | | |
|---|---|---|---|---|---|---|---|---|
| **A3** | Minneapolis International Hostel | **42 B2** | Moxy Minneapolis Uptown | **58 B4** | Sheraton Minneapolis Midtown | | |

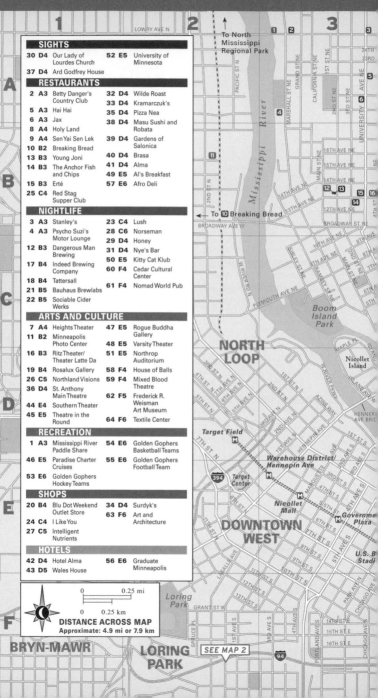

**SIGHTS**

| 30 | D4 | Our Lady of Lourdes Church | 52 | E5 | University of Minnesota |
| 37 | D4 | Ard Godfrey House | | | |

**RESTAURANTS**

| 2 | A3 | Betty Danger's Country Club | 32 | D4 | Wilde Roast |
| 5 | A3 | Hai Hai | 33 | D4 | Kramarczuk's |
| 6 | A3 | Jax | 35 | D4 | Pizza Nea |
| 8 | A4 | Holy Land | 38 | D4 | Masu Sushi and Robata |
| 9 | A4 | Sen Yai Sen Lek | 39 | D4 | Gardens of Salonica |
| 10 | B2 | Breaking Bread | 40 | D4 | Brasa |
| 13 | B3 | Young Joni | 41 | D4 | Alma |
| 14 | B3 | The Anchor Fish and Chips | 49 | E5 | Al's Breakfast |
| 15 | B3 | Erté | 57 | E6 | Afro Deli |
| 25 | C4 | Red Stag Supper Club | | | |

**NIGHTLIFE**

| 3 | A3 | Stanley's | 23 | C4 | Lush |
| 4 | A3 | Psycho Suzi's Motor Lounge | 28 | C6 | Norseman |
| 12 | B3 | Dangerous Man Brewing | 29 | D4 | Honey |
| | | | 31 | D4 | Nye's Bar |
| 17 | B4 | Indeed Brewing Company | 50 | E5 | Kitty Cat Klub |
| 18 | B4 | Tattersall | 60 | F4 | Cedar Cultural Center |
| 21 | B5 | Bauhaus Brewlabs | 61 | F4 | Nomad World Pub |
| 22 | B5 | Sociable Cider Werks | | | |

**ARTS AND CULTURE**

| 7 | A4 | Heights Theater | 47 | E5 | Rogue Buddha Gallery |
| 11 | B2 | Minneapolis Photo Center | 48 | E5 | Varsity Theater |
| 16 | B3 | Ritz Theater/ Theater Latte Da | 51 | E5 | Northrop Auditorium |
| 19 | B4 | Rosalux Gallery | 58 | F4 | House of Balls |
| 26 | C5 | Northland Visions | 59 | F4 | Mixed Blood Theatre |
| 36 | D4 | St. Anthony Main Theatre | 62 | F5 | Frederick R. Weisman Art Museum |
| 44 | E4 | Southern Theater | | | |
| 45 | E5 | Theatre in the Round | 64 | F6 | Textile Center |

**RECREATION**

| 1 | A3 | Mississippi River Paddle Share | 54 | E6 | Golden Gophers Basketball Teams |
| 46 | E5 | Paradise Charter Cruises | 55 | E6 | Golden Gophers Football Team |
| 53 | E6 | Golden Gophers Hockey Teams | | | |

**SHOPS**

| 20 | B4 | Blu Dot Weekend Outlet Store | 34 | D4 | Surdyk's |
| 24 | C4 | I Like You | 63 | F6 | Art and Architecture |
| 27 | C5 | Intelligent Nutrients | | | |

**HOTELS**

| 42 | D4 | Hotel Alma | 56 | E6 | Graduate Minneapolis |
| 43 | D5 | Wales House | | | |

0　　0.25 mi

0　　0.25 km

**DISTANCE ACROSS MAP**
Approximate: 4.9 mi or 7.9 km

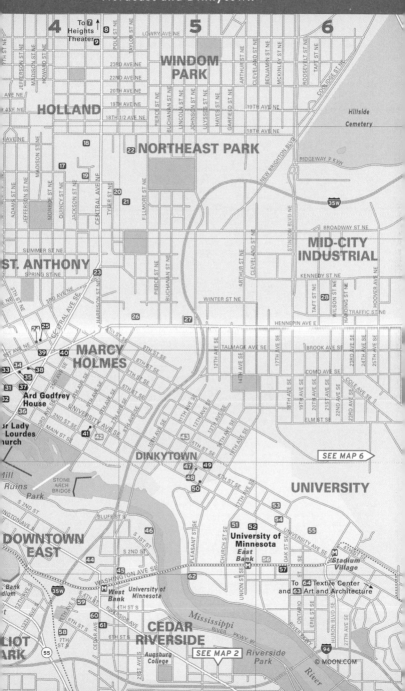

**SIGHTS**

| 5 | B2 | Western Sculpture Park |
| 6 | B3 | Minnesota State Capitol |
| 8 | C2 | Cathedral of St. Paul |
| 9 | C2 | Minnesota History Center |
| 28 | C4 | Union Depot |
| 30 | C6 | Indian Mounds Park |
| 48 | D3 | Rice Park |
| 51 | D3 | James J. Hill Center |
| 52 | D3 | St. Paul City Hall and Ramsey County Courthouse |
| 64 | F4 | Wabasha Street Caves |

**RESTAURANTS**

| 3 | B1 | Trieu Chau |
| 4 | B1 | Cheng Heng |
| 10 | C3 | Babani's Kurdish Restaurant |
| 15 | C3 | Mickey's Diner |
| 18 | C3 | Meritage |
| 22 | C4 | Buttered Tin |
| 24 | C4 | Salty Tart |
| 25 | C4 | OCTO fishbar |
| 26 | C4 | Saint Dinette |
| 31 | D1 | W.A. Frost and Company |
| 34 | D2 | Cossetta Alimentar |
| 40 | D3 | St. Paul Grill |
| 50 | D3 | Sakura Restaurant & Bar |
| 55 | E1 | Mancini's Char House |
| 58 | E2 | Forepaugh's |
| 62 | F1 | Mucci's Italian |
| 63 | F1 | Pajarito |
| 65 | F5 | Boca Chica |
| 66 | F5 | El Burrito Mercado |

**NIGHTLIFE**

| | | | | | | |
|---|---|---|---|---|---|---|
| **12 C3** | Tin Whiskers Brewing Company | **41 D3** | St. Paul Grill | **47 D3** | Amsterdam Bar and Hall |
| **32 D1** | The Commodore | **43 D3** | Vieux Carre | **56 E2** | Waldmann Brewery & Wurstery |

**ARTS AND CULTURE**

| | | | | | | |
|---|---|---|---|---|---|---|
| **11 C3** | Minnesota History Theatre | **20 C4** | Minnesota Museum of American Art | **38 D3** | Science Museum of Minnesota |
| **13 C3** | Fitzgerald Theater | **29 C5** | AZ Gallery | **39 D3** | Ordway Center for the Performing Arts |
| **14 C3** | Minnesota Children's Museum | **33 D2** | James J. Hill House | **44 D3** | Landmark Center |
| **16 C3** | Palace Theatre | **35 D2** | Alexander Ramsey House | | |
| **17 C3** | Park Square Theatre | **36 D3** | Xcel Energy Center | | |

**RECREATION**

| | | | | | | |
|---|---|---|---|---|---|---|
| **1 A4** | Gateway State Trail | **27 C4** | Mears Park | **60 E3** | Padelford Cruises |
| **2 A6** | Vertical Endeavors | **37 D3** | Minnesota Wild | **61 E3** | Harriet Island Regional Park |
| **23 C4** | St. Paul Saints | **45 D3** | Landmark Center Rink | | |

**SHOPS**

| | | | | | | |
|---|---|---|---|---|---|---|
| **46 D3** | Heimie's Haberdashery | **49 D3** | Subtext Books | **57 E2** | Scout Handsome Apparel and Gifts |

**HOTELS**

| | | | | | | |
|---|---|---|---|---|---|---|
| **7 B4** | Embassy Suites | **42 D3** | St. Paul Hotel | **59 E3** | Covington Inn Bed and Breakfast |
| **19 C3** | DoubleTree by Hilton | **53 D4** | Intercontinental St. Paul Riverfront | | |
| **21 C4** | Hyatt Place St. Paul Downtown | **54 D4** | Hotel 340 | | |

© MOON.COM

SEE MAP 6

SEE MAP 2

MIDWAY

Snelling Ave

Allianz Field

MERRIAM PARK

Mississippi Gorge Park

University of St. Thomas

Mississippi River

MACALESTER-GROVELAND

Macalester College

College of St. Catherine

Highland Nine Golf Course

HIGHLAND

Hidden Falls Park

© MOON.COM

DISTANCE ACROSS MAP
Approximate: 5.1 mi or 8.2 km

0　　0.25 mi

0　　0.25 km

SEE MAP 6

SEE MAP 4

## SIGHTS

**17 B5** Summit Avenue

## RESTAURANTS

**4 A5** Ngon Bistro
**7 B2** Izzy's Ice Cream Café
**8 B2** Stewart's
**25 B6** Moscow on the Hill
**27 C3** Grand Catch
**30 C4** Everest on Grand
**31 C4** The Lexington
**32 C5** Cafe Latte
**36 C5** Grand Ole Creamery
**38 D4** Casper & Runyon's Nook
**39 E2** Cecil's Delicatessen
**40 E2** Punch Pizza

## NIGHTLIFE

**1 A3** Turf Club
**2 A3** Town House
**10 B3** O'Gara's Bar and Grill
**24 B6** Happy Gnome
**41 E5** Summit Brewing Company

## ARTS AND CULTURE

**5 A6** Penumbra Theatre
**13 B5** SteppingStone Theatre
**37 D2** The O'Shaughnessy

## RECREATION

**3 A3** Minnesota United FC
**42 F1** Hidden Falls Park
**43 F4** Crosby Farm Park

## SHOPS

**6 B2** Choo Choo Bob's
**9 B3** Lula's Vintage Wear
**11 B3** Common Good Books
**12 B4** Baby Grand
**14 B5** Red Balloon Bookshop
**15 B5** Cooks of Crocus Hill
**16 B5** Garden of Eden
**18 B6** The Grand Hand
**19 B6** Primp
**20 B6** BlackBlue
**21 B6** Solo Vino
**22 B6** Corazon
**23 B6** Idun
**26 C2** Uncle Sven's Comic Shoppe
**28 C3** Poppy
**29 C4** Treadle Yard Goods
**33 C5** Quince
**34 C5** The Yarnery
**35 C5** Golden Fig

## 4  5  6

**CALIFORNIA AVE**
**IDAHO AVE**
**IOWA AVE**

## COMO

W CALIFORNIA AVE
W IOWA AVE
HOYT AVE W
W MONTANA AVE
W NEBRASKA AVE
W NEVADA AVE

Como Park
Golf Course

**Como Park Zoo
and Conservatory**

mo Town **7**

**9**

ARLINGTON AVE W
W PARKVIEW AVE
W COTTAGE AVE
IVY AVE W

**Cafesjian's Carousel**

**8**

Como

Lake

VAN SLYKE AVE

MARYLAND AVE W

Como
Park **11**

Loeb
Lake

JESSAMINE AVE W

JESSAMINE AVE W
W LAWSON AVE

COACH RD

**12**

W ORCHARD AVE

**13**

HATCH AVE

FRONT AVE

## NORTH END

ENERGY LN

W STINSON ST

BURGESS ST

**SEE MAP 4**

HEWITT AVE
W HUBBARD AVE
W SEMINARY AVE
W ENGLEWOOD AVE
W MINNEHAHA AVE
W VAN BUREN AVE

W PIERCE BUTLER RTE

## THOMAS-DALE

W BLAIR AVE
W LAFOND AVE

THOMAS AVE
EDMUND AVE
CHARLES AVE
SHERBURNE AVE

UNIVERSITY AVE W

Lexington
Pkwy

BIGELOW AVE

94

## SUMMIT-UNIVERSITY

Dunning
Field

### SIGHTS
**7**  **B4**  Como Town
**8**  **B4**  Cafesjian's Carousel
**9**  **B4**  Como Park Zoo and Conservatory

### RESTAURANTS
**5**  **B1**  Finnish Bistro
**16**  **D3**  Mirror of Korea
**17**  **E3**  Fasika

### NIGHTLIFE
**13**  **C5**  HalfTime Rec
**14**  **D1**  Surly Brewing Company
**15**  **D2**  Can Can Wonderland

### ARTS AND CULTURE
**2**  **A2**  Gibbs Museum of Pioneer and Dakotah Life
**3**  **A2**  Bell Museum of Natural History
**6**  **B2**  Goldstein Museum
**12**  **C4**  Twin City Model Railroad Museum

### RECREATION
**1**  **A1**  Les Bolstad University of Minnesota Golf Club
**10**  **B5**  Como Ski Center
**11**  **C4**  Como Park

### SHOPS
**4**  **B1**  Micawber's Books

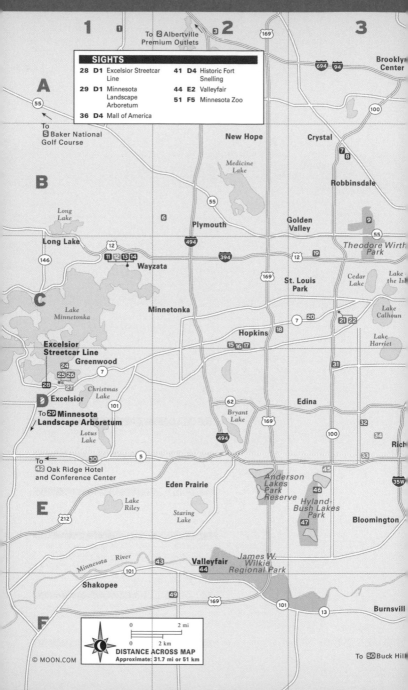

| SIGHTS | | |
|---|---|---|
| **28 D1** Excelsior Streetcar Line | **41 D4** Historic Fort Snelling | |
| **29 D1** Minnesota Landscape Arboretum | **44 E2** Valleyfair | |
| **36 D4** Mall of America | **51 F5** Minnesota Zoo | |

To 2 Albertville Premium Outlets

55

To 5 Baker National Golf Course

New Hope

Crystal

Brooklyn Center

694 94

100

7 8

Robbinsdale

Medicine Lake

Long Lake

6

Plymouth

55

Golden Valley

9

Theodore Wirth Park

55

Long Lake

12

146

11 12 13 14

Wayzata

494

394

12 19

169

St. Louis Park

Cedar Lake

Lake the Isl

**Minnetonka**

Lake Minnetonka

7 20

18

Hopkins

21 22

Lake Calhoun

**Excelsior Streetcar Line**

24

Greenwood

7

15 16 17

Lake Harriet

25 26

27

28

Christmas Lake

31

**Excelsior**

101

Bryant Lake

**Edina**

To 29 **Minnesota Landscape Arboretum**

62

32

Lotus Lake

169

100

34

Rich

33

30

5

45

35W

To 42 **Oak Ridge Hotel and Conference Center**

**Eden Prairie**

Anderson Lakes Park Reserve

46

212

Lake Riley

Staring Lake

Hyland-Bush Lakes Park

47

**Bloomington**

Minnesota River

43

**Valleyfair**

James W. Wilkie Regional Park

101

44

**Shakopee**

49

169

101

13

**Burnsville**

© MOON.COM

0 ——— 2 mi
0 ——— 2 km
**DISTANCE ACROSS MAP**
Approximate: 31.7 mi or 51 km

To 50 Buck Hill

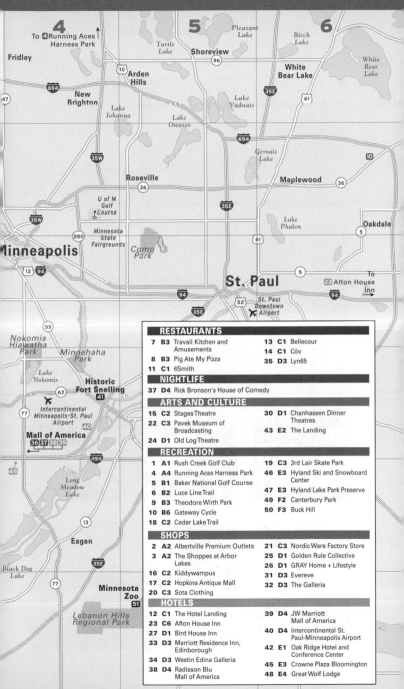

## RESTAURANTS

| 7 | B3 | Travail Kitchen and Amusements |
| 8 | B3 | Pig Ate My Pizza |
| 11 | C1 | 6Smith |
| 13 | C1 | Bellecour |
| 14 | C1 | Cöv |
| 35 | D3 | Lyn65 |

## NIGHTLIFE

| 37 | D4 | Rick Bronson's House of Comedy |

## ARTS AND CULTURE

| 15 | C2 | Stages Theatre |
| 22 | C3 | Pavek Museum of Broadcasting |
| 24 | D1 | Old Log Theatre |
| 30 | D1 | Chanhassen Dinner Theatres |
| 43 | E2 | The Landing |

## RECREATION

| 1 | A1 | Rush Creek Golf Club |
| 4 | A4 | Running Aces Harness Park |
| 5 | B1 | Baker National Golf Course |
| 6 | B2 | Luce Line Trail |
| 9 | B3 | Theodore Wirth Park |
| 10 | B6 | Gateway Cycle |
| 18 | C2 | Cedar Lake Trail |
| 19 | C3 | 3rd Lair Skate Park |
| 46 | E3 | Hyland Ski and Snowboard Center |
| 47 | E3 | Hyland Lake Park Preserve |
| 49 | F2 | Canterbury Park |
| 50 | F3 | Buck Hill |

## SHOPS

| 2 | A2 | Albertville Premium Outlets |
| 3 | A2 | The Shoppes at Arbor Lakes |
| 16 | C2 | Kiddywampus |
| 17 | C2 | Hopkins Antique Mall |
| 20 | C3 | Sota Clothing |
| 21 | C3 | Nordic Ware Factory Store |
| 25 | D1 | Golden Rule Collective |
| 26 | D1 | GRAY Home + Lifestyle |
| 31 | D3 | Evereve |
| 32 | D3 | The Galleria |

## HOTELS

| 12 | C1 | The Hotel Landing |
| 23 | C6 | Afton House Inn |
| 27 | D1 | Bird House Inn |
| 33 | D3 | Marriott Residence Inn, Edinborough |
| 34 | D3 | Westin Edina Galleria |
| 38 | D4 | Radisson Blu Mall of America |
| 39 | D4 | JW Marriott Mall of America |
| 40 | D4 | Intercontinental St. Paul-Minneapolis Airport |
| 42 | E1 | Oak Ridge Hotel and Conference Center |
| 45 | E3 | Crowne Plaza Bloomington |
| 48 | E4 | Great Wolf Lodge |

# MOON TRAVEL GUIDES TO EUROPE

MOON
AMALFI COAST
With Capri, Naples & Pompeii
LAURA THAYER

MOON
BARCELONA & MADRID
JESSICA JONES

MOON
CAMINO DE SANTIAGO
SACRED SITES, HISTORIC VILLAGES, LOCAL FOOD & WINE
BEEBE BAHRAMI

MOON
CROATIA & SLOVENIA
SHANN FOUNTAIN ALIPOUR

MOON
EDINBURGH, GLASGOW & THE ISLE OF SKYE
SALLY COFFEY

MOON
ICELAND
JENNA GOTTLIEB

MOON
IRELAND
CAMILLE DEANGELIS

MOON
NORMANDY & BRITTANY
With Mont-Saint-Michel
CHRIS NEWENS

MOON
NORWAY
DAVID NIKEL

MOON
PORTUGAL
CARRIE-MARIE BRATLEY

MOON
PRAGUE, VIENNA & BUDAPEST
JENNIFER D. WALKER
AUBON BHATTACHARYA

MOON
ROME, FLORENCE & VENICE
ALEXEI J. COHEN

# GO BIG AND GO BEYOND!

These savvy city guides include strategies to help you see the top sights and find adventure beyond the tourist crowds.

# OR TAKE THINGS ONE STEP AT A TIME

Advice on where to sleep, eat, and explore

Detailed driving directions including mileage and drive times

Itineraries for a range of timelines

## MOON
### NEW ENGLAND
*Road Trip*

BOSTON, ACADIA NATIONAL PARK, WHITE MOUNTAINS, BERKSHIRES, NEWPORT, AND CAPE COD

JEN ROSS SMITH

## MOON
### PACIFIC NORTHWEST
*Road Trip*

SEATTLE, VANCOUVER, VICTORIA, THE OLYMPIC PENINSULA, PORTLAND, THE OREGON COAST & MOUNT RAINIER

ALLISON WILLIAMS

## MOON
### ROUTE 66
*Road Trip*

JESSICA DUNHAM

## MOON
### SOUTH FLORIDA & THE KEYS
*Road Trip*

WITH MIAMI, WALT DISNEY WORLD, TAMPA & THE EVERGLADES

JASON FERGUSON

## MOON
### SOUTHWEST
*Road Trip*

LAS VEGAS, ZION & BRYCE, MONUMENT VALLEY, SANTA FE & TAOS, AND THE GRAND CANYON

TIM HULL

## MOON
### VANCOUVER & CANADIAN ROCKIES
*Road Trip*

VICTORIA, BANFF, JASPER, CALGARY, THE OKANAGAN, WHISTLER & THE SEA-TO-SKY HIGHWAY

CAROLYN B. HELLER

# Gear up for a bucket list vacation

or plan your next beachy getaway!

# MAP SYMBOLS

| | | | | | | | |
|---|---|---|---|---|---|---|---|
| ■ | Sights | ⊛ | National Capital | ▲ | Mountain | ═══ | Major Hwy |
| ■ | Restaurants | ⊚ | State Capital | ✦ | Natural Feature | ──── | Road/Hwy |
| ■ | Nightlife | ○ | City/Town | 🖋 | Waterfall | ──── | Pedestrian Friendly |
| ■ | Arts and Culture | ★ | Point of Interest | ▲ | Park | ------ | Trail |
| ■ | Sports and Activities | • | Accommodation | ⩘ | Archaeological Site | ⬚⬚⬚⬚ | Stairs |
| ■ | Shops | ▾ | Restaurant/Bar | ◧ | Trailhead | ·········· | Ferry |
| ■ | Hotels | ■ | Other Location | �ᴾ | Parking Area | ‑‑‑‑‑‑ | Railroad |

# CONVERSION TABLES

°C = (°F - 32) / 1.8
°F = (°C x 1.8) + 32
1 inch = 2.54 centimeters (cm)
1 foot = 0.304 meters (m)
1 yard = 0.914 meters
1 mile = 1.6093 kilometers (km)
1 km = 0.6214 miles
1 fathom = 1.8288 m
1 chain = 20.1168 m
1 furlong = 201.168 m
1 acre = 0.4047 hectares
1 sq km = 100 hectares
1 sq mile = 2.59 square km
1 ounce = 28.35 grams
1 pound = 0.4536 kilograms
1 short ton = 0.90718 metric ton
1 short ton = 2,000 pounds
1 long ton = 1.016 metric tons
1 long ton = 2,240 pounds
1 metric ton = 1,000 kilograms
1 quart = 0.94635 liters
1 US gallon = 3.7854 liters
1 Imperial gallon = 4.5459 liters
1 nautical mile = 1.852 km

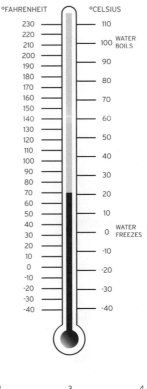

MOON MINNEAPOLIS & ST. PAUL
Avalon Travel
Hachette Book Group
1700 Fourth Street
Berkeley, CA 94710, USA
www.moon.com

Editor: Kristi Mitsuda
Series Manager: Leah Gordon
Copy Editor: Deana Shields
Graphics and Production Coordinator: Krista Anderson
Cover Design: Faceout Studios, Charles Brock
Interior Design: Megan Jones Design
Moon Logo: Tim McGrath
Map Editor: Kat Bennett
Cartographers: Karin Dahl, Lohnes+Wright
Proofreader: Anna Ho
Indexer: Rachel Kuhn

ISBN-13: 9781640492011

Printing History
1st Edition — 2009
4th Edition — May 2019
5 4 3 2 1

Front cover photo: Hiawatha light-rail in downtown Minneapolis © Wiskerke / Alamy Stock photo
Back cover photo: Minneapolis © Davel5957 / iStock Photo

Printed in China by RR Donnelley